CHRYSLER
MUSCLE CAR
PARTS INTERCHANGE MANUAL
1968-1974

Paul Herd

Motorbooks International
Publishers & Wholesalers ®

Acknowledgments

This book would have not been possible without the assistance of several individuals. First, thanks to all of those at the Chrysler legal-Ions staff who graciously allowed me to use the factory illustrations, and those at Chrysler Historical who supplied the factory photos. A very special thank you to John Justice and Kathy Slobe, and all those at R and R Auto Salvage, for all their help, and allowing me to photograph original parts. Thanks also to Barbara Hillick and all those at Year One for supplying photos, to the staff of Special Events, and to the Dodge and Plymouth car owners who allowed me to photograph their cars.

Finally, thank you to all of my family. To Ruth, Larry, Rodney, Joe, and Sue, who put up with my trips to the salvage yard and my long disappearances behind factory catalogs. It is to all of you that I dedicate this book. And a special thank you to my fiancée Kimberly; it's not always easy loving a car guy, but you always try.

First published in 1997 by Motorbooks International Publishers & Wholesalers, 729 Prospect Avenue, PO Box 1, Osceola, WI 54020-0001 USA

© Paul Herd, 1997

Motorbooks International books are also available at discounts in bulk quantity for industrial or sales-promotional use. For details write to Special Sales Manager at the Publisher's address

Library of Congress Cataloging-in-Publication Data

Herd, Paul A.
    Chrysler muscle car parts interchange manual, 1968-1974/ Paul Herd.
        p. cm.
    Includes index.
    ISBN 0-7603-0420-3 (paperback : alk. paper)
    1. Chrysler automobile--Parts--Catalogs. 2. Muscle cars--Parts--Catalogs. I. Title. II. Series: Motorbooks International powerpro series.
TL215.C55H47 1997
629.28'72--DC21   97-21849

On the front cover: Good things come in small-block packages. For 1971 Dodge combined its lightweight A-body with 275-horsepower to create the Demon 340. Quarter-mile times in the low 14s were the happy result. This Plum Crazy example belongs to Rich Berlisk. *Tom Shaw*

Printed in the United States of America

Contents

Introduction

Dodge and Plymouth are the kissing cousins of the Chrysler clan. They wear different nameplates and have their own distinct identities, but there is no mistaking that these two are kin, for a lot of their parts are interchangeable—which is what this book is about.

When one is restoring, rebuilding, or hot rodding, knowing what parts are interchangeable can be a blessing. It can save you money, as a part from a full-size car may not cost as much as a part from a muscle car, even though they are the same part. This knowledge is also valuable when replacing parts no longer available. It should be noted that this book is for parts that will appear and/or physically fit; it should be not be confused with a restoration guide for building a matching numbers car. Material for this manual was drawn mainly from original Chrysler master parts catalogs, service manuals, and salvage-yard personnel.

How to Use This Guide and Read VIN and Data Plates

This book is divided into 11 different sections, each of which is further divided into individual subdivisions that make up the entire section. For example, chapter 1 is divided by components such as cylinder block, short block, crankshaft, connecting rods, and so on.

At the beginning of each of these subdivisions is an interchange listing of the models, along with other necessary data to allow you to find the part you're looking for. It will look similar to this:

Hinges, Hood
Model Identification
Barracuda ....*Interchange Number*
1968–69 1
1970 3
1971 5
1972 8
1973–74...9
Belvedere/Charger/Coronet/Satellite
1968–69 2
1970 4
1971–74...6

By finding your model and model year in the chart, you will be able to find the interchange number that will list the models that the particular part can be found on. Then, trace through the interchange to find the interchange number you are looking for. The interchange is listed in numerical order. For example, if you were looking for hood hinges for your 1972 Charger, you would look for Interchange Number 6, where you will find a section like this:

Interchange Number: 6
Part Number(s): 3582536 (right), 352537 (left)
Usage: 1971–74 Charger, Coronet, Satellite, all models and body styles.

Part number(s)—if listed—are either the original or original replacement numbers. Usage lists the models that this part was used on. Notes list things to watch for during your interchange, such as body style restrictions or modifications that can be done to make

other parts fit. It may also give you a cross reference to another interchange that will also fit.

Mopar Family Groups

Chrysler grouped its models together in different lines, or family groups. For example, instead of listing Charger, Coronet, Super Bee, Road Runner, and GTX, it listed them all as B-bodies, and the 1970–74 Barracuda and Challenger were referred to as E-bodies. It is important to know this because parts are sometimes designed to fit the family groups. In other words, a part designed to fit a Coronet may also fit a Charger. The following is a complete listing of the family groups.

A-body: 1964–67 Barracuda; 1964–74 Dart; 1970–1974 Duster
B-body: 1966–74 Charger; 1966–74 Coronet; 1968–1974 Road Runner
B-body: 1966–74 Satellite; 1968–1971 Super Bee; 1967–72 GTX
C-body: 1964–74 full-size Plymouth or Dodge
E-body: 1970–74 Barracuda; 1970–74 Challenger

Many different sub-models were available under one model name. For example, the Plymouth Belvedere line includes the Belvedere, Satellite, Sport Satellite, Road Runner, and GTX. If the part in question will fit all Belvedere models, only the Belvedere name will be listed. If the part fits only specific sub-models—for example, Road Runner—then only the Road Runner name will be listed, and it can be assumed that it will not correctly fit other Belvedere models. Also note that Duster is listed in the interchange, but Demon or Dart Sport may not be listed. This is because the Dart Sport and Demon are considered Dart models. So if the Duster and Dart models are listed, you can assume that it will fit the fastback, unless otherwise indicated.

Decoding VIN Plates and Fender Tags

The model and sub-model can be determined by decoding the Vehicle Identification Number (VIN) that is located on the driver's side of the instrument panel. In addition to the sub-model, the original engine size was also coded into the VIN plate. Use the diagrams and charts to help you decode Chrysler VIN plates.

1968–74 Plymouth Barracuda and Dodge Challenger Body Numbers

Model/Sub-model	Body Numbers	Years Used
Barracuda two-door hardtop	BH23	1968–74
Barracuda two-door fastback	BH29	1968–69
Barracuda convertible	BH27	1968–71
Cuda two-door hardtop	BS23	1970–71
Cuda convertible	BS27	1970–71
Gran Coupe Barracuda	BP23	1970–71
Challenger two-door hardtop	JH23	1970–74
Challenger S.E.	JH29, JS29	1970–71
Challenger R/T two-door hardtop	JS23	1970–71
Challenger Rallye two-door hardtop	JS23	1972–74
Challenger convertible	JH27	1970–71
Challenger R/T convertible	JS27	1970–71

1968–74 Dodge Charger Body Numbers

Model/Sub-model	Body Numbers	Years Used
Charger	XP29	1966–70
Charger R/T	XS29	1968–70
Charger DaytonaCharger 500	XX29	1969
Charger two-door hardtop	WH23	1971–74
Charger two-door coupe	WL23	1971–74
Charger R/T	WS23	1971
Charger Rallye	WS23 or WH23	1972–74
Charger S.E.	WP29	1971–74
Charger 500	WP23	1971

1968–74 Dodge Coronet Body Numbers

Model/Sub Model	Body Numbers	Years Used
Coronet R/T two-door hardtop	WS23	1968–70
Coronet R/T convertible	WS27	1968–70
Super Bee two-door hardtop	WM23	1968–71
Super Bee coupe	WM21	1968–70
Coronet 440 coupe	WH21	1968–70
Coronet 440 two-door hardtop	WH23	1968–70
Coronet 440 convertible	WH23	1968–67
Coronet 440 four-door sedan	WH41	1968–70
Coronet 440 station wagon	WH45	1968–70
Coronet Deluxe coupe	WL21	1968–70
Coronet Deluxe four-door sedan	WI41	1968–70
Coronet Deluxe station wagon	WI45	1968–70
Coronet 500 two-door hardtop	WP23	1968–70
Coronet 500 four-door sedan	WP41	1968–70
Coronet 500 convertible	WP27	1968–70
Coronet Brougham four-door sedan	WP41	1971
Coronet Brougham station wagon	WP45	1971
Coronet Taxi four-door sedan	WT41	1968–74
Coronet police sedan	WK41	1966–74
Coronet four-door sedan	WL41	1971–74
Crestwood station wagon	WP45-2 seat; WP46-3 seat	1971–74
Coronet Custom sedan	WH41	1971–74
Coronet Custom station wagon	WH45	1971–74

1968–74 Dodge Dart Body Numbers

Model/Sub Model	Body Numbers	Years Used
Dart 170 two-door sedan	LL21	1968
Dart 170 four-door sedan	LL41	1968–74
Dart Swinger two-door hardtop	LL23	1969–74
Dart Swinger 340-ci	LM23	1969–74*
Dart 270 two-door sedan	LH21	1968
Dart 270 two-door hardtop	LH23	1968
Dart GT two-door hardtop	LP23	1968–69
Dart GT convertible	LP27	1968–69
Dart GTS two-door hardtop	LS23	1968–69
Dart GTS convertible	LS27	1968–69
Demon two-door fastback	LL29	1971–72
Demon 340-ci	LM29	1971–72
Dart Sport two-door fastback	LL29	1973–74
Dart Sport 340	LM29	1973–74

(*Dart Sport 360 in 1974)

1968–74 Plymouth Belvedere and Satellite Body Numbers

Model/Sub Model	Body Numbers	Years Used
Belvedere two-door sedan	RL21	1968–70
Belvedere four-door sedan	RL41	1968–70
Belvedere station wagon	RL45	1968–70
Satellite two-door hardtop	RH23	1968–70
Satellite four-door sedan	RH41	1968–70
Satellite station wagon	RH45	1968–70
Satellite convertible	RH27	1968–70
Sport Satellite two-door hardtop	RP23	1968–70
Sport Satellite convertible	RP27	1968–70
Sport Satellite station wagon	RP45	1968–70
GTX two-door hardtop	RS23	1968–71
GTX convertible	RS27	1968–69
Road Runner coupe	RM21	1968–71
Road Runner two-door hardtop	RM23	1968–74
Road Runner convertible	RM27	1969–70
Satellite four-door sedan	RL41	1971–74
Satellite station wagon	RL45	1971–74
Satellite two-door hardtop	RL23	1971–74
Satellite Sebring	RH23	1971–74
Satellite Sebring Plus	RP23	1971–74
Satellite Custom sedan	RH41	1971–74
Satellite Custom wagon	RH45 (six pass.); RH46 (nine pass.)	1971–74
Regent wagon	RP45 (six pass.); RP46 (nine pass.)	1971–74
Police sedan	RK41	1966–74
Taxi	RT41	1968–74

1968–74 Plymouth Valiant and Duster Body Numbers

Model	Body Numbers	Years Used
Valiant 100 four-door sedan	VL41	1968–74
Valiant 100 two-door sedan	VL21	1968–69
Valiant Signet two-door hardtop	VH23	1968–69
Duster, except 340-ci	VL29	1970–74
Duster 340-ci	VS29	1970–74
Scamp	VH23	1971–74

(*Duster 360 in 1974)

The fifth character in the VIN plate is a single letter that designates the original engine. Note that the original engine could have been replaced in the car you are interchanging from. Do not use the VIN code as the sole source in identifying a powerplant in a car. It is useful, however, in finding the correct suspension components. Use the chart to help decode the VIN engine code.

The sixth digit is the model year: 8 for 1968, 9 for 1969, 0 for 1970, and so on. The seventh digit is the assembly plant, and the eighth to the thirteenth digits are the serial number. The assembly plant and the serial number have very little effect on interchanging.

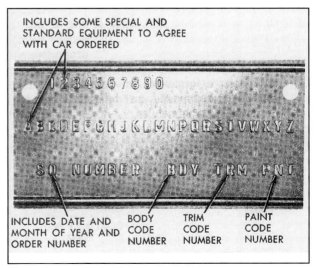

1968 fender tag.

When they do, it will be listed in the notes section of that particular interchange.

1968–74 Engine VIN Code Letters

Code Letter...........Engine Size/Type......................Years Used

A.....................170-ci six-cylinder.....................1968–69
B.....................225-ci six-cylinder, 1968–69
.....................198-ci six-cylinder, 1970–74........................#
C.....................Special-order six-cylinder, 1968–69
.....................225-ci six-cylinder, 1970–74........................#
D.....................273-ci two-barrel V-8.....................1968
E.....................Special-order six-cylinder, 1970–74........#
F.....................318-ci two-barrel V-8, 1967–69........#
G.....................383-ci two-barrel V-8, 1968–69
.....................318-ci two-barrel V-8, 1970–74........#
H.....................383-ci four-barrel, 1968–69
.....................340-ci four-barrel, 1970–73........#
J.....................426 Hemi, 1967–69
.....................340-ci triple-two-barrel V-8, 1970–71
.....................360-ci four-barrel, 1974........#

K.....................Special-order V-8, 1966
.....................440-ci four-barrel, 350 hp, 1968–69
.....................360-ci two-barrel V-8, 1971–74........#
L.....................440-ci four-barrel, 375 hp, 1968–69
.....................383-ci two-barrel V-8, 1970–71
.....................360-ci four-barrel, 245 hp, 1974........#
M.....................Special-order V-8, 1968–69
.....................400-ci two-barrel V-8, 1972–74........#
N.....................383-ci four-barrel, 1970–71
.....................400-ci four-barrel, 1974........
P.....................340-ci four-barrel, 1968–69
.....................400-ci four-barrel HP, 1972–74........#
R.....................426 Hemi........1970–71
T.....................440-ci four-barrel, except HP.....1970–74
U.....................440-ci four-barrel HP.....1970–74
V.....................440-ci triple-two-barrel........1970–72
Z.....................Special-order V-8........1970–74

#Some codes used on different engines on different model years. See engine/type column.

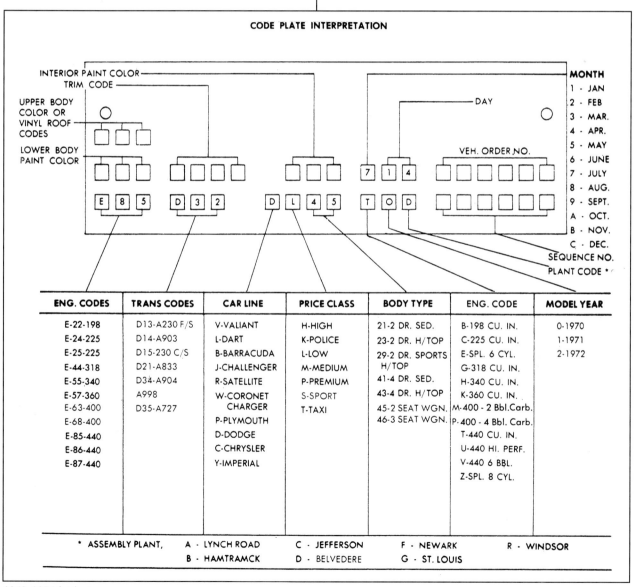

CODE PLATE INTERPRETATION

ENG. CODES	TRANS CODES	CAR LINE	PRICE CLASS	BODY TYPE	ENG. CODE	MODEL YEAR
E-22-198	D13-A230 F/S	V-VALIANT	H-HIGH	21-2 DR. SED.	B-198 CU. IN.	0-1970
E-24-225	D14-A903	L-DART	K-POLICE	23-2 DR. H/TOP	C-225 CU. IN.	1-1971
E-25-225	D15-230 C/S	B-BARRACUDA	L-LOW	29-2 DR. SPORTS	E-SPL. 6 CYL.	2-1972
E-44-318	D21-A833	J-CHALLENGER	M-MEDIUM	H/TOP	G-318 CU. IN.	
E-55-340	D34-A904	R-SATELLITE	P-PREMIUM	41-4 DR. SED.	H-340 CU. IN.	
E-57-360	A998	W-CORONET	S-SPORT	43-4 DR. H/TOP	K-360 CU. IN.	
E-63-400	D35-A727	CHARGER	T-TAXI	45-2 SEAT WGN.	M-400 - 2 Bbl.Carb.	
E-68-400		P-PLYMOUTH		46-3 SEAT WGN.	P-400 - 4 Bbl. Carb.	
E-85-440		D-DODGE			T-440 CU. IN.	
E-86-440		C-CHRYSLER			U-440 HI. PERF.	
E-87-440		Y-IMPERIAL			V-440 6 BBL.	
					Z-SPL. 8 CYL.	

* ASSEMBLY PLANT, A - LYNCH ROAD C - JEFFERSON F - NEWARK R - WINDSOR
B - HAMTRAMCK D - BELVEDERE G - ST. LOUIS

MONTH
1 - JAN
2 - FEB
3 - MAR.
4 - APR.
5 - MAY
6 - JUNE
7 - JULY
8 - AUG.
9 - SEPT.
A - OCT.
B - NOV.
C - DEC.
SEQUENCE NO.
PLANT CODE *

1969–1974 fender tag.

Chapter 1

Engine

Interchange here is the bare block without its internal components or cylinder heads. The displacement of the block can be determined by the engine serial number. The location and the way the ID number breaks down varies with model year and engine size.

With small blocks (318-ci, 340-ci, or 360-ci), the location of the engine serial number is on the front left side, just below the cylinder head. For the big blocks (383-ci, 400-ci, or 440-ci) and the 426 Hemi, the location is at the left rear of the block near the oil-pan flange. The location for big blocks would again change with the 1973 model year. For 400-ci engines, the ID code would now be located at the right front of the block near the distributor, while the location for the ID code on 440-ci engines is found at the left front of the block near the tappet rail. Location for the ID code on small blocks did not change in 1973.

The breakdown of the engine serial number for 1968–72 is as follows: The first two letters are the engine assembly plant. Either PM (Mound Road) or PT (Trenton) was used. The code for the assembly plant is followed by the cubic-inch displacement. After this is a four-digit code that represents the manufacture date, according to the 10, 000-day calendar. The date is followed by a four-digit code for the serial number, which is the unit number built that day. Assembly plant, build date, and serial number have little affect on the interchanging process. On those rare occasions it does, it will be listed in the notes section of that interchange.

The ID code in 1973 and 1974 begins with the last digit of the model year and/or a single letter for the engine assembly plant. The following codes were used for assembly plants: M (Mound Road), T (Trenton), and W (Windsor). If no code is used, then the engine was made at the Trenton plant. This is followed by the three-digit code for the cubic-inch displacement. A single- or two-letter code that depicts the engine type may follow the cubic-inch code. The following codes

were used: LC (low compression), P (premium fuel), R (regular fuel), or S (special engine). After this is the build date, which now uses a regular calendar date instead of the 10, 000-day calendar. Thus, the date of April 4 would be listed as 0404. On small blocks, some cores may end in the daily sequence number. Note that this usage was optional, so not all blocks will have the sequential number. However, big blocks end with a single number that indicates the shift. So, for example, the code 4T44008-12 3 would decode as a 440-ci built on August 12, 1973, at the Trenton plant by the third shift (the first number 4 indicates it is for a 1974 model).

Cylinder Blocks
Model Identification

318-ci	*Interchange Number*
1967–74	1
340-ci	*Interchange Number*
1968–73, except T/A	2
1968–73, T/A	3
360-ci	*Interchange Number*
1972–74	6
383-ci	*Interchange Number*
1968–71	4
400-ci	*Interchange Number*
1972–74	5
426-ci	*Interchange Number*
1968–71	8
440-ci	*Interchange Number*
1968–74	7

Interchange
Interchange Number: 1

Casting Number(s): 2466090
Usage: 1967–74, all Dodge, Plymouth models with 318-ci engines.
Note(s): Will not fit later styles due to casting methods.

Cylinder blocks can be identified by their casting number.

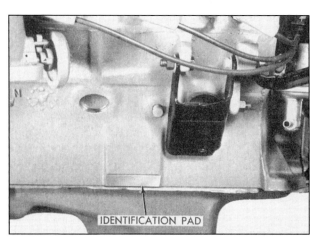

VIN pad location for V-8 engines.

Casting number for cylinder heads.

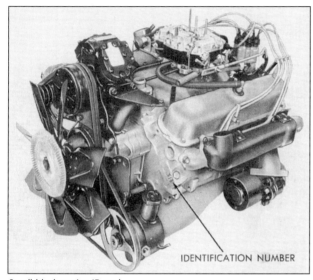

Small-block engine ID pad.

Interchange Number: 2
    Casting Number(s): 2780930
    Usage: 1968–73, all Dodge and Plymouth models with 340-ci, except 1970–71 Challenger T/A or Cuda AAR.
    Note(s): Has single carburetor.

Interchange Number: 3
    Casting Number(s): 3577130TA
    Usage: 1970–71 Challenger T/A and 1970–71 Cuda AAR.
    Note(s): Multi carburetors.

Interchange Number: 4
    Casting Number(s): 2468130
    Usage: 1968–71 Dodge and Plymouth models with 383-ci engine, includes Super Bee and Road Runner models.

Interchange Number: 5
    Casting Number(s): 3164230, 3698630
    Usage: 1971–74 Dodge and Plymouth models with 400-ci engine.

Interchange Number: 6
    Casting Number(s): 3418496
    Usage: 1971–74 Dodge and Plymouth models with 360-ci engine.

Interchange Number: 7
    Casting Number(s): 2536430
    Usage: All Dodge/Plymouth/Chrysler models with 440-ci engine, includes 440-ci triple-two-barrel versions.

Interchange Number: 8
    Casting Number(s): 2468330
    Usage: 1964–71 Dodge and Plymouth models with 426 Hemi.

Big-block upper engine ID pad.

Short Block
Model Identification

318-ci	***Interchange Number***
1968–73, all	1
1974, all	2
340-ci	***Interchange Number***
1968–71, except T/A	3
1968–71 T/A	11
1972–73, all	13
360-ci	***Interchange Number***
1974	12
383-ci	***Interchange Number***
1968–71 two-barrel	7
1968–71 four-barrel, 330 and 335 hp	8
400-ci	***Interchange Number***
1972–73, all	14
1974, all	15
426-ci	***Interchange Number***
1966–70 Hemi	6
1971 Hemi	9
440-ci	
1968–69, except high-performance	3
1968–69 high-performance	4
1968–69 440-ci triple-two-barrel	5
1970, except high-performance	20
1970 high-performance	21
1970 triple-two-barrel	5
1971, except high-performance	16
1971 high-performance	17
1971 440 triple-two-barrel	5
1972, except triple-two-barrel	18
1972 triple-two-barrel	5
1973–74, all	19

Interchange
Interchange Number: 1
    Displacement: 318-ci
    Horsepower: 230 at 4, 400 rpm
    Compression Ratio: 8.8:1
    Carburetor: Two-barrel

Usage: 1967–73 Barracuda, Charger, Coronet, Dart, Fury, Monaco, Polara, Satellite, and Valiant; 1973 Road Runner; 1970–73 Challenger and Duster.

Note(s): 1967 models are USA models only.

Interchange Number: 2
Displacement: 318-ci
Horsepower: 150 at 4,000 rpm
Compression Ratio: 8.6:1
Carburetor: Two-barrel
Usage: 1974 Barracuda, Challenger, Charger, Coronet, Fury, Monaco, Satellite, and Valiant

Interchange Number: 3
Displacement: 440-ci
Horsepower: 350 at 4,400 rpm
Compression Ratio: 10:1
Carburetor: Four-barrel
Usage: 1966–69 Chrysler, 1966–69 full-size Dodge, 1966–69 full-size Plymouth, and 1966–69 Imperial.
Note(s): Cam must be changed for 375-hp version. See Interchange Number 4 for more details.

Interchange Number: 4
Displacement: 440-ci
Horsepower: 375 at 4,600 rpm
Compression Ratio: 10:1
Carburetor: Four-barrel
Usage: 1967–69 Belvedere, Charger, and Coronet; 1969 Barracuda and Dart GTS.
Note(s): Interchange Number 3 will fit if camshaft is changed.

Interchange Number: 5
Displacement: 440-ci
Horsepower: 390 at 4,700 rpm
Compression Ratio: 10.5:1
Carburetor: Triple-two-barrel
Usage: 1969–71 Super Bee, 1969–72 Road Runner, 1970–72 Charger R/T, and 1970–71 Chrysler 300.
Note(s): 1972 block is painted blue.

Interchange Number: 6
Displacement: 426 Hemi
Horsepower: 425 at 5,000 rpm
Compression Ratio: 10.25:1
Carburetor: Twin-four-barrel
Usage: 1967–70 Belvedere, Charger, Coronet; 1970 Barracuda, Challenger.

Interchange Number: 7
Displacement: 383-ci
Horsepower: 290 at 4,400 rpm
Compression Ratio: 9.2:1
Carburetor: Two-barrel
Usage: 1968–71 Barracuda, Challenger, Charger, Coronet, Fury, Monaco, Newport, Polara, and Satellite.
Note(s): For two- or four-barrel in 1971 models.

Interchange Number: 8
Displacement: 383-ci
Horsepower: 330 at 5,000 rpm or 335 at 5, 500 rpm
Compression Ratio: 10:1
Carburetor: Four-barrel
Usage: 1968–69 Barracuda, Charger, Coronet, Dart GTS, Fury, Monaco, Newport, and Polara.
Note(s): 335-hp in Super Bee, Road Runner, Dart GTS, and Barracuda only. Has different camshaft.

Interchange Number: 9
Displacement: 426 Hemi
Horsepower: 425 at 5,000 rpm
Compression Ratio: 10.2:1
Carburetor: Twin-four-barrel
Usage: 1971 Barracuda, Challenger, Charger, Satellite.
Note(s): Has hydraulic camshaft.

Interchange Number: 10
Displacement: 340-ci
Horsepower: 275 at 5,000 rpm

Compression Ratio: 10.5:1
Carburetor: Four-barrel
Usage: 1968–71 Dart, Valiant; 1970–71 Duster; 1970–71 Barracuda, Challenger; 1971 Charger, Satellite.

Interchange Number: 11
Displacement: 340-ci
Horsepower: 290 at 5,000 rpm
Compression Ratio: 10.5:1
Carburetor: Triple-two-barrel
Usage: 1970–71 Cuda AAR; 1970–71 Challenger T/A.

Interchange Number: 12
Displacement: 360-ci
Horsepower: 245 at 4,800 rpm
Compression Ratio: 8.4:1
Carburetor: Four-barrel
Usage: 1974 Challenger; 1974 Charger; 1974 Road Runner; 1974–75 Duster; 1974–75 Dart Sport; 1975 Fury.

Interchange Number: 13
Displacement: 340-ci
Horsepower: 240 at 4,800 rpm
Compression Ratio: 8.5:1
Carburetor: Four-barrel
Usage: 1972–73 Barracuda, Challenger, Charger, Dart, and Duster.
Note(s): Early 1972 models (up to engine number HM34039118000) used a forged crankshaft; after this number a cast crankshaft is used. The letter "E" appears on the upper block pad.

Interchange Number: 14
Displacement: 400-ci
Horsepower: 255 at 4,800 rpm (two-barrel), or 265 at 4, 800 rpm (four-barrel).
Compression Ratio: 8.2:1
Carburetor: Two-barrel or four-barrel
Usage: 1972–73 Charger Coronet, Fury, Monaco, Newport, New Yorker, Polara, and Satellite.

Interchange Number: 15
Displacement: 400-ci
Horsepower: See Notes
Compression Ratio: 8.2:1
Carburetor: Two- or four-barrel
Usage: 1974–75 Charger, Coronet, Fury, Monaco, Newport, New Yorker, Polara, and Satellite.
Note(s): Two-barrel 185 hp at 4, 000 rpm; four-barrel 205 hp at 4, 400 rpm; four-barrel high-performance 250 hp at 4, 800 rpm. Camshafts may have to be interchanged when interchanging between regular and high-performance applications.

Interchange Number: 16
Displacement: 440-ci
Horsepower: 335 at 4,400 rpm
Compression Ratio: 8.5:1
Carburetor: Four-barrel
Usage: 1971 Fury, Monaco, Newport, and New Yorker.

Interchange Number: 17
Displacement: 440-ci
Horsepower: 370 at 4,600 rpm
Compression Ratio: 9.5:1
Carburetor: Four-barrel
Usage: 1971 Charger, Coronet, and Satellite.

Interchange Number: 18
Displacement: 440
Horsepower: See Notes
Compression Ratio: 8.2:1
Carburetor: Four-barrel
Usage: 1972 Charger, Coronet, Fury, Monaco, Newport, New Yorker, and Satellite.
Note(s): Many different rates. Camshafts may have to be swapped when interchanging between different ratings.

Interchange Number: 19
Displacement: 440
Horsepower: See Notes

Compression Ratio: 8.2:1
Carburetor: Four-barrel
Usage: 1973–74 Charger, Coronet, Fury, Monaco, Newport, New Yorker, and Satellite.
Note(s): 220 hp at 3,600 rpm regular; 275 hp at 4, 800 rpm high-performance. Camshafts must be changed when interchanging from regular to high-performance engine.

Interchange Number: 20
Displacement: 440-ci
Horsepower: 350 at 4,400 rpm
Compression Ratio: 9.7:1
Carburetor: Four-barrel
Usage: 1970 Fury, Monaco, Newport, and New Yorker.

Interchange Number: 21
Displacement: 440-ci
Horsepower: 375 at 4,600 rpm
Compression Ratio: 9.7:1
Carburetor: Four-barrel
Usage: 1970 Barracuda, Challenger, Charger, Coronet, and Satellite.
Note(s): Interchange Number 20 can be modified to fit by switching the rods, crankshaft, and camshaft to the high-performance parts.

Crankshafts

The type of transmission and the material the crankshaft is made from will affect the interchangeability. Those units from a car with manual transmission will fit a car with an automatic transmission without any modification, except the removal of the clutch pilot bushing. But a crankshaft from a car with an automatic transmission will not fit a car with a manual transmission unless the crankshaft is bored to accept the clutch pilot bushing.

Both forged-steel and cast-iron crankshafts were used, and the two are not interchangeable. Although a cast-iron crankshaft may fit, it should *never* take the place of a forged-steel unit, because the cast crankshaft cannot withstand the abuse a high-performance engine gives out. A forged-steel crankshaft, on the other hand, can take the place of a cast-iron unit, but the engine will have to be rebalanced.

Some crankshafts may have one or more connecting rod or main journals that are undersized. Undersized journals can be identified by special markings on the block and the crankshaft itself. Location of these markings varies with engine family group. On small blocks—the 273, 318, and 340—the markings are stamped on the milled, flat portion of the number eight counterweight of the crankshaft. For 0.001-inch undersized rods, the marking will be the letter "R" followed by the number or num-

ber(s) of those rod journals that are undersized. If all rod journals are undersized by 0.010 inch, then the marking is "RX." The letter "M" followed by number(s) indicates that those main journals are undersized 0.001 inch, while the code "MX" is an indication all main journals are undersized by .010 inch.

The location for big blocks—383-ci, 426-ci, and 440-ci—and Hemi engines is found on the number three counterweight of the crankshaft. The codes are the same as those used on small blocks, except when all rod or main journals are undersized by 0.010 inch, where the code "R10" for rod journals and "M10" for main journals is used.

A Maltese Cross on the upper engine pad is an indication that either rod or main journals are undersized by 0.001 inch, while a Maltese Cross and the letter "X" will mark that either rod or main journals are undersized by .010 inch.

Model Identification

Interchange

Interchange Number: 1
Part Number(s): 2268119
Forging Number(s): 2128278, 2128869, 2264182, 2465747, 253457, 2658268, 2658278, 26999910
Usage: 1964–69 273-ci; 1964–71 318-ci.

Interchange Number: 2
Part Number(s): 3698267
Usage: 1972–73 318-ci.

Interchange Number: 3
Part Number(s): 3751831
Usage: 1974 318-ci.

Interchange Number: 4
Part Number(s): 2843868
Forging Number(s): 2843868, 34044035
Usage: 1968 to early 1972 340-ci.
Note(s): Used up to engine serial number HM34039118000. Crankshaft is a forged-steel unit.

Interchange Number: 5
Part Number(s): 3751162
Usage: Late 1972–73 340-ci.
Note(s): Begins with block number HM34039118001; number six counterweight is painted orange with white stripe. A clock face

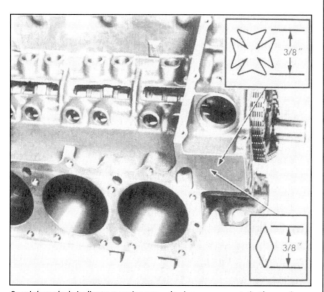

Special symbols indicate oversize or undersize components in the engine.

is cast into the number eight counterweight. Vibration damper is cast with the words "Use with 340 cast crank only."

Interchange Number: 6
Part Number(s): 3751602
Usage: 1974–75 360-ci.

Interchange Number: 7
Part Number(s): 2268114
Forging Number(s): 1737641, 2203155, 2206159
Usage: 1964–66 361-ci; 1964–71 383-ci; 1972–73 400-ci. See Notes.
Note(s): Forged crankshaft. Not used in two-barrel 383-ci with automatic transmission or 400-ci with automatic transmission.

Interchange Number: 8
Part Number(s): 3751162
Forging Number(s):
Usage: 1970–71 383-ci two-barrel with automatic transmission; 1972–73 400-ci two- or four-barrel with automatic transmission.
Note(s): Cast-iron crankshaft. *Do not use* in cars with manual transmission. Has an elliptical-shaped weight in front of the main member.

Interchange Number: 9
Part Number(s): 3751881
Usage: 1974 400-ci with manual transmission.

Interchange Number: 10
Part Number(s): 3751886
Usage: 1974 400-ci with automatic transmission.

Interchange Number: 11
Part Number(s): 2780533
Forging Number(s): 2780533
Usage: 1966–71 426 Hemi.

Interchange Number: 12
Part Number(s): 2536983
Usage: 1966–71 440-ci, except triple-two-barrel.

Interchange Number: 13
Part Number(s): 3671283
Usage: 1972–73 440-ci, except 1972 440-ci triple-two-barrel.
Note(s): 280-hp high-performance only in 1973.

Interchange Number: 14
Part Number(s): 3698460
Usage: 1973 440-ci, except high-performance.
Note(s): Cast-iron crankshaft. Has clock face in number one counterweight.

Interchange Number: 15
Part Number(s): 3671242
Usage: 1973 440-ci, except high-performance.
Note(s): Forged-steel crankshaft.

Interchange Number: 16
Part Number(s): 3751891
Usage: 1974 440-ci, except high-performance.
Note(s): Cast-iron crankshaft. Has clock face in number one counterweight.

Interchange Number: 17
Part Number(s): 3751891
Usage: 1974 440-ci, except high-performance.
Note(s): Forged-steel crankshaft.

Interchange Number: 18
Part Number(s): 3751899
Usage: 1974 440-ci high-performance.
Note(s): Forged crankshaft.

Interchange Number: 19
Part Number(s): 3512036
Usage: 1970–72 440-ci triple-two-barrel.
Note(s): Will fit 440-ci four-barrel. May require rebalancing high-performance crankshaft.

Flywheel
Model Identification

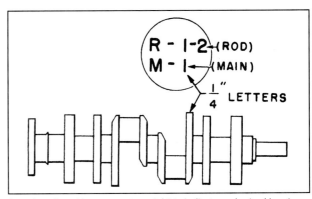

Location of marking on counterweight to indicate undersized bearings.

Interchange

Interchange Number: 1
Part Number(s): 2264597
Usage: 1966–69 273-ci; 1964–74 318-ci; 1968–early 1972 340-ci; 1964–66 361-ci; 1964–67 383-ci; 1970–1971 383-ci; 1972–74 400-ci; 1972–74 440-ci, except 440-ci triple-two-barrel; 1966 440-ci.
Note(s): Used only until engine number HM34039118000 on 1972 340-ci engines.

Interchange Number: 2
Part Number(s): 2463256
Usage: 1964–65 273-ci.

Interchange Number: 3
Part Number(s): 2402215
Usage: 1962–64 413-ci; 1963–64 426-ci, except Hemi.

Interchange Number: 4
Part Number(s): 2536400
Usage: 1964–65 426 Hemi.

Interchange Number: 5
Part Number(s): 2863069
Usage: 1966–69 426 Hemi.

Interchange Number: 6
Part Number(s): 2843211
Usage: 1967–69 440-ci; 1968–69 383-ci.
Note(s): Also found in 1969–74 Dodge pickups with 440-ci.

Interchange Number: 7
Part Number(s): 3410258
Usage: 1970–71 426 Hemi.

Interchange Number: 8
Part Number(s): 3410837
Usage: 1970–71 440-ci only.

Interchange Number: 9
Part Number(s): 3410916
Usage: 1974 360-ci.

Interchange Number: 10
Part Number(s): 3681639
Usage: Late 1972–73 340-ci.
Note(s): Beginning with block marked HM34039118001 or later.
Will *not fit* earlier models, due to change in crankshaft design.

Connecting Rods
Model Identification

Interchange
Interchange Number: 1
Part Number(s): 2406785
Forging Number(s): 1618699, 2406782
Usage: 1964–71 318-ci, all models; 1964–69 273-ci; 1968–71 340-ci.

Interchange Number: 2
Part Number(s): 2899495
Forging Number(s): 2899496
Usage: 1972 and certain 1973 318-ci, all models (See Notes); 1972–73 340-ci.
Note(s): Use only in 1973 318-ci engines with engine numbers from JM318R40209000 to JM318R40209999 and from JM318R41609000 to JM318R41609600.

Interchange Number: 3
Part Number(s): 2899061
Usage: 1973–74 318-ci; 1973–74 360-ci, all models (See Notes).
Note(s): Used only in 1973 318-ci engine marked up to JM318R40209000 and from engine serial numbers JM318R40209999 to JM318R 41609000 and then after JM318R41609600; all 1974 models used these rods. Interchange Number 2 will fit if swapped with pistons.

Interchange Number: 4
Part Number(s): 2406766
Forging Number(s): 1737692
Usage: 1964–71 383-ci; 1964–66 361-ci; 1972–1974 400-ci.

Interchange Number: 5
Part Number(s): 2406770
Forging Number(s): NA
Usage: 1966–69 440-ci, all models except 1969 440-ci triple-two-barrel; 1970–74 440-ci, except high-performance or triple-two-barrel; 1962–64 413-ci.; 1962–64 426-ci, except Hemi.

Interchange Number: 6
Part Number(s): 2951906
Usage: 1970–74 440-ci, high performance only; 1970–72 440-ci triple-two-barrel.

Interchange Number: 7
Part Number(s): 3462426
Usage: 1969 440-ci with triple-two-barrel.

Interchange Number: 8
Part Number(s): 2532709
Usage: 1964–65 426 Hemi.

Interchange Number: 9
Part Number(s): 2780531
Usage: 1966–71 426 Hemi.

Pistons

Interchange here is for standard-bore pistons. However, some powerplants may have come from the factory with over-bored pistons. Over-bored pistons can be identified by the letter A on the block. On small blocks, the letter "A" will follow the engine serial number, while on big blocks and the Hemi, the letter A will appear on the engine pad, at the front of the block. Interchange is the same with or without an over-bore; only the part number is different. Also note that some engines used different pistons for different banks. So follow the interchange carefully.

Model Identification

Interchange
Interchange Number: 1
Part Number(s): 3004509
Compression Ratio: 9.20:1
Usage: 1968–69 318-ci.

Interchange Number: 2
Part Number(s): 3420222
Compression Ratio: 8.60:1
Usage: 1970–72 318-ci; certain 1973 318-ci engines (See Notes).
Note(s): Use only in 1973 engines with engine serial numbers between JM31840209000 to JM31840209999 and between JM31841609000 to JM31841609600.

Interchange Number: 3
Part Number(s): 3685751
Compression Ratio: 8.60:1
Usage: Certain 1973 models and all 1974 318-ci engines.
Note(s): Used only in 1973 models with engines having serial number up to JM31840209000; then from JM31840209999 to JM31841609000; then after JM31841609600 until end of production in 1974.

Interchange Number: 4
Part Number(s): 3004524

Compression Ratio: 9.20:1
Usage: 1968–69 383-ci two-barrel, all models.
Interchange Number: 5
Part Number(s): 3004531
Compression Ratio: 10:1
Usage: 1968–69 383-ci four-barrel. Includes 330 hp and 335 hp.
Interchange Number: 6
Part Number(s): 3420206
Compression Ratio: 8.8:1
Usage: 1970–71 383-ci two-barrel.
Interchange Number: 7
Part Number(s): 3420210
Compression Ratio: 9.5:1
Usage: 1970–71 383-ci four-barrel.
Interchange Number: 8
Part Number(s): 3621356
Compression Ratio: 8.2:1
Usage: 1972–74 400-ci, all models.
Interchange Number: 9
Part Number(s): 3004535
Compression Ratio: 10.10:1
Usage: 1968–69 440-ci, all models.
Interchange Number: 10
Part Number(s): 3420214
Compression Ratio: 9.5:1
Usage: 1970 440-ci, except 370 hp or multi carburetors.
Interchange Number: 11
Part Number(s): 3549426
Compression Ratio: 9.5:1
Usage: 1970–71 440-ci 370-hp.
Interchange Number: 12
Part Number(s): 3420218
Compression Ratio: 10.5:1
Usage: 1970–72 440-ci triple-two-barrel.
Interchange Number: 13
Part Number(s): 3549528
Compression Ratio: 8.5:1
Usage: 1971 440-ci, except high-performance.
Interchange Number: 14
Part Number(s): 3579047
Compression Ratio: 8.2:1
Usage: 1972–74 440-ci, all models, except with triple-two-barrel.
Interchange Number: 15
Part Number(s): 3004516 odd, 3004517 even
Compression Ratio: 10.5:1
Usage: 1968–71 340-ci engine.
Interchange Number: 16
Part Number(s): 3621352
Compression Ratio: 8.5:1
Usage: 1972–73 340-ci.
Interchange Number: 17
Part Number(s): 3685737
Compression Ratio: 8.4:1
Usage: 1973–74 360-ci.
Interchange Number: 18
Part Number(s): 2808227 odd, 2808228 even
Compression Ratio: 10.25:1
Usage: 1966–71 426 Hemi.
Interchange Number: 19
Part Number(s): 3549528
Compression Ratio: 8.5:1
Usage: 1971 440-ci, except high-performance.

Camshafts
Model Identification

Interchange
Interchange Number: 1
Part Number(s): 2532190
Lifter Type: Hydraulic.
Usage: 1966–70 383-ci four-barrel, except in Road Runner,
Super Bee, Cuda; Dart GTS or Challenger R/T; 1964–65 413-
ci, except police cars; 1966–70 440-ci.
Note(s): Cast numbers: 1964–65: 2532190; 1966–70: 2532175
or 2532454.
Interchange Number: 2
Usage: 1968–69 273-ci; 1968–70 318-ci.
Interchange Number: 3
Part Number(s): 2899206
Lifter Type: Hydraulic
Usage: 1968–73 340-ci; 1974 360-ci in Charger, Road Runner,
Challenger, or Barracuda.
Interchange Number: 4
Part Number(s): 2843564
Lifter Type: Hydraulic
Usage: 1968–70 383-ci 335-hp four-barrel; 1968–70 440-ci
375 hp.
Interchange Number: 5
Part Number(s): 2899534
Lifter Type: Mechanical
Usage: 1968–69 426 Hemi.
Interchange Number: 6
Part Number(s): 3462355
Lifter Type: Hydraulic
Usage: 1970–71 426 Hemi.
Interchange Number: 7
Part Number(s): 3462038
Lifter Type: Hydraulic
Usage: 1969 440-ci triple-two-barrel.
Interchange Number: 8
Part Number(s): 3512033
Lifter Type: Hydraulic
Usage: 1970 440-ci triple-two-barrel.
Interchange Number: 9
Part Number(s): 3512635
Lifter Type: Hydraulic
Usage: 1971–74 318-ci, all models
Interchange Number: 10
Part Number(s): 3577181
Lifter Type: Hydraulic
Usage: 1971 383-ci two-barrel; 1971–74 440-ci four-barrel,

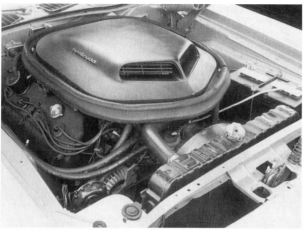

The 426 Hemi used unique valve covers. The 1970–1971 style is shown.

except high-performance or multi carburetors; 1972–74 400-ci two-barrel; 1974 400-ci four-barrel, except 250 hp.

Interchange Number: 11
Part Number(s): 3512907
Lifter Type: Hydraulic
Usage: 1971 383-ci four-barrel, all models; 1971–74 440-ci high-performance; 1972–73 400-ci four-barrel; 1974 400-ci 250 hp.

Interchange Number: 12
Part Number(s): 3512903
Lifter Type: Hydraulic
Usage: 1971–72 440-ci triple-two-barrel.

Cylinder Heads
Model Identification

Interchange

Interchange Number: 1
Part Number(s): 2780557
Casting Number: 2780559
Usage: 1966–71 426 Hemi.

Interchange Number: 2
Part Number(s): 2843674
Casting Number: 2843675
Usage: 1968–69 273-ci; 1968–71 318-ci.

Interchange Number: 3
Part Number(s): 2531902
Casting Number: 2531894
Usage: 1968–71 340-ci, except triple-two-barrel.

Interchange Number: 4
Part Number(s): 2843904
Casting Number: 2843906
Usage: 1968–71 383-ci, all outputs; 1968–71 440-ci, all outputs.

Interchange Number: 5
Part Number(s): 3671637
Casting Number: 2843675
Usage: 1972 318-ci.

Interchange Number: 6
Part Number(s): 3577053
Casting Number: 3418915
Usage: 1970–71 340-ci triple-two-barrel.

Interchange Number: 7
Part Number(s): 3671639
Casting Number: 3418915
Usage: 1972 340-ci; 1972 360-ci.

Interchange Number: 8
Part Number(s): 3462344
Casting Number: 3423246
Usage: 1972 400-ci; 1972 440-ci.

Interchange Number: 9
Part Number(s): 3698615
Casting Number: 2843675
Usage: 1973 318-ci.

Interchange Number: 10
Part Number(s): 3698617
Casting Number: 3671587
Usage: 1973 340-ci; 1973–74 360-ci, except with California emissions.

Interchange Number: 11
Part Number(s): 3671640
Casting Number: 37512213
Usage: 1973–74 400-ci; 1973–74 440-ci, all outputs.

Interchange Number: 12
Part Number(s): 3751661
Casting Number: 2843675
Usage: 1974 318-ci, all models.

Interchange Number: 13
Part Number(s): 3671873
Casting Number: 3671587
Usage: 1973 360-ci with California emissions; 1974 360-ci, all states.

Interchange Number: 14
Part Number(s): 3769910
Casting Number: 3769901
Usage: 1974 400-ci, 440-ci, all outputs.

Valve Covers
Model Identification

Interchange

Interchange Number: 1
Position: Driver's side
Part Number(s): 2465383
Usage: 1965–68 273-ci two-barrel in all models; 1967–68 318-ci (1967 USA 318-ci only); 1968 340-ci.

Interchange Number: 2
Position: Passenger's side
Part Number(s): 2806072
Usage: 1966–68 273-ci two-barrel, all models; 1967–68 318-ci, all models (1967 USA 318-ci only).
Note(s): 1967 318-ci engine marked C318.

Interchange Number: 3
Position: Passenger's side
Part Number(s): 2806659
Usage: 1966–69 426 Hemi, all models.

Interchange Number: 4
Position: Driver's side
Part Number(s): 2806661
Usage: 1966–69 426 Hemi, all models.

Interchange Number: 5
Position: Driver's side
Part Number(s): 2899045
Usage: 1967–69 Dart GTS or Barracuda with 383-ci.

Interchange Number: 6
Position: Passenger's side
Part Number(s): 2780911
Usage: 1967 383-ci, all models; 1967 440-ci, except 375-hp models; 1968 383-ci two-barrel; 1968 440-ci, except 375-hp version.

Interchange Number: 7
Position: Passenger's side
Part Number(s): 2946466
Usage: 1968–69 340-ci, all models.

Interchange Number: 8
Position: Passenger's side
Part Number(s): 2806996
Usage: 1968 383-ci four-barrel; 1968 440-ci 375-hp version.

Interchange Number: 9
Position: Driver's side
Part Number(s): 2899052
Usage: 1968–69 383-ci two-barrel in Coronet or Belvedere only; 1968–69 440-ci 375 hp, all models.

Interchange Number: 10
Position: Driver's side
Part Number(s): 2899016
Usage: 1968 383-ci four-barrel in Barracuda, Dart GTS, Coronet, or Belvedere; 1968–69 383-ci two-barrel or four-barrel in full-size models; 1968–69 440-ci in full-size models.

Interchange Number: 11
Position: Passenger's side
Part Number(s): 2946450
Usage: 1969 273-ci, 318-ci, or 340-ci engines, all models.

Interchange Number: 12
Position: Driver's side
Part Number(s): 2946451
Usage: 1969 273-ci or 318-ci, all models.

Interchange Number: 13
Position: Passenger's side
Part Number(s): 2946463
Usage: 1969 383-ci in Dart or Barracuda models only.

Interchange Number: 14
Position: Passenger's side
Part Number(s): 2946464
Usage: 1969 383-ci or 440-ci, all models, all outputs.

Interchange Number: 15
Position: Passenger's side
Part Number(s): 2946008
Usage: 1970 318-ci, all models.

Interchange Number: 16
Position: Passenger's side
Part Number(s): 3577636
Usage: 1971–72 318-ci; 1971–72 360-ci, all models; 1971–72 340-ci four-barrel.

Interchange Number: 17
Position: Driver's side
Part Number(s): 2946011
Usage: 1970–71 318-ci; 1971–74 360-ci, all models; 1972 318-ci without electronic ignition.

Interchange Number: 18
Position: Passenger's side
Part Number(s): 3462684
Usage: 1970 340-ci four-barrel, all models.

Interchange Number: 19
Position: Driver's side
Part Number(s): 3462913
Usage: 1970 340-ci four-barrel.

Interchange Number: 20
Position: Driver's side
Part Number(s): 3577807

Usage: 1971–72 340-ci four-barrel or triple-two-barrel; 1972 318-ci with electronic ignition; 1972 360-ci, all models.

Interchange Number: 21
Position: Passenger's side
Part Number(s): 3577222
Usage: 1970 340-ci triple-two-barrel.

Interchange Number: 22
Position: Driver's side
Part Number(s): 3577223
Usage: 1970–71 340-ci triple-two-barrel.

Interchange Number: 23
Position: Passenger's side
Part Number(s): 3577253
Usage: 1971 340-ci triple-two-barrel.

Interchange Number: 24
Position: Passenger's side
Part Number(s): 2946057
Usage: 1970–71 383-ci; 1972 400-ci; 1970–72 440-ci, all models.

Interchange Number: 25
Position: Driver's side
Part Number(s): 2946070
Usage: 1970–71 383-ci; 1970–72 440-ci; 1972 400-ci, all except full-size models.

Interchange Number: 26
Position: Passenger's side

Part Number(s): 2946072
Usage: 1970–71 426 Hemi, all models.

Interchange Number: 27
Position: Driver's side
Part Number(s): 2946075
Usage: 1970–71 426 Hemi, all models.

Interchange Number: 28
Position: Passenger's side
Part Number(s): 3671341
Usage: 1973–74 318-ci; 1973–74 360-ci, all models.

Interchange Number: 29
Position: Driver's side
Part Number(s): 3671372
Usage: 1973–74 318-ci; 1973 340-ci; 1974 360-ci, all models.

Interchange Number: 30
Position: Passenger's side
Part Number(s): 3698818
Usage: 1973 340-ci, all models.

Interchange Number: 31
Position: Passenger's side
Part Number(s): 3751024
Usage: 1973–74 400-ci or 440-ci, all models, all outputs.

Interchange Number: 32
Position: Driver's side
Part Number(s): 3698821
Usage: 1973–74 400-ci or 440-ci, all models, all outputs.

Chapter 2

Fuel Systems

Fuel Tanks
Model Identification

Interchange
Interchange Number: 1
   Part Number(s): 2880417
   Capacity: 18 gallons
   Usage: 1968–69 Barracuda, Dart, and Valiant, all body styles, all models.
Interchange Number: 2
   Part Number(s): 2880435
   Capacity: 19 gallons
   Usage: 1968–69 Charger, all models.
Interchange Number: 3
   Part Number(s): 2880434
   Capacity: 19 gallons
   Usage: 1968–69 Belvedere, Coronet, all engines, all body styles except station wagon.
Interchange Number: 4
   Part Number(s): 3404493

Capacity: 18 gallons
Usage: 1970 Barracuda with E.E.C; 1971–early 1972 Barracuda, all models.
Note(s): Used until March 1972.
Interchange Number: 5
   Part Number(s): 3404509
   Capacity: 18 gallons
   Usage: 1970 Barracuda without E.E.C. Will not fit California cars.
Interchange Number: 6
   Part Number(s): 3404494
   Capacity: 18 gallons
   Usage: 1970 Challenger with E.E.C.; 1971 Challenger, all models.
Interchange Number: 7
   Part Number(s): 3404510
   Capacity: 18 gallons
   Usage: 1970 Challenger without E.E.C. Not for California cars.
Interchange Number: 8
   Part Number(s): 3404393
   Capacity: 19 gallons
   Usage: 1970 Charger with E.E.C.
Interchange Number: 9
   Part Number(s): 3404492
   Capacity: 19 gallons
   Usage: 1970 Charger without E.E.C.
Interchange Number: 10
   Part Number(s): 3404951
   Capacity: 21 gallons
   Usage: 1971–early 1972 Charger, Coronet, and Satellite, all models and body styles except station wagon.
   Note(s): Up to build date April 30, 1972.
Interchange Number: 11
   Part Number(s): 3642103
   Capacity: 19 1/2 gallons
   Usage: Late 1972–73 Charger, Coronet, Satellite, all models and body styles except station wagon.
   Note(s): After April 30, 1972, only.
Interchange Number: 12
   Part Number(s): 3726425
   Capacity: 19 1/2 gallons
   Usage: 1974 Charger, Coronet, Satellite, all models and body styles except station wagon.
Interchange Number: 13
   Part Number(s): 3404220
   Capacity: 18 gallons
   Usage: 1970–early 1972 Dart, Duster, Demon, and Valiant, all models, body styles, and engines with E.E.C.
   Note(s): E.E.C. standard all 50 states in 1971–72. Used until April 15, 1972.
Interchange Number: 14
   Part Number(s): 3583522
   Capacity: 16 gallons
   Usage: Late 1972–74 Dart, Duster, and Valiant, all models, body styles, and engines.
   Note(s): Used after April 15, 1972.

Interchange Number: 15
    Part Number(s): 3404478
    Capacity: 18 gallons
    Usage: 1970 Dart, Duster, and Valiant, all models, body styles, and engines, all without E.E.C.
    Note(s): Not for California cars.

Interchange Number: 16
    Part Number(s): 3583569
    Capacity: 16 1/2 gallons
    Usage: Late 1972–74 Barracuda.
    Note(s): Used After March 1972.

Interchange Number: 17
    Part Number(s): 3404491
    Capacity: 19 gallons
    Usage: 1970 Coronet and Satellite without E.E.C., all models and body styles except station wagon.
    Note(s): Not for California cars.

Interchange Number: 18
    Part Number(s): 3404392
    Capacity: 19 gallons
    Usage: 1970 Coronet, Satellite with E.E.C., all models and body styles except station wagon.

Interchange Number: 19
    Part Number(s): 3583570
    Capacity: 18 gallons
    Usage: Early 1972 Challenger, all models.
    Note(s): Used until March 1972.

Interchange Number: 20
    Part Number(s): 3642139
    Capacity: 18 gallons
    Usage: Late 1972–74 Challenger, all models.
    Note(s): Used after March 1972.

Gas Caps
Model Identification

Interchange

Interchange Number: 1
    Part Number(s): 2823339
    Usage: 1967 GTX; 1967–68 Barracuda; 1968 Charger.
    Note(s): Flip-top cap.

Interchange Number: 2
    Part Number(s): 2823328
    Usage: 1967–69 Dart, Valiant, all models, all body styles.

Interchange Number: 3
    Part Number(s): 2925697
    Usage: 1968–69 Belvedere, Coronet, all models and body styles except station wagon.

Interchange Number: 4
    Part Number(s): 2925878
    Usage: 1969–70 Charger; 1969 Barracuda.
    Note(s): Flip-top cap. Imprinted "FUEL."

Interchange Number: 5
    Part Number(s): 3404534
    Usage: 1970 Duster without E.C.S.
    Note(s): Four-door or two-door hardtop Valiant models will not fit.

Interchange Number: 6
    Part Number(s): 3404529
    Usage: 1970 Duster with E.C.S.; early–1971 Duster; early 1971 Demon
    Note(s): Used until May 1971.

Interchange Number: 7
    Part Number(s): 3404478
    Usage: 1970 Dart, Valiant, all body styles except fastback, without E.C.S. only.

Interchange Number: 8
    Part Number(s): 3404180
    Usage: 1970–late 1971 Dart, Valiant, all body styles except fastback, with E.C.S. only.
    Note(s): Up to May 1971.

Interchange Number: 9
    Part Number(s): 3642004
    Usage: Late 1971 Dart and Valiant, all models except Duster and Demon.
    Note(s): After May 1971 only.

Interchange Number: 10
    Part Number(s): 3642007
    Usage: Late 1971 Duster and Demon.
    Note(s): After May 1971 only.

Interchange Number: 11

The 1968 Charger's gas cap was used on a variety of models.

Part Number(s): 2962213
Usage: 1970–early 1971 Barracuda with E.C.S.
Note(s): Used until June 1971.

Interchange Number: 12
Part Number(s): 3583573
Usage: Late 1971 Barracuda.
Note(s): After June 1971 only.

Interchange Number: 13
Part Number(s): 3404677
Usage: 1970 Challenger without E.C.S.

Interchange Number: 14
Part Number(s): 3404531
Usage: 1970–early 1971 Challenger with E.C.S.
Note(s): Up to June 1971.

Interchange Number: 15
Part Number(s): 3583575
Usage: Late 1971–74 Challenger.
Note(s): After June 1971 only.

Interchange Number: 16
Part Number(s): 2856332
Usage: 1970 Coronet, Satellite without E.C.S., all models and body styles except station wagon.

Interchange Number: 17
Part Number(s): 3404382
Usage: 1970 Coronet, Satellite with E.C.S., all models and body styles except station wagon.
Note(s): Used in California car only.

Interchange Number: 18
Part Number(s): 3404202
Usage: 1970 Charger with E.C.S.

Interchange Number: 19
Part Number(s): 3466426
Usage: 1971 Charger; 1971 Satellite. Two-door models only.

Interchange Number: 20
Part Number(s): 3549077
Usage: 1972 Dart, Duster, Demon, and Valiant, all models and body styles.

Interchange Number: 21
Part Number(s): 3549089
Usage: 1970–74 Challenger.
Note(s): Chrome cap.

Interchange Number: 22
Part Number(s): 3549088
Usage: 1972–74 Barracuda; late 1972 Charger, Coronet, Fury, Monaco, Newport, New Yorker, Polara, Satellite, all models and body styles except station wagon.
Note(s): Used after February 1972 for all models except Barracuda.

Interchange Number: 23
Part Number(s): 3466825
Usage: Early 1972 Charger, Coronet, and Satellite, all models, all body styles except station wagon.
Note(s): Up to February 1972 only.

Interchange Number: 24
Part Number(s): 3642192
Usage: 1973–74 Dart, Duster, and Valiant, all models and body styles.

Interchange Number: 25
Part Number(s): 3549087
Usage: 1973–74 Charger, Coronet, and Satellite, all models and body styles.

Interchange Number: 26
Part Number(s):
Usage: 1970 Barracuda without E.E.C., all models and body styles.

Fuel Pumps
Model Identification

318-ci	Interchange Number
1964–74	1
340-ci	**Interchange Number**
1968–71	1
1972–73	2

The word "Fuel" is imprinted on the 1969–1970 gas cap.

360-ci	Interchange Number
1971–74	2
361-ci	**Interchange Number**
1964–66	3
383-ci	**Interchange Number**
1964–68	3
1969–71	6
400-ci	**Interchange Number**
1972	9
1973–74, except high-performance	11
1973–74 high-performance	12
426-ci	**Interchange Number**
1968–71	5
440-ci	**Interchange Number**
1966–68, except high-performance	3
1966–68 high-performance	8
1969–71, except high-performance	6
1969–71 high-performance	7
1972, except high-performance	9
1972 high-performance	10
1972, except high-performance	11
1972 high-performance	12

Fuel pump used with the high-performance 383-ci V-8. Year One

Fuel pump used with the high-performance 440-ci V-8. Year One

Hemi fuel pump. Year One

Interchange
Interchange Number: 1
> Part Number(s): 3744806
> ID Number(s): M3673 , M3962S
> Usage: 1964–74 318-ci; 1964–69 273-ci; 1968-71 340-ci, all models.

Interchange Number: 2
> Part Number(s): 3744805
> ID Number(s): 6450S
> Usage: 1972–73 340-ci; 1971–74 360-ci, except two-barrel in 1974.

Interchange Number: 3
> Part Number(s): 2495528
> ID Number(s): M3672
> Usage: 1964–66 361-ci; 1964–68 383-ci, all outputs; 1966–67 440-ci, except 375 hp; 1965 426-ci, except Hemi.
> Note(s): Interchange Number 8 will fit and provide better performance.

Interchange Number: 4
> Part Number(s): 2421466
> ID Number(s): M3446
> Usage: 1964 426-ci, except Hemi.
> Note(s): Interchange Number 8 may fit.

Interchange Number: 5
> Part Number(s): 2585118
> ID Number(s): M4024
> Usage: 1964–71 426 Hemi.

Interchange Number: 6
> Part Number(s): 3621675
> ID Number(s): 4589SA
> Usage: 1969–71 383-ci, all outputs; 1969–71 440-ci, except 375 hp or 390 hp.
> Note(s): Interchange Number 7 will fit and provide better performance.

Interchange Number: 7
> Part Number(s): 3420835
> ID Number(s): 4845S
> Usage: 1970–71 440-ci 375 hp or triple-two-barrel.

Interchange Number: 8
> Part Number(s): 3004107
> ID Number(s): 4434
> Usage: 1967–69 440-ci 375 hp or triple-two-barrel.

Interchange Number: 9
> Part Number(s): 3621609
> ID Number(s): 6415S
> Usage: 1972 440-ci; 1972 440-ci, all except high-performance 440-ci.
> Note(s): Interchange Number 10 will fit and provide better performance.

Interchange Number: 10
> Part Number(s): 3621610
> ID Number(s): 6190
> Usage: 1972 440-ci high-performance only.

Interchange Number: 11
> Part Number(s): 3685799
> ID Number(s): 6415S
> Usage: 1973–74 400 or 440-ci, all outputs except high-performance.
> Note(s): Interchange Number 12 will fit and provide better performance.

Interchange Number: 12
> Part Number(s): 3685800
> ID Number(s): 6416S
> Usage: 1973–74 400- or 440-ci high-performance.
> Note(s): Found in Charger or Road Runner models.

Intake Manifolds

All intake manifolds are made of cast iron with two exceptions: Hemi and the 1969 440-ci triple-two-barrel powerplants. These two engines used a cast aluminum intake. Manifolds can be identified by their casting number, which can be found on the intake runners. You may also find a casting date below the casting number. The casting date has no effect on the interchange. The interchange here is based on part number. Note that options like emission controls may affect the interchange.

Model Identification

Interchange

Interchange Number: 1
Part Number(s): 2468959
Casting Number: 2468960
Usage: 1967–69 318-ci two-barrel, all models except 1967
  Canadian-built powerplant.
Note(s): Canadian engine blocks are marked CC318.

Interchange Number: 2
Part Number(s): 2780542
Casting Number: 2780543
Usage: 1966–71 426 Hemi, all models.

Interchange Number: 3
Part Number(s): 2843031
Casting Number: 2806178
Usage: 1967–69 440-ci four-barrel, all makes; all outputs except
  triple-two-barrel.

Interchange Number: 4
Part Number(s): 2843683
Casting Number: 2843681
Usage: 1968–69 383-ci two-barrel, all makes.

Interchange Number: 5
Part Number(s): 2843684
Casting Number: 2806301
Usage: 1968–69 383-ci four-barrel, all makes, all outputs.

Interchange Number: 6
Part Number(s): 3412046
Casting Number: 3412048
Usage: 1969 440-ci triple-two-barrel.
Note(s): (1) Used originally on Road Runner and Super Bee
  models. But can be adapted to all 440-ci. Interchange with
  camshaft and distributor. (2) Aluminum intake. Interchange
  Number 21 will fit but is cast iron.

Interchange Number: 7
Part Number(s): 2951184
Casting Number: 2951185
Usage: 1970–71 318-ci two-barrel, all makes, all models.

Interchange Number: 8
Part Number(s): 3614020
Casting Number: 2951670
Usage: 1970–71 383-ci two-barrel; 1972 400-ci two-barrel
  without A.I.R. emissions.

Interchange Number: 9
Part Number(s): 2951665

The casting number can identify the intake manifold.

Casting Number: 2951666
Usage: 1970–71 383-ci four-barrel, all makes, all outputs.

Interchange Number: 10
Part Number(s): 2951737
Casting Number: 2951736
Usage: 1970 440-ci four-barrel, all makes, all outputs.

Interchange Number: 11
Part Number(s): 2946275
Casting Number: 2946276
Usage: 1970–72 44-ci triple-two-barrel.

Interchange Number: 12
Part Number(s): 2531914
Casting Number: 2531915
Usage: 1968–69 340-ci four-barrel.

Interchange Number: 13
Part Number(s): 3462847
Casting Number: 3462848
Usage: 1970 340-ci four-barrel.

Interchange Number: 14
Part Number(s): 3512099
Casting Number: 3512100
Usage: 1971 340-ci four-barrel.

Interchange Number: 15
Part Number(s): 3418681
Casting Number: 3418682
Usage: 1970–71 340-ci triple-two-barrel.

Interchange Number: 16
Part Number(s): 3614032
Casting Number: NA
Usage: 1972 318-ci two-barrel without NOX emissions system.

Interchange Number: 17
Part Number(s): 3671466
Casting Number: NA
Usage: 1972 318-ci two-barrel with NOX emission systems.

Interchange Number: 18
Part Number(s): 3671878
Casting Number: NA
Usage: 1972 340-ci four-barrel with NOX emission systems.

Interchange Number: 19
Part Number(s): 3671462
Casting Number: NA
Usage: 1972 340-ci four-barrel without NOX emission systems.

Interchange Number: 20
Part Number(s): 3614047
Casting Number: 3614046
Usage: 1972 400-ci four-barrel without A.I.R. emissions.

Interchange Number: 21
Part Number(s): 3614048
Casting Number: NA
Usage: 1972 400-ci four-barrel with NOX emissions.

Interchange Number: 22
Part Number(s): 3614015
Casting Number: 3614014
Usage: 1971 440-ci four-barrel, all makes, all outputs; 1972
  440-ci four-barrel without NOX emissions only.

Interchange Number: 23
 Part Number(s): 3614016
 Casting Number: NA
 Usage: 1972 440-ci four-barrel with NOX emissions only.

Interchange Number: 24
 Part Number(s): 3751760
 Casting Number: 3698431
 Usage: 1973 318-ci two-barrel, all makes, all models.

Interchange Number: 25
 Part Number(s): 3698656
 Casting Number: 3671918
 Usage: 1973 340-ci four-barrel, all makes.

Interchange Number: 26
 Part Number(s): 3671880
 Casting Number: 3671879
 Usage: 1973 400-ci four-barrel, all makes, all outputs.

Interchange Number: 27
 Part Number(s): 3698585
 Casting Number: 3698444
 Usage: 1973 440-ci four-barrel, all makes, all outputs.

Interchange Number: 28
 Part Number(s): 3698583
 Casting Number: 3698440
 Usage: 1973 400-ci two-barrel, all makes.

Interchange Number: 29
 Part Number(s): 3769991
 Casting Number: NA
 Usage: 1974 318-ci two-barrel, all makes, all models.

Interchange Number: 30
 Part Number(s): 3698435
 Casting Number: NA
 Usage: 1974 360-ci four-barrel.

Interchange Number: 31
 Part Number(s): 3751729
 Casting Number: NA
 Usage: 1974 440-ci four-barrel, all makes, all outputs.

Interchange Number: 32
 Part Number(s): 3830019
 Casting Number: NA
 Usage: 1974 400-ci two-barrel, all makes.

Interchange Number: 33
 Part Number(s): 3698584
 Casting Number: NA
 Usage: 1974 400-ci four-barrel, all outputs.

Carburetors

Carburetors are identified by appearance and number of venturi. They are also identified by a stamping number on the body or a tag that is attached to the carburetor. Holley, Carter, Rochester, and Bendix (Stromberg) brands were used. Factors that will affect the interchange can include type of transmission and certain options such as air conditioning and forced-air induction.

Interchange is not based on the ID number but instead the original replacement part number. As carburetors got older they were grouped together; thus, there may be more than one year and several different engines that the carburetor can fit.

Model Identification

Interchange

Interchange Number: 1
  ID Number(s): 4420
  Type: Carter BBD two-barrel
  Usage: 1968 318-ci two-barrel with manual transmission.

Interchange Number: 2
  ID Number(s): 4421
  Type: Carter BBD two-barrel
  Usage: 1968 318-ci two-barrel with automatic transmission.

Interchange Number: 3
  ID Number(s): 4607
  Type: Carter BBD two-barrel
  Usage: 1969 318-ci two-barrel with manual transmission.
  Note(s): Salvage-yard dealers report that Interchange Number
    16 will fit.

Interchange Number: 4
  ID Number(s): 4608
  Type: Carter BBD two-barrel
  Usage: 1969 318-ci two-barrel with automatic transmission.

Interchange Number: 5
  ID Number(s): 4721
  Type: Carter BBD two-barrel
  Usage: 1970 318-ci two-barrel with manual transmission,
    without E.E.C.

Interchange Number: 6
  ID Number(s): 4722
  Type: Carter BBD two-barrel
  Usage: 1970 318-ci two-barrel with automatic transmission,
    without E.E.C

Interchange Number: 7
  ID Number(s): 4957
  Type: Carter BBD two-barrel
  Usage: 1971 318-ci two-barrel with manual transmission.

Interchange Number: 8
  ID Number(s): 4958
  Type: Carter BBD two-barrel
  Usage: 1971 318-ci two-barrel with automatic transmission,
    except with air conditioning.

Interchange Number: 9
  ID Number(s): 7041180
  Type: Rochester two-barrel
  Usage: 1971 318-ci two-barrel with automatic transmission and
    air conditioning.

Interchange Number: 10
  ID Number(s): 4959
  Type: Carter BBD two-barrel
  Usage: 1970–73 318-ci two-barrel export cars only with manual
    transmission.

Interchange Number: 11
  ID Number(s): 4960

Type: Carter BBD two-barrel
Usage: 1970–73 318-ci two-barrel export cars only with
automatic transmission.

Interchange Number: 12
ID Number(s): 6149
Type: Carter BBD two-barrel
Usage: 1972 318-ci two-barrel with manual transmission
without NOX.

Interchange Number: 13
ID Number(s): 6150
Type: Carter BBD two-barrel
Usage: 1972 318-ci two-barrel with automatic transmission
without NOX.

Interchange Number: 14
ID Number(s): 6151
Type: Carter BBD two-barrel
Usage: 1972 318-ci with manual transmission and NOX.

Interchange Number: 15
ID Number(s): 6152
Type: Carter BBD
Usage: 1972 318-ci with automatic and NOX.

Interchange Number: 16
ID Number(s): 6316
Type: Carter BBD two-barrel
Usage: 1973 318-ci two-barrel with manual transmission,
except cars sold in California.

Interchange Number: 17
ID Number(s): 6317
Type: Carter BBD two-barrel
Usage: 1973 318-ci two-barrel with automatic transmission,
except cars sold in California.

Interchange Number: 18
ID Number(s): 6343
Type: Carter BBD two-barrel
Usage: 1973 California cars with a 318-ci two-barrel with
manual transmission.

Interchange Number: 19
ID Number(s): 6344
Type: Carter BBD two-barrel
Usage: 1973 California cars with a 318-ci two-barrel with
automatic transmission.

Interchange Number: 20
ID Number(s): 6464
Type: Carter BBD two-barrel
Usage: 1974 318-ci two-barrel with manual transmission, all
models except Road Runner, or export models.

Interchange Number: 21
ID Number(s): 8010S
Type: Carter BBD two-barrel
Usage: 1974 318-ci two-barrel in Road Runner only.

Interchange Number: 22
ID Number(s): 8028
Type: Carter BBD two-barrel
Usage: 1974 318-ci two-barrel with automatic transmission,
except export or cars sold in California.

Interchange Number: 23
ID Number(s): 6467
Type: Carter BBD two-barrel
Usage: 1974 California cars with 318-ci two-barrel and
automatic transmission.

Interchange Number: 24
ID Number(s): 6491
Type: Carter BBD two-barrel
Usage: 1974 318-ci export cars only with manual transmission.

Interchange Number: 25
ID Number(s): 6492
Type: Carter BBD two-barrel
Usage: 1974 318-ci export cars with automatic transmission.

Interchange Number: 26
ID Number(s): TQ9000S

Type: Carter Thermo-Quad four-barrel
Usage: 1974 Dodge Dart 318-ci four-barrel export only.

Interchange Number: 27
ID Number(s): 8009S
Type: Carter BBD two-barrel

Interchange Number: 28
ID Number(s): 4424
Type: Carter AVS four-barrel
Usage: 1968 340-ci four-barrel with manual transmission.

Interchange Number: 29
ID Number(s): 4425
Type: Carter AVS four-barrel
Usage: 1968 340-ci four-barrel with automatic transmission.

Interchange Number: 30
ID Number(s): 4611, 4638
Type: Carter AVS four-barrel
Usage: 1969 340-ci four-barrel with manual transmission.

Interchange Number: 31
ID Number(s): 4612, 4639
Type: Carter AVS four barrel
Usage: 1969 340-ci four-barrel with automatic transmission.

Interchange Number: 32
ID Number(s): 4933S
Type: Carter AVS
Usage: 1970 340-ci four-barrel with manual transmission
without E.E.C.

Interchange Number: 33
ID Number(s): 4934S
Type: Carter AVS
Usage: 1970 340-ci four-barrel with automatic transmission
without E.E.C., except with air conditioning.

Interchange Number: 34
ID Number(s): 4935
Type: Carter AVS
Usage: 1970 340-ci four-barrel with automatic transmission
with air conditioning without E.E.C.

Interchange Number: 35
ID Number(s): 4936
Type: Carter AVS four-barrel
Type: 1970 340-ci four-barrel with manual transmission with E.E.C.

Interchange Number: 36
ID Number(s): 4937
Type: Carter AVS four-barrel
Usage: 1970 340-ci four-barrel with automatic transmission
with E.E.C.

Interchange Number: 37
ID Number(s): R4789A
Type: Holley two-barrel (front carburetor)
Usage: 1970–71 340-ci triple-two-barrel.

Interchange Number: 38
ID Number(s): R4790A
Type: Holley two-barrel (rear carburetor)
Usage: 1970–71 340-ci triple-two-barrel.

Interchange Number: 39
ID Number(s): R4791A
Type: Holley two-barrel (center carburetor)
Usage: 1970–71 340-ci triple-two-barrel with manual
transmission.

Interchange Number: 40
ID Number(s): R4792A
Type: Holley two-barrel (center carburetor)
Usage: 1970–71 340-ci triple-two-barrel with automatic
transmission.

Interchange Number: 41
ID Number(s): 4872
Type: Carter Thermo-Quad four-barrel
Usage: 1971 340-ci four-barrel with manual transmission.

Interchange Number: 42
ID Number(s): 4973
Type: Carter Thermo-Quad four-barrel

Usage: 1971 340-ci four-barrel with automatic transmission.

Interchange Number: 43
ID Number(s): 6138
Type: Carter Thermo-Quad four-barrel
Usage: 1972 340-ci four-barrel with manual transmission.

Interchange Number: 44
ID Number(s): 6139
Type: Carter Thermo-Quad four-barrel
Usage: 1972 340-ci four-barrel with automatic transmission.

Interchange Number: 45
ID Number(s): 6318
Type: Carter Thermo-Quad four-barrel
Usage: 1973 340-ci four-barrel with manual transmission, except cars sold in California.

Interchange Number: 46
ID Number(s): 6319
Type: Carter Thermo-Quad four-barrel
Usage: 1973 340-ci four-barrel with automatic transmission, except cars sold in California.

Interchange Number: 47
ID Number(s): 6339
Type: Carter Thermo-Quad four-barrel
Usage: 1973 California cars with a 340-ci four-barrel with manual transmission.

Interchange Number: 48
ID Number(s): 6340
Type: Carter Thermo-Quad four-barrel
Usage: 1973 California cars with 340-ci four-barrel with automatic transmission.

Interchange Number: 49
ID Number(s): 6452
Type: Carter Thermo-Quad four-barrel
Usage: 1974 360-ci four-barrel in Charger, Road Runner, Cuda, Challenger, Dart, or Duster models only with manual transmission, except cars sold in California.

Interchange Number: 50
ID Number(s): 6453
Type: Carter Thermo-Quad four-barrel
Usage: 1974 360-ci four-barrel in Charger, Road Runner, Cuda, Challenger, Dart, or Duster models only with automatic transmission, except cars sold in California.

Interchange Number: 51
ID Number(s): 6454
Type: Carter Thermo-Quad four-barrel
Usage: 1974 360-ci four-barrel in Charger, Road Runner, Cuda, Challenger, Dart, or Duster models only sold in California with manual transmission.

Interchange Number: 52
ID Number(s): 6455
Type: Carter Thermo-Quad four-barrel
Usage: 1974 360-ci four-barrel in Charger, Road Runner, Cuda, Challenger, Dart, or Duster models only sold in California with automatic transmission.

Interchange Number: 53
ID Number(s): 4426
Type: Carter AFB four-barrel
Usage: 1968 383-ci four-barrel with manual transmission, except Road Runner or Super Bee models.

Interchange Number: 54
ID Number(s): 4401
Type: Carter AFB four-barrel
Usage: 1968 383-ci four-barrel with automatic transmission, except with air conditioning.

Interchange Number: 55
ID Number(s): 4635
Type: Carter AFB four-barrel
Usage: 1968 383-ci four-barrel with automatic transmission with air conditioning.

Interchange Number: 56
ID Number(s): 4615
Type: Carter AFB four-barrel
Usage: 1969 383-ci four-barrel with manual transmission, all models except Road Runner or Super Bee.

Interchange Number: 57
ID Number(s): 4616, 4638
Type: Carter AFB four-barrel
Usage: 1969 383-ci four-barrel with automatic transmission.

Interchange Number: 58
ID Number(s): R4440
Type: Holley 4160 four-barrel
Usage: 1969 383-ci four-barrel with automatic transmission, except Road Runner, Super Bee, Cuda, or Dart GTS models.

Interchange Number: 59
ID Number(s): 4711
Type: Carter AVS four-barrel
Usage: 1968–69 Super Bee, 1968–69 Road Runner, 1968–69 Dart GTS, 1968–69 Barracuda with 383-ci four-barrel (335 hp) with manual transmission.

Interchange Number: 60
ID Number(s): 4682
Type: Carter AVS four-barrel
Usage: 1969 Super Bee, 1969 Road Runner, 1969 Dart GTS, 1969 Barracuda with 383-ci four-barrel (335 hp) with automatic transmission.

Interchange Number: 61
ID Number(s): R4367A
Type: Holley 4160 four-barrel
Usage: 1970 Cuda, Challenger R/T, Road Runner, Super Bee with 383-ci 335-hp four-barrel with manual transmission without E.E.C., without fresh-air hood.
Note(s): Do not confuse with lesser-powered 383-ci, 330-hp that was available in base Barracuda and Challenger models.

Interchange Number: 62
ID Number(s): R4217A
Type: Holley 4160 four-barrel
Usage: 1970 Cuda, Challenger R/T, Road Runner, Super Bee with 383-ci 335-hp four-barrel with manual transmission with E.E.C., without fresh-air hood.
Note(s): For cars sold in California only.

Interchange Number: 63
ID Number(s): 4736
Type: Carter AVS four-barrel
Usage: 1970 383-ci 330-hp four-barrel with automatic transmission without E.E.C., except with air conditioning.

Interchange Number: 64
ID Number(s): 4732
Type: Carter AVS four-barrel
Usage: 1970 383-ci four-barrel, all outputs with automatic transmission with air conditioning without E.E.C.

Interchange Number: 65
ID Number(s): 4734
Type: Carter AVS four-barrel
Usage: 1970 383-ci 330-hp four-barrel with automatic transmission with E.E.C., except with air conditioning.

Interchange Number: 66
ID Number(s): R4368A
Type: Holley 4160 four-barrel
Usage: 1970 Cuda, Challenger R/T, Road Runner, Super Bee with 383-ci 335-hp four-barrel with automatic transmission without E.E.C., without fresh-air hood.

Interchange Number: 67
ID Number(s): R47371A
Type: Holley 4160 four-barrel
Usage: 1970 Cuda, Challenger R/T, Road Runner, Super Bee with 383-ci 335-hp four-barrel with automatic transmission with fresh-air hood.

Interchange Number: 68
ID Number(s): R4218A
Type: Holley 4160 four-barrel
Usage: 1970 Cuda, Challenger R/T, Road Runner, Super Bee

with 383-ci 335-hp four-barrel with automatic transmission with E.E.C.

Note(s): For cars sold in California only.

Interchange Number: 69
ID Number(s): R4369A
Type: Holley 4160 four-barrel
Usage: 1970 Cuda, Challenger R/T, Road Runner, Super Bee with 383-ci 335-hp four-barrel with automatic transmission and air conditioning.

Interchange Number: 70
ID Number(s): R47361A
Type: Holley 4160 four-barrel
Usage: 1970 Cuda, Challenger R/T, Road Runner, Super Bee with 383-ci 335-hp four-barrel with manual transmission with fresh-air hood without E.E.C.

Interchange Number: 71
ID Number(s): R47381A
Type: Holley 4160 four-barrel
Usage: 1970 Cuda, Challenger R/T, Road Runner, Super Bee with 383-ci 335-hp four-barrel with manual transmission with fresh-air hood with E.E.C.

Interchange Number: 72
ID Number(s): R47391A
Type: Holley 4160 four-barrel
Usage: 1970 Cuda, Challenger R/T, Road Runner, Super Bee with 383-ci 335-hp four-barrel with automatic transmission with fresh-air hood with E.E.C.

Interchange Number: 73
ID Number(s): R4667A
Type: Holley 4160 four-barrel
Usage: 1971 Cuda, Challenger R/T, Road Runner, Super Bee with 383-ci four-barrel with manual transmission without fresh-air hood.

Interchange Number: 74
ID Number(s): R4668A
Type: Holley 4160 four-barrel
Usage: 1971 Cuda, Challenger R/T, Road Runner, Super Bee with 383-ci four-barrel with automatic transmission without fresh-air hood.

Interchange Number: 75
ID Number(s): R4734A
Type: Holley 4160 four-barrel
Usage: 1971 Cuda, Challenger R/T, Road Runner, Super Bee with 383-ci four-barrel with manual transmission with fresh-air hood.

Interchange Number: 76
ID Number(s): R4735A
Type: Holley 4160 four-barrel
Usage: 1971 Cuda, Challenger R/T, Road Runner, Super Bee with 383-ci four-barrel with automatic transmission with fresh-air hood.

Interchange Number: 77
ID Number(s): TQ6140S
Type: Carter Thermo-Quad four-barrel
Usage: 1972 Charger, 1972 Road Runner with 400-ci four-barrel and manual transmission without A.I.R.

Interchange Number: 78
ID Number(s): TQ6165S
Type: Carter Thermo-Quad four-barrel
Usage: 1972 Charger, 1972 Road Runner with 400-ci four-barrel and manual transmission with A.I.R.

Interchange Number: 79
ID Number(s): TQ6090S
Type: Carter Thermo-Quad four-barrel
Usage: 1972 Charger, 1972 Road Runner, 1972 Fury, 1972 Polara or Monaco, 1972 Coronet, 1972 Satellite with 400-ci four-barrel, and automatic transmission without A.I.R.

Interchange Number: 80
ID Number(s): TQ6166S
Type: Carter Thermo-Quad four-barrel

Usage: 1972 Charger, 1972 Road Runner, 1972 Fury, 1972 Polara or Monaco, 1972 Coronet, 1972 Satellite with 400-ci four-barrel, and automatic transmission with A.I.R.

Interchange Number: 81
ID Number(s): TQ6321S
Type: Carter Thermo-Quad four-barrel
Usage: 1973 Charger, 1973 Road Runner, 1973 Fury, 1973 Polara or Monaco, 1973 Coronet, 1973 Satellite with 400-ci four-barrel, and automatic transmission without A.I.R.

Interchange Number: 82
ID Number(s): TQ6342S
Type: Carter Thermo-Quad four-barrel
Usage: 1973 Charger, 1973 Road Runner, 1973 Fury, 1973 Polara or Monaco, 1973 Coronet, 1973 Satellite with 400-ci four-barrel, and automatic transmission with A.I.R.
Note(s): California cars only.

Interchange Number: 83
ID Number(s): TQ6341S
Type: Carter Thermo-Quad four-barrel
Usage: 1972 Charger, 1972 Road Runner with 400-ci four-barrel and manual transmission with A.I.R.
Note(s): For cars sold in California only.

Interchange Number: 84
ID Number(s): TQ6320S
Type: Carter Thermo-Quad four-barrel
Usage: 1972 Charger, 1972 Road Runner with 400-ci four-barrel and manual transmission without A.I.R.

Interchange Number: 85
ID Number(s): TQ6457S
Type: Carter Thermo-Quad four-barrel
Usage: 1972 Charger, 1972 Road Runner, 1972 Fury police or ambulance, 1972 Monaco police sedan, 1972 Satellite coupe with 400-ci 250-hp four-barrel and automatic transmission.
Note(s): Don't confuse with lower power 400 that was optional in this line. Only police cars in Fury and Monaco used this carburetor.

Interchange Number: 86
ID Number(s): TQ6503S
Type: Carter Thermo-Quad four-barrel
Usage: 1974 Charger export cars with manual transmission.

Interchange Number: 87
ID Number(s): TQ6456S
Type: Carter Thermo-Quad four-barrel
Usage: 1974 Charger, 1974 Road Runner with 400-ci 250-hp four-barrel and manual transmission, all applications.

Interchange Number: 88
ID Number(s): 4430 (front)
Type: Carter AFB four-barrel
Usage: 1968 426 Hemi, all applications.

Interchange Number: 89
ID Number(s): 4431 (rear)
Type: Carter AFB four-barrel
Usage: 1968 426 Hemi with manual transmission.

Interchange Number: 90
ID Number(s): 4432 (rear)
Type: Carter AFB four-barrel
Usage: 1968 426 Hemi with automatic transmission.

Interchange Number: 91
ID Number(s): 4619 (front)
Type: Carter AFB four-barrel
Usage: 1969 426 Hemi, all applications.

Interchange Number: 92
ID Number(s): 4620 (rear)
Type: Carter AFB four-barrel
Usage: 1969 426 Hemi with manual transmission.

Interchange Number: 93
ID Number(s): 4621 (rear)
Type: Carter AFB four-barrel
Usage: 1969 426 Hemi with automatic transmission.

Interchange Number: 94
 ID Number(s): 4742 (front)
 Type: Carter AFB four-barrel
 Usage: 1970–early 1971 426 Hemi, all applications.
Interchange Number: 95
 ID Number(s): 4745 (rear)
 Type: Carter AFB four-barrel
 Usage: 1970–early 1971 426 Hemi with manual transmission.
Interchange Number: 96
 ID Number(s): 4746 (rear)
 Type: Carter AFB four-barrel
 Usage: 1970 426 Hemi with automatic transmission.
Interchange Number: 97
 ID Number(s): 4971 (front)
 Type: Carter AFB four-barrel
 Usage: Late 1971 426 Hemi, all applications.
Interchange Number: 98
 ID Number(s): 4970 (rear)
 Type: Carter AFB four-barrel
 Usage: Late 1971 426 Hemi with automatic transmission.
Interchange Number: 99
 ID Number(s): 4669 (rear)
 Type: Carter AFB four-barrel
 Usage: Late 1971 426 Hemi with manual transmission.
Interchange Number: 100
 ID Number(s): 4428
 Type: Carter AVS four-barrel
 Usage: 1968 Coronet R/T, 1968 GTX, 1968 Charger R/T, 1968
   Sport Fury, 1968 Monaco 500 with 440-ci 375-hp four-
   barrel with manual transmission.
Interchange Number: 101
 ID Number(s): 4429
 Type: Carter AVS four-barrel
 Usage: 1968 Coronet R/T, 1968 GTX, 1968 Sport Fury, 1968
   Monaco 500, 1968 Charger R/T, 1968 Chrysler 300 with
   440-ci 375-hp four-barrel with automatic transmission.
Interchange Number: 102
 ID Number(s): 4330
 Type: Carter AVS four-barrel
 Usage: 1968 Coronet R/T, 1968 GTX, 1968 Sport Fury, 1968
   Monaco 500, 1969 Charger R/T, 1968 Chrysler 300, all with
   440-ci four-barrel and with automatic transmission and air
   conditioning.
 Note(s): Watch out for Holley carburetors on full-size models.
   This is for the lesser-powered 350-hp version and will not
   interchange.
Interchange Number: 103
 ID Number(s): 4617
 Type: Carter AVS four-barrel
 Usage: 1969 Coronet R/T, 1969 GTX, 1969 Sport Fury, 1969
   Monaco 500, 1969 Charger R/T, 1969 Charger 500, 1969
   Charger Daytona with 440-ci 375-hp four-barrel with
   manual transmission.
Interchange Number: 104
 ID Number(s): 4618, 4610
 Type: Carter AVS four-barrel
 Usage: 1969 Coronet R/T, 1969 GTX, 1969 Sport Fury, 1969
   Monaco 500, 1969 Charger R/T, 1969 Charger 500, 1969
   Charger Daytona with 440-ci 375-hp four-barrel with
   automatic transmission.
 Note(s): Be careful when interchanging from full-size models.
   Those with a Holley 4160 will not interchange, but will fit
   with some loss in power.
Interchange Number: 105
 ID Number(s): R4393A (front)
 Type: Holley two-barrel (triple-two-barrel)
 Usage: 1969 Super Bee, 1969 Road Runner with 440-ci triple-
   two-barrel, all applications.
Interchange Number: 106
 ID Number(s): R4391A (center)

 Type: Holley two-barrel (triple-two-barrel)
 Usage: 1969 Super Bee, 1969 Road Runner with 440-ci triple-
   two-barrel with manual transmission.
Interchange Number: 107
 ID Number(s): R4392A (center)
 Type: Holley two-barrel (triple-two-barrel)
 Usage: 1969 Super Bee, 1969 Road Runner with 440-ci triple-
   two-barrel with automatic transmission.
Interchange Number: 108
 ID Number(s): R4394A (rear)
 Type: Holley two-barrel (triple-two-barrel)
 Usage: 1969 Super Bee, 1969 Road Runner with 440-ci triple-
   two-barrel, all applications.
Interchange Number: 109
 ID Number(s): 4737S
 Type: Carter AVS four-barrel
 Usage: 1970 Cuda, 1970 Challenger R/T, 1970 Charger R/T,
   1970 Road Runner, 1970 Superbird, 1970 GTX with 440-ci
   four-barrel 375 hp with manual transmission, without E.E.C.
Interchange Number: 110
 ID Number(s): 4739S
 Type: Carter AVS four-barrel
 Usage: 1970 Cuda, 1970 Challenger R/T, 1970 Charger R/T,
   1970 Road Runner, 1970 Superbird, 1970 Coronet R/T,
   1970 GTX, with 440-ci four-barrel 375 hp with manual
   transmission, with E.E.C.
Interchange Number: 111
 ID Number(s): 4738S
 Type: Carter AVS four-barrel
 Usage: 1970 Cuda, 1970 Challenger R/T, 1970 Charger R/T,
   1970 Road Runner, 1970 Coronet R/T, 1970 Superbird,
   1970 Fury GT, 1970 Fury S-23, 1970 Chrysler 300, 1970
   GTX with 440-ci four-barrel 375 hp with automatic
   transmission, without E.E.C., without air conditioning.
 Note(s): Watch out when interchanging from full-size models;
   those with a Holley 4160 will not interchange.
Interchange Number: 112
 ID Number(s): 4741S
 Type: Carter AVS four-barrel
 Usage: 1970 Cuda, 1970 Challenger R/T, 1970 Charger R/T,
   1970 Road Runner, 1970 Superbird, 1970 Fury GT, 1970
   Fury S-23, 1970 Chrysler 300, 1970 Coronet R/T, 1970 GTX
   with 440-ci four-barrel 375 hp with automatic transmission
   and with air conditioning, without E.E.C.
 Note(s): Watch out when interchanging from full-size models;
   those with a Holley 4160 will not interchange.
Interchange Number: 113
 ID Number(s): 4740S
 Type: Carter AVS four-barrel
 Usage: 1970 Cuda, 1970 Challenger R/T, 1970 Charger R/T,
   1970 Road Runner, 1970 Superbird, 1970 Fury GT, 1970
   Fury S-23, 1970 Chrysler 300, 1970 Coronet R/T, 1970 GTX
   with 440-ci four-barrel 375-hp with automatic transmission
   and with air conditioning, with E.E.C.
 Note(s): Watch out when interchanging from full-size models;
   those with a Holley 4160 will not interchange.
Interchange Number: 114
 ID Number(s): R4382A (front)
 Type: Holley two-barrel (triple-two-barrel)
 Usage: 1970 Cuda, 1970 Challenger R/T, 1970 Charger R/T,
   1970 Road Runner, 1970 Superbird, 1970 Fury GT, 1970 Fury
   S-23, 1970 Super Bee, 1970 Coronet R/T, 1970 GTX with
   440-ci triple-two-barrel all applications, except with E.E.C.
Interchange Number: 115
 ID Number(s): R4175A (front)
 Type: Holley two-barrel (triple-two-barrel)
 Usage: 1970 Cuda, 1970 Challenger R/T, 1970 Charger R/T,
   1970 Road Runner, 1970 Superbird, 1970 Fury GT, 1970
   Fury S-23, 1970 Super Bee, 1970 Coronet R/T, 1970 GTX
   with 440-ci triple-two-barrel, all applications with E.E.C.

Interchange Number: 116
ID Number(s): R4375A (center)
Type: Holley two-barrel (triple-two-barrel)
Usage: 1970 Cuda, 1970 Challenger R/T, 1970 Charger R/T, 1970 Road Runner, 1970 Superbird, 1970 Fury GT, 1970 Fury S-23, 1970 Super Bee, 1970 Coronet R/T, 1970 GTX with 440-ci triple-two-barrel with manual transmission without E.E.C.

Interchange Number: 117
ID Number(s): R4374A (center)
Type: Holley two-barrel (triple-two-barrel)
Usage: 1970 Cuda, 1970 Challenger R/T, 1970 Charger R/T, 1970 Road Runner, 1970 Superbird, 1970 Fury GT, 1970 Fury S-23, 1970 Super Bee, 1970 Coronet R/T, 1970 GTX with 440-ci triple-two-barrel with manual transmission with E.E.C.

Interchange Number: 118
ID Number(s): R4376A (center)
Type: Holley two-barrel (triple-two-barrel)
Usage: 1970 Cuda, 1970 Challenger R/T, 1970 Charger R/T, 1970 Road Runner, 1970 Superbird, 1970 Fury GT, 1970 Fury S-23, 1970 Super Bee, 1970 Coronet R/T, 1970 GTX with 440-ci triple-two-barrel with automatic transmission without E.E.C.

Interchange Number: 119
ID Number(s): R4144A
Type: Holley two-barrel (triple-two-barrel)
Usage: 1970 Cuda, 1970 Challenger R/T, 1970 Charger R/T, 1970 Road Runner, 1970 Superbird, 1970 Fury GT, 1970 Fury S-23, 1970 Super Bee, 1970 Coronet R/T, 1970 GTX with 440-ci triple-two-barrel with automatic transmission with E.E.C.

Interchange Number: 120
ID Number(s): R4383A (rear)
Type: Holley two-barrel (triple-two-barrel)
Usage: 1970 Cuda, 1970 Challenger R/T, 1970 Charger R/T, 1970 Road Runner, 1970 Superbird, 1970 Fury GT, 1970 Fury S-23, 1970 Super Bee, 1970 Coronet R/T, 1970 GTX with 440-ci triple-two-barrel, all applications, except with E.E.C.

Interchange Number: 121
ID Number(s): R4365A (rear)
Type: Holley two-barrel (triple-two-barrel)
Usage: 1970 Cuda, 1970 Challenger R/T, 1970 Charger R/T, 1970 Road Runner, 1970 Superbird, 1970 Fury GT, 1970 Fury S-23, 1970 Super Bee, 1970 Coronet R/T, 1970 GTX, with 440-ci triple-two-barrel, all applications, with E.E.C.

Interchange Number: 122
ID Number(s): 4967
Type: Carter AVS four-barrel
Usage: 1971 Charger R/T, 1971 Road Runner, 1971 GTX, with 440-ci four-barrel and manual transmission.

Interchange Number: 123
ID Number(s): 4968
Type: Carter AVS four-barrel
Usage: 1971 Charger R/T, 1971 Road Runner, 1971 GTX, 1971 Fury GT, 1971 Monaco 500, 1970 Chrysler 300 with 440-ci four-barrel and automatic transmission.
Note(s): Be careful when interchanging from full-size models; be sure of the ID numbers. Carter's used on lower-powered cars (Fury, New Yorker, and so on) will not interchange but will fit with some loss of horsepower.

Interchange Number: 124
ID Number(s): R4671A (front)
Type: Holley two-barrel (triple-two-barrel)
Usage: 1971 Charger R/T, 1971 Road Runner, 1971 GTX, 1971 Cuda, 1971 Challenger R/T, 1972 Charger Rallye, 1972 Road Runner with 440-ci triple-two-barrel, all applications.

Interchange Number: 125
ID Number(s): R4669A (center)
Type: Holley two-barrel (triple-two-barrel)
Usage: 1971 Charger R/T, 1971 Road Runner, 1971 GTX, 1971 Cuda, 1971 Challenger R/T, 1972 Charger Rallye, 1972 Road Runner with 440-ci triple-two-barrel with manual transmission.

Interchange Number: 126
ID Number(s): R4670A (center)
Type: Holley two-barrel (triple-two-barrel)
Usage: 1971 Charger R/T, 1971 Road Runner, 1971 GTX, 1971 Cuda, 1971 Challenger R/T; 1972 Charger Rallye, 1972 Road Runner with 440-ci triple-two-barrel with automatic transmission.

Interchange Number: 127
ID Number(s): R4668A (rear)
Type: Holley two-barrel (triple-two-barrel)
Usage: 1971 Charger R/T, 1971 Road Runner, 1971 GTX, 1971 Cuda, 1971 Challenger R/T, 1972 Charger Rallye, 1972 Road Runner with 440-ci triple-two-barrel, all applications.

Interchange Number: 128
ID Number(s): R6254AAS
Type: Holley 4160 four-barrel
Usage: 1972 Charger, 1972 Satellite coupe (includes Road Runner/GTX models) with 440-ci four-barrel with manual transmission, except with A.I.R.

Interchange Number: 129
ID Number(s): R6256AAS
Type: Holley 4160 four-barrel
Usage: 1972 Charger, 1972 Satellite coupe (includes Road Runner/GTX models) with 440-ci four-barrel with manual transmission, with A.I.R.

Interchange Number: 130
ID Number(s): R6255AAS
Type: Holley 4160 four-barrel
Usage: 1972 Charger, 1972 Satellite coupe (includes Road Runner/GTX models) with 440-ci four-barrel with automatic transmission, except with A.I.R.

Interchange Number: 131
ID Number(s): R6257AAS
Type: Holley 4160 four-barrel
Usage: 1972 Charger, 1972 Satellite coupe (includes Road Runner/GTX models), 1972 Fury, 1972 Dodge Monaco, 1972 New Yorker with 440-ci four-barrel with manual transmission, with A.I.R.

Interchange Number: 132
ID Number(s): TQ6324S
Type: Carter Thermo-Quad four-barrel
Usage: 1973 Charger, 1973 Satellite coupe (includes Road Runner/GTX models), 1973 New Yorker, 1973 Fury, 1973 Dodge Monaco with 440-ci four-barrel with automatic transmission, except with A.I.R.

Interchange Number: 133
ID Number(s): TQ6324S
Type: Carter Thermo-Quad four-barrel
Usage: 1973 Charger, 1973 Satellite coupe (includes Road Runner/GTX models), 1973 Fury police car, 1973 Dodge Monaco police car with 440-ci four-barrel with automatic transmission, except with A.I.R.
Note(s): Be careful when interchanging from full-size cars. Lesser-powered versions will not interchange.

Interchange Number: 134
ID Number(s): TQ6411S
Type: Carter Thermo-Quad four-barrel
Usage: 1973 Charger, 1973 Satellite coupe (includes Road Runner/GTX models), 1973 Fury police car, 1973 Dodge Monaco police car with 440-ci four-barrel with automatic transmission, with A.I.R.
Note(s): Be careful when interchanging from full-size cars. Lesser-powered versions will not interchange.

Interchange Number: 135
ID Number(s): TQ6463S–early, TQ9016–late
Type: Carter Thermo-Quad four-barrel
Usage: 1974 Charger, 1974 Satellite coupe (includes Road

Hemi air cleaner for cars without the fresh-air hood.

This unsilenced air cleaner was used on many different engines.

Runner/GTX models), 1974 Fury police car, 1974 Dodge Monaco police car with 440-ci four-barrel with automatic transmission, with A.I.R.

Note(s): Be careful when interchanging from full-size cars. Lesser-powered versions will not interchange.

Interchange Number: 136
ID Number(s): TQ6462–early, TQ9015S–late
Type: Carter Thermo-Quad four-barrel
Usage: 1974 Charger, 1974 Satellite coupe (includes Road Runner/GTX models), 1974 Fury police car, 1974 Dodge Monaco police car with 440-ci four-barrel with automatic transmission, with A.I.R.
Note(s): Be careful when interchanging from full-size cars. Lesser-powered versions will not interchange.

Interchange Number: 137
ID Number(s): 4723S
Type: Carter BBD two-barrel
Usage: 1970 318-ci with manual transmission with A.I.R. emissions.

Interchange Number: 138
ID Number(s): 4724S
Type: Carter BBD two-barrel
Usage: 1970 318-ci with automatic transmission with A.I.R. emissions.

Interchange Number: 139
ID Number(s): TQ6489S
Type: Carter Thermo-Quad four-barrel
Usage: 1974 400-ci with automatic transmission, except high-performance or California cars.

Interchange Number: 140
ID Number(s): TQ6463S
Type: Carter Thermo-Quad four-barrel
Usage: 1974 California cars with 400-ci four-barrel with automatic transmission, except with high-performance.

Interchange Number: 141
ID Number(s): TQ 6459S
Type: Carter Thermo-Quad
Usage: 1974 400-ci four-barrel, 250 hp, with automatic transmission with A.I.R.

Air Cleaners

Air cleaners are identified by their basic shape and design. Those units with ram air (fresh air) usually required a special unit that used a system of ducts and seals to direct the cold outside air down into the carburetor. Note that only the air cleaner assembly itself is the interchange here. Duct work that was bolted to the underside of the hood is not included in this interchange.

Listed below are the terms *silenced* and *unsilenced*. The term *silenced* means that the air cleaner has one or more tube-shaped snorkels that air was drawn through. Most high-performance models in 1968 and 1969 used unsilenced versions, which have no snorkel.

Model Identification

Barracuda	*Interchange Number*
1968 318-ci	2
1968 340-ci	8
1968 383-ci, silenced	4
1968 383-ci, unsilenced	8
1969 318-ci	9
1969 340-ci	8
1969 383-ci	8
1969 440-ci	8
1970 318-ci	16
1970 340-ci four-barrel without fresh air	8
1970 340-ci four-barrel with shaker hood	27
1970 340-ci triple-two-barrel	26
1970 383-ci two-barrel	38
1970 383-ci four-barrel without shaker hood	39
1970 383-ci four-barrel with shaker hood	27
1970 440-ci four-barrel without shaker hood	39
1970 440-ci four-barrel with shaker hood	27
1970 440-ci triple-two-barrel without shaker hood	22
1970 440-ci triple-two-barrel with shaker hood	23
1970 440 Hemi	19
1971 318-ci	16
1971 340-ci four-barrel without shaker hood	33
1971 383-ci two-barrel	36
1971 383-ci four-barrel	37
1971 440-ci triple-two-barrel without shaker hood	22
1971 440-ci triple-two-barrel with shaker hood	23
1971 Hemi	19
1972 318-ci	16
1972 340-ci	40
1973 318-ci	43
1973 340-ci up to December 1972	40
1973 340-ci after December 1972	44
1974 318-ci	46
1974 360-ci	47
Belvedere, Charger, Coronet, and Satellite	*Interchange Number*
1968 318-ci	2
1968 383-ci two-barrel	6
1968 383-ci four-barrel	5
1968 Road Runner and Super Bee	3

The hood scoop formed part of the air cleaner with the shaker hood.

The air cleaner used with 3x2-barrel setup and the fiberglass hood.

Interchange

Interchange Number: 1
Part Number(s): 2658852
Usage: 1966–68 426 Hemi in Charger, Coronet, or Belvedere; 1969–70 Charger R/T with 426 Hemi.

Interchange Number: 2
Part Number(s): 2899405
Usage: 1968 273-ci two-barrel or 318-ci two-barrel, all models.

Interchange Number: 3
Part Number(s): 2946172
Usage: 1968 Road Runner or Super Bee with 383-ci 335-hp; 1968 GTX or Coronet R/T with 440-ci 375 hp; 1968 Fury Sport or full-size Dodge with 440-ci 375-hp; 1968 Barracuda or Dart with 383-ci.
Note(s): Unsilenced air cleaner. Swap without pie tins. Cover in Interchange Number 27 will fit.

Interchange Number: 4
Part Number(s): 2899133
Usage: 1968 Barracuda or Dart 383-ci four-barrel.
Note(s): Dual snorkel design.

Interchange Number: 5
Part Number(s): 2863307
Usage: 1968 Coronet, Belvedere, full-size Dodge, Plymouth, or Newport, with 383-ci four-barrel.
Note(s): Dual snorkel design.

Interchange Number: 6
Part Number(s): 2863341
Usage: 1968 Coronet, Belvedere, full-size Dodge, Plymouth, or Newport, with 383-ci two-barrel.
Note(s): Single snorkel design.

Interchange Number: 7
Part Number(s): 2899133
Usage: 1968 Coronet R/T, GTX with California sound-reduction package; 1968 full-size Plymouth or Dodge with 440-ci, all states.
Note(s): Dual snorkel design.

Interchange Number: 8
Part Number(s): 2863319
Usage: 1968–69 Barracuda or Dart with 340-ci four-barrel; 1969 Super Bee or Road Runner with 383-ci 335-hp; 1969 GTX, Charger R/T, Coronet R/T, full-size Dodge or Plymouth with 440-ci 375-hp four-barrel, without fresh-air hood.
Note(s): Cover in Interchange Number 22 will fit. Retainers will not swap.

Interchange Number: 9
Part Number(s): 2946179
Usage: 1969 318-ci two-barrel, all models.

Interchange Number: 10
Part Number(s): 2946156
Usage: 1969 Belvedere, Coronet, Charger, full-size Plymouth, Dodge, or Chrysler models with 383-ci two-barrel.
Note(s): Single snorkel design.

Interchange Number: 11
Part Number(s): 2946159
Usage: 1969 Coronet, Belvedere, full-size Plymouth, Dodge, Chrysler with 383-ci four-barrel, except Super Bee and Road Runner models; 1969 full-size Dodge, Plymouth, or Chrysler with 440-ci.
Note(s): Dual snorkel design.

Interchange Number: 12
Part Number(s): 2951362
Usage: 1969 Super Bee or Road Runner with 383-ci 335-hp and fresh-air hood package.
Note(s): Cover in Interchange Numbers 32 and 33 will fit.

Interchange Number: 13
Part Number(s): 2951353
Usage: 1969 Coronet R/T, GTX, Super Bee or Road Runner with 426 Hemi.

Note(s): Cover in Interchange Numbers 31 and 33 will fit.

Interchange Number: 14
Part Number(s): 2951361
Usage: 1969 Coronet R/T or GTX with 440-ci with fresh-air hood.
Note(s): Cover in Interchange 31 and 32 will fit.

Interchange Number: 15
Part Number(s):
Usage: 1969 Road Runner or Super Bee with 440-ci triple-two-barrel.

Interchange Number: 16
Part Number(s): 2951675
Usage: 1970–72, all car lines with a 318-ci two-barrel.

Interchange Number: 17
Part Number(s): 3418722
Usage: 1970 Coronet R/T, 1970–71 GTX, 1971 Charger R/T with 440-ci four-barrel with fresh-air hood.

Interchange Number: 18
Part Number(s): 3418723
Usage: 1970–71 Super Bee, 1970–71 Road Runner with 383-ci four-barrel and fresh-air hood.

Interchange Number: 19
Part Number(s): 3418652
Usage: 1970 Cuda with 426 Hemi.
Note(s): shaker hood scoop

Interchange Number: 20
Part Number(s): 3418715
Usage: 1970 Challenger R/T 426 Hemi without shaker hood, 1970 Charger R/T with 426 Hemi.

Interchange Number: 21
Part Number(s): 3418686
Usage: 1970 Road Runner, GTX, Super Bee, or Coronet R/T with 426 Hemi.
Note(s): Used with fresh-air hood only.

Interchange Number: 22
Part Number(s): 3418717
Usage: 1970–71 Road Runner, GTX, Super Bee, Coronet R/T, Cuda, Challenger R/T, Fury with 440 triple-two-barrel without fresh-air hood.

Interchange Number: 23
Part Number(s): 2946394
Usage: 1970–71 Cuda with 440-ci triple-two-barrel, 1971 Challenger R/T 440-ci triple-two-barrel, with shaker hood.

Interchange Number: 24
Part Number(s): 2946389
Usage: 1970 GTX or Road Runner with 440-ci triple-two-barrel, with fresh-air hood.

Interchange Number: 25
Part Number(s): 3512764
Usage: 1971 Barracuda, Challenger with 340-ci with E.C.S.

Interchange Number: 26
Part Number(s): 3577385
Usage: 1970–71 Challenger T/A with 340-ci triple-two-barrel, 1970–71 Challenger R/T with 440-ci triple-two-barrel with fiberglass hood.
Note(s): Factory ran out of shaker hoods. Fiberglass T/A hoods were used instead.

Interchange Number: 27
Part Number(s): 3462485
Usage: 1970–71 Barracuda 1970–71 Challenger 340-ci, 383- or 440-ci four-barrel with shaker hood.

Interchange Number: 28
Part Number(s): 3577354
Usage: 1971 Challenger R/T with 426 Hemi without shaker hood.

Interchange Number: 29
Part Number(s): 3577464
Usage: 1971 Challenger R/T with 426 Hemi with shaker hood.

Interchange Number: 30
Part Number(s): 3577394
Usage: 1971 Challenger R/T with 426 Hemi with fiberglass hood.
Note(s): shaker hood, shortage fiberglass hood used instead.

Interchange Number: 31
Part Number(s): 3577357
Usage: 1971 Charger R/T, Super Bee, GTX, or Road Runner with 426 Hemi.
Note(s): Fresh-air hood standard with these models.

Interchange Number: 32
Part Number(s): 3418709
Usage: 1971 Charger R/T, Super Bee, GTX, or Road Runner with 440-ci triple-two-barrel with fresh-air hood.

Interchange Number: 33
Part Number(s): 3462467
Usage: 1970–71 Barracuda, Challenger, Charger, Dart, Duster, Super Bee, Road Runner, or Valiant with 340-ci four-barrel.
Note(s): Without fiberglass hood on Challenger models.

Interchange Number: 34
Part Number(s): 3577457
Usage: 1970–71 Challenger with 340-ci four-barrel with fiberglass hood.

Interchange Number: 35
Part Number(s): 3577458
Usage: 1970–71 Challenger with 383-ci four-barrel with fiberglass hood.

Interchange Number: 36
Part Number(s): 3577470
Usage: 1971, all car lines with a 383-ci two-barrel or 360-ci two-barrel.

Interchange Number: 37
Part Number(s): 3577467
Usage: 1971, all car lines with a 383-ci four-barrel or 440-ci four-barrel, without fresh-air hood, except full-size Chrysler models without high-performance engine.

Interchange Number: 38
Part Number(s): 2951761
Usage: 1970, all car lines with 383-ci two-barrel, except export models

Interchange Number: 39
Part Number(s): 2951765
Usage: 1970, all car lines with 383-ci four-barrel or 440-ci four-barrel, except full-size Chrysler models, or those models with fresh-air hood.
Note(s): (1) Dual snorkel design. (2) Air cleaner from full-size Chrysler station wagon will fit.

Interchange Number: 40
Part Number(s): 3614908
Usage: 1972–early 1973 Charger Rallye, Road Runner, Dart, Duster, Challenger, Barracuda, and Valiant, full-size Dodge or Plymouth, with 340-ci or 440-ci four-barrel.
Note(s): Unsilenced unit. Some 1972 cars with 440-ci also used Interchange Number 41. Used until build date December 1972 on cars with a 340-ci engine.

Interchange Number: 41
Part Number(s): 3671364
Usage: 1972 Charger, Satellite, full-size Dodge or Plymouth with 400-ci four-barrel; 1973 Charger, Satellite with 400-ci four-barrel.
Note(s): Silenced unit. Some 1972 models also used Interchange Number 40. Unit from full-size Chrysler models will not fit.

Interchange Number: 42
Part Number(s): 3462496
Usage: 1972 Charger, Satellite with 400-ci two-barrel; 1972 full-size Dodge or Plymouth with 360-ci two-barrel.
Note(s): Unit from a full-size model with a 400-ci engine will not interchange.

Interchange Number: 43
Part Number(s): 3577760
Usage: 1973, all car lines with 318-ci two-barrel, except exports.

Interchange Number: 44
Part Number(s): 3769046
Usage: Late 1973 Barracuda, Challenger, Charger, Dart Duster, Road Runner, or Valiant with 340-ci four-barrel.
Note(s): After December 1972.

Interchange Number: 45
Part Number(s): 3751208
Usage: 1973 Charger, Satellite with 400-ci two-barrel; 1973 full-size Dodge or Plymouth with 360-ci two-barrel, except export models.
Note(s): full-size models with 400-ci will not fit.

Interchange Number: 46
Part Number(s): 3769024
Usage: 1974, all car lines with 318-ci two-barrel, except export models.

Interchange Number: 47
Part Number(s): 4006500
Usage: 1974 Barracuda, Challenger Duster, Dart, or Valiant with 360-ci four-barrel.

Interchange Number: 48
Part Number(s): 3769008
Usage: 1974 Charger, Satellite, full-size Dodge, Plymouth, or Chrysler with 360-ci four-barrel or 400-ci two-barrel.

Interchange Number: 49
Part Number(s): 3769004
Usage: 1974 Charger, Satellite, full-size Dodge, Plymouth, or Chrysler with 360-ci four-barrel

Interchange Number: 50
Part Number(s): 3769020
Usage: 1974 Charger, Satellite, full-size Dodge or Plymouth with 400-ci four-barrel or high-output 440-ci four-barrel.
Note(s): Unit from full-size Chrysler will not fit. Nor will police model.

Interchange Number: 51
Part Number(s): 3830036
Usage: 1974 Coronet, Satellite, full-size Dodge, or Plymouth police car with 440-ci engine.

1970 dual snorkel air cleaner.

426 Hemi Challengers without a fresh-air hood used this air cleaner.

Chapter 3

Oiling and Cooling Systems

Oil Pans
Model Identification

Interchange
Interchange Number: 1
Part Number(s): 2806393
Usage: 1965–66 Barracuda, Dart, and Valiant with 273-ci; 1967–69 Barracuda, Dart, and Valiant with 318-ci or 340-ci; 1965–69 Belvedere, Coronet with 273-ci or 318-ci; 1966–69 Charger with 318-ci.
Interchange Number: 2
Part Number(s): 2863892
Usage: 1967–68 Barracuda, Dart GTS with 383-ci.
Interchange Number: 3
Part Number(s): 3671693
Usage: 1970–71 Barracuda, Challenger with 383-ci; 1966–71 Belvedere/Satellite, Charger, Coronet with 383-ci; 1967–69 Belvedere, Charger, Coronet with 440-ci; 1966 Belvedere, Charger, Coronet with 361-ci; 1972 Charger, Coronet, and Satellite with 400-ci.
Interchange Number: 4
Part Number(s): 3671852
Usage: 1966–71 426 Hemi, all models; 1970–71 Barracuda, Challenger with 440-ci; 1970–72 Charger, with 440-ci; 1970 Coronet with 440-ci; 1970–72 Satellite with 440-ci.
Interchange Number: 5
Part Number(s): 3614227
Usage: 1970–74 Barracuda, Challenger, Charger, Coronet, Dart, Duster, Fury, Monaco, Satellite, and Valiant with 318-ci; 1970–73 Barracuda, Challenger, Dart, Duster, and Valiant with 340-ci; 1971–73 Charger, Satellite with 340-ci.
Interchange Number: 6
Part Number(s): 3614970
Usage: 1973–74 Charger, Coronet, and Satellite with 400-ci or 440-ci.
Interchange Number: 7
Part Number(s): 3751954
Usage: 1974 Barracuda, Challenger, Charger, Dart, Duster, Satellite, and Valiant with 360-ci.
Interchange Number: 8
Part Number(s): 2946706
Usage: 1969 Barracuda, Dart with 383-ci or 440-ci.

Oil Pumps
Model Identification

Radiator core identification number location.

Interchange

Interchange Number: 1
    Part Number(s): 2806270
    Usage: 1964–68 273-ci, all models; 1967–74 318-ci, all models;
        1968–73 240-ci, all models; 1971–74 360-ci, all models.
Interchange Number: 2
    Part Number(s): 2808510
    Usage: 1968–71 426 Hemi; 1970–72 440-ci triple-two-barrel;
        1971–72 440-ci four-barrel, all models; 1971 383-ci; 1972
        400-ci.
Interchange Number: 3
    Part Number(s): 2808509
    Usage: 1968–70 383-ci; 1968–70 440-ci
Interchange Number: 4
    Part Number(s): 3685652
    Usage: 1973–74 400-ci or 440-ci, all models, all outputs.

Radiator Core

The radiator core is identified by an ID number that is stamped into the top of the core's tank, near the filler neck opening. Factors that may have influence on the interchanging of cores are model, model year, engine size, and certain options such as air conditioning and maximum cooling. Width of the core is given when known, but you should not rely on this. Watch when swapping a core from a car with manual transmission to a car with automatic transmission. Those models with a manual transmission have no provisions for transmission cooling lines on the core. A unit from a car with automatic will fit a car with manual transmission, if the cooling line provisions are shut off. Also note there was a change in

radiator design on late 1973 models; after March 15, 1973, the tank switch was moved to the top. Early design and later style will not interchange for this reason.

Model Identification

Barracuda..Interchange Number
1968 318-ci without air conditioning............................1
1968 318-ci with air conditioning............................2
1968 318-ci with maximum cooling............................2
1968 340-ci without air conditioning............................1
1968 340-ci with air conditioning............................2
1968 340-ci with maximum cooling............................2
1968 383-ci, all............................3
1969 318-ci without air conditioning............................10
1969 318-ci with air conditioning............................17
1969 318-ci with maximum cooling............................21
1969 340-ci without air conditioning............................12
1969 340-ci with air conditioning............................18
1969 340-ci with maximum cooling............................21
1969 383-ci or 440-ci, all............................13
1970 318-ci without air conditioning............................24
1970 318-ci with air conditioning............................26
1970 318-ci with maximum cooling............................26
1970 340-ci without air conditioning............................26
1970 340-ci with air conditioning............................26
1970 340-ci with maximum cooling............................26
1970 383-ci or 440-ci without air conditioning............................29
1970 383-ci or 440-ci with air conditioning............................30
1970 383-ci or 440-ci with maximum cooling............................31
1970 Hemi without air conditioning............................31
1971 318-ci without air conditioning............................34
1971 318-ci with air conditioning............................36
1971 318-ci with maximum cooling............................37
1971 340-ci without air conditioning............................37
1971 340-ci with air conditioning............................36
1971 340-ci with maximum cooling............................37
1971 383-ci or 440-ci without air conditioning............................39
1971 383-ci or 440-ci with air conditioning............................40
1971 383-ci or 440-ci with maximum cooling............................40
1971 Hemi, all............................40
1972 318-ci without air conditioning............................42
1972 318-ci with air conditioning............................44
1972 318-ci with maximum cooling............................45
1972 340-ci without air conditioning............................45, 47
1972 340-ci with air conditioning............................44
1972 340-ci with maximum cooling............................45, 47
1973 318-ci without air conditioning............................42, 64
1973 318-ci with air conditioning............................54, 67
1973 318-ci with maximum cooling............................54, 69
1973 340-ci without air conditioning............................56, 72
1973 340-ci with air conditioning............................54, 67
1973 340-ci with maximum cooling............................56, 69
1974 318-ci without air conditioning............................82
1974 318-ci with air conditioning............................79
1974 318-ci with maximum cooling............................83
1974 360-ci without air conditioning............................78
1974 360-ci with air conditioning............................79
1974 360-ci with maximum cooling............................83
Belvedere, Charger,
Coronet, and Satellite............................Interchange Number
1968 318-ci without air conditioning............................5
1968 318-ci with air conditioning............................6
1968 318-ci with maximum cooling............................6
1968 383-ci or 440-ci without air conditioning............................4
1968 383-ci or 440-ci with air conditioning............................8
1968 383-ci or 440-ci with maximum cooling............................7
1968 Hemi, all............................9
1969 318-ci without air conditioning............................11
1969 318-ci with air conditioning............................19
1969 318-ci with maximum cooling............................22

Interchange

Interchange Number: 1
   Part/ID Number(s): 2898028
   Width: 22 in
   Usage: 1968 Barracuda, Dart, and Valiant with 318-ci or 340-ci
      without air conditioning or maximum cooling.
Interchange Number: 2
   Part/ID Number(s): 2949068
   Width: 22 in

Usage: 1968 Barracuda, Dart, and Valiant with 318-ci, 340-ci
   with air conditioning or maximum cooling.
Interchange Number: 3
   Part/ID Number(s): 2898033
   Width: 22 in
   Usage: 1968 Barracuda, Dart with 383-ci.
Interchange Number: 4
   Part/ID Number(s): 2949053
   Width: 22 in
   Usage: 1968 Coronet, Charger, Belvedere with 383-ci or 440-ci
      without air conditioning or maximum cooling.
Interchange Number: 5
   Part/ID Number(s): 2898038
   Width: 22 in
   Usage: 1968 Coronet, Charger, Belvedere with 318-ci without
      air conditioning or maximum cooling.
Interchange Number: 6
   Part/ID Number(s): 2898041
   Width: 26 in
   Usage: 1968 Coronet, Charger, Belvedere with 318-ci with air
      conditioning.
Interchange Number: 7
   Part/ID Number(s): 2949054
   Width: 26 in
   Usage: 1968 Coronet, Charger, Belvedere with 383-ci or 440-ci
      with maximum cooling.
Interchange Number: 8
   Part/ID Number(s): 2898047
   Width: 26 in
   Usage: 1968 Coronet, Charger, Belvedere with 383-ci or 440-ci
      with air conditioning.
Interchange Number: 9
   Part/ID Number(s): 2898048
   Width: 26 in
   Usage: 1968 Coronet, Charger, Belvedere with 426 Hemi.
   Note(s): Interchange Number 8 will fit.
Interchange Number: 10
   Part/ID Number(s): 2949031
   Width: 19 in
   Usage: 1969 Barracuda, Dart, and Valiant with 318-ci without
      air conditioning or maximum cooling.
Interchange Number: 11
   Part/ID Number(s): 2949060
   Width: 19 in
   Usage: 1969 Coronet, Charger, Belvedere with 318-ci without
      air conditioning or maximum cooling.
Interchange Number: 12
   Part/ID Number(s): 2949066
   Width: 22 in
   Usage: 1969 Barracuda, Dart, and Valiant with 340-ci without
      air conditioning or maximum cooling.
Interchange Number: 13
   Part/ID Number(s): 2949065
   Width: 22 in
   Usage: 1969 Barracuda or Dart with 383-ci or 440-ci.
Interchange Number: 14
   Part/ID Number(s): 2949053
   Width: 22 in
   Usage: 1969 Coronet, Charger, and Belvedere with 383-ci or
      440-ci without air conditioning or maximum cooling.
Interchange Number: 15
   Part/ID Number(s): 2949054
   Width: 26 in
   Usage: 1969 Coronet, Charger, and Belvedere with 426 Hemi;
      1969 Coronet, Charger, Belvedere with 383-ci or 440-ci
      with maximum cooling.
   Note(s): Interchange Numbers 16 and 20 will fit.
Interchange Number: 16
   Part/ID Number(s): 2949052
   Width: 26 in

Usage: 1969 Coronet or Belvedere police car with 383-ci or 440-ci.

Interchange Number: 17
Part/ID Number(s): 2949067
Width: 22 in
Usage: 1969 Barracuda, Dart, and Valiant with 318-ci with air conditioning; 1969 Coronet, Charger, Belvedere with 225-ci six-cylinder, with maximum cooling.

Interchange Number: 18
Part/ID Number(s): 2949068
Width: 22 in
Usage: 1969 Barracuda, Dart with 340-ci with air conditioning.

Interchange Number: 19
Part/ID Number(s): 2949059
Width: 226 in
Usage: 1969 Coronet, Charger, and Belvedere with 318-ci with air conditioning.

Interchange Number: 20
Part/ID Number(s): 2949055
Width: 26 in
Usage: 1969 Coronet, Charger, and Belvedere with 383-ci or 440-ci with air conditioning.

Interchange Number: 21
Part/ID Number(s): 2949068
Width: 22 in
Usage: 1969 Barracuda, Valiant, and Dart with 318-ci with maximum cooling; 1969 Barracuda, Dart with 340-ci with maximum cooling.

Interchange Number: 22
Part/ID Number(s): 2949058
Width: 26 in
Usage: 1969 Coronet, Charger, and Belvedere with 318-ci with maximum cooling.

Interchange Number: 23
Part/ID Number(s): 2998943
Width: 19 in
Usage: 1970 Duster, Dart, and Valiant with 318-ci without air conditioning or maximum cooling.

Interchange Number: 24
Part/ID Number(s): 2998947, 2998946, 2998973
Width: 19 in
Usage: 1970 Barracuda, Challenger, Coronet, Charger, and Belvedere with 318-ci without air conditioning or maximum cooling.

Interchange Number: 25
Part/ID Number(s): 2998944
Width: 22 in
Usage: 1970 Duster, Dart, and Valiant with 318-ci with air conditioning.

Interchange Number: 26
Part/ID Number(s): 2998948, 2998974, 2998949
Width: 26 in
Usage: 1970 Barracuda, Challenger with 318-ci with air conditioning; 1970 Barracuda, Challenger with 340-ci with maximum cooling; 1970 Barracuda, Challenger, Coronet, Charger, and Belvedere with 318-ci with maximum cooling.

Interchange Number: 27
Part/ID Number(s): 2998945
Width: 22 in
Usage: 1970 Duster, Dart, and Valiant with 318-ci with maximum cooling.

Interchange Number: 28
Part/ID Number(s): 2998978
Width: 22 in
Usage: 1970 Duster, Dart, and Valiant with 340-ci.

Interchange Number: 29
Part/ID Number(s): 2998954, 299857, 2998960
Width: 22 in
Usage: 1970 Barracuda, Challenger, Charger, Coronet, and Belvedere with 383-ci or 440-ci without maximum cooling.

Interchange Number: 30
Part/ID Number(s): 2998956
Width: 26 in
Usage: 1970 Barracuda, Challenger, Charger, Coronet, and Belvedere with 383-ci or 440-ci with air conditioning.
Note(s): Interchange Number 31 may also fit.

Interchange Number: 31
Part/ID Number(s): 2998958, 2998961
Width: 26 in
Usage: 1970 Challenger, Barracuda, Coronet, Charger, and Belvedere with 383-ci or 440-ci with maximum cooling.
Note(s): Interchange Number 30 may also fit.

Interchange Number: 32
Part/ID Number(s): 2998959
Width: 26 in
Usage: 1970 Challenger, Barracuda, Charger, Coronet, and Belvedere with 383-ci with maximum cooling.

Interchange Number: 33
Part/ID Number(s): 3443978
Width: 19 in
Usage: Dart, Duster, and Valiant with 318-ci without air conditioning or maximum cooling.

Interchange Number: 34
Part/ID Number(s): 3443972, 3443973, 3443968
Width: 19 in.
Usage: 1971 Barracuda, Challenger, Charger, and Satellite with 318-ci without air conditioning or maximum cooling.

Interchange Number: 35
Part/ID Number(s): 3443976, 3443977
Width: 22 in
Usage: 1971 Dart, Duster, and Valiant with 318-ci or 340-ci with air conditioning.

Interchange Number: 36
Part/ID Number(s): 3443971, 3443969, 3443960
Width: 26 in
Usage: 1971 Barracuda, Challenger, Coronet, Charger, and Satellite with 318-ci or 340-ci with air conditioning.

Interchange Number: 37
Part/ID Number(s): 3443970
Width: 26 in
Usage: 1971 Barracuda, Challenger, Charger, Coronet, and Satellite with 318-ci or 340-ci with maximum cooling.

Interchange Number: 38
Part/ID Number(s): 3443975
Width: 22 in
Usage: 1971 Dart, Duster, and Valiant with 318-ci or 340-ci with maximum cooling.

Interchange Number: 39
Part/ID Number(s): 3443961, 3443962, 3443938, 3443961
Width: 22 in
Usage: 1971 Barracuda, Challenger, Coronet, and Satellite with 383-ci or 440-ci without air conditioning or maximum cooling.

Interchange Number: 40
Part/ID Number(s): 3443940, 3443959, 3443960
Width: 26 in
Usage: 1971 Barracuda, Challenger, Charger, Coronet, and Satellite with 383-ci or 440-ci with air conditioning; 1971 Barracuda, Challenger, Charger, and Road Runner with 426 Hemi.

Interchange Number: 41
Part/ID Number(s): 3574635, 35744637
Width: 19 in
Usage: 1972 Dart, Duster, and Valiant with 318-ci without air conditioning.
Note(s): ID number 3574635 originally with manual transmission.

Interchange Number: 42
Part/ID Number(s): 3574633, 3574631
Width: 19 in

Usage: 1972 Barracuda, Challenger, Charger, Coronet, and Satellite with 318-ci without air conditioning.
Note(s): ID number 3574633 originally with manual transmission.

Interchange Number: 43
Part/ID Number(s): 3574658, 3574634
Width: 22 in
Usage: 1972 Dart, Duster, and Valiant with 318-ci or 340-ci with air conditioning or maximum cooling.

Interchange Number: 44
Part/ID Number(s): 3574626, 3574627
Width: 26 in
Usage: 1972 Barracuda, Challenger, Charger, Coronet, and Satellite with 318-ci or 340-ci with air conditioning.

Interchange Number: 45
Part/ID Number(s): 3574624
Width: 26 in
Usage: 1972 Barracuda, Challenger, Coronet, Charger, and Satellite with 318-ci or 340-ci with maximum cooling.

Interchange Number: 46
Part/ID Number(s): 3574636
Width: 22 in
Usage: 1972 Dart, Duster with 340-ci with manual transmission with maximum cooling.

Interchange Number: 47
Part/ID Number(s): 3574628
Width: 22 in
Usage: 1972 Barracuda, Challenger, Charger, Road Runner with 340-ci with manual transmission with maximum cooling.

Interchange Number: 48
Part/ID Number(s): 3574614, 3574616
Width: 22 in
Usage: 1972 Charger, Road Runner, Satellite, and Coronet with 400-ci with manual or automatic transmission without air conditioning; 1972 Charger, Road Runner with 440-ci with automatic transmission without air conditioning.
Note(s): ID number 3574616 originally used with manual transmission.

Interchange Number: 49
Part/ID Number(s): 3574611, 3574612, 3574613
Width: 26 in
Usage: 1972 Charger, Satellite, and Coronet with 400-ci with air conditioning; 1972 Charger, Road Runner with 440-ci with four-speed transmission; 1972 Charger, Road Runner with 440-ci with air conditioning.

Interchange Number: 50
Part/ID Number(s): 3673913, 3673914
Width: 19 in
Usage: 1973 Dart, Duster, and Valiant with 318-ci without air conditioning.
Note(s): ID number 3673913 originally with manual transmission.

Interchange Number: 51
Part/ID Number(s): 3673922, 3673926
Width: 19 in
Usage: 1972 Charger, Coronet, and Satellite with 318-ci without air conditioning.
Note(s): ID number 3673922 originally with manual transmission.

Interchange Number: 52
Part/ID Number(s): 3673915
Width: 26 in
Usage: 1973 Dart, Duster, and Valiant with 318-ci with air conditioning; 1973 Dart, Duster with 340-ci with automatic transmission.

Interchange Number: 53
Part/ID Number(s): 3673921
Width: 26 in
Usage: 1972 Dart, Duster, and Valiant with 318-ci with maximum cooling; 1972 Dart, Duster, and Valiant with 340-ci with air conditioning.

Interchange Number: 54
Part/ID Number(s): 3673924
Width: 26 in
Usage: 1973 Barracuda, Challenger with 318-ci or 340-ci with air conditioning.

Interchange Number: 55
Part/ID Number(s): 3673927
Width: 26 in
Usage: 1973 Charger, Coronet, and Satellite with 318-ci or 340-ci with air conditioning.

Interchange Number: 56
Part/ID Number(s): 3673925
Width: 26 in
Usage: 1973 Barracuda, Challenger with 340-ci with maximum cooling.

Interchange Number: 57
Part/ID Number(s): 3673928
Width: 28 in
Usage: 1973 Charger, Coronet, and Satellite with 318-ci or 340-ci with maximum cooling.

Interchange Number: 58
Part/ID Number(s): 3673916
Width: 26 in
Usage: 1973 Dart Sport, Duster with 340-ci and manual transmission.

Interchange Number: 59
Part/ID Number(s): 3673931, 3673932
Width: 22 in
Usage: 1973 Charger, Road Runner with 340-ci without air conditioning.
Note(s): ID number 3673931 originally with manual transmission.

Interchange Number: 60
Part/ID Number(s): 3673947, 3673952
Width: 28 in
Usage: 1973 Charger, Coronet, and Satellite with 400-ci or 440-ci with air conditioning.

Interchange Number: 61
Part/ID Number(s): 3673961
Width: 26 in
Usage: 1973 Charger, Coronet, and Satellite with 400-ci or 440-ci without air conditioning.

Interchange Number: 62
Part/ID Number(s): 3673953
Width:28 in
Usage: 1973 Charger, Coronet, and Satellite with 400-ci or 440-ci with maximum cooling.

Interchange Number: 63
Part/ID Number(s): 3673013, 3673014
Width: 19 in
Usage: Late 1973 Dart, Duster, and Valiant with 318-ci without air conditioning.
Note(s): ID number 367013 originally used with manual transmission.

Interchange Number: 64
Part/ID Number(s): 3673022, 3673026
Width: 19 in
Usage: Late 1973 Barracuda, Challenger, Charger, Coronet, and Satellite with 318-ci without air conditioning.
Note(s): ID number 3673022 originally used with manual transmission.

Interchange Number: 65
Part/ID Number(s): 3673015
Width: 26 in
Usage: Late 1973 Dart, Duster, and Valiant with 318-ci with air conditioning; late 1973 Dart Sport, Duster 340-ci with automatic transmission.

Interchange Number: 66
Part/ID Number(s): 3673021
Width: 26 in
Usage: Late 1973 Dart, Duster, and Valiant with 318-ci with maximum cooling; late 1973 Dart, Duster, and Valiant with 340-ci with air conditioning.

Interchange Number: 67
 Part/ID Number(s): 3673024
 Width: 26 in
 Usage: Late 1973 Barracuda, Challenger with 318-ci or 340-ci with air conditioning.
Interchange Number: 68
 Part/ID Number(s): 3673027
 Width: 26 in
 Usage: Late 1973 Charger, Coronet, and Satellite with 318-ci or 340-ci with air conditioning.
Interchange Number: 69
 Part/ID Number(s): 3673025
 Width: 26 in
 Usage: Late 1973 Barracuda, Challenger with 318-ci or 340-ci with maximum cooling.
Interchange Number: 70
 Part/ID Number(s): 3673028
 Width: 28 in
 Usage: Late 1973 Charger, Coronet, and Satellite with 318-ci or 340-ci with maximum cooling.
Interchange Number: 71
 Part/ID Number(s): 3673016
 Width: 26 in
 Usage: Late 1973 Dart Sport, Duster with 340-ci with manual transmission.
Interchange Number: 72
 Part/ID Number(s): 3673031, 3673032
 Width: 22 in
 Usage: Late 1973 Barracuda, Challenger, Charger, Coronet, and Satellite with 340-ci.
 Note(s): ID number 3673031 originally used with manual transmission.
Interchange Number: 73
 Part/ID Number(s): 3673047, 3673052
 Width: 28 in
 Usage: Late 1973 Charger, Coronet, and Satellite with 400-ci or 440-ci with air conditioning.
Interchange Number: 74
 Part/ID Number(s): 3673098
 Width: 28 in
 Usage: Late 1973 Charger, Coronet, and Satellite with 400-ci or 440-ci without air conditioning.
Interchange Number: 75
 Part/ID Number(s): 3673053
 Width: 28 in
 Usage: Late 1973 Charger, Coronet, and Satellite with 400-ci or 440-ci with maximum cooling.
Interchange Number: 76
 Part/ID Number(s): 3692913, 3692914
 Width: 19 in
 Usage: 1974 Dart, Duster, and Valiant with 318-ci without air conditioning.
 Note(s): ID number 3692913 originally used with manual transmission.
Interchange Number: 77
 Part/ID Number(s): 3692905
 Width: 22 in
 Usage: 1974 Charger, Coronet, and Satellite with 318-ci with air conditioning.
Interchange Number: 78
 Part/ID Number(s): 3692932
 Width: 26 in
 Usage: 1974 Barracuda, Challenger with 360-ci without air conditioning.
Interchange Number: 79
 Part/ID Number(s): 3692935
 Width: 26 in
 Usage: 1974 Barracuda, Challenger with 318-ci or 360-ci with air conditioning.
Interchange Number: 80
 Part/ID Number(s): 3692915, 3692923
 Width: 26 in
 Usage: 1974 Dart, Duster, and Valiant with 318-ci or 360-ci with air conditioning.
Interchange Number: 81
 Part/ID Number(s): 3692912
 Width: 26 in
 Usage: 1974 Dart Sport, Duster with 360-ci; 1974 Dart, Duster, and Valiant with 318-ci with maximum cooling.
Interchange Number: 82
 Part/ID Number(s): 3692926
 Width: 119 in
 Usage: 1974 Barracuda, Challenger with 318-ci without air conditioning.
Interchange Number: 83
 Part/ID Number(s): 3692925
 Width: 26 in
 Usage: 1974 Barracuda, Challenger with 318-ci or 360-ci with maximum cooling.
Interchange Number: 84
 Part/ID Number(s): 3692934
 Width: 19 in
 Usage: 1974 Charger, Coronet, and Satellite with 318-ci without air conditioning.
Interchange Number: 85
 Part/ID Number(s): 3692942, 369227
 Width: 28 in
 Usage: 1974 Charger, Coronet, and Satellite with 318-ci or 360-ci with air conditioning.
Interchange Number: 86
 Part/ID Number(s): 3692944
 Width: 28 in
 Usage: 1974 Charger, Coronet, and Satellite with 318-ci or 360-ci with air conditioning with maximum cooling.
 Note(s): Best cooling core for a small block for the 1971–74 models.
Interchange Number: 87
 Part/ID Number(s): 3692947
 Width: 28 in
 Usage: 1974 Charger, Coronet, and Satellite with 400-ci with air conditioning; 1974 Charger, Coronet, and Satellite with 440-ci without air conditioning.
Interchange Number: 88
 Part/ID Number(s): 3692947
 Width: 28 in
 Usage: 1974 Charger, Satellite with 440-ci with air conditioning.
Interchange Number: 89
 Part/ID Number(s): 3692953
 Width: 28 in
 Usage: 1974 Charger, Coronet, and Satellite with 400-ci or 440-ci with air conditioning with maximum cooling.
 Note(s): Best core for big blocks in 1971–1974 models.

Fan Blades

Fan blades are identified by the number of blades and the diameter of the assembly. Options such as maximum cooling or air conditioning may affect the interchange of the fan assembly. The interchange is the fan without the spacer or fan clutch assembly.

Note that a larger diameter fan will provide better cooling for your car. And in many cases, the larger-diameter fan will fit models that originally came with a smaller-diameter fan. For example the large, 20-inch fans used in 1974 models will fit the 1971–73 models, which used 18-inch-diameter fans, without any problems. Use the shroud and fan clutch that was used with the larger-diameter fan when making these swaps.

Model Identification

Dart, Duster, and Valiant ....Interchange Number

Interchange

Interchange Number: 1
Part Number(s): 2265034
Number of Blades: 6

Usage: 1964–65 Belvedere, Coronet, Polara, Fury, Newport,
    New Yorker, or Imperial with V-8 engine except 426-ci;
    1966–68 Coronet, Charger, Belvedere, Fury, and Polara with
    all engines without C.A.P., air conditioning, or trailer
    package; 1969 Barracuda, Valiant, Belvedere, Coronet,
    Charger, Fury, Monaco, and Polara with 318-ci without air
    conditioning; 1970 Barracuda, Challenger, Coronet,
    Charger, Satellite, Fury, Polara, Monaco, Newport, New
    Yorker, and Chrysler 300, all engines except 340-ci or Hemi
    without air conditioning.

Interchange Number: 2
Part Number(s): 2658984
Number of Blades: 4
Usage: 1966–67 Barracuda, Dart, and Valiant with 273-ci
    without air conditioning without C.A.P. without trailer
    package.

Interchange Number: 3
Part Number(s): 2780920
Number of Blades: 4
Usage: 1966–68 Coronet, Charger, and Belvedere with 318-ci
    V-8 without air conditioning, without C.A.P. without trailer
    package; 1966 Coronet, Belvedere, Fury, and Polara with
    six-cylinder with C.A.P.; 1970 Fury, Polara, and Monaco with
    225-ci six-cylinder without air conditioning; 1970–71
    Barracuda, Challenger, Coronet, Belvedere, and Charger
    with 225-ci six-cylinder with air conditioning.

Interchange Number: 4
Part Number(s): 2863227
Number of Blades: 7
Usage: 1968–72 Barracuda, Dart, Valiant, Belvedere, Coronet,
    Charger, Fury, Polara, and Monaco with all V-8s with
    maximum cooling.

Interchange Number: 5
Part Number(s): 2863224
Number of Blades: 7
Diameter: 18
Usage: 1968–69 Barracuda, Dart, and Valiant with 318-ci V-8
    without air conditioning; 1969–70 Belvedere, Coronet,
    Charger, Fury, Polara, Monaco, Newport, and New Yorker
    with all V-8s, except Hemi; 1971–73 Barracuda, Challenger,
    Coronet, Satellite, Fury, Polara, and Monaco, with 318-ci V-8
    without air conditioning; 1973 Dart, Duster, and Valiant
    with 318-ci V-8 without air conditioning; 1973–74 Dart,
    Coronet, Charger, and Satellite with 225-ci six-cylinder with
    air conditioning; 1974 Dart, Fury, Polara, and Monaco with
    225-ci six-cylinder without air conditioning.

Interchange Number: 6
Part Number(s): 2863213
Number of Blades: 7
Diameter: 18
Usage: 1968–69 Barracuda, Dart GTS with 340-ci or 383-ci V-8
    without air conditioning; 1968 Fury with 225-ci six-cylinder,
    except taxi or police car; 1969 Belvedere, Coronet, Charger,
    Fury, and Polara with 225-ci six-cylinder with maximum
    cooling.
Note(s): Has 1-in pitch.

Interchange Number: 7
Part Number(s): 2863215
Number of Blades: 7
Diameter: 18
Usage: 1968–69 Barracuda, Dart, and Valiant with 318-ci or
    340-ci with air conditioning; 1968 Coronet, Belvedere,
    Charger, Fury, and Polara with 318-ci with air conditioning;
    1968–69 426 Hemi; 1969 GTX, Coronet R/T, Charger,
    Super Bee, and Road Runner with 440-ci with manual
    transmission.

Interchange Number: 8
Part Number(s): 2863216
Number of Blades: 7
Diameter: 18 1/2

Usage: 1968–71 Belvedere, Coronet, and Charger with 383-ci or 440-ci with maximum cooling and air conditioning; 1969–71 Fury, Polara, and Monaco with all V-8 engines with air conditioning; 1970–73 340-ci or Hemi without air conditioning; 1973 Dart, Duster, Valiant, Barracuda, and Challenger with 318-ci or 340-ci with air conditioning; 1973 Charger, Coronet, Satellite, Fury, Monaco, and Polara with 318-ci with 2.94 axle with air conditioning; 1973 Fury, Polara, Monaco police car, or taxi with 360-ci.

Interchange Number: 9
Part Number(s): 2863228
Number of Blades: 7
Usage: 1968 Belvedere, Coronet, Charger, Fury, Monaco, and Polara with 318-ci with air conditioning and maximum cooling.

Interchange Number: 10
Part Number(s): 2863223
Number of Blades: 7
Usage: 1968–69 Coronet, Belvedere, Charger, Fury, Polara, Monaco, Newport, New Yorker, and Imperial with 383-ci or 440-ci without air conditioning with trailer package.

Interchange Number: 11
Part Number(s): 3462150
Number of Blades: 5
Diameter: 18 1/4
Usage: 1971–72 Barracuda, Challenger, Charger, Coronet, Satellite, Fury, Monaco, and Polara with 318-ci with 2.71 or 2.76 axle; 1972 Charger, Coronet, Satellite, Fury, Polara, Monaco, Newport, and New Yorker with 400-ci or 440-ci without air conditioning with California emissions, in full-size cars.
Note(s): Flex fan.

Interchange Number: 12
Part Number(s): 3462139
Number of Blades: 5
Diameter: 18 1/2
Usage: Late 1972 Fury, Polara, Monaco, Newport, and New Yorker with a 400-ci or 440-ci without air conditioning; 1973 Charger, Coronet, Satellite, Fury, Polara, Monaco, Newport, New Yorker, and Chrysler 300 with 400-ci or 440-ci without air conditioning; 1973 Barracuda, Challenger, Charger, Coronet, Satellite, Fury, Polara, and Monaco with 318-ci with 2.71 or 2.76 axle with air conditioning.

Interchange Number: 13
Part Number(s): 3462149
Number of Blades: 7
Diameter: 20
Usage: 1973 Charger, Satellite, Coronet, Fury, Monaco, and Polara with 318-ci or 360-ci with air conditioning; 1973 Imperial; 1973 Charger, Satellite, Coronet, Fury, Monaco, Polara, Newport, New Yorker, and Chrysler 300 with all engines with maximum cooling; 1974 Dart, Duster, Valiant, Barracuda, Challenger, Charger, Coronet, Fury, Polara, Monaco, Newport, and New Yorker with 318-ci*, 360-ci, 400-ci, or 440-ci without air conditioning; 1974 Charger, Satellite, and Coronet with 318-ci with air conditioning without heavy-duty transmission; 1974 Charger, Coronet, and Satellite with 318-ci with maximum cooling.
Note(s): Aluminum blades. Will fit 1971–72 models using 1973 shroud and provide better cooling.
*With heavy-duty fan or transmission only with 318-ci.

Interchange Number: 14
Part Number(s): 2863214
Number of Blades: 4
Diameter: 18 1/2
Usage: 1974 Dart, Duster, Valiant, Barracuda, Challenger, Charger, Satellite, and Coronet with 318-ci without air conditioning or heavy-duty fan.

Interchange Number: 15
Part Number(s): 3462190
Number of Blades: 5
Diameter: 20

Usage: 1974 Charger, Coronet, Satellite, Monaco, Polara, Newport, and New Yorker with 360-ci, 400-ci, or 440-ci without air conditioning; 1974 Dart, Duster, Valiant, Barracuda, and Challenger with 318-ci with air conditioning; 1974 Charger, Coronet, and Satellite with 318-ci with manual transmission with air conditioning.
Note(s): Flex blades.

Interchange Number: 16
Part Number(s): 3462186
Number of Blades: 7
Diameter: 20
Usage: 1974 Charger, Coronet, Satellite, Fury, Polara, Monaco, Newport, and New Yorker with 318-ci*, 360-ci, 400-ci, or 440-ci with air conditioning.
Note(s): *With heavy-duty automatic transmission only on 318-ci.

Interchange Number: 17
Part Number(s): 1985513
Usage: 1968 Charger, Coronet, Satellite, Fury, Polara, Monaco, Newport, and New Yorker with 383-ci with air conditioning.

Fan Drives
Model Identification

Interchange

Interchange Number: 1
Part Number(s): 2536675
Type: Thermal drive
Usage: 1964–68 273-ci or 318-ci with air conditioning; 1968 383-ci or 440-ci with Leece-Nevill alternator.
Note(s): Change in design on full-size models after March 1968. Later style will not interchange.

Interchange Number: 2
Part Number(s): 2658456
Type: Thermal drive
Usage: 1966–66 361-ci, 1966–69 383-ci or 440-ci with air conditioning; 1970 Charger, Coronet, and Belvedere with 383-ci or 440-ci with air conditioning.

Interchange Number: 3
Part Number(s): 2806070
Type: Fluid drive
Usage: 1967–70 426 Hemi; 1967–70 440-ci with four-speed transmission without air conditioning.

Interchange Number: 4
Part Number(s): 2863231
Type: Thermal drive
Usage: 1968 340-ci with air conditioning.

Interchange Number: 5
Part Number(s): 2863263
Type: Thermal drive
Usage: 1969 340-ci with air conditioning; 1969 318-ci with air conditioning, except with 2.76 rear axle.

Interchange Number: 6
Part Number(s): 2863266
Type: Thermal drive
Usage: 1969 318-ci with air conditioning with 2.76 rear axle ratio.

Interchange Number: 7
Part Number(s): 2863259
Type: Fluid drive
Usage: 1969 340-ci without air conditioning.

Interchange Number: 8
Part Number(s): 3462108
Type: Thermal drive

Usage: 1970–71 318-ci or 360-ci, except in Dart, Duster, or Valiant models, with air conditioning with a 2.71, 2.76, or 2.94 rear axle.
Note(s): 6-in diameter. Easy to confuse with Interchange Number 9; they will not interchange.

Interchange Number: 9
Part Number(s): 3462106
Type: Thermal drive
Usage: 1970–72 Dart, Duster, or Valiant with 318-ci with air conditioning with 2.71 or 2.76 axle.
Note(s): 6-in diameter. Easy to confuse with Interchange Number 8; they will not interchange.

Interchange Number: 10
Part Number(s): 3462105
Type: Thermal drive
Usage: 1970–71 Dart, Duster, and Valiant with 318-ci with air conditioning with 2.94 rear axle.
Note(s): 7-in diameter

Interchange Number: 11
Part Number(s): 3462107
Type: Thermal drive
Usage: 1970–72 Barracuda, Challenger, Charger, Coronet, Satellite, Fury, Monaco, Polara, Newport, and New Yorker with air conditioning, all engine sizes except 318-, 340-, or 360-ci with 2.71, 2.76, or 2.94 rear axle.

Interchange Number: 12
Part Number(s): 2863233
Type: Fluid drive
Usage: 1970–72 Dart, Duster with 340-ci without air conditioning.

Interchange Number: 13
Part Number(s): 3462112
Type: Fluid drive
Usage: 1971 426 Hemi; 1971 440-ci with four-speed without air conditioning; 1970–72 340-ci in Barracuda, Challenger, Charger, or Road Runner; 1972 400-ci or 440-ci with four-speed without air conditioning.

Interchange Number: 14
Part Number(s): 2863260
Type: Torque drive
Usage: 1970–71 383-ci with air conditioning; 1970–72 440-ci with air conditioning; 1972 400-ci with air conditioning with 2.71, 2.76, or 3.23 rear axle.

Interchange Number: 15
Part Number(s): 3462108
Type: Thermal drive
Usage: 1972 318-ci or 360-ci with air conditioning with 2.71, 2.76, and 29.4 rear axle or with California emissions, all models except Dart, Duster, or Valiant.

Interchange Number: 16
Part Number(s): 3462168
Type: Fluid drive
Usage: Early 1973 Barracuda, Challenger with 340-ci without air conditioning.
Note(s): Used until build date March 9, 1973.

Interchange Number: 17
Part Number(s): 3462183
Type: Fluid drive
Usage: Late 1973 Barracuda, Challenger with 340-ci without air conditioning.
Note(s): Used after build date March 9, 1973.

Interchange Number: 18
Part Number(s): 3462180
Type: Fluid drive
Usage: Early 1973 Dart, Duster, and Charger Road Runner with 340-ci without air conditioning; early 1973, all models with 318-ci, 360-ci, 400-ci, or 440-ci with maximum cooling without air conditioning.
Note(s): Used until build date March 9, 1973.

Interchange Number: 19
Part Number(s): 33462182
Type: Fluid drive

Usage: Late 1973 Dart, Duster, and Charger Road Runner with 340-ci without air conditioning; late 1973, all models with 318-ci, 360-ci, 400-ci, or 440-ci with maximum cooling without air conditioning.

Note(s): Used after build date March 9, 1973.

Interchange Number: 20
Part Number(s): 3462179

Type: Thermal drive

Usage: 1973, all models, except Imperial, all engines with air conditioning, except with 2.71, 2.76, or 2.94 rear axle.

Interchange Number: 21
Part Number(s): 3462174

Type: Thermal drive

Usage: 1973 models with V-8 engine with air conditioning with 2.71, 2.76, or 2.94 rear axle.

Interchange Number: 22
Part Number(s): 3769614

Type: Fluid drive

Usage: 1974 Dart, Duster, Barracuda, Challenger, Charger, Satellite, and Coronet, all V-8 engines with maximum cooling, without air conditioning.

Note(s): Unit from full-size models will *not* interchange.

Interchange Number: 23
Part Number(s): 3769616

Type: Thermal drive

Usage: 1974 Dart, Duster, Barracuda, Challenger, Charger, Satellite, and Coronet, all V-8 engines with air conditioning.

Note(s): Unit from full-size models will *not* fit.

Water Pumps
Model Identification

318-ci	*Interchange Number*
1968 without air conditioning	1
1968 with air conditioning	2
1969 without air conditioning	5
1969 with air conditioning	6
1970–73 without air conditioning	7
1970–73 with air conditioning	8
1974, all	10

340-ci	*Interchange Number*
1968 without air conditioning	1
1968 with air conditioning	2
1969 without air conditioning	5
1969 with air conditioning	6
1970–73 without air conditioning	7
1970–73 with air conditioning	8

360-ci	*Interchange Number*
1974, all	11

383-ci	*Interchange Number*
1968–71 without air conditioning	3
1968–71 with air conditioning	4
1972–73, all	9
1974, all	12

400-ci	*Interchange Number*
1972–73, all	9
1974, all	12

426 Hemi	*Interchange Number*
1968–71	4

440-ci	*Interchange Number*
1968–71 without air conditioning	3
1968–71 with air conditioning	4
1972–73, all	9
1974, all	12

Interchange

Interchange Number: 1
Part Number(s): 2448315

Usage: 1964–67 273-ci or 318-ci with or without air conditioning, except Barracuda, Dart, or Valiant models with air conditioning; 1967 273-ci or 318-ci without C.A.P. with or without air conditioning; 1968 340-ci without air conditioning.

Note(s): Casting number 2402794

Interchange Number: 2
Part Number(s): 2585385

Usage: 1967 273-ci or 318-ci with C.A.P. with air conditioning; 1968 318-ci with air conditioning.

Interchange Number: 3
Part Number(s): 2808680

Usage: 1968–69 383-ci or 440-ci without air conditioning.

Interchange Number: 4
Part Number(s): 2808681

Usage: 1968–69 383-ci or 440-ci with air conditioning; 1968–69 426 Hemi.

Interchange Number: 5
Part Number(s): 3004991

Usage: 1969 318-ci, 340-ci without air conditioning.

Interchange Number: 6
Part Number(s): 3004763

Usage: 1969 318-ci or 340-ci with air conditioning.

Interchange Number: 7
Part Number(s): 3420038

Usage: 1970–73 318-ci, 340-ci, or 360-ci without air conditioning.

Interchange Number: 8
Part Number(s): 3420037

Usage: 1970–73 318-ci, 340-ci, 360-ci with air conditioning.

Interchange Number: 9
Part Number(s): 3683834

Usage: 1972–73 440-ci or 440-ci with or without air conditioning.

Interchange Number: 10
Part Number(s): 3780108

Usage: 1974 318-ci with or without air conditioning.

Interchange Number: 11
Part Number(s): 3780109

Usage: 1974 360-ci with or without air conditioning.

Interchange Number: 12
Part Number(s): 3780127

Usage: 1974 400-ci or 440-ci with or without air conditioning.

Chapter 4

Exhaust Systems

Exhaust Manifolds

Manifolds can be identified by their casting numbers, which will appear on the outer side of the unit. It will be followed by a casting date. The casting date is not of importance in interchanging. Note that model and engine output have effects on interchanging, as sometimes does transmission type and emission packages.

Exhaust manifolds are largely interchangeable in the engine family. High-performance types of manifolds can be adapted to fit non-high-performance heads for better performance.

Model Identification

Barracuda...Interchange Number
1968 318-ci, passenger's side 1
1968 318-ci, driver's side 12
1968 340-ci, passenger's side 8
1968 340-ci, driver's side 9
1968 383-ci, passenger's side 10
1968 383-ci, driver's side 14
1969 318-ci, passenger's side 13
1969 318-ci, driver's side 12
1969 340-ci, passenger's side 8
1969 340-ci, driver's side 9
1969, 383-ci or 440-ci, passenger's side 10
1969, 383-ci or 440-ci, driver's side 14
1970 318-ci, passenger's side 15
1970 318-ci, driver's side 17
1970 340-ci, passenger's side 8
1970 340-ci, driver's side 9
1970 383-ci, two-barrel, passenger's side 21
1970 383-ci, two-barrel, driver's side 22
1970 383-ci, four-barrel, passenger's side................................23
1970 383-ci, four-barrel, driver's side......................................24
1970 426 Hemi, passenger's side..4
1970 426 Hemi, driver's side..26
1970 440-ci, four-barrel, passenger's side................................23
1970 440-ci, four-barrel, driver's side......................................22
1970 440-ci, triple-two-barrel, passenger's side 24
1970 440-ci, triple-two-barrel, driver's side............................22
1971 318-ci, passenger's side 15
1971 318-ci, driver's side 18
1971 340-ci, passenger's side 19
1971 340-ci, driver's side 20
1971 383-ci, two-barrel, passenger's side 21
1971 383-ci, two-barrel, driver's side 22
1971 383-ci, four-barrel, passenger's side 23
1971 383-ci, four-barrel, driver's side......................................24
1971 426 Hemi, passenger's side..25
1971 426 Hemi, driver's side..26
1971 440-ci, triple-two-barrel, passenger's side 24
1971 440-ci, triple-two-barrel, driver's side............................22
1972 318-ci, passenger's side 13
1972 318-ci, driver's side 18
1972 340-ci, passenger's side 19
1972 340-ci, driver's side 20
1973 318-ci, passenger's side 13

1973 318-ci, driver's side 18
1973 340-ci, passenger's side 19
1973 340-ci, driver's side 35
1974 318-ci, passenger's side 42
1974 318-ci, driver's side 18
1974 360-ci, passenger's side 44
1974 360-ci, driver's side 35
Belvedere, Coronet, Charger,
and Satellite.....................................Interchange Number
1968 318-ci, passenger's side 1
1968 318-ci, driver's side 6
1968 383-ci, two-barrel, passenger's side 2
1968 383-ci, two-barrel, driver's, automatic 3
1968 383-ci, two-barrel, driver's, manual 11
1968 383-ci, four-barrel, passenger's side 7
1968 383-ci, four-barrel, driver's side 11
1968 426 Hemi, passenger's side..4
1968 426 Hemi, driver's side..5
1968 440-ci, passenger's side 7
1968 440-ci, driver's side 11
1969 318-ci, passenger's side 13
1969 318-ci, driver's side 6
1969 383-ci, two-barrel, passenger's side 2
1969 383-ci, two-barrel, driver's side 3
1969 383-ci, four-barrel, passenger's side 7
1969 383-ci, four-barrel, driver's side 11
1969 426 Hemi, passenger's side..4
1969 426 Hemi, driver's side..5
1969 440-ci passenger's side 7
1969 440-ci driver's side 11
1970 318-ci, passenger's side 15
1970 318-ci, driver's side 17
1970 383-ci, two-barrel, passenger's side 21
1970 383-ci, two-barrel, driver's side 22
1970 383-ci, four-barrel, passenger's side 23
1970 383-ci, four-barrel, driver's side 24
1970 426 Hemi, passenger's side..4
1970 426 Hemi, driver's side..26
1970 440-ci, four-barrel, passenger's side 23
1970 440-ci, four-barrel, driver's side 22
1970 440-ci, triple-two-barrel, passenger's side 24
1970 440-ci, triple-two-barrel, driver's side............................22
1971 318-ci, passenger's side 15
1971 318-ci, driver's side 18
1971 340-ci, passenger's side 19
1971 340-ci, driver's side 20
1971 383-ci, two-barrel, passenger's side 21
1971 383-ci, two-barrel, driver's side 22
1971 383-ci, four-barrel, passenger's side 23
1971 383-ci, four-barrel, driver's side 24
1971 426 Hemi, passenger's side..25
1971 426 Hemi, driver's side..26
1971 440-ci, triple-two-barrel, passenger's side 24
1971 440-ci, triple-two-barrel, driver's side............................22
1972 318-ci, passenger's side 13

Interchange

Interchange Number: 1
    Part Number(s): 2465766
    Casting Number: 2465769
    Side: Passenger's
    Usage: 1964–68 Barracuda, Dart, and Valiant with 273-ci;
        1965–67 Coronet, Belvedere with 273-ci; 1967 USA 318-ci,
        all models; 1968 Coronet, Charger, Belvedere, Fury, Polara,
        and Monaco with 318-ci.
    Note(s): 1967 USA engine is coded C-318.

Interchange Number: 2
    Part Number(s): 2532459
    Casting Number: 253246
    Side: Passenger's
    Usage: 1966 361-ci, 1966–67 383-ci, except Barracuda or Dart;
        1966–67 440-ci, except high-performance; 1968–69 383-ci
        two-barrel.
    Note(s): Unit from Imperial will *not* interchange. Coronet R/T,
        GTX models will *not* interchange. Number 7 will fit and
        provide better power.

Interchange Number: 3
    Part Number(s): 2532625
    Casting Number: 2532626
    Side: Driver's
    Usage: 1966–67 Belvedere, Coronet, and Charger with 361-ci
        or 383-ci; 1968–69 Belvedere, Charger, and Coronet with
        383-ci two-barrel and automatic transmission.

Interchange Number: 4
    Part Number(s): 2780506
    Casting Number: 2780508

Casting numbers help identify exhaust manifolds.

Side: Passenger's
Usage: 1966–70 Belvedere, Coronet, and Charger with 426
    Hemi; 1970 Barracuda, Challenger with 426 Hemi.

Interchange Number: 5
Part Number(s): 2780502
Casting Number: 2780501
Side: Driver's
Usage: 1966–69 Belvedere, Coronet, and Charger with 426 Hemi.

Interchange Number: 6
Part Number(s): 2465718
Casting Number: 2465719
Side: Driver's
Usage: 1964–67 Coronet, Belvedere with 273-ci; 1967, all models
    with 318-ci, except Canadian-built models; 1968–69 Belvedere,
    Coronet, Charger, Fury, Polara, and Monaco with 318-ci V8.
Note(s): 1967 engine block must be coded C-318.

Interchange Number: 7
Part Number(s): 2806898
Side: Passenger's
Usage: 1967–69 Coronet R/T, GTX, Fury, Polara, Monaco, and full-
    size Chrysler with 440-ci high-performance (375 hp); 1968–69
    383-ci four-barrel, all car lines except Barracuda or Dart.

Interchange Number: 8
Part Number(s): 2863545
Side: Passenger's
Usage: 1968–70 Barracuda, Dart with 340-ci; 1970 Duster,
    Challenger with 340-ci.

Interchange Number: 9
Part Number(s): 2863552
Side: Driver's
Usage: 1968–70 Barracuda, 1968–71 Dart with 340-ci;
    1970–71 Duster with 340-ci; and 1970 Challenger.

Interchange Number: 10
Part Number(s): 2863897
Side: Passenger's
Usage: 1968–69 Barracuda or Dart GTS with 383-ci; 1969
    Barracuda or Dart with 440-ci.

Interchange Number: 11
Part Number(s): 2843991
Side: Driver's
Usage: 1968 Belvedere, Coronet, and Charger with 383-ci two-
    barrel with four-speed transmission; 1968–69 383-ci four-barrel;
    1968–69 Coronet R/T, Charger R/T, and GTX with 440-ci.

Interchange Number: 12
Part Number(s): 2780946
Side: Driver's
Usage: 1968–69 Barracuda, Dart, and Valiant with 318-ci.

Interchange Number: 13
Part Number(s): 2843966
Side: Passenger's
Usage: 1969 318-ci, all models; 1972 318-ci, all models; 1973
    318-ci, all models except Road Runner.

Interchange Number: 14
Part Number(s): 2946728
Side: Driver's
Usage: 1968–69 Barracuda, Dart with 383-ci; 1969 Barracuda
    or Dart with 440-ci.

Interchange Number: 15
Part Number(s): 2946084
Side: Passenger's
Usage: 1970–71 318-ci, all car lines.

Interchange Number: 16
Part Number(s): 2951124
Side: Driver's
Usage: 1970–71 Dart, Duster, and Valiant with 318-ci.

Interchange Number: 17
Part Number(s): 2951915
Side: Driver's
Usage: 1970 Barracuda, Challenger, Charger, Coronet,
    Belvedere, Fury, Polara, and Monaco with 318-ci V-8.

Interchange Number: 18
Part Number(s): 3512076
Side: Driver's
Usage: 1971–74 Barracuda, Challenger, Charger, Coronet,
    Satellite, Fury, Polara, and Monaco with 318-ci.

Interchange Number: 19
Part Number(s): 3418624
Side: Passenger's
Usage: 1971–73 Barracuda, Challenger, Dart, Duster, Charger,
    and Road Runner with 340-ci; 1971–73 Fury, Polara, and
    Monaco with 360-ci without California emissions.

Interchange Number: 20
Part Number(s): 3418620
Side: Driver's
Usage: 1971–72 Barracuda, Challenger, Charger, and Road Runner
    with 340-ci; 1971–72 Fury, Monaco, and Polara with 360-ci.

Interchange Number: 21
Part Number(s): 2899954
Side: Passenger's
Usage: 1970–71 383-ci two-barrel, all car lines; 1970–71 Fury,
    Polara, Monaco, Newport, and New Yorker with 440-ci,
    except high-performance triple-two-barrel setup; 1972 400-
    ci two-barrel without California emissions.

Interchange Number: 22
Part Number(s): 2951864
Side: Driver's
Usage: 1970–71 Barracuda, Challenger, Charger, Coronet, and
    Satellite with 383-ci two-barrel; 1970–71 Barracuda,
    Challenger, Charger, Coronet, and Satellite with 440-ci
    including triple-two-barrel setups.

Interchange Number: 23
Part Number(s): 2899968
Side: Passenger's
Usage: 1970–71 383-ci four-barrel, all car lines; 1970–71 440-ci
    high-performance, all car lines, except triple-two-barrel set-ups;
    1973 400-ci four-barrel or 440-ci without California emissions.

Interchange Number: 24
Part Number(s): 2951864
Side: Driver's
Usage: 1970–71 Barracuda, Challenger, Charger, Coronet, and
    Satellite with 383-ci four-barrel; 1970–71 Barracuda,
    Challenger, Charger, Coronet, and Satellite with 440-ci
    triple-two-barrel.

Interchange Number: 25
Part Number(s): 3577282
Side: Passenger's
Usage: 1971 Barracuda, Challenger, Charger, Coronet, and
    Satellite with 426 Hemi.

Interchange Number: 26
Part Number(s): 3418452
Side: Driver's
Usage: 1970–71 Barracuda, Challenger, Charger, Coronet, and

Satellite with 426 Hemi.

Interchange Number: 27
Part Number(s): 3614396
Side: Driver's
Usage: 1972–74 Dart, Duster, and Valiant with 318-ci.

Interchange Number: 28
Part Number(s): 3614367
Side: Driver's
Usage: 1972–73 Dart, Duster with 340-ci; 1974 Dart, Duster with 360-ci.

Interchange Number: 29
Part Number(s): 3614340
Side: Passenger's
Usage: 1972 Charger, Coronet, and Satellite with 400-ci four-barrel or 440-ci with California emissions.

Interchange Number: 30
Part Number(s): 3614997
Side: Passenger's
Usage: 1972 Charger, Coronet, and Satellite with 400-ci two-barrel with California emissions.

Interchange Number: 31
Part Number(s): 3671594
Casting Number:
Side: Driver's
Usage: 1972 Charger, Coronet, and Satellite with 400- or 440-ci without California emissions.

Interchange Number: 32
Part Number(s): 3614801
Side: Driver's
Usage: 1972 Charger, Coronet, and Satellite with 400- or 440-ci with California emissions.

Interchange Number: 33
Part Number(s): 3671396
Side: Passenger's
Usage: 1973 Road Runner with 318-ci.
Note(s): Dual exhaust.

Interchange Number: 34
Part Number(s): 3671399
Side: Driver's
Usage: 1973–74 Road Runner with 318-ci; 1974 export full-size Dodge with 318-ci.
Note(s): Dual exhaust.

Interchange Number: 35
Part Number(s): 3751083
Side: Driver's
Usage: 1973 Barracuda, Challenger, Charger, and Road Runner with 340-ci; 1973 360-ci without California emissions; 1974 360-ci, all models except Dart or Duster.

Interchange Number: 36
Part Number(s): 3671634
Side: Passenger's
Usage: 1973 360-ci with California emissions.

Interchange Number: 37
Part Number(s): 3671583
Side: Driver's
Usage: 1973 360-ci with California emissions.

Interchange Number: 38
Part Number(s): 3751072
Side: Passenger's
Usage: 1973 Charger, Coronet, and Satellite with 400-ci two-barrel; 1973 Fury, Monaco, and Polara with 440-ci four-barrel.

Interchange Number: 39
Part Number(s): 3751069
Side: Passenger's
Usage: 1973 Charger, Coronet, and Satellite with 400-ci four-barrel or 440-ci high-performance.

Interchange Number: 40
Part Number(s): 3751067
Side: Driver's
Usage: 1973–74 Charger, Coronet, and Satellite with 400-ci or 440-ci.
Note(s): Fits two-barrel or four-barrel.

Interchange Number: 41
Part Number(s): 3751072
Side: Passenger's
Usage: 1973 Charger, Coronet, and Satellite with 400-ci two-barrel; 1973 Fury, Monaco, and Polara with 440-ci four-barrel.

Interchange Number: 42
Part Number(s): 3751607
Side: Passenger's
Usage: 1974 318-ci, all models except Road Runner or export in full-size Dodge.

Interchange Number: 43
Part Number(s): 3769406
Side: Passenger's
Usage: 1974 Road Runner with 318-ci; 1974 export full-size Dodge with 318-ci.
Note(s): Dual exhaust.

Interchange Number: 44
Part Number(s): 3751393
Side: Passenger's
Usage: 1974 360-ci, all models.

Interchange Number: 45
Part Number(s): 3751791
Side: Passenger's
Usage: 1974 Charger, Coronet, and Satellite with 400-ci two-barrel; 1974 Monaco, Newport, Fury, and New Yorker with 440-ci without California emissions, except with high-performance.
Note(s): 440-ci high-performance was of limited production in full-size models.

Interchange Number: 46
Part Number(s): 3751795
Side: Passenger's
Usage: 1974 Charger, Coronet, and Satellite with 400-ci four-barrel or 440-ci; 1974 Fury, Monaco, Newport, and New Yorker with 440-ci.
Note(s): 440-ci high-performance was of limited production in full-size models.

Mufflers
Model Identification

Barracuda	Interchange Number
1968–69 single	3
1968–69 dual, 340-ci or 383-ci, original	4
1968–69 dual, 340-ci or 383-ci, replacement	5
1970–71 single, 318-ci	8
1970–71 dual, 340-ci four-barrel	14
1970–71 dual, 340-ci triple-two-barrel	13
1970–71 dual, 383-ci, except Cuda	15
1970–71 dual, 383-ci, Cuda	14
1970–71 Hemi, dual	16
1970–71 Hemi, dual	14
1970–71 dual, 440-ci, four-barrel	14
1970–71 440-ci triple-two-barrel, except California	14
1970–71 440-ci triple-two-barrel, California	38
1972 340-ci, driver's side	14
1972 340-ci, passenger's side	14
1973 340-ci, driver's side	14
1973 340-ci, passenger's side	14
1974 360-ci, driver's side	14
1974 360-ci, passenger's side	36

Belvedere, Charger, Coronet, and Satellite	Interchange Number
1968–69 single, 318-ci, replacement	1
1968–69 single, 318-ci, 383-ci two-barrel	1
1968–69 dual, 383-ci four-barrel, original	7
1968–69 dual, 383-ci four-barrel, replacement	6
1968–69 dual, Hemi	2
1968–69 dual, 440-ci	2
1970 single, 318-ci	1

Interchange

Interchange Number: 1
Part Number(s): 2781265 (aluminized); 2781266 (zinc-coated)
Usage: 1966–70 Belvedere, Charger, and Coronet with 318-ci, or 1966 Belvedere, Charger, and Coronet with 361-ci, all with single exhaust; 1972–73 Charger, Coronet, and Satellite with 318-ci with single exhaust, zinc-coated muffler only.
Note(s): Will not fit 1973 Road Runner with 318-ci.

Interchange Number: 2
Part Number(s): 2781300
Usage: 1966–69 Belvedere, Charger, and Coronet with 426 Hemi; 1967–70 Charger, GTX, and Coronet R/T with 440-ci.
Note(s): Fits either side.

Interchange Number: 3
Part Number(s): 2460823 (aluminized); 2460824 (zinc-coated)
Usage: 1966–69 Barracuda, Dart, and Valiant with 318-ci with single exhaust; 1970–71–74 Dart, Duster, and Valiant with 318-ci with single exhaust, zinc-coated muffler only.

Interchange Number: 4
Part Number(s): 285639 (passenger); 2856398 (driver)
Usage: 1968 Barracuda or Dart with 340-ci or 383-ci and dual exhaust.
Note(s): Mufflers are aluminized.

Interchange Number: 5
Part Number(s): 2856399
Usage: 1968 Barracuda, Dart with 340-ci or 383-ci with dual exhaust.
Note(s): (1) Mufflers are zinc-coated. (2) Fits either side.

Interchange Number: 6
Part Number(s): 2925771 (aluminized); 2883912 (zinc-coated)
Usage: 1969–70 Belvedere, Charger, and Coronet with 383-ci two-barrel with single exhaust; 1968–69 Belvedere, Charger, and Coronet with 383-ci four-barrel with dual exhaust, zinc-coated muffler only; 1970–74 Charger, Coronet, and Satellite with 440-ci, zinc-coated muffler only; 1972–73 Charger, Coronet, and Satellite with 400-ci two-barrel with single exhaust, zinc-coated muffler only; 1972 Charger, Coronet, and Satellite with 340-ci with dual exhaust, zinc-coated muffler only.
Note(s): Fits either side.

Interchange Number: 7
Part Number(s): 2883910 (passenger); 2883911 (driver)
Usage: 1968–70 Belvedere, Charger, and Coronet with 383-ci four-barrel with dual exhaust; 1971–73 Charger, Road Runner with 340-ci or 440-ci without noise reduction. Includes 44-ci triple-two-barrel in 1970–72; 1971 Charger, Coronet, and Satellite with 383-ci four-barrel with dual exhaust.
Note(s): Mufflers are aluminized.

Interchange Number: 8
Part Number(s): 3404266
Usage: 1970–74 Barracuda, Challenger with 318-ci with single exhaust.
Note(s): Original unit came with tailpipe.

Interchange Number: 9

Part Number(s): 3466243 (passenger); 3466242 (driver)
Usage: 1970 Dart, Duster with 340-ci with dual exhaust.
Note(s): Mufflers are aluminized.

Interchange Number: 10
Part Number(s): 3466244
Usage: 1970 Dart, Duster with 340-ci with dual exhaust.
Note(s): (1) Mufflers are zinc-coated. (2) Fits either side.

Interchange Number: 11
Part Number(s): 3466960 (passenger); 3466959 (driver)
Usage: 1971 Dart, Duster with 340-ci with dual exhaust.

Interchange Number: 12
Part Number(s): 3466961
Usage: 1971 Dart, Duster with 340-ci with dual exhaust.

Interchange Number: 13
Part Number(s): 3466913
Usage: 1970–71 Challenger T/A; 1970 AAR Cuda.

Interchange Number: 14
Part Number(s): 3404557 (passenger); 3404558 (driver)
Usage: 1970–71 Barracuda, Challenger with 340-ci four-barrel with dual exhaust; 1970 Barracuda, Challenger with 440-ci four-barrel with dual exhaust; 1970 Barracuda, Challenger with 440-ci triple-two-barrel, except in California; 1970–71 Cuda, Challenger R/T with 383-ci four-barrel; 1970–71 Cuda, Challenger R/T with 426, Hemi passenger-side only; 1972 Barracuda, Challenger with 340-ci with dual exhaust, passenger-side only; 1973 Barracuda, Challenger with 340-ci with dual exhaust; 1974 Barracuda, Challenger with 360-ci with dual exhaust, driver's side only.
Note(s): (1) Original units came with tailpipes. (2) Will not fit base Barracuda or Challenger models with a 383-ci four-barrel.

Interchange Number: 15
Part Number(s): 3404288 (passenger); 3404289 (driver)
Usage: 1970–71 Barracuda, Challenger with 383-ci four-barrel.
Note(s): Will not fit Cuda and Challenger R/T models.

Interchange Number: 16
Part Number(s): 3466608
Usage: 1970–71 Cuda, Challenger R/T with 426 Hemi, except California cars.
Note(s): Driver's side only. See Interchange Number 19 for passenger's side.

Interchange Number: 17
Part Number(s): 3466298 (passenger); 3466297 (driver)
Usage: 1970–71 Charger, Coronet, and Satellite with 383-ci four-barrel with dual exhaust with noise reduction.
Note(s): Mufflers are aluminized.

Interchange Number: 18
Part Number(s): 3466299
Usage: 1970–71 Charger, Coronet, and Satellite with 383-ci four-barrel with dual exhaust with noise reduction.
Note(s): (1) Mufflers are zinc-coated. (2) Fits either side.

Interchange Number: 19
Part Number(s): 3409839
Usage: 1970–71 Charger, Coronet, and Satellite with 426 Hemi.

Interchange Number: 20
Part Number(s): 3583904
Usage: 1972 Charger, Coronet, and Satellite with 318-ci.
Note(s): Mufflers are aluminized.

Interchange Number: 21
Part Number(s): 3583836
Usage: 1972–73 Charger, Coronet, and Satellite with 400-ci two-barrel with single exhaust.
Note(s): Muffler are aluminized.

Interchange Number: 22
Part Number(s): 3583714 (passenger); 3583819 (driver)
Usage: 1972–73 Dart, Duster with 340-ci with dual exhaust.
Note(s): Mufflers are aluminized.

Interchange Number: 23
Part Number(s): 3583718
Usage: 1972–73 Dart, Duster with 340-ci with dual exhaust.

Note(s): (1) Mufflers are zinc-coated (2) Fits either side.

Interchange Number: 24
Part Number(s): 3583826 (passenger); 3583827 (driver)
Usage: 1972–73 Charger, Coronet, and Satellite with 400-ci four-barrel with dual exhaust; 1973 Road Runner with 318-ci with dual exhaust; 1973 Charger, Road Runner with 340-ci with dual exhaust.

Interchange Number: 25
Part Number(s): 3583829
Usage: 1972–74 Charger, Coronet, and Satellite with 400-ci four-barrel with dual exhaust; 1973–74 Road Runner with 318-ci with dual exhaust; 1973 Road Runner, Charger with 340-ci with dual exhaust.
Note(s): (1) Mufflers are zinc-coated. (2) Fits either side.

Interchange Number: 26
Part Number(s): 3579548
Usage: 1970–74 Dart, Duster, and Valiant with 318-ci.
Note(s): Aluminized unit.

Interchange Number: 27
Part Number(s): 3583985
Usage: 1973 Charger, Coronet, and Satellite with 318-ci with single exhaust.
Note(s):(1) Mufflers are aluminized. (2) Will not fit Road Runner.

Interchange Number: 28
Part Number(s): 3726737
Usage: 1974 Charger, Coronet, and Satellite, except Road Runner, with 318-ci, with single exhaust.

Interchange Number: 29
Part Number(s): 3726739
Usage: 1974 Charger, Coronet, and Satellite, except Road Runner, with 318-ci, with single exhaust.
Note(s): Mufflers are zinc-coated.

Interchange Number: 30
Part Number(s): 3726924
Usage: 1974 Charger, Coronet, and Satellite with 400-ci two-barrel.
Note(s): Used only until January 7, 1974.

Interchange Number: 31
Part Number(s): 3818228
Usage: Late 1974 Charger, Coronet, and Satellite with 400-ci two-barrel.
Note(s): Used after January 7, 1974.

Interchange Number: 32
Part Number(s): 3726899
Usage: 1974 Charger, Coronet, and Satellite with 400-ci two-barrel, with single exhaust.

Interchange Number: 33
Part Number(s): 3642562 (passenger); 3642561 (driver)
Usage: 1974 Dart, Duster with 360-ci.

Interchange Number: 34
Part Number(s): 3642560
Usage: 1974 Dart, Duster with 340-ci with dual exhaust.
Note(s): Mufflers are zinc-coated.

Interchange Number: 35
Part Number(s): 3726732 (passenger)
Usage: 1974 Barracuda, Challenger with 360-ci with dual exhaust, passenger-side only.
Note(s): For driver's side, see Interchange Number 19.

Interchange Number: 36
Part Number(s): 3726972 (passenger); 3726973 (driver)
Usage: 1974 Road Runner with 318-ci with dual exhaust; 1974 Charger, Coronet, and Satellite with 360-ci four-barrel or 400-ci four-barrel with dual exhaust.

Interchange Number: 37
Part Number(s): 3726898 (passenger); 3726891 (driver)
Usage: 1974 Charger, Coronet, and Satellite with 440-ci four-barrel.

Interchange Number: 38
Part Number(s): 3466610 (passenger); 3466609 (driver)
Usage: 1970–71 Cuda, or Challenger R/T with Hemi or 440-ci triple-two-barrel, sold in California.

Chapter 5

Transmissions and Drive Lines

Transmissions

In order to conserve space and because of their lack of popularity with collectors, the three-speed manual transmissions will not be covered here. Only four-speed and automatic transmissions will be covered. Only one type of four-speed was used, the A833, and three different types of automatic transmissions were used. Small-block 318-ci V-8s used the A904LA type, while big blocks used the A727B type. Small blocks with a heavy-duty transmission, or with high-performance high applications—like the 340-ci—used the heavy-duty small-block transmission known as 727A.

These are only general types, and engine size and output greatly affects the interchange in both automatic and four-speed applications. For example, while a transmission from a production-line big block will fit a Hemi, the components inside the transmission are not as strong as those in a transmission made specifically for a Hemi. Thus, the production line transmission would not last long behind the Hemi and would not be considered interchangeable.

Automatic transmission type can be identified by the family code that appears in raised letters that are 3/8 inch high on the lower-left-hand side of the bell housing. This will only indicate the family group; as reported earlier, there are internal differences. Thus, a transmission serial number can further identify the transmission and should be used for the purposes of identification. This number is located on the oil pan side rail on the driver's side of the transmission. The serial number will begin with two letters that indicate the transmission assembly plant. This is not a big concern of the interchange process. Next will be a seven-digit part number; the interchange is based on this number. After the part number is a four-digit code that represents the build date; following this is a four-digit code that is the daily sequential number. Each day begins with 0001. The last four numbers of this 17-digit serial number are of little importance to interchanging, except in certain-circumstances where the transmission was changed in production. If that is the case, then those changes will be noted in the interchange.

A serial number also appears on the four-speed transmission, but it is not of as great importance in interchanging as that on the automatic transmission. This code is located on the front portion of the case on the passenger's side just below the centerline.

The code will begin with two letters that identify the assembly plant. Either PP (New Process) or PK (Kokomo) will be used. Next is a three-digit number that indicates the type of transmission; all four-speeds will have the code 833. After the transmission type code is the build date, followed by the four-digit daily sequential production number. Interchange in this guide is based on the original part number, which does not appear on the manual transmission. All transmissions that were originally installed at the factory will have the car's VIN, or the last eight digits of the VIN, stamped on the same pad as the serial number. Replacement transmissions will have the serial number, but not the VIN.

Model Identification

IDENTIFICATION PAD

Manual transmission ID pad location.

Interchange

Interchange Number: 1
Part Number(s): 2892032
Type: A727A Automatic
Usage: 1968 Barracuda, Dart with 340-ci.

Interchange Number: 2
Part Number(s): 2892028
Type: A904LA automatic
Usage: 1968 Dart, Valiant, Belvedere, and Coronet with 273-ci until build date February 1, 1968.
Note(s): Up to transmission number PK289202823801000.

Interchange Number: 3
Part Number(s): 2892071
Type: A904LA automatic
Usage: Late 1968 Dart, Valiant, Belvedere, and Coronet with 273-ci.
Note(s): Used after build date February 1, 1968.

Interchange Number: 4
Part Number(s): 2892029
Type: A904-1 automatic
Usage: Early 1968 Barracuda, Dart, Valiant, Belvedere, Coronet, Charger, Fury, Monaco, and Polara with 318-ci.
Note(s): Used until build date February 1, 1968. Up to transmission number PK28920291000.

Interchange Number: 5
Part Number(s): 2892072
Type: A904-1
Usage: Late 1968 Barracuda, Dart, Valiant, Belvedere, Coronet, Charger, Fury, Polara, and Monaco with 318-ci.
Note(s): Used after build date February 1, 1968, but before March 18, 1968. Up to transmission number PK289207224831000.

Interchange Number: 6
Part Number(s): 2892080
Type: A904-1 automatic
Usage: Very late 1968-69 Barracuda, Dart, Valiant, Belvedere, Coronet, Charger, Fury, Polara, and Monaco with 318-ci.
Note(s): Used after build date March 15, 1968.

Interchange Number: 7
Part Number(s): 2892031
Type: A727B
Usage: 1968 Barracuda, Dart, Belvedere, Coronet, Charger, Fury, Monaco, Polara, and Newport with 383-ci four-barrel, except Road Runner, or Super Bee.

Interchange Number: 8
Part Number(s): 2801544
Type: A727B automatic
Usage: 1967–68 Belvedere, Charger, and Coronet with 426 Hemi.

Interchange Number: 9
Part Number(s): 2801539
Type: A727A
Usage: 1967–68 Belvedere, Coronet, Charger, Fury, Polara, and Monaco with 318-ci with heavy-duty transmission, or trailer package.

Interchange Number: 10
Part Number(s): 2801541
Type: A727B automatic
Usage: 1967–early 1968 Belvedere, Charger, and Coronet with 440-ci; 1967–early 1968 Fury, Polara, Monaco, Newport, and New Yorker with 440-ci high-performance; early 1968 Super Bee or Road Runner with 383-ci 335-hp.
Note(s): (1) Used until March 15, 1968. (2) Up to transmission number PK280154124831000. (Police cars in full-size models.)

Interchange Number: 11
Part Number(s): 2801543 ——
Type: A727B automatic
Usage: 1967 Polara, Monaco, Newport, and police car with 383-ci; 1968 Belvedere, Coronet, Charger, Fury, Monaco, Polara, and Newport with 383-ci two-barrel.

Interchange Number: 12
Part Number(s): 2892093
Type: A727B automatic
Usage: Late 1968–69 Belvedere, Charger, and Coronet with 440-ci; late 1968–69 Fury, Monaco, Polara, and New Yorker, 300, with 440-ci high-performance; late 1968 Super Bee, Road Runner with 383-ci 335-hp.
Note(s): Used after build date March 15, 1968. Warning: Do not use a non-high-performance unit, be particularly careful when swapping from full-size models. Look in police cars and high-performance models.

Interchange Number: 13
Part Number(s): 2892042
Type: A833 four-speed
Usage: 1968 Barracuda, Dart, and Valiant, with 273-ci, 318-ci, 340-ci, or 383-ci with four-speed transmission.

Interchange Number: 14
Part Number(s): 2892049, 3410609
Type: A833 four-speed
Usage: 1968–69 Belvedere, Coronet, Charger, Fury, Polara, and Monaco with 383-ci with four-speed transmission.
Note(s): (1) 1969 models used only part number 3410609. (2) 3410609 will replace 2892049 but not vice-versa.

Interchange Number: 15
Part Number(s): 2892047
Type: A833 four-speed
Usage: 1968 Belvedere, Charger, Coronet, Fury, Polara, and Monaco with 440-ci; 1968 Belvedere, Charger, and Coronet with 426 Hemi.

Interchange Number: 16
Part Number(s): 2892089

Type: A727A automatic
Usage: 1969 Barracuda, Dart with 340-ci.
Interchange Number: 17
Part Number(s): 2892091
Type: A727B
Usage: 1969 Barracuda, Dart, Belvedere, Coronet, Charger, Fury, Monaco, Polara, and Newport with 383-ci four-barrel, except Road Runner or Super Bee.
Interchange Number: 18
Part Number(s): 2892087
Type: A727A automatic
Usage: 1969–early 1970 Belvedere, Coronet, Charger, Fury, and Polara with 318-ci with heavy-duty transmission or trailer package; early 1970 Barracuda, Challenger, Dart, and Duster with 340-ci.
Note(s): Used until build date April 27, 1970.
Interchange Number: 19
Part Number(s): 2892090
Type: A727B
Usage: 1969 Belvedere, Coronet, Charger, Newport, Monaco, Polara, and Fury with 383-ci two-barrel.
Interchange Number: 20
Part Number(s): 2892094, 3410671
Type: A727B automatic
Usage: 1969–70 Belvedere, Charger, and Coronet with 426 Hemi.
Note(s): (1) Part number 3410671 used in 1970 models, service part for 1969 models. (2) Part number 2892094 will not fit 1970 models.
Interchange Number: 21
Part Number(s): 3410608
Type: A833 four-speed
Usage: 1969 Barracuda, Dart, and Valiant with 273-ci, 318-ci, 340-ci, or 383-ci with four-speed transmission.
Interchange Number: 22
Part Number(s): 3410610
Type: A833 four-speed
Usage: 1969 Belvedere, Charger, and Coronet with 440-ci or Hemi; 1969 Super Bee, Road Runner with 426 Hemi.
Interchange Number: 23
Part Number(s): 3410681
Type: A833 four-speed
Usage: 1970 Dart, Duster with 318-ci or 340-ci.
Interchange Number: 24
Part Number(s): 3410697
Type: A833 four-speed
Usage: 1970 Barracuda, Challenger with 318-ci or 340-ci four-barrel with four-speed.
Interchange Number: 25
Part Number(s): 3410790
Type: A833 four-speed
Usage: 1970 AAR Cuda, Challenger T/A with 340-ci triple-two-barrel.
Interchange Number: 26
Part Number(s): 3410763
Type: A833 four-speed
Usage: 1971–73 Barracuda, Challenger, Charger, and Road Runner with 340-ci four-barrel; 1973 Road Runner or Charger Rallye with 318-ci.
Interchange Number: 27
Part Number(s): 3410682
Type: A833 four-speed
Usage: 1970 Barracuda, Challenger, Charger, Coronet, and Satellite with 383-ci.
Interchange Number: 28
Part Number(s): 3410760
Type: A833 four-speed
Usage: 1971 Barracuda, Challenger, Charger, Coronet, and Satellite with 383-ci.
Interchange Number: 29
Part Number(s): 3410683

Type: A833 four-speed
Usage: 1970 Barracuda, Challenger, Charger, Coronet, and Satellite with 440-ci or Hemi.
Interchange Number: 30
Part Number(s): 3410761
Type: A833 four-speed
Usage: 1971 Barracuda, Challenger, Charger, Coronet, and Satellite with 440-ci or Hemi.
Interchange Number: 31
Part Number(s): 3410637, 3410779
Type: A904-1 automatic
Usage: 1970 Barracuda, Challenger, Charger, Coronet, Satellite, Dart, Duster, Valiant, Fury, and Polara with 318-ci.
Note(s): Interchange Number 32 will also fit.
Interchange Number: 32
Part Number(s): 3515852
Type: 904-1 automatic
Usage: Late 1970–71 Barracuda, Challenger, Charger, Coronet, Satellite, Fury, Polara, Dart, Duster, and Valiant with 318-ci.
Interchange Number: 33
Part Number(s): 3410767
Type: A727A automatic
Usage: Late 1970 Barracuda, Challenger, Dart, and Duster with 340-ci.
Interchange Number: 34
Part Number(s): 3515842
Type: A727A
Usage: 1971 Barracuda, Challenger, Charger, Dart, Duster, and Road Runner with 340-ci; 1971 Barracuda, Challenger, Charger, Coronet, Satellite, Fury, and Polara with 318-ci with heavy-duty transmission or trailer package.
Interchange Number: 35
Part Number(s): 3410667
Type: A727B automatic
Usage: Early 1970 Barracuda, Challenger, Charger, Coronet, Fury, Monaco, Newport, Polara, and Satellite with 383-ci two-barrel.
Note(s): Used until April 27, 1970.
Interchange Number: 36
Part Number(s): 3515815
Type: A727B automatic
Usage: Late 1970 Barracuda, Challenger, Charger, Coronet, Satellite, Fury, Monaco, Polara, and Newport with 383-ci two-barrel; 1970 Barracuda (except Cuda), Challenger (except R/T), Coronet, (except Super Bee), Charger, Satellite (except Road Runner), Fury, Monaco, Polara, and Newport with 383-ci four-barrel.
Note(s): Used after build date April 27, 1970, with two-barrel powerplant.
Interchange Number: 37
Part Number(s): 3410670
Type: A727B automatic
Usage: 1970 Barracuda, Challenger, Charger, Coronet, and Satellite with 383-ci 335-hp four-barrel or 440-ci, except triple-two-barrel; 1970 Chrysler 300, Fury, Polara, Monaco, and New Yorker, with 440-ci four-barrel high-performance.
Note(s): Warning: Non-high-performance unit will not fit.
Interchange Number: 38
Part Number(s): 3410672
Type: A727B automatic
Usage: 1970 Barracuda, Challenger, Charger, Coronet, and Satellite with 440-ci triple-two-barrel.
Note(s): Warning: Normal 440-ci unit or high-performance unit will not fit.
Interchange Number: 39
Part Number(s): 3515845
Type: A727B automatic
Usage: 1971 Barracuda, Challenger, Charger, Coronet, Satellite, Fury, Polara, Monaco, and Newport with 383-ci two-barrel; early 1972 Charger, Coronet, Satellite, Fury, Polara, Monaco, and Newport with 400-ci two-barrel.

Interchange Number: 40
   Part Number(s): 3515846
   Type: A727B automatic
   Usage: 1971 Barracuda, Challenger, Charger, Coronet, Satellite,
      Fury, Polara, Monaco, and Newport with 383-ci four-barrel;
      early 1972 Charger, Coronet, Satellite, Fury, Polara, and
      Monaco with 400-ci four-barrel.
   Note(s): Interchange Number 41 will fit.

Interchange Number: 41
   Part Number(s): 3515848
   Type: A727B automatic
   Usage: 1971–early 1972 Charger, Road Runner, Coronet police
      car, Fury police car, Polara police car, Monaco police car,
      Satellite police car with 440-ci four-barrel high-performance;
      1971 Super Bee; GTX with 440-ci four-barrel.
   Note(s): Watch when interchanging from full-size models. Non-
      high-performance model will not fit.

Interchange Number: 42
   Part Number(s): 3515850
   Type: A727B automatic
   Usage: 1971 Barracuda, Challenger, Charger, Coronet, and
      Satellite with 440-ci triple-two-barrel; 1972 Charger, Satellite
      with 440-ci triple-two-barrel.

Interchange Number: 43
   Part Number(s): 3515849
   Type: A727B automatic
   Usage: 1971 Barracuda, Challenger, Charger, Coronet, and
      Satellite with 426 Hemi.

Interchange Number: 44
   Part Number(s): 3515873
   Type: A904-1 automatic
   Usage: Early 1972 Barracuda, Challenger, Charger, Coronet,
      Dart, Duster, Fury, Monaco, Polara, and Satellite with 318-ci.
   Note(s): Date varies at each factory.

Interchange Number: 45
   Part Number(s): 3681063
   Type: A904-1 automatic
   Usage: Late 1972–73 Barracuda, Challenger, Charger,
      Coronet, Dart, Duster, Fury, Monaco, Polara, and Satellite
      with 318-ci.
   Note(s): Date varies at each factory.

Interchange Number: 46
   Part Number(s): 3515843
   Type: A727A automatic
   Usage: Early 1972 Barracuda, Challenger, Charger, Dart, Duster,
      and Road Runner with 340-ci.
   Note(s): Date of change not known.

Interchange Number: 47
   Part Number(s): 3681052
   Type: A727A automatic
   Usage: Late 1972–73 Barracuda, Challenger, Charger, Dart,
      Duster, and Road Runner with 340-ci.

Interchange Number: 48
   Part Number(s): 3515844
   Type: A727A automatic
   Usage: Early 1972 Charger, Coronet, Fury, Monaco, Polara, and
      Satellite with 318-ci with heavy-duty transmission or trailer
      package; early 1972 Fury, Monaco, Newport, and Polara
      with 360-ci.
   Note(s): Date of change is not known.

Interchange Number: 49
   Part Number(s): 33681053
   Type: A727A automatic
   Usage: Late 1972–73 Charger, Coronet, Fury, Monaco, Polara,
      and Satellite with 318-ci with heavy-duty transmission or
      trailer package; late 1972–73 Fury, Monaco, Newport, and
      Polara with 360-ci.
   Note(s): Date of change is not known.

Interchange Number: 50
   Part Number(s): 3681054
   Type: A727B automatic
   Usage: Late 1972–73 Charger, Coronet, Satellite, Fury, Polara,
      Monaco, and Newport with 400-ci two-barrel.

Interchange Number: 51
   Part Number(s): 3681055
   Type: A727B automatic
   Usage: Late 1972–73 Charger, Coronet, Satellite, Fury, Polara,
      and Monaco with 400-ci four-barrel.
   Note(s): Date of change is not known.

Interchange Number: 52
   Part Number(s): 3681057
   Type: A727B automatic
   Usage: Late 1972–73 Charger, Coronet, and Satellite, Fury,
      Monaco, and Satellite with 440-ci four-barrel high-
      performance.
   Note(s): Warning: Do not use unit from full-size Chrysler or
      non-emergency full-size model.

Interchange Number: 53
   Part Number(s): 3515857
   Type: A833 four-speed
   Usage: 1972–73 Charger, Satellite with 400-ci four-barrel.
   Note(s): Rare find.

Interchange Number: 54
   Part Number(s): 3515858
   Type: A833 four-speed
   Usage: 1972 Charger, Satellite 440-ci four-barrel.

Interchange Number: 55
   Part Number(s): 3410759
   Type: A833 four-speed
   Usage: 1972–73 Dart, Duster with 340-ci; 1971–72 Dart,
      Duster, and Valiant with 318-ci, export cars only; 1974 Dart,
      Duster with 360-ci four-barrel.

Interchange Number: 56
   Part Number(s): 3681897
   Type: A833 four-speed
   Usage: 1974 Dart, Duster, and Valiant with 318-ci with
      four-speed.
   Note(s): Interchange Number 55 will fit and is stronger.

Interchange Number: 57
   Part Number(s): 3780235
   Type: A833 four-speed
   Usage: 1974 Barracuda, Challenger, Charger, and Satellite with
      360-ci four-barrel; 1974 Charger, and Satellite with 318-ci.

Interchange Number: 58
   Part Number(s): 3780234
   Type: A833 four-speed
   Usage: 1974 Charger, Satellite with 400-ci four-barrel.

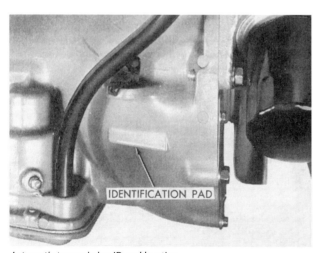

Automatic transmission ID pad location.

Interchange Number: 59
   Part Number(s): 3681843
   Type: A904-1 automatic.
   Usage: Early 1974 Dart, Duster, Valiant, Barracuda, Challenger, Charger, Coronet, and Satellite with 318-ci.
   Note(s): Used up until December 3, 1974.

Interchange Number: 60
   Part Number(s): 3743423
   Type: A904-1 automatic
   Usage: Late 1974 Barracuda, Challenger, Dart, Duster, Charger, Coronet, and Satellite with 318-ci.
   Note(s): Used after December 3, 1973.

Interchange Number: 61
   Part Number(s): 3681863
   Type: A727A automatic
   Usage: 1974 Barracuda, Challenger, Charger, Dart, Duster, and Satellite with 360-ci four-barrel;
   Note(s): Caution: Watch when swapping from Satellite or Coronet line; a non-high-performance unit will not fit. Do not swap from full-size models.

Interchange Number: 62
   Part Number(s): 3681864
   Type: A727B automatic
   Usage: 1974 Charger, Coronet, Satellite, Fury, Monaco, Newport, and New Yorker with 400-ci two-barrel.

Interchange Number: 63
   Part Number(s): 3681865
   Type: A727B automatic
   Usage: 1974 Charger, Coronet police car, Fury police car, Monaco police car, Road Runner, and Satellite police car with 400-ci four-barrel.
   Note(s): Watch when interchanging; use only the models listed.

Interchange Number: 64
   Part Number(s): 3681867
   Type: A727B automatic
   Usage: 1974 Charger, Road Runner, Satellite police car, Coronet police car, Fury police car, and Monaco police car with 440-ci four-barrel high-performance.
   Note(s): Warning: Be particularly careful when interchanging from full-size models. Only police cars used this transmission. Other models will not fit.

Interchange Number: 65
   Part Number(s): 3515851
   Type: A727A automatic
   Usage: 1970–71 Challenger T/A; 1970 Cuda AAR with 340-ci triple-two-barrel.
   Note(s): Warning: Do not use 340 four-barrel unit.

Gear Shift Levers
Model Identification

Barracuda	Interchange Number
1968 four-speed without console, Inland	1
1968 four-speed without console, Hurst	2
1968 four-speed with console, Inland	3
1968 four-speed with console, Hurst	4
1968 automatic, column	20
1968 automatic, console	21
1969 four-speed without console	
before January 17, 1969	2
after January 17, 1969	9
1969 four-speed with console	8
1969 automatic, column	20
1969 automatic, console	22
1970 four-speed	10
1970 automatic, column, chrome	27
1970 automatic, column, flat black	8
1970 automatic, floor	29
1971 four-speed	10
1971 automatic, column	24
1971 automatic, console	26
1972–74 four-speed	13
1972–74 automatic, column	24

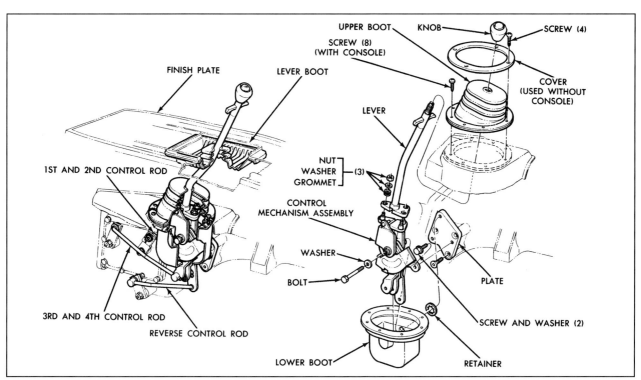

1968 Inland shifter.

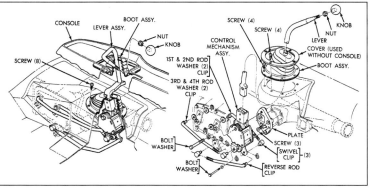

1969 Hurst shifter.

Interchange

Interchange Number: 1
Part Number(s): 2660370
Manufacturer: Inland
Usage: 1966–68 Barracuda, Dart, and Valiant with four-speed without console.

Interchange Number: 2
Part Number(s): 2950054
Manufacturer: Hurst
Usage: 1968–early 1969 Barracuda, Dart, and Valiant with four-speed without console.
Note(s): Used until January 17, 1969.

Interchange Number: 3
Part Number(s): 2800820
Manufacturer: Inland
Usage: 1967–68 Barracuda, Dart with four-speed with console.

Interchange Number: 4
Part Number(s): 2950055
Manufacturer: Hurst
Usage: 1968–69 Barracuda, Dart with four-speed with console.

Interchange Number: 5
Part Number(s): 2800955
Manufacturer: Inland
Usage: 1968 Belvedere, Coronet, and Charger with four-speed without console.

Interchange Number: 6
Part Number(s): 2950056
Manufacturer: Hurst
Usage: 1968–69 Belvedere, Charger, and Coronet with four-speed without console.

Interchange Number: 7
Part Number(s): 2800954
Manufacturer: Inland
Usage: 1968–Belvedere, Charger, and Coronet with four-speed with console.

Interchange Number: 8
Part Number(s): 2950057
Manufacturer: Hurst
Usage: 1968–69 Belvedere, Charger, and Coronet with four-speed with console.

Interchange Number: 9
Part Number(s): 2996313
Manufacturer: Hurst
Usage: Late 1969 Barracuda, Dart, and Valiant with four-speed without console; 1970–71 Dart, Duster, and Valiant with four-speed without console.
Note(s): Used after January 17, 1969, in 1969 models.

Interchange Number: 10
Part Number(s): 2996461
Manufacturer: Hurst (pistol grip)
Usage: 1970–71 Barracuda, Challenger with four-speed with or without console; 1971 Charger, Coronet, and Satellite with four-speed with bucket seats without center armrest.

Interchange Number: 11
Part Number(s): 2996462
Manufacturer: Hurst (pistol grip)
Usage: 1970 Charger, Coronet, and Satellite with four-speed without console.

Interchange Number: 13
Part Number(s): 2996463
Manufacturer: Hurst (pistol grip)
Usage: 1970 Charger, Coronet, and Satellite with four-speed with console.

Interchange Number: 14
Part Number(s): 3467638
Manufacturer: Hurst (pistol grip)
Usage: 1971 Charger, Satellite with four-speed with bucket seats with center cushion.

Interchange Number: 15
Part Number(s): 2996314
Manufacturer: Hurst
Usage: 1970–71 Dart, Duster, and Valiant with four-speed with console.

Interchange Number: 16
Part Number(s): 3467740
Manufacturer: Hurst
Usage: 1972–74 Dart, Duster, and Valiant with four-speed without console.

Interchange Number: 17
Part Number(s): 3467736
Manufacturer: Hurst
Usage: 1972–74 Dart, Duster, and Valiant with four-speed with console.

Interchange Number: 18
Part Number(s): 3467732
Manufacturer: Hurst (pistol grip)
Usage: 1972–74 Charger, Satellite with four-speed without center fold-down armrest.

Interchange Number: 19
Part Number(s): 3467733
Manufacturer: Hurst (pistol grip)
Usage: 1972–74 Charger, Satellite with four-speed with center fold-down armrest.

Interchange Number: 20
Part Number(s): 2883435
Location: Column
Usage: 1968–69 Barracuda, Dart, Valiant, Belvedere, Coronet, and Charger with automatic.

Interchange Number: 21
Part Number(s): 2643914
Location: Floor
Usage: 1966–68 Barracuda, Dart, Valiant, Belvedere, Coronet, Charger, Fury, Polara, and Monaco with automatic with console.

Interchange Number: 22
Part Number(s): 2950207
Location: Floor
Usage: 1969 Barracuda, Dart, Belvedere, Charger, Coronet, Fury, Polara, and Monaco.

Interchange Number: 23
Part Number(s): 3575036
Location: Column
Usage: 1971–72 Coronet, Charger, Chrysler 300, Fury, Polara, Monaco, Dart, Valiant, Newport, New Yorker, and Imperial, all with automatic.
Note(s): Warning: Lever from Barracuda or Challenger will not interchange.

Interchange Number: 24
Part Number(s): 3575038
Location: Column
Usage: 1971–72 Barracuda, Challenger with automatic.

Interchange Number: 25
Part Number(s): 3467641
Location: Floor
Usage: 1970–72 Dart, Duster, and Fury with automatic transmission with console.

Interchange Number: 26
Part Number(s): 3467001

Location: Floor
Usage: 1971–72 Barracuda, Challenger, Charger, and Satellite with automatic transmission with console.

Interchange Number: 27
Part Number(s): 2950971
Location: Column
Usage: 1970 Barracuda, Challenger with automatic transmission.
Note(s): Chrome-plated. Interchange Number 28 will fit.

Interchange Number: 28
Part Number(s): 2950970
Location: Column
Usage: 1970 Barracuda, Challenger with automatic transmission.
Note(s): Flat black.

Interchange Number: 29
Part Number(s): 3467627
Location: Floor
Usage: 1970 Barracuda, Challenger with automatic transmission with console.

Interchange Number: 30
Part Number(s): 3467642
Location: Floor
Usage: 1970 Charger, Coronet, and Satellite with automatic transmission with console.

Interchange Number: 31
Part Number(s): 2950965
Location: Column
Usage: 1970 Charger, Coronet, Satellite, Dart, Duster, and Valiant with automatic transmission.

Knobs, Shift Lever
Model Identification

Barracuda	Interchange Number
1968 four-speed, Inland	7
1968 four-speed, Hurst	5
1968 automatic, column	8
1968 automatic, console	1
1969 four-speed	5
1969 automatic, column	3
1969 automatic, console	2
1970 four-speed	6
1970 automatic, column	3
1970 automatic, console	2
1971 four-speed	6
1971 automatic, column	3
1971 automatic, console	8
1972–74 four-speed	6
1972–74 automatic, column	3
1972–74 automatic, console	7

Belvedere, Charger, Coronet, and Satellite	Interchange Number
1968 four-speed, Inland	7
1968 four-speed, Hurst	5
1968 automatic, column	8
1968 automatic, console	1
1969 four-speed	5
1969 automatic, column	3
1969 automatic, console	2
1970 four-speed	6
1970 automatic, column	3
1970 automatic, console	2
1971 four-speed	6
1971 automatic, column	3
1971 automatic, console	8
1972–74 four-speed	6
1972–74 automatic, column	3
1972–74 automatic, console	7

Challenger	Interchange Number
1970 four-speed	6

Dart, Duster, and Valiant.........................Interchange Number

Interchange

Interchange Number: 1
Part Number(s): 2660357
Usage: 1966–68 Barracuda, Dart, Belvedere, Charger, Coronet, Chrysler 300, Fury, Polara, and Monaco with automatic transmission *with* console; 1969 Fury, Polara, and Monaco with automatic transmission *with* console, *Canadian* cars only.
Note(s): Diecast knob and button.

Interchange Number: 2
Part Number(s): 2950713
Usage: 1969–70 Barracuda, Belvedere, Charger, and Coronet; 1969–71 Chrysler 300 Fury, Polara, Monaco, and Newport, with automatic transmission *with* console; 1972 Fury with automatic transmission *with* console; 1969–73 Dart, Duster with automatic transmission *with* console.
Note(s): Woodgrain knob.

Interchange Number: 3
Part Number(s): 2883402
Usage: 1969–74 Belvedere, Barracuda, Charger, Coronet, Chrysler 300, Fury, Monaco, Newport, New Yorker, Satellite, and Valiant with automatic shift on the column.

Interchange Number: 4
Part Number(s): 3467760
Usage: 1972–74 Barracuda, Challenger, Charger, and Satellite with automatic transmission *with* console.

Interchange Number: 5
Part Number(s): 2950213

Inland shift knob. Year One

Usage: 1968–69 Barracuda, Belvedere, Charger, and Coronet; 1969–74 Dart, Duster, and Valiant with four-speed transmission; 1968 Fury, Polara, and Monaco with Hurst four-speed.
Note(s): Woodgrain shifter. Used with Hurst shifter only in 1968 models.

Interchange Number: 6
Part Number(s): 2996466–right, 2996467–left
Usage: 1970–1974 Barracuda, Challenger, Charger, and Satellite with four-speed.
Note(s): Woodgrain pistol grips.

Interchange Number: 7
Part Number(s): 2643887
Usage: 1966–68 Barracuda, Dart, Valiant, Belvedere, Charger, Coronet, Fury, Polara, and Monaco with four-speed *with* Inland shifter.
Note(s): Black plastic knob. Use with T-bar shifter handle.

Interchange Number: 8
Part Number(s): 3467051
Usage: 1971 Barracuda, Challenger, Charger, and Satellite with automatic in the floor.

Shift Patterns and Dials
Model Identification

Barracuda.....................................Interchange Number

Belvedere, Charger, Coronet, and Satellite......Interchange Number

*Not available on Coronet sedans.

Challenger.....................................Interchange Number

*Not available on Valiant, except Duster.

Interchange
Interchange Number: 1
Part Number(s): 2781381
Usage: 1967–69 Barracuda, Belvedere, Charger, Cornet, Dart, and Valiant, with automatic transmission on the column.
Interchange Number: 2
Part Number(s): 3488555
Usage: 1972–late 1974 Charger, Coronet, Dart, Duster, Satellite, and Valiant, with automatic transmission on the column.
Note(s): Up to January 30, 1974, in 1974 models.
Interchange Number: 3
Part Number(s): 3488556
Usage: 1972–73 Barracuda, Challenger with automatic transmission on the column.

Interchange Number: 4
Part Number(s): 3488158
Usage: 1971–73 Coronet, Charger, and Satellite with automatic transmission on the column with tilt steering.
Interchange Number: 5
Part Number(s): 37646921
Usage: Late 1974 Charger, Coronet, Dart, Duster, Satellite, and Valiant with automatic transmission on the column.
Interchange Number: 6
Part Number(s): 3746922
Usage: Late 1974 Barracuda, Challenger with automatic transmission on the column.
Interchange Number: 7
Part Number(s): 2820756
Usage: 1967–69 Barracuda; 1967–70 Belvedere, Coronet; 1967–71 Fury, Polara, Monaco, Newport, and New Yorker, 300 series with automatic transmission on the floor; 1968–70 Charger with automatic transmission on the floor; 1970–74 Dart, Duster with automatic transmission on the floor; 1972 Fury with automatic transmission on the floor.
Note(s): 1967 Charger unit will *not* interchange.
Interchange Number: 8
Part Number(s): 3488485
Usage: 1972 Barracuda, Challenger, Charger, and Satellite with automatic transmission on the floor.
Interchange Number: 9
Part Number(s): 3488535
Usage: Late 1971–74 Barracuda, Challenger, Charger, and Satellite with automatic transmission on the floor.
Note(s): After December 1970 in 1971 models.
Interchange Number: 10
Part Number(s): 2996464
Usage: 1972–74 Barracuda, Challenger, Charger, and Satellite with four-speed transmission on the floor.
Interchange Number: 11
Part Number(s): 2947903
Usage: 1970–71 Barracuda, Challenger with automatic transmission on the column.

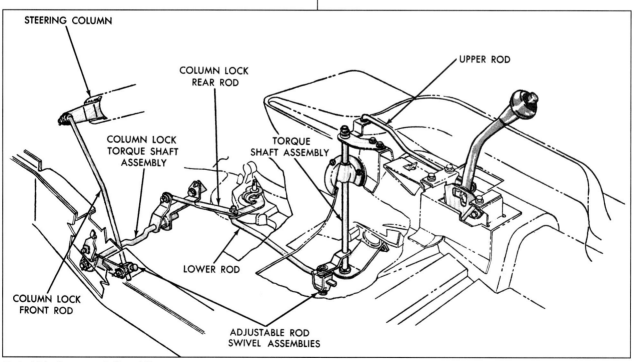

Typical A-body automatic floor shift.

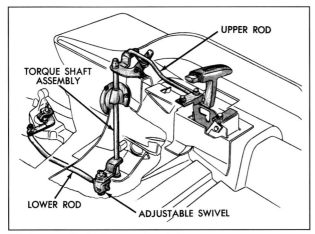

1970–1974 B-body automatic floor shifter.

Interchange Number: 12
Part Number(s): 2947944
Usage: 1970 Barracuda, Challenger with automatic transmission on the floor.

Interchange Number: 13
Part Number(s): 3488485
Usage: Early 1971 Barracuda, Challenger, Charger, and Satellite with automatic transmission on the floor.
Note(s): Used until December 1970.

Interchange Number: 14
Part Number(s): 2947724
Usage: 1970–71 Charger, Coronet, Dart, Duster, Satellite, and Valiant with automatic transmission on the column *without* tilt steering.

Shift Boots
Model Identification

Interchange

Interchange Number: 1
Part Number(s): 2660422
Usage: 1968–69 Barracuda, 1968–74 Dart, Duster with four-speed with console.
Note(s): Fits either Hurst or Inland shifters.

Interchange Number: 2
Part Number(s): 2660390
Usage: 1968 Barracuda, Dart, and Valiant with Inland four-speed without console.

Interchange Number: 3
Part Number(s): 2950201
Usage: 1968–71 Barracuda, Dart, and Valiant with *Hurst* four-speed without console; 1970–71 Challenger with four-speed Hurst shifter without console.

Interchange Number: 4
Part Number(s): 2534510
Usage: 1968 Belvedere, Charger, Coronet, Fury, Polara, and Monaco with Inland four-speed without console.

Interchange Number: 5
Part Number(s): 2950074
Usage: 1968–70 Belvedere, Charger, Coronet, Fury, Monaco, and Polara with *Hurst* four-speed without console.

Interchange Number: 6
Part Number(s): 2660394
Usage: 1968 Belvedere, Charger, Coronet, Fury, Monaco, and Polara with four-speed with console.
Note(s): Fits either Hurst or Inland shifters.

Interchange Number: 7
Part Number(s): 2996454
Usage: 1969 Belvedere, Charger, Coronet with four-speed with console; 1970 Charger, Coronet, and Satellite with three-speed or four-speed with console.

Interchange Number: 8
Part Number(s): 3467764
Usage: 1972–74 Dart, Duster, and Valiant with threespeed or four-speed floor shift without console.

Interchange Number: 9
Part Number(s): 3467766
Usage: 1972–74 Charger, Satellite four-speed without center seat cushion; 1972 Barracuda, Challenger with four-speed, all applications.

Interchange Number: 10
Part Number(s): 3467755
Usage: 1972–74 Charger, Satellite with four-speed with center seat cushion.

Interchange Number: 11
Part Number(s): 2996405
Usage: 1970–71 Barracuda, Challenger with console; 1971 Charger, Satellite with three-speed or four-speed with console.

Interchange Number: 12
Part Number(s): 3467644
Usage: 1971 Charger, Satellite with four-speed without console.

Drive Shafts

Factors that can determine the interchange can include engine size, engine output, transmission type, rear axle type, and model. Though many items in this book will interchange between Plymouths and Dodges, drive shafts for the most part will not, due to a difference in the length of the wheelbase.

Two different types of drive shafts were used: the type 7260 and the type 7290. Each shaft can be identified by the width of the inside yoke. Type 7260 was 2 1/8 inches wide, while the type 7290 was 2 5/8 inches wide. Most high-performance models used the 7290 unit.

Model Identification

Interchange

Interchange Number: 1
    Part Number(s): 2852206
    Type: 7290
    Length: 48.60
    Diameter: 2 3/4
    Usage: 1968–69 Barracuda, Valiant with four-speed
        transmission and 8 3/4-in axle, all engine sizes.

Interchange Number: 2
    Part Number(s): 2852109
    Type: 7260
    Length: 52.27
    Diameter: 3.00
    Usage: 1968 Dart with 318-ci with automatic transmission with
        8 3/4-in axle.

Interchange Number: 3
    Part Number(s): 2852212
    Type: 7290
    Length: 51.53
    Diameter: 3.00
    Usage: 1968–69 Dart with V-8 engine with four-speed
        transmission with 8 3/4-in axle, all engine sizes.

Interchange Number: 4
    Part Number(s): 2852216
    Type: 7290
    Length: 48.60
    Diameter: 2 3/4
    Usage: 1968–69 Barracuda with 383-ci with automatic transmission;
        1969 Barracuda with 340-ci with automatic transmission.

Interchange Number: 5
    Part Number(s): 2852228
    Type: 7290
    Length: 47.81
    Diameter: 3 1/4

Usage: 1968–69 Dart with 340-ci or 383-ci with automatic transmission.

Interchange Number: 6
Part Number(s): 2781952
Type: 7260
Length: 49.27
Diameter: 2 3/4
Usage: 1968–69 Barracuda, Valiant with 318-ci with automatic transmission.

Interchange Number: 7
Part Number(s): 2852268
Type: 7260
Length: 56.47
Diameter: 3.00
Usage: 1968–69 Belvedere 273-ci or 318-ci with automatic transmission with 8 3/4-in axle, all models except police car, taxi, or station wagon.

Interchange Number: 8
Part Number(s): 2852161, 2883560
Type: 7290
Length: 51 1/2
Diameter: 3.00
Usage: 1968–69 Belvedere with 383-ci, all transmissions, or with 426 Hemi or 440-ci powerplants with automatic transmission and 8 3/4-in axle, all models except station wagon.
Note(s): Interchange Number 19 is the same length and type but is 3 1/4 in in diameter; it is rumored to fit. (2) For 383-ci four-barrel only in 1968 models, two-barrel and four-barrel 383-ci in 1969 models.

Interchange Number: 9
Part Number(s): 2852347
Type: 7290
Length: 50.39
Diameter: 3.00
Usage: 1968 Belvedere with 426 Hemi or 440-ci with four-speed transmission and 9 3/4-in axle, except station wagons.

Interchange Number: 10
Part Number(s): 2852286
Type: 7260
Length: 56.17
Diameter: 3.00
Usage: 1968–69 Coronet, Charger with six-cylinder, 273-ci or 318-ci with automatic transmission with 8 3/4-in axle, except station wagons or models with axle ratio above 2.76; 1968–69 Belvedere station wagon with 273-ci or 318-ci with automatic transmission.

Interchange Number: 11
Part Number(s): 2852162
Type: 7290
Length: 52.07
Diameter: 3.00
Usage: 1968–69 Coronet, Charger with 383-ci four-barrel, 426 Hemi, or 440-ci with automatic or four-speed transmission with 8 3/4-in axle, except station wagons; 1968–69 Belvedere station wagon with 383-ci four-barrel with automatic or four-speed transmission.

Interchange Number: 12
Part Number(s): 2852293
Type: 7260
Length: 52.03
Diameter: 3.00
Usage: 1968 Coronet, Charger with 383-ci two-barrel with four-speed with 8 3/4-in axle; 1968–69 Coronet, Charger with 318-ci with three-speed manual transmission .... with 8 3/4-in axle: 1968–69 Belvedere station wagon with 318-ci or 383-ci with manual transmission except station wagons.

Interchange Number: 13
Part Number(s): 2883581
Type: 7290

Drive shaft identification.

Length: 50.96
Diameter: 3.00
Usage: 1968–69 Charger, Coronet with 426 Hemi or 440-ci with automatic transmission or four-speed transmissions with 9 3/4-in axle, except station wagons.

Interchange Number: 14
Part Number(s): 2660683
Type: 7260
Length: 52.03
Diameter: 3 1/4
Usage: 1968 Charger, Coronet with 318-ci with heavy-duty automatic transmission; 1969 Charger, Coronet with 383-ci with four-speed transmission.

Interchange Number: 15
Part Number(s): 2883608
Type: 7290
Length: 49.27
Diameter: 2 3/4
Usage: 1969 Barracuda, Valiant with 318-ci with automatic transmission with 8 3/4-in axle.

Interchange Number: 16
Part Number(s): 2883633
Type: 7290
Length: 52.27
Diameter: 3.00
Usage: 1969 Dart with 318-ci with automatic transmission with 8 3/4-in axle.

Interchange Number: 17
Part Number(s): 2852333
Type: 7260
Length: 55.47
Diameter: 3.00
Usage: 1969 Belvedere with 318-ci or 225-ci six-cylinder with automatic transmission with 8 3/4-in axle, all body styles except station wagon.
Note(s): All ratios except 2.94.

Interchange Number: 18
Part Number(s): 2996560
Type: 7290
Length: 50.39
Diameter: 3 1/4
Usage: 1969 Belvedere with 440 or 426 Hemi with four-speed or automatic transmission with 9 3/4-in axle.

Interchange Number: 19
Part Number(s): 2996161
Type: 7290
Length: 51 1/2
Diameter: 3 1/4
Usage: 1970 Belvedere with 383-ci, 440-ci with four-speed or automatic transmission; 1970 Belvedere with 426 Hemi and automatic transmission without axle package, with 8 3/4-in axle, all body styles except station wagon.

Interchange Number: 20
Part Number(s): 2996182
Type: 7260
Length: 51.44
Diameter: 3 1/4

Usage: 1969 Belvedere with 383-ci two-barrel with automatic transmission; 1969 Belvedere with 318-ci V-8 with heavy-duty automatic transmission, with 8 3/4-in axle.

Interchange Number: 21
Part Number(s): 2852242
Type: 7260
Length: 51.44
Diameter: 3.00
Usage: 1969 Belvedere 318-ci with heavy-duty automatic transmission, with 8 3/4-in axle.
Note(s): Interchange Number 30 is the same length and type but is larger in diameter. It is rumored to fit.

Interchange Number: 22
Part Number(s): 2852343
Type: 7260
Length: 55.47
Diameter: 2 3/4
Usage: 1969 Belvedere with 318-ci with automatic transmission, except heavy-duty transmission or station wagon models, with 8 1/4-in axle. Used with 2.94 rear axle.

Interchange Number: 23
Part Number(s): 2996581
Type: 7290
Length: 50.96
Diameter: 3 1/4
Usage: 1969 Charger, Coronet with 426 Hemi or 440-ci with four-speed or automatic transmission with 9 3/4-in axle.

Interchange Number: 24
Part Number(s): 2996162
Type: 7290
Length: 52.07
Diameter: 3 1/4
Usage: 1969–70 Charger, Coronet with 383-ci four-barrel or 440-ci with four-speed or automatic transmission with 8 3/4-in axle; 1969–70 Charger, Coronet with 426 Hemi with automatic without axle package; 1969–70 Belvedere station wagon with 383-ci four-barrel, 440-ci and automatic transmission with 8 3/4-in axle.

Interchange Number: 25
Part Number(s): 2883563
Type: 7260
Length: 56.83
Diameter: 3.00
Usage: 1969 Charger, Coronet with 318-ci with automatic transmission, except heavy-duty transmission with 8 3/4-in axle.

Interchange Number: 26
Part Number(s): 2660635
Type: 7260
Length: 52.03
Diameter: 2 3/4
Usage: 1968–69 Charger, Coronet with 383-ci two-barrel with automatic transmission with 8 3/4-in axle, except station wagons; 1968–69 Belvedere station wagon with 383-ci and automatic transmission.

Interchange Number: 27
Part Number(s): 2660550
Type: 7260
Length: 56.17
Diameter: 3.00
Usage: 1969 Charger, Coronet with 318-ci V-8 or six-cylinder with automatic transmission with 8 3/4-in axle, except station wagon or models with heavy-duty transmission.

Interchange Number: 28
Part Number(s): 2883739
Type: 7260
Length: 48.89
Diameter: 3.00
Usage: 1970–73 Valiant, Duster with automatic transmission with 8 3/4-in axle; 1971–72 Demon with automatic transmission; 1973 Dart Sport 318-ci with automatic transmission.

Interchange Number: 29
Part Number(s): 2883690
Type: 7260
Length: 44.99
Diameter: 3.00
Usage: 1970–early 1973 Valiant Duster 340 with automatic transmission and 8 3/4-in axle; 1971–72 Demon with 340-ci with automatic transmission; early 1973 Dart Sport 340-ci with automatic transmission
Note(s): Up to October 1972 in 1973 models.

Interchange Number: 30
Part Number(s): 2883760
Type: 7260
Length: 48.96
Diameter: 2 3/4
Usage: 1970–early 1973 Duster 340-ci with four-speed transmission with 8 3/4-in axle; 1970–71–early 1973 Valiant with 318-ci with four-speed export models only; 1971–72 Demon with 340-ci with four-speed transmission; Early 1973 Dart Sport with 340-ci four-speed.
Note(s): Up to October 1972 in 1973 models.

Interchange Number: 31
Part Number(s): 2996203
Type: 7260
Length: 51.89
Diameter: 3.00
Usage: 1970–71 Duster, Valiant with six-cylinder or 318-ci with automatic transmission with 8 3/4-in axle.

Interchange Number: 32
Part Number(s): 2883758
Type: 7260
Length: 51.96
Diameter: 3.00
Usage: 1970–71 Valiant Scamp with 318-ci with four-speed transmission with 8 3/4-in axle; 1970–71 Dart with 318-ci with four-speed transmission, all models except Demon.

Interchange Number: 33
Part Number(s): 2883778
Type: 7260
Length: 52.27
Diameter: 3.00
Usage: 1970–72 Dart except Demon, all engines, all transmissions except four-speed; 1972 Valiant Scamp; used with 8 3/4-in axle.

Interchange Number: 34
Part Number(s): 2883760
Type: 7260
Length: 48.96
Diameter: 2 3/4
Usage: 1970–71 Dart 340 with four-speed transmission and 8 3/4-in axle.

Interchange Number: 35
Part Number(s): 2883693
Type: 7260
Length: 44.99
Diameter: 3.00
Usage: 1970–71 Dart 340 with heavy-duty automatic transmission (727A) and 8 3/4-in axle.

Interchange Number: 36
Part Number(s): 2883768
Type: 7260
Length: 47.95
Diameter: 3 1/4
Usage: 1970–72 Barracuda with 318-ci with automatic transmission.
Note(s): With small sliding spline in 1972 models.

Interchange Number: 37
Part Number(s): 2996138
Type: 7260
Length: 47.89

Diameter: 3 1/4
Usage: 1970–early 1973 Barracuda with six-cylinder or 318-ci
with automatic transmission, including heavy-duty, except
in 1972 models.
Note(s): Up to February 1973 in 1973 models.

Interchange Number: 38
Part Number(s): 2883769
Type: 7290
Length: 43.85
Diameter: 3 1/4
Usage: 1970 Barracuda with 318-ci with manual transmission,
or 340-ci, or with 383-ci two-barrel, all applications.

Interchange Number: 39
Part Number(s): 2883636
Type: 7290
Length: 43.60
Diameter: 3 1/4
Usage: 1970–72 Barracuda with 340-ci or 383-ci four-barrel, all
transmissions; 1970 Barracuda, with 440-ci with automatic
transmission or Hemi with automatic transmission with 8
3/4-in rear axle.

Interchange Number: 40
Part Number(s): 2883779
Type: 7290
Length: 49.95
Diameter: 3 1/4
Usage: 1970–72 Challenger with 318-ci with automatic
transmission, including heavy-duty, with 8 3/4-in axle.

Interchange Number: 41
Part Number(s): 2996146
Type: 7260
Length: 49.89
Diameter: 3 1/4
Usage: 1971–early 1973 Challenger with 318-ci or 225-ci six-
cylinder with automatic transmission and 8 3/4-in axle,
except heavy-duty transmission.
Note(s): Up to February 1973 in 1973 models.

Interchange Number: 42
Part Number(s): 2883782
Type: 7290
Length: 45.85
Diameter: 3 1/4
Usage: 1970 Challenger with 318-ci with four-speed or with
340-ci, all transmissions, or with 383-ci two-barrel, all
transmissions. Used with 8 3/4-in axle.

Interchange Number: 43
Part Number(s): 2996142
Type: 7260
Length: 45.79
Diameter: 3 1/4
Usage: 1970–74 Challenger with 318-ci with manual
transmission; 1971 Challenger with 383-ci or 1970–73
Challenger with 340-ci, all transmissions with 8 3/4-in axle;
1974 Challenger 360-ci, all transmissions.

Interchange Number: 44
Part Number(s): 2883791
Type: 7260
Length: 55.47
Diameter: 3 1/4
Usage: 1970 Belvedere with six-cylinder or 318-ci with
automatic transmission, except heavy-duty, all body styles
except station wagon or police car.

Interchange Number: 45
Part Number(s): 2996109
Type: 7260
Length: 50.80
Diameter: 3 1/4
Usage: 1971–early 1974 Charger, Satellite, except sedans or
wagons, with three-speed manual with 8 1/4-in axle and 225-
ci six-cylinder, or 318-ci with heavy-duty automatic
transmission with 8 3/4-in axle; 1971 Charger or Satellite,
except sedans or wagons, with 383-ci two-barrel with
automatic transmission and 2.45 or 2.95 gears; 1972–early
1974 Charger, Satellite with 400-ci two-barrel with automatic
transmission; early 1974 Charger, Satellite with 360-ci.
Note(s): Used until September 1973 in 1974 models.

Interchange Number: 46
Part Number(s): 2996101
Type: 7290
Length: 50.68
Diameter: 3 1/4
Usage: 1971–74 Charger, Satellite, except sedans or wagons,
with all engines and four-speed transmission, except 440-ci
or 426 Hemi; 1971–74 Charger, Satellite with 340-ci, 383-ci
(1971 only), 440-ci, or 426 Hemi (1971 only) with automatic
transmission with 8 3/4-in axle; 1972–74 Charger, Satellite,
except sedan or wagon, with 400-ci with automatic
transmission; 1974 Charger Road Runner with 360-ci four-
barrel with four-speed or automatic transmission; 1971
Charger, Satellite hardtop with 318-ci and 3.23 rear axle.

Interchange Number: 47
Part Number(s): 2996105
Type: 7290
Length: 49 1/2
Diameter: 3 1/4
Usage: 1971 Charger, Satellite, except sedans or wagons, with
440-ci or 426 Hemi with four-speed or automatic
transmission with 9 3/4-in axle.

Interchange Number: 48
Part Number(s): 2883775
Type: 7290
Length: 42.60
Diameter: 3 1/4
Usage: 1970–71 Barracuda with 440-ci or 426 Hemi with four-
speed or automatic transmission with 9 3/4-in axle.

Interchange Number: 49
Part Number(s): 2883667
Type: 7290
Length: 44.60
Diameter: 3 1/4
Usage: 1970–71 Challenger with 440-ci or 426 Hemi with four-
speed or automatic transmission with 9 3/4-in axle.

Interchange Number: 50
Part Number(s): 2996581
Type: 7290
Length: 50.96
Diameter: 3 1/4
Usage: 1970 Charger, Coronet with 440-ci or 426 Hemi with
four-speed or automatic transmission and 9 3/4-in axle.
Must have axle package with automatic transmission.

Interchange Number: 51
Part Number(s): 2996560
Type: 7 290
Length: 50.39
Diameter: 3 1/4
Usage: 1969–70 Belvedere with 440-ci or 426 Hemi with four-
speed or automatic transmission with 9 3/4-in axle. Must
have axle package with automatic.

Interchange Number: 52
Part Number(s): 2996101
Type: 7290
Length: 50.68
Diameter: 3 1/4
Usage: 1971 Charger, Satellite, except sedans or wagons, with
340-ci or 383-ci, all transmissions; or 318-ci with heavy-duty
automatic transmission and 3.23 gears or with 440-ci or 426
Hemi with automatic transmission with 8 3/4-in axle.

Interchange Number: 53
Part Number(s): 2996201
Type: 7260

Length: 54.92
Diameter: 3 1/4
Usage: 1971–74 Charger, Satellite, except sedans or wagons, with 225-ci six-cylinder or 318-ci with automatic transmission and 8 3/4-in axle, except with heavy-duty automatic transmission.

Interchange Number: 54
Part Number(s): N/A
Type: 7260
Length: 54.86
Diameter: 3 1/4
Usage: 1971 Charger, Satellite, except sedans or wagons, with 318-ci with automatic transmission, except heavy-duty, with 3.21 or 3.55 gears.
Note(s): Discontinued during year, replaced with Interchange Number 63.

Interchange Number: 55
Part Number(s): 2883792
Type: 7260
Length: 56.17
Diameter: 3 1/4
Usage: 1970 Charger, Coronet with 225-ci six-cylinder or 318-ci with automatic transmission, except heavy-duty, all models including station wagon; 1970 Belvedere station wagon with 383-ci two-barrel with automatic or three-speed manual transmission.

Interchange Number: 56
Part Number(s): 2883789
Type: 7260
Length: 52.03
Diameter: 3 1/4
Usage: 1970 Charger, Coronet with 318-ci with heavy-duty automatic transmission or with 383-ci two-barrel and automatic transmission, all body styles including station wagon; 1970 Belvedere station wagon with 318-ci two-barrel with heavy-duty automatic transmission or 383-ci two-barrel with automatic transmission.

Interchange Number: 57
Part Number(s): 2883788
Type: 7260
Length: 51.44
Diameter: 3 1/4
Usage: 1970 Belvedere with 318-ci with heavy-duty automatic transmission or with 383-ci two-barrel with automatic transmission, all body styles except station wagon.

Interchange Number: 58
Part Number(s): 3578798
Type: 7260
Length: 54.13
Diameter: 3 1/4
Usage: 1972 Valiant Scamp, and Dart, except Demon, with six-cylinder or 318-ci with automatic transmission.

Interchange Number: 59
Part Number(s): 2883752
Type: 7260
Length: 49.27
Diameter: 2 3/4
Usage: 1971–72 Demon, Duster, and Valiant with 318-ci or 340-ci, except Scamp automatic or three-speed manual transmissions.

Interchange Number: 60
Part Number(s): 2996134
Type: 7260
Length: 43.79
Diameter: 3 1/4
Usage: 1972–73 Barracuda with 340-ci with four-speed or automatic transmission or with 318-ci with heavy-duty automatic transmission; 1974 Barracuda with 360-ci four-barrel, all transmissions.

Interchange Number: 61
Part Number(s): 2883656

Type: 7290
Length: 45.60
Diameter: 3 1/4
Usage: 1971–72 Challenger with 340-ci with three-speed, four-speed, or automatic; 1970–71 Challenger with 383-ci three-speed, four-speed or automatic; 1970–71 Challenger 440-ci or 426 Hemi with automatic transmission without axle package; 8-in axle.

Interchange Number: 62
Part Number(s): 2996207
Type: 7260
Length: 54.92
Diameter: 3 1/4
Usage: 1972–early 1974 Charger, Satellite, except sedans or wagons, with six-cylinder or 318-ci and automatic transmission, except heavy-duty.
Note(s): (1) Uses 7290 type at rear. (2) Used up to September 1973 in 1974 models.

Interchange Number: 63
Part Number(s): 3578690
Type: 7260
Length: 44.99
Diameter: 3.00
Usage: Late 1973 Dart Sport, Duster with 340-ci with automatic transmission; 1974 Dart Sport, Duster with 360-ci with automatic transmission.

Interchange Number: 64
Part Number(s): 2996157
Type: 7260
Length: 48.89
Diameter: 3 1/4
Usage: 1973–early 1974 Dart Sport, Valiant, except Scamp or Brougham models with automatic transmission; early Duster, Dart Sport with 360-ci with three-speed manual.
Note(s): Up to May 1974 in 1974 models.

Interchange Number: 65
Part Number(s): 2996137
Type: 7260
Length: 51.89
Diameter: 3 1/4
Usage: 1973–early 1974 Dart, except Sport; 1973–early 1974 Valiant Scamp or Brougham with automatic or three-speed manual transmission.
Note(s): Used until May 1974 in 1974 models.

Interchange Number: 66
Part Number(s): 3578138
Type: 7260
Length: 47.40
Diameter: 3.00
Usage: Late 1973–74 Barracuda with 318-ci with automatic transmission, except heavy-duty.

Interchange Number: 67
Part Number(s): 3578146
Type: 7260
Length: 49.40
Diameter: 3.00
Usage: Late 1973–74 Challenger with 318-ci and automatic transmission, except heavy-duty.
Note(s): Used after February 1973.

Interchange Number: 68
Part Number(s): 3578760
Type: 7260
Length: 48.96
Diameter: 2 3/4
Usage: 1974 Dart Sport, Duster with 318-ci or 360-ci with four-speed transmission.

Interchange Number: 69
Part Number(s): 3467151
Type: 7260
Length: 49.90

Diameter: 3 1/4
Usage: Late 1974 Dart Sport or Duster, with six-cylinder 318-ci with automatic or three-speed manual transmission; 1974 Dart Sport or Duster with 360-ci and three-speed manual transmission.
Note(s): Used after May 1974.

Interchange Number: 70
Part Number(s): 3578301
Type: 7260
Length: 54.92
Diameter: 3 1/4
Usage: Late 1974 Charger, Satellite, except sedans or wagons, with 318-ci and automatic transmission, except heavy-duty.

Interchange Number: 71
Part Number(s): 3578305
Type: 7260
Length: 50.80
Diameter: 3 1/4
Usage: Late 1974 Charger, Satellite, except sedans or wagons, with three-speed manual with 318-ci and 225-ci six-cylinder and 8 1/4-in axle, or 318-ci with heavy-duty automatic transmission with 8 3/4-in axle; late 1974 Charger, Satellite with 400-ci two-barrel with automatic transmission; late 1974 Charger, Satellite with 360-ci.
Note(s): Used after September 1973 in 1974 models.

Interchange Number: 72
Part Number(s): N/A
Type: 7260
Length: 5.1.44
Diameter: 2.75
Usage: 1968 Belvedere with 383-ci two-barrel with four-speed or automatic transmissions, all body styles except station wagon.

Interchange Number: 73
Part Number(s): 2996130
Type: 7260
Length: 50.80
Diameter: 3.00
Usage: 1971 Charger, Satellite, except sedans or wagons, with 318-ci with 2.94 or 3.55 rear axle or with 383-ci two-barrel with 2.45 or 2.95 rear axle.

Interchange Number: 74
Part Number(s): 2883569
Type: 7260
Length: 56.17
Diameter: 2 3/4
Usage: 1968 Charger, Coronet with 318-ci and automatic transmission with rear axle ratio higher than 2.76, except with heavy-duty transmission, all body styles except station wagon; 1968 Belvedere station wagon with 318-ci, except with heavy-duty transmission.

Interchange Number: 75
Part Number(s): 3467155
Type: 7260
Length: 52.70
Diameter: 3 1/4
Usage: Late 1974–76 Dart, except Sport, with 318-ci or 360-ci with automatic transmission; late 1974 Valiant Scamp or Brougham with six-cylinder or 318-ci, all transmissions except four-speed.

Axle Housing

Three different axle housings are covered here. Each can be identified by sight. The 8 3/4-inch axle can be quickly identified by its lack of a removable cover, and its removable carrier. Called a banjo axle because of its shape, it is the most common axle under the Mopars used in this book. The 8 1/4- and 9 3/4-inch axles both have removable covers. The 8 1/4-inch axle has a round-shaped cover that is held on with 10 bolts. If it is still there, and it rarely is, a small tag with the ratio is attached to one of the bolts.

The 9 3/4-inch axle, commonly called a Dana 60 axle, can be identified by its hexagon-shaped cover that is held on with 10 bolts. The 7-inch axle is not listed, because it was used with low-powered six-cylinder models, which are not covered in this guide.

Model Identification

Interchange

Interchange Number: 1
Part Number(s): 2800227
Axle Type: 8 3/4-in ring gear
Usage: 1966–69 Barracuda, Dart, and Valiant, all body styles with V-8 engine.

Interchange Number: 2
Part Number(s): 2852838
Axle Type: 8 3/4-in ring gear
Usage: 1968–70 Belvedere, Charger, and Coronet, all body styles with V-8, except 273-ci or Hemi with four-speed.

Interchange Number: 3
Part Number(s): 2881003
Axle Type: 9 3/4-in Dana 60 axle
Usage: 1968–69 Belvedere, Charger, and Coronet with 426 Hemi and four-speed transmission; 1969 Belvedere, Charger, and Coronet with 440-ci with Super Track Pack.

Interchange Number: 4
Part Number(s): 2881055
Axle Type: 8 1/4-in ring gear
Usage: 1969–70 Belvedere, Charger, and Coronet with 318-ci and 2.71:1 gears, all body styles.

Interchange Number: 5
Part Number(s): 3432295
Axle Type: 8 3/4-in ring gear.
Usage: 1970–72 Dart, Duster, and Valiant with V-8 engine.
Note(s): Axle assembly is 52 37/64 in wide.

Interchange Number: 6
Part Number(s): 2852882
Axle Type: 8 3/4-in ring gear
Usage: 1970–74 Barracuda, Challenger with V-8 engine, except Hemi or 440-ci with four-speed.

Interchange Number: 7
Part Number(s): 3412212
Axle Type: 9 3/4-in Dana 60 axle

Usage: 1970–71 Barracuda, Challenger with 426 Hemi or 440-ci with axle package.

Interchange Number: 8
Part Number(s): 3507527
Axle Type: 8 1/4-in ring gear
Usage: 1971 Charger, Coronet, and Satellite with 318-ci with 2.45, 2.71, or 3.21 gears only.
Note(s): Small shaft bearings.

Interchange Number: 9
Part Number(s): 3507168
Axle Type: 8 1/4-in ring gear
Usage: 1971–72 Charger, Coronet, and Satellite with 318-ci with 2.45, 2.71, or 3.21 gears only.
Note(s): Large shaft bearings.

Interchange Number: 10
Part Number(s): 3507502
Axle Type: 8 3/4-in rear gear
Usage: 1971–72 Charger, Coronet, and Satellite with V-8 engine, except Hemi with four-speed, all models except station wagon.

Interchange Number: 11
Part Number(s): 3432555
Axle Type: 9 3/4-in Dana 60 axle
Usage: 1970 Belvedere, Charger, and Coronet with 426 Hemi or 440-ci with Super Track Pack.

Interchange Number: 12
Part Number(s): 3507530
Axle Type: 9 3/4-in Dana 60 axle
Usage: 1971–72 Charger, Satellite with 426 Hemi or 440-ci with Super Track Pack.

Interchange Number: 13
Part Number(s): 3507899
Axle Type: 8 3/4-in ring gear
Usage: 1973–76 Dart, Duster, and Valiant, all body styles with a V-8.

Interchange Number: 14
Part Number(s): 3507629
Axle Type: 8 3/4-in ring gear.
Usage: 1973–74 Charger, Coronet, and Satellite, all body styles except station wagon.

Interchange Number: 15
Part Number(s): 3723054
Axle Type: 8 1/4-in ring gear
Usage: 1973–74 Charger, Coronet, and Satellite with 318-ci, all body styles except station wagon.

Interchange Number: 16
Part Number(s): 3723106
Axle Type: 8 1/4-in rear axle
Usage: 1974–76 Dart, Duster, and Valiant with V-8.

Differentials and Carriers

The 8 3/4-inch ring gear axles, commonly called banjo axles, used a removable carrier. These carriers are interchangeable, regardless of the make or model. Those carriers used on a full-size model, for example, will fit a 1969 Barracuda or 1970 Challenger.

However, several different carriers were used. A casting number located 2 inches below the yoke is used for identification of the pinion shaft diameter. The proper pinion should be used that was originally in the car.

Those carriers with a 1 3/8-inch-diameter pinion shaft will have the casting numbers of 1820657 or 2070741. Those with a 1 3/4-inch diameter shaft will have the casting numbers of 1634985 or 2070742. In 1969 the pinion grew to a 1 7/8-inch diameter, and it will have the casting numbers of either 2881488 or 2881489. Note that 1969 full-size models built in the United States used the 1 7/8-inch-diameter pinion only, while those 1969 models built in Canada but sold in the United States used the 1 3/4-inch-diameter pinion only.

Axle Shafts
Model Identification

Interchange
Interchange Number: 1
Part Number(s): 2800182
Axle Type: 8 3/4 in
Length: 27 11/16 in
Usage: 1967–69 Barracuda; 1967–72 Dart, Valiant; 1970–72 Duster; 1971–72 Demon with V-8 engine.
Note(s): Axles have 30 splines.

Interchange Number: 2
Part Number(s): 2852826
Axle Type: 8 3/4 in
Length: 29 7/32 in
Usage: 1968–69 Belvedere, Charger, and Coronet, all body styles and models except Hemi or 440-ci with four-speed or automatic transmission with axle package.

Interchange Number: 3
Part Number(s): 2881010 (right), 2881011 (left)
Axle Type: 9 3/4-in Dana 60
Length: 28 5/16 in (right), 29 11/16 in (left)
Usage: 1968–early 1970 Belvedere, Charger, and Coronet with 426 Hemi or 440-ci with four-speed or with Hemi or 440-ci with automatic transmission and axle package.

Interchange Number: 4
Part Number(s): 2852884
Axle Type: 8 1/4 in
Usage: 1969 Belvedere, Charger, and Coronet with 318-ci.

Interchange Number: 5
Part Number(s): 3432780
Axle Type: 8 3/4 in
Length: 29 31/32 in
Usage: 1970–74 Barracuda, Challenger with V-8 engine, except Hemi or 440-ci with four-speed transmission or with axle package.

Interchange Number: 6
Part Number(s): 3432209 (right), 3432210 (left)
Axle Type: 9 3/4-in Dana 60
Usage: 1970–71 Barracuda, Challenger with 426 Hemi or 440-ci with four-speed transmission or Hemi or 440-ci with automatic transmission and axle package.

Interchange Number: 7
Part Number(s): 3432820
Axle Type: 8 1/4 in
Length: 29 37/64 in
Usage: 1970 Charger, Coronet, and Satellite with 318-ci.

Interchange Number: 8
Part Number(s): 3507475

Axle Type: 8 1/4 in

Length: 31 in

Usage: 1971 Charger, Coronet, and Satellite, all body styles with 318-ci.

Note(s): Early style.

Interchange Number: 9

Part Number(s): 3507160 (right), 3507161 (left)

Axle Type: 9 3/4-in Dana 60

Length: 29 9/32 in (right), 29 21/32 in (left)

Usage: Late 1970 Charger, Coronet, and Satellite with 426 Hemi or 440-ci with four-speed or with automatic transmission with axle package.

Interchange Number: 10

Part Number(s): 3507507 (right), 3507508 (left)

Axle Type: 9 3/4-in Dana 60

Usage: 1971–72 Charger, Satellite with 440-ci with four-speed or with automatic transmission with axle package; 1971 Charger, Satellite with 426 Hemi with four-speed or automatic transmission with axle package.

Note(s): Has 35 splines.

Interchange Number: 11

Part Number(s): 3432774

Axle Type: 8 3/4 in

Length: 29 1/8 in

Usage: 1970 Charger, Coronet, and Satellite with V-8 engine, all models and body styles except with Hemi or 440-ci with four-speed transmission or with axle package.

Interchange Number: 12

Part Number(s): 3432830

Axle Type: 8 3/4 in

Length: 30 5/8 in

Usage: 1971 Charger, Coronet, Chrysler 300, Fury, Newport, New Yorker, and Satellite with V-8 engine, all models and body styles except station wagon or those models with a 426 Hemi or 440-ci and four-speed or automatic transmission and axle package; 1972–74 Charger, Coronet, and Satellite with V-8 engine except 440-ci with four-speed transmission.

Note(s): (1) Those axles from a full-size 1971 Dodge (Monaco/Polara) model will not fit. (2) Axles from 1972–73 full-size models will not fit.

Interchange Number: 13

Part Number(s): 2931864

Axle Type: 8 1/4 in

Length: 30 63/64 in

Usage: 1971–74 Charger, Coronet, and Satellite with 318-ci, all models except station wagon.

Note(s): Late style.

Interchange Number: 14

Part Number(s): 3723100

Axle Type: 8 1/4 in

Usage: 1973–74 Dart, Duster, and Valiant with V-8 engine.

Torque Converters
Model Identification
Interchange Number

Interchange
Interchange Number: 1

Part Number(s): 2801762

Usage: 1968–74 Barracuda, Belvedere, Charger, Coronet, Dart, Monaco, Polara, Valiant, and Satellite with 318-ci; 1970–74 Challenger, Duster with 318-ci, except with heavy-duty transmission.

Interchange Number: 2

Part Number(s): 2843586

Usage: 1968–74 Barracuda, Belvedere, Charger, Coronet, Dart, Monaco, Polara, Satellite, and Valiant with 318-ci and heavy-duty transmission: 1969–71 Fury, Monaco, Newport, and Polara with 383-ci two-barrel; 1969 Belvedere, Charger, Coronet, Monaco, Newport, New Yorker, and Polara with 383-ci two-barrel or 440-ci; 1970–74 Fury, Newport, New Yorker, and Monaco with 440-ci except high-performance; 1972–74 Charger, Coronet, Fury, Monaco, and Newport with 400-ci two-barrel without cast crankshaft; 1972–73 Charger, Coronet, Fury, Monaco, Newport, New Yorker, and Satellite with 440-ci, except triple-two-barrel.

Note(s): (1) Cast crankshaft only in 1970–71 models with 383-ci two-barrel. (2) Don't use unit from full-size model with 440-ci with cast crankshaft in 1973 and 1974. (3) Used in 1974 400-ci engines marked between 4T400103 and 4T400108.

Interchange Number: 3

Part Number(s): 2801764

Usage: 1968–72 Barracuda, Dart with 340-ci; 1970–72 Challenger, Duster with 340-ci; 1968–71 Barracuda, Belvedere, Charger, Coronet, Fury, Monaco, Newport, and Polara with 383-ci four-barrel; 1970–71 Barracuda, Challenger, Charger, Coronet, Fury, Monaco, Polara, Satellite, and Valiant models with 318-ci with 727A transmission, but not heavy-duty; 1973 Charger, Satellite with 440-ci four-barrel; 1974 Road Runner or Charger Rallye with 318-ci and 727A transmission.

Note(s): Unit from full-size 1968 models will not interchange. (2) Forged crankshaft in 1972 340-ci only.

Interchange Number: 4

Part Number(s): 2801766

Usage: 1968–71 Belvedere, Charger, and Coronet with 426 Hemi.

Interchange Number: 5

Part Number(s): 2801359

Usage: 1968 Belvedere, Charger, and Coronet with 383-ci two-barrel; 1968 Fury, Monaco, Newport, and Polara with 383-ci two-barrel or 440-ci, non-high-performance.

Interchange Number: 6

Part Number(s): 3410839

Usage: 1970–71 Barracuda, Challenger, Charger, Coronet, and Satellite with 440-ci high-performance or with triple-two-barrel setup; 1972 Charger, Road Runner with 440-ci triple-two-barrel.

Interchange Number: 7
Part Number(s): 3681641
Usage: 1972 Barracuda, Challenger, Charger, Dart, Duster, Satellite, and Valiant with 340-ci with cast crankshaft only; 1973 Barracuda, Challenger, Charger, Dart, Duster, Satellite, and Valiant with 340-ci.

Interchange Number: 8
Part Number(s): 3515282
Usage: 1972 Charger, Coronet, Fury, Monaco, Newport, and Polara with 400-ci two-barrel with cast-type crankshaft only; 1973 Charger, Coronet, Fury, Monaco, Newport, and Satellite models with 400-ci two-barrel; 1974 Charger, Coronet, Fury, Monaco, Newport, and Satellite with 400-ci (see notes), except high-performance versions.
Note(s): (1) Converter will have two weights welded to it on each side of the drain plug. (2) For 1974 400-ci engine marked up to 4T400103 and after 4T400108.

Interchange Number: 9
Part Number(s): 3681145
Usage: All 1972–74 Charger, Satellite with 400-ci four-barrel.

Interchange Number: 10
Part Number(s): 3515499
Usage: 1974 Charger, Coronet, Fury, Monaco, Newport, and Satellite with a 360-ci two-barrel.

Interchange Number: 11
Part Number(s): 3410918
Usage: 1974 Barracuda, Challenger, Charger, Coronet, Fury, Monaco, Newport, and Satellite with 360-ci four-barrel.

Clutch Pedals
Model Identification
Barracuda...Interchange Number
1968–69..1
1970 5
1971–72..6
1973–74..10

Belvedere, Charger, Coronet,
and Satellite...................................Interchange Number
1968–69..2
1970 7
1971–72..6
1973–74..10

Challenger.....................................Interchange Number
1970 5
1971–72..6
1973–74..10

Dart, Duster, Demon, and Valiant ....Interchange Number
1968–69..1
1970 3
1971, except 340-ci 3
1971 with 340-ci 4
1972, except with 340-ci 8
1972 with 340-ci 4
1973 318-ci, early 8
1973 318-ci, late 9
1973 340-ci...4
1974 318-ci...11
1974 360-ci...12

Interchange
Interchange Number: 1
Part Number(s): 2883457
Usage: 1968–69 Barracuda, Dart, and Valiant with manual transmission and V-8 engine.

Note(s): Pedal is different with six-cylinder; will not interchange.
Interchange Number: 2
Part Number(s): 2823607
Usage: 1968–69 Belvedere, Charger, and Coronet with manual transmission and V-8 engine; 225-ci six-cylinder with heavy-duty three-speed manual.
Note(s): Unit from standard three-speed and six-cylinder will not interchange.

Interchange Number: 3
Part Number(s): 3467082
Usage: 1970 Dart, Duster, and Valiant with manual transmission; 1971 Dart, Duster, and Valiant, except with 340-ci.

Interchange Number: 4
Part Number(s): 3467987
Usage: 1971–73 Duster 340, Dart 340, and Demon 340 with manual transmission.

Interchange Number: 5
Part Number(s): 3467098
Usage: 1970 Barracuda, Challenger with V-8 engine with manual transmission; 1970 Barracuda, Challenger with six-cylinder and four-speed transmission.

Interchange Number: 6
Part Number(s): 3575111
Usage: 1971–72 Barracuda, Challenger with V-8 engine and manual transmission; 1971–72 Charger, Coronet, and Satellite with V-8 engine and manual transmission; 1971–72 Charger, Coronet, and Satellite with six-cylinder with heavy-duty manual transmission.
Note(s): Unit from standard three-speed and six-cylinder will not fit.

Interchange Number: 7
Part Number(s): 3467087
Usage: 1970 Charger, Coronet, and Satellite with V-8 engine and manual transmission.
Note(s): Unit from a car with a six-cylinder will not fit.

Interchange Number: 8
Part Number(s): 3575150
Usage: 1972 Dart, Duster, Demon, and Valiant with all engines except 340-ci; early 1973 Dart, Duster, and Valiant with 318-ci engine; early 1973 Dart, Duster, and Valiant with six-cylinder and 10-in clutch.
Note(s): (1) Used until June 1, 1973, in 1973 models. (2) Unit from a standard six-cylinder in 1973 will not fit.

Interchange Number: 9
Part Number(s): 3575150
Usage: Late 1973 Dart, Duster, and Valiant with 318-ci engine; late 1973 Dart, Duster, and Valiant with six-cylinder and 10-in clutch.
Note(s): (1) Used after June 1, 1973, in 1973 models. (2) Unit from a standard six-cylinder in 1973 will not fit.

Interchange Number: 10
Part Number(s): 3575177
Usage: 1973–74 Barracuda, Challenger, Charger, Coronet, and Satellite with V-8 engine and manual transmission; 1973–74 Charger, Coronet, and Satellite with six-cylinder and 10-in clutch.
Note(s): Unit from standard six-cylinder will not fit.

Interchange Number: 11
Part Number(s): 3748052
Usage: 1974 Dart, Duster, and Valiant with 318-ci engines; 1974 Dart, Duster, and Valiant with six-cylinder and 10-in clutch.
Note(s): (1) Unit from a standard six-cylinder will not fit.

Interchange Number: 12
Part Number(s): 3748056
Usage: 1974 Dart, Duster, and Valiant with 360-ci and manual transmission.

Chapter 6

Suspension and Steering

K-Members

The K-member was used to support the engine and the front suspension. K-members were usually designed for a particular line of car, such as A–body, B–body, etc. Body style has little effect on the interchange, but engine size and model year does.

Model Identification

Barracuda.....................................Interchange Number

1968, except 383-ci	1
1968 383-ci, without power steering	2
1968 383-ci, with power steering	3
1969, except 383-ci or 440-ci	6
1969 383-ci or 440-ci	7
1970, except Hemi or 340-ci triple-two-barrel	11
1970 340-ci triple-two-barrel	12
1970 Hemi	13
1971, except Hemi	15
1971 Hemi	14
1972, all	19
1973, all	15
1974, all	23

Belvedere, Charger, Coronet, and Satellite.........Interchange Number

1968, except Hemi	5
1968 Hemi	4
1969, except Hemi	8
1969 Hemi	9
1970, except Hemi or 440-ci	16
1970 Hemi	17
1970 440-ci	18
1971, except Hemi	15
1971 Hemi	14
1972, all	19
1973 318-ci or 340-ci	21
1973 400-ci or 440-ci	22
1974 318-ci or 360-ci	
before October 15, 1973	21
after October 15, 1973	24
1973 400-ci or 440-ci	
before October 15, 1973	22
after October 15, 1973	25

Challenger......................................Interchange Number

1970, except Hemi or 340-ci triple-two-barrel	11
1970 340-ci triple-two-barrel	12
1970 Hemi	13
1971, except Hemi or 340-ci triple-two-barrel	15
1971 340-ci triple-two-barrel	12
1971 Hemi	14
1972, all	19
1973, all	15
1974, all	23

Dart, Duster, Demon, and Valiant......................................Interchange Number

1970, all	6
1971–72, all	10
1973–74, all	20

Interchange

Interchange Number: 1
Part Number(s): 2883980
Usage: 1968 Barracuda, Dart, and Valiant with V-8 engine, except 383-ci.

Interchange Number: 2
Part Number(s): 2883984
Usage: 1968 Barracuda, Dart with 383-ci without power steering.

Interchange Number: 3
Part Number(s): 2883999
Usage: 1968 Barracuda, Dart with 383-ci with power steering.

Interchange Number: 4
Part Number(s): 2883994
Usage: 1968 Belvedere, Charger, and Coronet with 426 Hemi.
Note(s): Features a skid plate.

Interchange Number: 5
Part Number(s): 2883990
Usage: 1968 Belvedere, Charger, and Coronet with V-8 engine, except Hemi.

Interchange Number: 6
Part Number(s): 2925976
Usage: 1969 Barracuda; 1969–70 Dart, Valiant with V-8 engine, except 383-ci or 440-ci.

Interchange Number: 7
Part Number(s): 2925946
Usage: 1969 Barracuda, Dart with 383-ci or 440-ci engine.
Note(s): Excellent replacement in 1970 Duster for big-block conversion.

Interchange Number: 8
Part Number(s): 2925930
Usage: 1969 Belvedere, Charger, and Coronet with V-8 engine, except Hemi.

Interchange Number: 9
Part Number(s): 2925934
Usage: 1969 Belvedere, Charger, and Coronet with 426 Hemi.
Note(s): Has skid plate.

Interchange Number: 10
Part Number(s): 3583064
Usage: 1971–72 Dart, Duster, and Valiant with V-8 engine.

Interchange Number: 11
Part Number(s): 3466477
Usage: 1970 Barracuda, Challenger with V-8 engine, except Hemi or 340-ci triple-two-barrel.

Interchange Number: 12
Part Number(s): 3583052
Usage: 1970 Cuda AAR; 1970–71 Challenger T/A with 340-ci triple-two-barrel.
Note(s): Mopar salvage dealer says Interchange Number 11 will fit.

Interchange Number: 13
Part Number(s): 2962014
Usage: 1970 Barracuda, Challenger with 426 Hemi.

Interchange Number: 14
Part Number(s): 3583076
Usage: 1971 Barracuda, Challenger, Charger, and Satellite with 426 Hemi.

Interchange Number: 15
> Part Number(s): 3583074
> Usage: 1971 Barracuda, Challenger, Charger, Coronet, and Satellite with V-8 engine, except Hemi; 1973 Barracuda, Challenger with V-8 engine.
> Note(s): 1972 models or 1973 B-body's will *not* interchange.

Interchange Number: 16
> Part Number(s): 2962090
> Usage: 1970 Charger, Coronet, and Satellite with V-8 engine, except Hemi or 440-ci.

Interchange Number: 17
> Part Number(s): 2962094
> Usage: 1970 Charger, Coronet, and Satellite with 426 Hemi.

Interchange Number: 18
> Part Number(s): 3466479
> Usage: 1970 Charger, Coronet, and Satellite with 440-ci.

Interchange Number: 19
> Part Number(s): 3583078
> Usage: 1972 Barracuda, Challenger, Charger, and Coronet with V-8 engine.

Interchange Number: 20
> Part Number(s): 3466471
> Usage: 1973–74 Dart, Duster, and Valiant with V-8 engine.

Interchange Number: 21
> Part Number(s): 3642745
> Usage: 1973–early 1974 Charger, Coronet, and Satellite with 318-ci or 340-ci only.
> Note(s): (1) Big-block K-members will not interchange. (2) Used up to October 15, 1973, in 1974 models.

Interchange Number: 22
> Part Number(s): 3642749
> Usage: 1973–early 1974 Charger, Coronet, and Satellite with 400-ci or 440-ci.
> Note(s): (1) Small-block 318-ci or 340-ci K-members will not interchange. (2) Used until October 15, 1973, in 1974 models.

Interchange Number: 23
> Part Number(s): 3726799
> Usage: 1974 Barracuda, Challenger, all models.

Interchange Number: 24
> Part Number(s): 3817139
> Usage: Late 1974 Charger, Coronet, and Satellite with 318-ci or 360-ci.
> Note(s): (1) Used after October 15, 1973. (2) Big-block (400-ci or 440-ci) K-members will not interchange.

Interchange Number: 25
> Part Number(s): 3817135
> Usage: Late 1974 Charger, Coronet, and Satellite with 400-ci or 440-ci.
> Note(s): (1) Used after October 15, 1973. (2) Small-block (318-ci or 360-ci) K-members will not interchange.

Control Arms, Front
Model Identification

Interchange

Interchange Number: 1
> Part Number(s): 2071456 (right), 2071457 (left)
> Position: Upper
> Usage: 1968–69 Barracuda; 1968–72 Dart, Valiant; 1970–72 Duster; 1971–72 Demon, all makes, models, and options.

Interchange Number: 2
> Part Number(s): 1857856 (right), 1857857 (left)
> Position: Upper
> Usage: 1966–72 Belvedere, Charger, Coronet, and Satellite; 1970–74 Barracuda, Challenger, all makes, models, and options.

Interchange Number: 3
> Part Number(s): 3402702 (right), 3402703 (left)
> Position: Upper
> Usage: 1973 Dart, Duster, and Valiant, all models and options; 1974 Dart, Duster, and Valiant with disc brakes only.

Interchange Number: 4
> Part Number(s): 3722420 (right), 3722421 (left), without rear isolators; 3722690 (right), 3722691 (left), with rear isolators
> Position: Upper
> Usage: 1973–74 Charger, Coronet, and Satellite, all models and options.
> Note(s): Came with both styles of arms. Models with isolators are not interchangeable with those models without isolators.

Interchange Number: 5
> Part Number(s): 3722460 (right), 3722461 (left)
> Position: Upper
> Usage: 1974 Dart, Duster, and Valiant with drum brakes only.

Interchange Number: 6
> Part Number(s): 2535364 (right), 2535365 (left)
> Position: Lower
> Usage: 1967–69 Barracuda; 1967–72, Dart, Valiant, all models and options.

Interchange Number: 7
> Part Number(s): 2535366 (right), 2535367 (left)
> Position: Lower
> Usage: 1967–69 Belvedere, Charger, and Coronet without sway bar only.
> Note(s): Will *not* fit Charger R/T, Coronet R/T, GTX, Super Bee, or Road Runner models.

Interchange Number: 8
> Part Number(s): 2535368 (right), 2535369 (left)
> Position: Lower
> Usage: 1967–69 Belvedere, Charger, and Coronet with sway bar.
> Note(s): Standard part on Charger R/T, Coronet R/T, GTX, Super Bee, and Road Runner models.

Interchange Number: 9
> Part Number(s): 2535878 (right), 2535879
> Position: Lower
> Usage: 1970–72 Barracuda, Challenger, Charger, Coronet, and

Satellite without sway bar.

Note(s): Will *not* fit Challenger R/T, Charger R/T, Coronet, Cuda, Super Bee, GTX, Charger Rallye, Challenger Rallye, or Road Runner.

Interchange Number: 10
Part Number(s): 2535974 (right), 2535975 (left)
Position: Lower
Usage: 1970–72 Barracuda, Challenger, Charger, Coronet, and Satellite with sway bar.
Note(s): Standard part on Cuda, Challenger R/T, Charger R/T, GTX, Super Bee, Road Runner, Charger Rallye, Challenger Rallye models.

Interchange Number: 11
Part Number(s): 2948572 (right), 2948573 (left)
Position: Lower
Usage: 1973–74 Dart, Duster, and Valiant, all models and options.

Interchange Number: 12
Part Number(s): 3402934 (right), 3402935 (left)
Position: Lower
Usage: 1973–74 Barracuda, Challenger, all models and options.

Interchange Number: 13
Part Number(s): 3722474 (right), 3722475 (left)
Position: Lower
Usage: 1973 Charger, Coronet, Satellite, all models, body styles, and options.

Interchange Number: 14
Part Number(s): 3722636 (right), 3722637 (left), with rear isolators; 3815406 (right), 3815407 (left), without rear isolators
Position: Lower
Usage: 1974 Charger, Coronet, and Satellite, all models, body styles, and options.
Note(s): Both types of arms were used; they are not interchangeable with each other.

Torsion Bars

All Dodge and Plymouth models used front torsion bars as a front spring. Torsion bars vary in diameter and stiffness according to model, engine, and options. Torsion bars are stamped with the last three digits of their part numbers on the anchoring end of the bar. Part numbers that end with an even digit (2, 4, 6, 8, 0) are for the passenger's side, and those that end with an odd digit (1, 3, 5, 7, 9) are for the driver's side. Note that larger-diameter torsion bars will interchange, and provide for better handling, provided they are from the same basic model. For example, those from a Charger with a 440-ci will fit a Coronet with a 318-ci V-8. Be warned that the ride will be harsher, though.

Model Identification

Barracuda..Interchange Number
1968–69 318-ci, standard/heavy-duty 2
1968–69 340-ci, standard/heavy-duty 2
1968–69 383-ci, standard/heavy-duty 3
1970 318-ci, standard..4
1970 318-ci, heavy-duty..5
1970 340-ci, standard/heavy-duty...5
1970 383-ci two-barrel, standard..4
1970 383-ci two-barrel, heavy-duty...5
1970 383-ci four-barrel, standard/heavy-duty................................5
1970 426 Hemi or 440-ci, standard/heavy-duty 6
1971 318-ci, standard..7
1971 318-ci, heavy-duty..5
1971 340-ci, standard/heavy-duty...5
1971 383-ci two-barrel, standard..4
1971 383-ci two-barrel, heavy-duty...5
1971 383-ci four-barrel, standard/heavy-duty................................5
1971 426 Hemi or 440-ci, standard...5
1971 426 Hemi or 440-ci, heavy-duty 6
1972–74, all, standard 7
1972–74, all, heavy-duty..5

Belvedere, Charger, Coronet,
and Satellite....................................Interchange Number
1968 318-ci or 383-ci,
except Charger, Super Bee, and Road Runner
standard...4
heavy-duty...5
1968 318-ci or 383-ci, Charger, Super Bee, and Road Runner
standard/heavy-duty..5
1968 426 Hemi or 440-ci, standard/heavy-duty 6
1969–70 318-ci or 383-ci,
except Charger, Super Bee, and Road Runner
standard...4
heavy-duty...5
1969–70 318-ci or 383-ci, Super Bee and Road Runner
standard/heavy-duty..5
1969–70 318-ci or 383-ci, Charger
standard/heavy-duty..5
soft-rate suspension (with 318-ci only)...............................4
1969–70 426 Hemi or 440-ci, standard/heavy-duty.....................6
1971 318-ci or 383-ci,
except Charger, Super Bee, and Road Runner
standard...4
heavy-duty...5
1971 318-ci or 383-ci, Super Bee, and Road Runner
standard/heavy-duty..5
1971 318-ci or 383-ci, Charger
standard/heavy-duty..5
soft-rate suspension (with 318-ci only)...............................4
1971 426 Hemi or 440-ci, standard
1971 426 Hemi or 440-ci, heavy-duty 6
1972, all, standard 4
1972, all, heavy-duty..5
1973, all, standard 8
1973, all, heavy-duty
before March 15, 1973 9
after March 15, 1973 10
1974, all, standard 9
1974, all, heavy-duty..9, 10

Dart, Duster, Demon, and Valiant ....Interchange Number
1968–69 318-ci, standard/heavy-duty 2
1968–69 340-ci, standard/heavy-duty 2
1968–69 383-ci, standard/heavy-duty 3
1970–74 318-ci, standard without air conditioning 1
1970–74 318-ci, standard with air conditioning 2
1970–74 318-ci, standard heavy-duty...2
1970–73 340-ci or 1974 360-ci, standard/heavy-duty...................2

Interchange

Interchange Number: 1
Part Number(s): 2535890 (right), 2535891 (left)
Usage: 1968 Barracuda, Dart, and Valiant with six-cylinder or 273-ci V-8; 1970–74 Dart, Duster, and Valiant with 318-ci V-8 without air conditioning.
Note(s): ID numbers are 890 (right) and 891 (left)

Interchange Number: 2
Part Number(s): 2535892 (right), 2535893 (left)
Usage: 1968–69 Barracuda, Dart with 318-ci or 340-ci or with 273-ci with handling package; 1970–74 Dart, Duster, and Valiant with 318-ci with air conditioning; 1970–73 Dart, Duster, Demon with 340-ci; 1968–74 Dart with heavy-duty suspension; 1970–74 Duster with heavy-duty suspension; 1974 Dart, Duster with 360-ci.
Note(s): ID numbers are 892 (right) and 893 (left).

Interchange Number: 3
Part Number(s): 2535894 (right), 2535895 (left)
Usage: 1968–69 Barracuda, Dart with 383-ci.
Note(s): ID numbers are 894 (right) and 895 (left).

Interchange Number: 4
Part Number(s): 1857776 (right), 1857777 (left)
Usage: 1968–71 Belvedere, Coronet, and Satellite, except

station wagon with; 1969–70 Charger with soft-rate suspension; 1970 Barracuda, Challenger with 318-ci; 1970–71 Barracuda, Challenger with 383-ci two-barrel; 1971 Charger with 318-ci, 340-ci, or 383-ci, except Super Bee; 1972 Charger, Coronet, and Satellite, all models with a V-8 engine, except with heavy-duty suspension.

Note(s): (1) ID number 776 (right) and 777 (left). (2) Will not fit Coronet R/T, Charger, GTX, or Road Runner.

Interchange Number: 5

Part Number(s): 1857778 (right), 1857779 (left)

Usage: 1968–69 Charger, except R/T; 1968–69 Super Bee, Road Runner, Coronet police car, Belvedere police car with six-cylinder; 1970–71 Barracuda, Challenger with 340-ci or 383-ci four-barrel; 1971 Barracuda, Challenger with 440-ci, or 426 Hemi; 1970–71 Road Runner, Super Bee with 340-ci or 383-ci; 1971 Charger, Coronet, and Satellite with 440-ci or 426 Hemi; 1970–71 Charger, Coronet, and Satellite with heavy-duty suspension, except with 440-ci or Hemi; 1972 Charger, Coronet, and Satellite with heavy-duty suspension, including 440-ci; 1972–74 Barracuda, Challenger, all models with heavy-duty suspension.

Note(s): ID numbers are 778 (right) and 779 (left).

Interchange Number: 6

Part Number(s): 1857780 (right), and 1857781 (left)

Usage: 1968–70 Belvedere, Charger, and Coronet with 440-ci or 426 Hemi; 1968–69 Belvedere or Coronet police car with V-8; 1968–69 Road Runner Super Bee with 426 Hemi or heavy-duty suspension; 1968–69 Belvedere, Charger, or Coronet with extreme-duty suspension; 1970 Barracuda, Challenger with 440-ci or 426-ci; 1971 Barracuda, Challenger, Charger, and Satellite with 440-ci or 426 Hemi and heavy-duty suspension.

Note(s): ID numbers are 780 (right) and 781 (left).

Interchange Number: 7

Part Number(s): 1857774 (right), 1857775 (left)

Usage: 1971 Barracuda, Challenger with 318-ci; 1968–71 Belvedere, Coronet, Charger, and Satellite with six-cylinder; 1972–74 Barracuda, Challenger, all models except with heavy-duty suspension.

Note(s): ID numbers are 774 (right), 775 (left).

Interchange Number: 8

Part Number(s): 3402658 (right), 3402659 (left)

Usage: 1973 Charger, Coronet, and Satellite, all engines, all models except with heavy-duty suspension.

Note(s): ID numbers are 658 (right) and 659 (left).

Interchange Number: 9

Part Number(s): 3402660 (right), 3420661 (left)

Usage: Early 1973 Charger, Coronet, and Satellite, all models with heavy-duty suspension; 1974 Charger with standard suspension or heavy-duty suspension without rear isolators.

Note(s): (1) Used until May 5, 1973. (2) ID number 660 (right), 661 (left).

Interchange Number: 10

Part Number(s): 3402664 (right), 3402665 (left)

Usage: Late 1973–74 Charger, Coronet, and Satellite, all models with heavy-duty suspension.

Note(s): (1) Used after May 5, 1973. (2) ID numbers 664 (right), 665 (left). (3) 1974 models have rear isolators on the front control arms.

Rear Leaf Springs

All Mopars in this manual used rear leaf springs. Factors that will affect the interchange are model, engine size and output, and in some cases, the body style. Also certain options, such as Rallye suspension and air conditioning can affect some models. Note not all stiffer springs have more leaves than the standard units. In most cases the stiffer springs will interchange onto a car that was originally built with softer rated springs, and provide better handling. When swapping springs, also replace them in pairs.

Model Identification

1971 340-ci or 383-ci, except Road Runner or Super Bee
    standard 4
    heavy-duty 8
    extra heavy-duty 10
1971 340-ci or 383-ci, Road Runner or Super Bee, standard
    without trailer package 30
    with trailer package 8
1971 426 Hemi or 440-ci, standard
    right 7
    left 10
1971 426 Hemi or 440-ci, heavy-duty
    right/left 31
1972 318, 340, or 400-ci,
except Road Runner or Charger Rallye
    standard 29
    heavy-duty 8
1972 318-ci or 340 or 400-ci, Road Runner or Charger Rallye
    standard 30
    heavy-duty 8
1972 440-ci with 8 3/4-in axle 8
1972 440-ci with 9 3/4-in axle 9
1973–74 318, 340, or 400-ci,
except Road Runner with 340 or 400-ci
    standard 34
    heavy-duty, without sway bar 38
    with sway bar 36
1973–74 Road Runner with 340 or 400-ci
    standard 38
1973–74 440-ci, standard 39
1973–74 440-ci, heavy-duty 40

Challenger ....*Interchange Number*
1970 318-ci, hardtop, standard 17
1970 318-ci, hardtop, heavy-duty 21
1970 318-ci, convertible, standard 19
1970 318-ci, convertible, heavy-duty 22
1970 340-ci four-barrel hardtop, standard 21
1970 340-ci four-barrel hardtop, heavy-duty 25
1970 340-ci triple-two-barrel hardtop, all 23
1970 340-c,i convertible, standard...................22
1970 340-ci, convertible, heavy-duty 25
1970 383-ci two-barrel, standard 17
1970 383-ci two-barrel, heavy-duty 21
1970 383-ci four-barrel, standard 21
1970 383-ci four-barrel, heavy-duty 25
1970 426 Hemi or 440-ci, all 25
1971 318-ci, hardtop, standard 18
1971 318-ci, hardtop, heavy-duty 22
1971 318-ci, convertible, standard 20
1971 318-ci, convertible, heavy-duty 24
1971 340-ci, hardtop, standard 22
1971 340-ci, hardtop, heavy-duty 25
1971 340-ci, convertible, standard 24
1971 340-ci, convertible, heavy-duty 25
1971 383-ci two-barrel, hardtop, standard 18
1971 383-ci two-barrel, hardtop, heavy-duty 22
1971 383-ci two-barrel, convertible, standard 20
1971 383-ci two-barrel, convertible, heavy-duty 24
1971 383-ci four-barrel, hardtop, standard 22
1971 383-ci four-barrel, hardtop, heavy-duty 25
1971 383-ci four-barrel, convertible, standard 24
1971 383-ci four-barrel, convertible, heavy-duty 25
1971 426 Hemi or 440-ci, all 25
1972 318- or 340-ci, standard 18
1972 318- or 340-ci, heavy-duty.......................22
1973 318- or 340-ci or 1974 360-ci
    standard 18
    heavy-duty 26

Dart, Duster, Demon, and Valiant ....*Interchange Number*
1968–69 318-ci or 340-ci, standard 3
1968–69 318-ci or 340-ci, heavy-duty 3

1968–69 383-ci (or 440-ci, 1969 only), standard 3
1968–69 383-ci (or 440-ci, 1969 only), heavy-duty 2
1970–72 318-ci, standard 15
1970–72 318-ci, heavy-duty 16
1970–72 340-ci, standard 16
1973–74 318-ci, except Duster or Dart Sport
    standard 33
    heavy-duty 37
1973–74 318-ci, Duster or Dart Sport
    standard 32
    heavy-duty 37
1973 only, 340-ci, standard 26
1974 only, 360-ci, standard 26

Interchange

Interchange Number: 1
Part Number(s): 3004588
Number of Leaves: 6
Usage: 1968–69 Barracuda, with 318-ci, 340-ci with heavy-duty or standard springs; 1968 Barracuda with 383-ci with standard springs.

Interchange Number: 2
Part Number(s): 2808677
Number of Leaves: 6
Usage: 1968–69 Barracuda, Dart with 383-ci and heavy-duty suspension.

Interchange Number: 3
Part Number(s): 3004584
Number of Leaves: 6
Usage: 1968 Dart GT with 318-ci or 340-ci with standard or heavy-duty springs; 1968 Dart GT with 383-ci and standard springs; 1968–69 Valiant or Dart with heavy-duty suspension except Dart GTS with 383-ci; 1969 Dart, Valiant with 318-ci or 340-ci with standard suspension.

Interchange Number: 4
Part Number(s): 3004766
Number of Leaves: 4 1/2
Usage: 1968–70 Belvedere, Coronet, with 318-ci with standard suspension, all two-door models except convertible; 1971–72 Charger, Satellite two-door models only with 318-ci, 340-ci, or 383-ci, except Road Runner or Super Bee with heavy-duty suspension; 1972 Charger or Satellite two-door models only with 340-ci or 400-ci four-barrel with standard suspension.

Interchange Number: 5
Part Number(s): 3004654
Number of Leaves: 4 1/2
Usage: 1968–69 Belvedere, Coronet convertible with 318-ci or 383-ci with standard suspension.

Interchange Number: 6
Part Number(s): 30047655
Number of Leaves: 4 1/2
Usage: 1968 Charger with 318-ci or 383-ci with standard suspension; 1968–69 Belvedere, Coronet taxi.

Interchange Number: 7
Part Number(s): 3004768 right
Number of Leaves: 5 full and 2 half
Usage: 1968 Belvedere, Charger, and Coronet with 426 Hemi or 440-ci with standard suspension; 1970 Charger, Coronet, and Satellite with 426 Hemi or 440-ci and standard suspension; 1971 Charger, Satellite with 426 Hemi or 440-ci.

Interchange Number: 8
Part Number(s): 2585640
Number of Leaves: 4 1/2
Usage: 1968 Belvedere, Coronet two-door or four-door sedan with 318-ci or 383-ci, with heavy-duty suspension; 1968–70 Belvedere convertible with six-cylinder and heavy-duty suspension; 1970 Super Bee, Road Runner coupe or hardtop with 383-ci four-barrel with standard suspension; 1971 Super Bee, Road Runner with 340-ci or 383-ci with standard

suspension and trailer package; 1971 Charger, Coronet, and Satellite with 318-ci, 340-ci, or 383-ci with heavy-duty suspension, all models except station wagon; 1972 Charger, Satellite with 440-ci with 8 3/4-in rear axle or all engines with heavy-duty suspension.

Interchange Number: 9
Part Number(s): 2585641
Number of Leaves: 4
Usage: 1968 Belvedere, Coronet convertible with 318-ci or 383-ci with heavy-duty suspension; 1968–69 Super Bee, Road Runner with 383-ci; 1969–70 Belvedere, Coronet two-door or four-door with 318-ci or 383-ci with heavy-duty suspension, except station wagon; 1970 Super Bee, Road Runner convertible with 383-ci four-barrel and standard suspension; 1970 Coronet, Satellite taxi; 1972 Charger, Satellite with 440-ci four-barrel with 9 3/4-in axle.

Interchange Number: 10
Part Number(s): 3004767
Number of Leaves: 6
Usage: 1968 and 1970 Belvedere, Charger, and Coronet with 426 Hemi or 440-ci with standard or heavy-duty suspension; 1968–71 Belvedere, Charger, and Coronet with 318-ci or 383-ci with extreme-duty suspension; 1968–69 Belvedere, Coronet police car; 1971 Charger, Satellite with 426 Hemi or 440-ci.
Note(s): (1) Used on both sides on models with extreme-duty suspension. On right side on cars with Hemi or 440-ci. (2) Used on 383-ci two-barrel with extreme-duty suspension in 1969 only and for four-barrel 383-ci; see Interchange Numbers 12 and 13.

Interchange Number: 11
Part Number(s): 3004653
Number of Leaves: 4 1/2
Usage: 1969–70 Charger with 318-ci with soft-rate suspension.

Interchange Number: 12
Part Number(s): 2808366
Number of Leaves: 6
Usage: 1969 Belvedere, Charger, and Coronet with 426 Hemi or 440-ci; 1969 Belvedere, Coronet, and Charger with 383-ci four-barrel with extreme-duty suspension.

Interchange Number: 13
Part Number(s): 2808367
Number of Leaves: 5 full and 1 half
Usage: 1969 Belvedere, Charger, and Coronet with 426 Hemi or 440-ci; 1969 Belvedere, Charger, and Coronet with 383-ci four-barrel with extreme-duty suspension.

Interchange Number: 14
Part Number(s): 2585642
Number of Leaves: 4 1/2
Usage: 1969–70 Belvedere, Coronet convertible with 318-ci or 383-ci with heavy-duty suspension.

Interchange Number: 15
Part Number(s): 3420181
Number of Leaves: 5
Usage: 1970–72 Dart two-door hardtop, Valiant two-door hardtop, Duster; 1971–72 Demon with 318-ci or 225-ci six-cylinder with standard suspension.
Note(s): Four-door models will not interchange.

Interchange Number: 16
Part Number(s): 3420183
Number of Leaves: 6
Usage: 1970–72 Duster with 340-ci; 1971–72 Demon with 340-ci; 1970–72 Dart Swinger with 340-ci with standard suspension; 1970 Dart, Duster, and Valiant two-door models with 318-ci, only with heavy-duty suspension; 1971–72 Dart, Duster, Demon, and Valiant two-door or four-door models with 318-ci with heavy-duty suspension.

Interchange Number: 17
Part Number(s): 3420174
Number of Leaves: 4 1/2

Usage: 1970 Barracuda, Challenger hardtop with 318-ci or 383-ci, except Cuda or R/T models, with standard suspension; 1970 Barracuda, Challenger convertible with six-cylinder and standard suspension.

Interchange Number: 18
Part Number(s): 3579297
Number of Leaves: 4 1/2
Usage: 1971 Barracuda, Challenger hardtop with 318-ci or 383-ci two-barrel with standard suspension; 1971–72 Barracuda, Challenger convertible with six-cylinder and standard suspension; 1972–74 Barracuda, Challenger with 225-ci six-cylinder or V-8 with standard suspension.

Interchange Number: 19
Part Number(s): 3420175
Number of Leaves: 4 1/2
Usage: 1970 Barracuda, Challenger convertible with 318-ci or 383-ci, except Cuda or Challenger R/T models, with standard suspension.

Interchange Number: 20
Part Number(s): 3579298
Number of Leaves: 4 1/2
Usage: 1971 Barracuda, Challenger convertible with 318-ci or 383-ci two-barrel with standard suspension.

Interchange Number: 21
Part Number(s): 3420179
Number of Leaves: 4 1/2
Usage: 1970 Barracuda, Challenger with 340-ci; 1970 Cuda, Challenger R/T with 340-ci or 383-ci four-barrel with standard suspension; 1970 Barracuda, Challenger convertible with six-cylinder with heavy-duty suspension; 1970 Barracuda, Challenger hardtop with 318-ci or 383-ci two-barrel with heavy-duty suspension.

Interchange Number: 22
Part Number(s): 3420180
Number of Leaves: 4 1/2
Usage: 1971 Barracuda, Challenger hardtop with 340-ci or 383-ci four-barrel with standard suspension; 1970 Barracuda, Challenger convertible with 340-ci; 1970 Cuda, Challenger R/T convertible with 340-ci or 383-ci four-barrel; 1971 Barracuda, Challenger with six-cylinder, 318-ci or 383-ci two-barrel and heavy-duty suspension; 1972 Barracuda, Challenger with heavy-duty suspension.

Interchange Number: 23
Part Number(s): 3579511
Number of Leaves: 4 1/2
Usage: 1970 Cuda AAR with 340-ci triple-two-barrel; 1970–71 Challenger T/A with 340-ci triple-two-barrel.
Note(s): Springs are specially arched for clearance of exhaust.

Interchange Number: 24
Part Number(s): 3514244
Number of Leaves: 4 1/2
Usage: 1971 Barracuda, Challenger convertible with 340-ci or 383-ci four-barrel with standard suspension; 1971 Barracuda, Challenger convertible with 318-ci or 383-ci two-barrel with heavy-duty suspension.

Interchange Number: 25
Part Number(s): 3420176 right, 3420177 left
Number of Leaves: 5 1/2
Usage: 1970 Barracuda, Challenger with 426 Hemi or 440-ci with standard suspension; 1970–71 Barracuda, Challenger with 340-ci; 1970–71 Challenger R/T or Cuda with 340-ci or 383-ci four-barrel with extreme-duty suspension.

Interchange Number: 26
Part Number(s): 3549059
Number of Leaves: 5 1/2
Usage: 1971 Barracuda, Challenger with 426 Hemi or 440-ci with standard suspension; 1973 Dart, Duster with 340-ci; 1973–74 Barracuda, Challenger with 340-ci or 318-ci with heavy-duty suspension; 1974 Barracuda, Challenger with 360-ci.

Interchange Number: 27
Part Number(s): 3579502
Number of Leaves: 4 1/2
Usage: 1970 Charger with 225-ci six-cylinder, 318-ci, or 383-ci with standard suspension.

Interchange Number: 28
Part Number(s): 3004652
Number of Leaves: 4 1/2
Usage: 1970 Coronet, Satellite convertible or four-door sedan with 318-ci or 383-ci.

Interchange Number: 29
Part Number(s): 3004651
Number of Leaves: 4 1/2
Usage: 1971–72 Charger, Satellite two-door models only with 225-ci six-cylinder or 318-ci with standard suspension; 1971 Charger, Satellite with 400-ci two-barrel, *except* Road Runner or Charger with Rallye package.

Interchange Number: 30
Part Number(s): 3004655
Number of Leaves: 4 1/2
Usage: 1971 Super Bee, 1971–72 Road Runner with 340-ci or 383-ci with standard suspension without trailer package; 1970–71 Charger, Coronet, and Satellite with six-cylinder and heavy-duty suspension; 1972 Charger with Rallye Package.

Interchange Number: 31
Part Number(s): 3549073 right, 3549072 left
Number of Leaves: 5 full and 2 half (left), 6 (right)
Usage: 1971 Charger, Coronet, and Satellite with 383-ci four-barrel, 426 Hemi, or 440-ci with extra heavy-duty suspension.

Interchange Number: 32
Part Number(s): 3744421
Number of Leaves: 5
Usage: 1973–74 Dart Sport, Duster with 318-ci and standard suspension.
Note(s): Other two-door models or four-door models will *not* interchange.

Interchange Number: 33
Part Number(s): 3744415
Number of Leaves: 5
Usage: 1973–74 Dart, Valiant two-door hardtop models with 318-ci and standard suspension.
Note(s): Duster, Dart Sport, or four-door models will *not* interchange.

Interchange Number: 34
Part Number(s): 3744405
Number of Leaves: 5
Usage: 1973–74 Charger, Satellite two-door models only with 225-ci six-cylinder, 318-ci, or 400-ci two-barrel with standard suspension.

Interchange Number: 35
Part Number(s): 3744406
Number of Leaves: 4 1/2
Usage: 1973–74 Charger, Satellite two-door models only with 340-ci or 400-ci four-barrel, except Road Runner or Charger with Rallye package.

Interchange Number: 36
Part Number(s): 3744404
Number of Leaves: 6
Usage: 1973–74 Charger, Satellite with heavy-duty suspension and with sway bar, all models except station wagon or those with 440-ci; 1973–74 Road Runner with standard suspension and 340-ci or 400-ci.

Interchange Number: 37
Part Number(s): 3744417
Number of Leaves: 6
Usage: 1973–74 Dart, Duster, and Valiant two-door hardtop or fastback body styles only with 318-ci with heavy-duty suspension.
Note(s): Four-door models will *not* interchange.

Interchange Number: 38
Part Number(s): 3744409
Number of Leaves: 5
Usage: 1973–74 Charger, Coronet, and Satellite with heavy-duty suspension and no sway bar, all body styles and models except station wagon, Road Runner, Charger with Rallye package or models with a 440-ci.

Interchange Number: 39
Part Number(s): 3744410
Number of Leaves: 6
Usage: 1973–74 Charger, Coronet, and Satellite with heavy-duty suspension and 440-ci with *non-high-performance sway bar,* all body styles and models except station wagon, Road Runner, Charger with Rallye package.

Interchange Number: 40
Part Number(s): 3744403
Number of Leaves: 6
Usage: 1973–74 Charger, Satellite, or Coronet with 440-ci with high-performance sway bar, all body styles except station wagon.

Sway Bars, Front and Rear
Models Identification

Interchange

Interchange Number: 1
Part Number(s): 2535533
Usage: 1968 Barracuda, Dart, and Valiant.

Interchange Number: 2
Part Number(s): 2462884
Usage: 1968 Belvedere, Charger, and Coronet.

Interchange Number: 3
Part Number(s): 2535534
Usage: 1969 Barracuda; 1969–72 Dart, Valiant; 1970–72 Duster; 1971–72 Demon.

Interchange Number: 4
Part Number(s): 2462885
Usage: 1969 Belvedere, Charger, and Coronet.

Interchange Number: 5
Part Number(s): 2984723

Usage: 1970–71 Challenger T/A; 1970 Cuda AAR.
Interchange Number: 6
Part Number(s): 2835862
Usage: 1970–74 Barracuda, Challenger; 1970–71 Charger, Satellite, and Coronet.
Interchange Number: 7
Part Number(s): 3402049
Usage: 1970–74 Barracuda, Challenger.
Note(s): Rear bar.
Interchange Number: 8
Part Number(s): 3643801
Usage: 1971–early 1972 Charger Satellite, except with 9 3/4-in axle.
Note(s): Rear bar used until January 1972.
Interchange Number: 9
Part Number(s): 3643980
Usage: Late 1972–74 Charger, Satellite, except with 9 3/4-in axle.
Note(s): (1) Rear bar used after January 1972. (2) Without rear isolators on 1973 models.
Interchange Number: 10
Part Number(s): 3643501
Usage: 1971–72 Charger, Satellite with 9 3/4-in axle.
Note(s): Rear bar.
Interchange Number: 11
Part Number(s): 2948568
Usage: 1973–74 Dart, Duster, and Valiant.
Interchange Number: 12
Part Number(s): 3402891
Usage: 1973–74 Charger, Coronet, and Satellite, except with 400-ci or 440-ci or station wagons.
Interchange Number: 13
Part Number(s): 3722411
Usage: 1973–74 Charger, Coronet, and Satellite with 400-ci or 440-ci; 1973 Coronet, Satellite station wagon, all engines.
Note(s): 1974 police car uses even a larger-diameter bar and will fit.
Interchange Number: 14
Part Number(s): 3722990
Usage: 1973 Charger, Satellite.
Note(s): Rear bar with rear isolators.
Interchange Number: 15
Part Number(s): 3845007
Usage: 1974 Charger, Coronet, and Satellite, all models except police car.
Note(s): Rear bar. Police car has stiffer bar and will fit.

Steering Gearbox
Model Identification

Barracuda ....*Interchange Number*
1968 manual...1
1968 power, early...14
1968 power, late...13
1969 manual, quick ratio 2
1969 manual, except quick ratio................................3
1969 power 13
1970 manual..4
1970 power, except AAR..10
1970 power, AAR..11
1971 manual..4
1971 power...12
1972 manual..5
1972 power...8
1973 manual..6
1973 power 7, 9
1974 manual..6
1974 power 7

Belvedere, Charger, Coronet, and Satellite.....*Interchange Number*
1968 manual..1
1968 power, early...14
1968 power, late...13
1969 manual, quick ratio 2
1969 manual, except quick ratio................................3

1969 power 13
1970 manual..4
1970 power 10
1971 manual..4
1971 power...12
1972 manual..5
1972 power...8
1973 manual..6
1973 power 7, 9
1974 manual..6
1974 power 7

Challenger..*Interchange Number*
1970 manual..4
1970 power, except T/A..10
1970 power, T/A..11
1971 manual..4
1971 power...12
1972 manual..5
1972 power...8
1973 manual..6
1973 power 7, 9
1974 manual..6
1974 power 7

Dart, Duster, Demon, and Valiant ....*Interchange Number*
1968 manual..1
1968 power, early...14
1968 power, late...13
1969 manual, quick ratio 2
1969 manual, except quick ratio................................3
1969 power 13
1970 manual..4
1970 power 10
1971 manual..4
1971 power...12
1972 manual..5
1972 power...8
1973 manual..6
1973 power 7, 9
1974 manual..6
1974 power 7

Interchange
Interchange Number: 1
Part Number(s): 2537346
Type: Manual
Usage: 1967–68 Barracuda, Belvedere, Charger, Coronet, Dart, and Valiant, except with six-cylinder in Barracuda, Dart or Valiant.
Note(s): 16 to 1 ratio.
Interchange Number: 2
Part Number(s): 2537728
Type: Manual
Usage: 1969 Barracuda, Dart, and Valiant with V-8 and quick ratio steering.
Note(s): 16 to 1 ratio.
Interchange Number: 3
Part Number(s): 2537726
Type: Manual
Usage: 1969 Barracuda, Belvedere, Charger, Coronet, Dart, and Valiant, except with six-cylinder in Barracuda, Dart, or Valiant models or quick ratio steering.
Interchange Number: 4
Part Number(s): 2537726
Type: Manual
Usage: 1970–71 Barracuda, Challenger, Charger, Coronet, Dart, Satellite, and Valiant, all models except with power steering, or Dart, Duster, and Valiant models with six-cylinder.
Interchange Number: 5
Part Number(s): 2537347
Type: Manual
Usage: 1972 Barracuda, Challenger, Charger, Coronet, Dart,

Satellite, and Valiant, all models except with power steering or Dart, Duster, and Valiant models with six-cylinder.

Interchange Number: 6
Part Number(s): 2948812
Type: Manual
Usage: 1973–74 Barracuda, Challenger, Charger, Coronet, Dart, Satellite, and Valiant, all models except with power steering, or Dart, Duster, and Valiant models with six-cylinder.

Interchange Number: 7
Part Number(s): 3643013
Type: Power
Usage: 1973–74 Barracuda, Challenger, Charger, Coronet, Dart, Duster, Satellite, and Valiant models with power steering, all models except police cars.
Note(s): 1973 models also used Interchange Number 9. The two are not interchangeable

Interchange Number: 8
Part Number(s): 2948991
Type: Power
Usage: 1972 Barracuda, Challenger, Charger, Coronet, Dart, Duster, and Valiant with power steering , all models.

Interchange Number: 9
Part Number(s): 3579526
Type: Power
Usage: 1973 Barracuda, Challenger, Charger, Coronet, Dart, Duster, Fury, Monaco, Newport, New Yorker, Satellite, and Valiant with power steering. (See Notes for details.)
Note(s): (1) Identify unit by the letter "A" stamped on the date tag in place of the numeral 3. (2) Also Interchange Number 7 was used; the two are not interchangeable.

Interchange Number: 10
Part Number(s): 2537397
Type: Power
Usage: 1970 Barracuda, Challenger, Charger, Coronet, Dart, Satellite, and Valiant, all models except AAR and Challenger T/A models.

Interchange Number: 11
Part Number(s): 2948900
Type: Power
Usage: 1970 Cuda AAR, Challenger T/A with 340-ci triple-two-barrel.

Interchange Number: 12
Part Number(s): 2984991
Type: Power
Usage: 1971 Barracuda, Challenger, Charger, Coronet, Dart, Satellite, and Valiant, all models.

Interchange Number: 13
Part Number(s): 2537397
Type: Power
Usage: Late 1968–69 Barracuda, Belvedere, Charger, Coronet, Dart, and Valiant, all models.
Note(s): Has 2-in outside-diameter cover.

Interchange Number: 14
Part Number(s): 2537354
Type: Power
Usage: Early 1968 Barracuda, Belvedere, Charger, Coronet, Dart, and Valiant, all models.
Note(s): Has 2.1703-in outside-diameter cover.

Pumps, Power Steering

Some production line models used more than one pump design. To help identify the pumps and the different designs, the following descriptions should be used; all interchanges are without pulleys.

.94 displacement pump	Key slotted pump shaft
.96 displacement pump	Plain-end shaft with 4 5/8-in diameter reservoir
1.06 displacement pump	3/8-in threaded hole in end of shaft with 4 7/8-in diameter reservoir

Model Identification

Interchange

Interchange Number: 1
Part Number(s): 2585532
Pump Type: Plain end
Usage: 1966–68 Barracuda, Belvedere, Charger, Coronet, Fury, Monaco, and Polara.

Interchange Number: 2
Part Number(s): 2537664
Pump Type: Key slotted
Usage: 1967–68 Belvedere, Charger, Coronet, Fury, Monaco, and Polara, with V-8 only in full-size models and 1967 mid-sized models.

Interchange Number: 3
Part Number(s): 2891122
Pump Type: Key slotted
Usage: 1969 Barracuda, Dart, and Valiant with V-8 engine, except 383-ci or 440-ci.

Interchange Number: 4
Part Number(s): 3004801
Pump Type: Threaded hole shaft
Usage: 1969 Barracuda, Dart GTS with 383-ci; 1969 Barracuda, Belvedere, Charger, Coronet, Dart, and Valiant with six-cylinder; 1970–72 Barracuda, Challenger, Charger, Coronet,

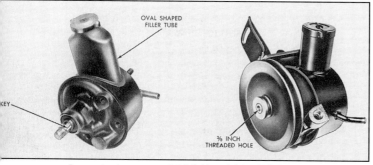

Power steering pumps, 0.94 (left) and 1.06 (right).

Dart, Duster, Demon, Satellite, Valiant with six-cylinder; 1970–72 Dart, Duster, Demon, and Valiant with V-8 engine.

Interchange Number: 5
Part Number(s): 2891123
Pump Type: Key slotted
Usage: 1969 Belvedere, Charger, and Coronet with V-8 engine, except Hemi; 1970–71 Barracuda, Challenger, Charger, Coronet, and Satellite with V-8, except 318-ci or 340-ci; 1972 Barracuda, Challenger, Charger, Coronet, and Satellite with V-8, except 318-ci.

Interchange Number: 6
Part Number(s): 3004800
Pump Type: Threaded hole shaft
Usage: 1969 Belvedere, Charger, and Coronet with V-8 engine, including Hemi; 1969 Fury, Polara with six-cylinder or V-8; 1970–71 Charger, Coronet, Dart, Duster, Satellite, and Valiant with 318-ci or 340-ci V-8; 1970–72 Fury, Polara, and Monaco, with six-cylinder or 318-ci or 360-ci V-8; 1970 Cuda AAR; 1970–71 Challenger T/A with 340-ci triple-two-barrel V-8; 1972 Dart, Duster, Valiant, Charger, Coronet, and Satellite with V-8 engine; 1973–74 Dart, Duster, and Valiant, all models, all engines; 1973 Barracuda, Challenger with V-8 engine.

Interchange Number: 7
Part Number(s): 2891218
Pump Type: Key slotted
Usage: 1970–71 Barracuda, Challenger, Charger, Coronet, and Satellite with 318-ci or 340-ci; 1972 Barracuda, Challenger, Charger, Coronet, and Satellite with 318-ci.

Interchange Number: 8
Part Number(s): 2891463
Pump Type: Threaded hole shaft
Usage: 1973–74 Charger, Coronet, Fury, Polara, Monaco, Newport, and New Yorker with V-8 engine; 1974 Imperial with V-8 engine.

Interchange Number: 9
Part Number(s): 2891435
Pump Type: Key slotted
Usage: 1973 Barracuda, Challenger with V-8 engine; 1973 Dart, Duster, and Valiant with six-cylinder.

Interchange Number: 10
Part Number(s): 2891436
Pump Type: Key slotted
Usage: 1973 Charger, Coronet, and Satellite with V-8 engine or six-cylinder without air conditioning.

Interchange Number: 11
Part Number(s): 2891471
Pump Type: Key slotted
Usage: 1974 Barracuda, Challenger, Dart, Duster, and Valiant, all engines.

Interchange Number: 12
Part Number(s): 2891472
Pump Type: Key slotted
Usage: 1974 Charger, Coronet, Fury, Monaco, Newport, and New Yorker, all models, all engines.

Steering Wheels

Steering wheels were molded in color to match the interior trim. However, interchange here is not based on color. Instead, all wheels are grouped together under the black or basic part number.

All wheels can be painted to match your trim, or you can look for a matching color. Interchange is the bare wheel without the horn cap and/or shroud.

Model Identification

Barracuda	Interchange Number
1968 with horn button	2
1968 with horn ring	1
1968 wood rim	3
1969 without horn ring	2
1969 with horn ring	5
1969 woodgrain	3
1969 padded horn button	4
1970 black wheel	8
1970 tan/black	11
1970 woodgrain	12
1971 tan/black	11
1971 woodgrain	12
1971 coachman grain	13
1972–73, all	15
1974, all	9

Belvedere, Charger, Coronet, and Satellite	Interchange Number
1968 with horn button	2
1968 with horn ring	1
1968 wood rim	3
1969 without horn ring	2
1969 with horn ring	5
1969 woodgrain	3
1970 padded horn button	6
1970 with horn ring	5
1970 rim blow	10
1970 woodgrain	3
1970 soft rim	13
1971 padded horn button	7
1971 three horn buttons	9
1971 woodgrain	3
1971 soft rim	13
1971 tan/black	11
1971 tilt wheel	16
1972–73 padded horn button	7
1972–73 three horn buttons	9
1972–73 soft rim	13
1972–73 tilt wheel	16
1974 three spoke	18
1974 soft rim	20

Dart, Duster, Demon, and Valiant	Interchange Number
1968 with horn button	2
1968 with horn ring	1
1968 wood rim	3
1969 without horn ring	2
1969 with horn ring	5
1969 woodgrain	3
1970 padded horn button	6
1970 with horn ring	5
1970 rim blow	10
1970 woodgrain	3
1970 soft rim	13
1971 padded horn button	7
1971 three horn button	9
1971 woodgrain	3
1971 soft rim	13
1971 tan/black	11
1972–73 padded horn button	7
1972–73 three horn buttons	9
1972–73 soft rim	13
1974 padded horn button	17

Interchange

Interchange Number: 1
Part Number(s): 4007DX9
Wheel Type: Three spoke with horn ring
Usage: 1967–68 Barracuda, Belvedere, Charger, Coronet, Dart, and Valiant; 1967–68 Fury or Polara police cars.

Interchange Number: 2
Part Number(s): 4018DX9
Wheel Type: With horn button
Usage: 1967–69 Barracuda, Belvedere, Charger, Coronet, Dart, and Valiant.

Interchange Number: 3
Part Number(s): 4016DDT

Wheel Type: Simulated wood rim
Usage: 1967–69 Barracuda, Belvedere, Charger, Coronet, Dart, and Valiant; 1970–71 Charger, Coronet, Fury, Polara, Monaco, and Satellite.

Interchange Number: 4
Part Number(s): 4072EX9
Wheel Type: Three spoke with padded horn button
Usage: 1969 Barracuda only.

Interchange Number: 5
Part Number(s): 4008FX9
Wheel Type: Three spoke with horn ring
Usage: 1969 Barracuda; 1969–70 Belvedere, Charger, Coronet, Dart, and Valiant.

Interchange Number: 6
Part Number(s): 4017FX9
Wheel Type: With padded horn button

1967–1968 three-spoke steering wheel.

Simulated woodgrain steering wheel for 1968 and 1969 models.

Three-spoke steering wheel used in a variety of 1969 and 1970 models.

Standard steering wheel for the 1970 E-body.

Simulated woodgrain steering wheel for 1970–1971 E-bodies.

1972–1974 E-body steering wheel.

This steering wheel can be found in most 1969–1973 models, particularly A-bodies.

Padded steering wheel for 1974 models.

Usage: 1970 Charger, Coronet, Dart, Satellite, and Valiant.

Interchange Number: 7
Part Number(s): 4054GX9
Wheel Type: With padded horn button
Usage: 1969–70 Fury, Monaco, Newport, New Yorker, Chrysler 300; 1971–73 Charger, Coronet, Dart, Duster, Satellite, and Valiant.

Interchange Number: 8
Part Number(s): 4087FX9
Wheel Type: With padded horn button
Usage: 1970 Barracuda, Challenger only.

Interchange Number: 9
Part Number(s): 4025GX9
Wheel Type: With three horn buttons
Usage: 1971–73 Charger, Coronet, Dart, Duster, Satellite, and Valiant.
Note(s): Also used in some full-sized models, but be careful when swapping from a full-size car as another similar steering wheel was also used in these models.

Interchange Number: 10
Part Number(s): 4010FX9
Wheel Type: Horn rim switch
Usage: 1970 Charger, Coronet, Dart, and Duster; 1970–73, Fury, Monaco, Newport, New Yorker, Chrysler 300, and Polara.

Interchange Number: 11
Part Number(s): 4020FTX
Wheel Type: Tan/black wheel
Usage: 1970–71 Barracuda, Challenger; 1971 Charger, Dart, Demon, Duster, Satellite, and Valiant.
Note(s): More commonly found on Barracuda and Challengers.

Interchange Number: 12
Part Number(s): 4004FTT
Wheel Type: Simulated woodgrain
Usage: 1970–71 Barracuda, Challenger.

Interchange Number: 13
Part Number(s): 4026GX9
Wheel Type: Coachman grain steering wheel.
Usage: 1971 Barracuda, Challenger models only.

Interchange Number: 14
Part Number(s): 4039FX9
Wheel Type: Soft rim
Usage: 1970–73 Charger, Coronet, Dart, Demon, Duster, Satellite, and Valiant.

Interchange Number: 15
Part Number(s): 4019GX9
Wheel Type: Two spoke
Usage: 1972–73 Barracuda, Challenger only.

Interchange Number: 16
Part Number(s): 4012FX9
Wheel Type: With horn rim and tilt steering
Usage: 1971–72 Charger, Coronet Satellite; 1970–73 Fury, Monaco, Polara, Newport, New Yorker, and Chrysler 300.
Note(s): Must have tilt steering. Look on full-size models where it is more commonly found.

Interchange Number: 17
Part Number(s): P000JX9
Wheel Type: Padded horn button
Usage: 1974 Dart, Duster, and Valiant.

Interchange Number: 18
Part Number(s): P002KX9
Wheel Type: Three spoke
Usage: 1974 Charger, Coronet, Dart, Duster, Fury, Monaco, Satellite, and Valiant.

Interchange Number: 19
Part Number(s): P005JX9
Wheel Type: Two spoke
Usage: 1974 Barracuda, Challenger.

Interchange Number: 20
Part Number(s): P006JX9
Wheel Type: Soft rim
Usage: 1974 Charger, Coronet, Dart, Duster, Satellite, and Valiant.

Steering Columns

Type and location of shift lever will greatly affect the interchange of the steering column. Those with a floor shifter, either automatic or manual, are usually interchangeable, but those with a three-speed manual on the column are not interchangeable with those with an automatic on the column. In 1971–74 the tilt steering wheel will also affect the interchange. Note that the type of steering will also affect the interchange; those columns from a car without power steering will not fit a car with power steering; to conserve space no mention of power steering is given. The interchange model listing is the same, just be sure if your car has power steering (most did) that you interchange from a car that also has power steering or vice versa. Also to conserve space, and due to their lack of popularity, three-speed manuals on the steering columns are not listed.

Model Identification

Interchange
Interchange Number: 1
Type/Location: Automatic column
Usage: 1968 Barracuda, Dart, and Valiant.
Interchange Number: 2
Type/Location: All/floor
Usage: 1968 Barracuda, Dart, and Valiant with floor shift,
    except those models with 383-ci and four-speed
    transmission.
Interchange Number: 3
Type/Location: Four-speed/floor
Usage: 1968 Barracuda, Dart with 383-ci and four-speed
    transmission.
Interchange Number: 4
Type/Location: Automatic/column
Usage: 1968 Belvedere, Charger, and Coronet with automatic
    transmission, except with console.
Interchange Number: 5
Type/Location: All/floor
Usage: 1968 Belvedere, Charger, and Coronet with floor shift.
Interchange Number: 6
Type/Location: Automatic/column

Usage: 1969 Barracuda, Dart, and Valiant, except those with
    383-ci or 440-ci.
Interchange Number: 7
Type/Location: All/floor
Usage: 1969 Barracuda, Dart, and Valiant with floor shift,
    except models with 383-ci or 440-ci.
Interchange Number: 8
Type/Location: All/floor
Usage: 1969 Barracuda, Dart, with 383-ci or 440-ci.
Interchange Number: 9
Type/Location: Automatic/column
Usage: 1969 Belvedere, Charger, and Coronet with automatic
    transmission, except with console.
Interchange Number: 10
Type/Location: All/floor
Usage: 1969 Belvedere, Charger, and Coronet with floor shift,
    all models, all transmissions.
Interchange Number: 11
Type/Location: Automatic/column
Usage: 1970 Dart, Duster, and Valiant, all models except with
    floor shift.
Interchange Number: 12
Type/Location: All/floor
Usage: 1970 Dart, Duster, and Valiant, all models with floor shift.
Interchange Number: 13
Type/Location: Automatic/column
Usage: 1971–73 Dart, Duster, Demon, and Valiant, all models
    except with floor shift.
Interchange Number: 14
Type/Location: All/floor
Usage: 1971–73 Dart, Duster, Demon, and Valiant, all models
    with floor shift.
Interchange Number: 15
Type/Location: Automatic/column
Usage: 1970 Barracuda, Challenger with automatic on the column.
Interchange Number: 16
Type/Location: All/floor
Usage: 1970 Barracuda, Challenger with floor shift, all
    transmissions.
Interchange Number: 17
Type/Location: Automatic/column
Usage: 1971–73 Barracuda, Challenger with automatic on the
    column.
Interchange Number: 18
Type/Location: All/floor
Usage: 1971–73 Barracuda, Challenger with floor shift, all
    transmissions.
Interchange Number: 19
Type/Location: Automatic/Column
Usage: 1970 Charger, Coronet, and Satellite with automatic on
    the column, all body styles.
Interchange Number: 20
Type/Location: All/floor
Usage: 1970 Charger, Coronet, and Satellite, all models, all
    body styles with floor shift.
Note(s): Usually not found in sedans and wagons.
Interchange Number: 21
Type/Location: Automatic/column
Usage: 1971–72 Charger, Coronet, and Satellite with automatic
    on the column without tilt steering.
Interchange Number: 22
Type/Location: All/floor
Usage: 1971–72 Charger, Coronet, all models with floor shift,
    without tilt steering.
Note(s): Usually not found in sedans and wagons.
Interchange Number: 23
Type/Location: Automatic/column/tilt wheel
Usage: 1971–72 Charger, Coronet, and Satellite with automatic
    on column and tilt steering.
Note(s): More commonly found in sedans and wagons.

Interchange Number: 24
    Type/Location: All/floor/tilt wheel
    Usage: 1971–72 Charger, Coronet, and Satellite with tilt
        steering and floor shift.
    Note(s): Rare column.
Interchange Number: 25
    Type/Location: Automatic/column
    Usage: 1973 Charger, Coronet, and Satellite with automatic on
        the column without tilt steering until November 3, 1972.
Interchange Number: 26
    Type/Location: All/floor
    Usage: 1973 Charger, Coronet, and Satellite with floor shift
        without tilt steering until November 3, 1972.
Interchange Number: 27
    Type/Location: Automatic/column
    Usage: 1973 Charger, Coronet, and Satellite with automatic on
        the column with tilt steering until November 3, 1972.
Interchange Number: 28
    Type/Location: All/floor
    Usage: 1973 Charger, Coronet, and Satellite with floor shift
        with tilt steering until November 3, 1972.
Interchange Number: 29
    Type/Location: Automatic/column
    Usage: 1973 Charger, Coronet, and Satellite with automatic on
        the column without tilt steering after November 3, 1972.
Interchange Number: 30
    Type/Location: All/floor
    Usage: 1973 Charger, Coronet, and Satellite with floor shift
        without tilt steering after November 3, 1972.
Interchange Number: 31
    Type/Location: Automatic/column
    Usage: 1973 Charger, Coronet, and Satellite with automatic on
        the column with tilt steering after November 3, 1972.
Interchange Number: 32
    Type/Location: All/floor
    Usage: 1973 Charger, Coronet, and Satellite with floor shift
        with tilt steering after November 3, 1972.
Interchange Number: 33
    Type/Location: Automatic/column
    Usage: 1974 Dart, Duster, and Valiant with automatic on the column.
Interchange Number: 34
    Type/Location: All/floor
    Usage: 1974 Dart, Duster, and Valiant with floor shift.
Interchange Number: 35
    Type/Location: Automatic/column
    Usage: 1974 Charger, Coronet, and Satellite with automatic on
        the column without tilt steering.
Interchange Number: 36
    Type/Location: All/floor
    Usage: 1974 Charger, Coronet, and Satellite with floor shift
        without tilt steering.
Interchange Number: 37
    Type/Location: Automatic/column
    Usage: 1974 Charger, Coronet, and Satellite with automatic on
        the column with tilt steering.
Interchange Number: 38
    Type/Location: All/floor
    Usage: 1974 Charger, Coronet, and Satellite with floor shift
        with tilt steering.
Interchange Number: 39
    Type/Location: Automatic/column
    Usage: 1974 Barracuda, Challenger with automatic on the column.
Interchange Number: 40
    Type/Location: All/floor
    Usage: 1974 Barracuda, Challenger with floor shift.

Steering Knuckle
Model Identification

Interchange
Interchange Number: 1
    Part Number(s): 2071650 (right), 2071651 (left)
    Brake Type: 10-in drum brakes
    Usage: 1965–69 Barracuda, Dart, and Valiant with 10-in
        brake drums.
Interchange Number: 2
    Part Number(s): 1858084
    Brake Type: Drum
    Usage: 1965–69 Belvedere, Charger, and Coronet, all models.
    Note(s): Fits either side.
Interchange Number: 3
    Part Number(s): 2269798 (right), 2269799 (left)
    Brake Type: Disc
    Usage: 1966–69 Barracuda, Dart, and Valiant with disc
        brakes only.
Interchange Number: 4
    Part Number(s): 2535072 (right), 2535073 (left)
    Brake Type: Disc
    Usage: 1966–69 Belvedere, Charger, and Coronet, all models
        with disc brakes.
Interchange Number: 5
    Part Number(s): 2835972 (right), 2835973 (left)
    Brake Type: Drum
    Usage: 1970–72 Dart, Duster, and Valiant with drum brakes,
        except six-cylinder with 9-in brakes.
    Note(s): Look on V-8-equipped cars.
Interchange Number: 6
    Part Number(s): 2535697
    Brake Type: Drum
    Usage: 1970–72 Barracuda, Challenger, Charger, Coronet, and
        Satellite, all models with drum brakes.
    Note(s): Fits either side.
Interchange Number: 7
    Part Number(s): 2269798 (right), 2269799 (left)
    Brake Type: Disc
    Usage: 1970–72 Dart, Duster, Valiant with disc brakes.
Interchange Number: 8
    Part Number(s): 2535694 (right), 2535695 (left)
    Brake Type: Disc
    Usage: 1970–72 Barracuda, Challenger, Charger, Coronet, and
        Satellite.
Interchange Number: 9
    Part Number(s): 3402628 (right), 3402629 (left)
    Brake Type: Disc
    Usage: 1973–74 Barracuda, Challenger, Dart, Duster, and
        Valiant with disc brakes.
    Note(s): Look on V-8-equipped cars.
Interchange Number: 10
    Part Number(s): 3402640 (right), 3402641 (left)
    Brake Type: Disc
    Usage: 1973–74 Charger, Coronet, Satellite, all models, all engines.

Chapter 7

Brake Systems and Parking Brakes

Master Cylinder

Interchange is based on part number. Factors that can affect the interchange are the type of front brakes and, in some cases, model and engine size. For example, those models with a 426 Hemi and disc brakes require a special master cylinder. Those with disc brakes will not interchange to a car with drum brakes.

Model Identification

Interchange

Interchange Number: 1
Part Number(s): 2808599
Type: Drum
Usage: 1967–69 Barracuda, Fury, Monaco, Newport, New Yorker, and Polara; 1967–68 Belvedere, Charger, and Coronet, with drum brakes. Used in both power- and nonpower-assisted applications.

Interchange Number: 2
Part Number(s): 2883058
Type: Disc
Usage: 1968–69 Belvedere, Charger, and Coronet, all engines except 426 Hemi.

Interchange Number: 3
Part Number(s): 2808600
Type: Disc
Usage: 1967–69 Barracuda; 1967–70 Dart, Valiant; 1970 Duster with front disc brakes. Used with power- and nonpower-assisted applications.

Interchange Number: 4
Part Number(s): 2881868
Type: Disc
Usage: 1968 Belvedere, Charger, and Coronet, with 426 Hemi and front disc brakes; 1967 Belvedere, Charger, and Coronet, all models with disc brakes.

Interchange Number: 5
Part Number(s): 2944376
Type: Disc
Usage: 1969 Belvedere, Charger, and Coronet, all models with 426 Hemi and front disc brakes.

Interchange Number: 6
Part Number(s): 2808577
Type: Drum
Usage: 1969–70 Belvedere, Charger, and Coronet, all models except 1969 station wagon with power drum brakes. Used with power and nonpower-assisted applications, except as listed.

Interchange Number: 7
Part Number(s): 3461178
Type: Disc
Usage: 1971–72, Dart, Duster, and Valiant with front disc brakes.

Interchange Number: 8
Part Number(s): 2944476
Type: Disc
Usage: 1970–71 Barracuda, Challenger, Charger, Coronet, and Satellite with 426 Hemi and front disc brakes.

Interchange Number: 9
Part Number(s): 2944453
Type: Disc
Usage: 1970 Barracuda, Challenger with disc brakes, except models with 426 Hemi.

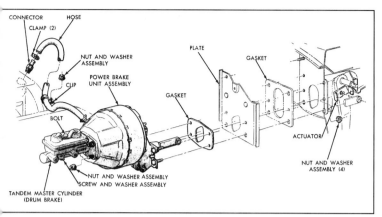

Typical Bendix brake setup.

Interchange Number: 10
Part Number(s): 2944477
Type: Disc
Usage: 1970 Charger, Coronet, and Satellite, all models except those with 426 Hemi.

Interchange Number: 11
Part Number(s): 3461176
Type: Disc
Usage: 1971–74 Barracuda, Challenger, Charger, Coronet, Fury, Monaco, Newport, New Yorker, Chrysler 300, and Imperial with disc brakes, all body styles and models except those with 426 Hemi.

Interchange Number: 12
Part Number(s): 3420961
Type: Drum
Usage: 1970 Dart, Duster, and Valiant, all models with drum brakes. Used in both power and nonpower-assisted applications.

Interchange Number: 13
Part Number(s): 3461184
Type: Drum
Usage: 1971–72 Barracuda, Challenger, Charger, Coronet, Dart, Duster, Satellite, and Valiant with drum brakes. Used in both power- and nonpower-assisted applications.
Note(s): (1) For 10- and 11-in drum brakes only. Unit from car with 9-in drum brakes will *not* interchange. (2) For Nonpower drum brakes on 1972 Charger and Coronet models only.

Interchange Number: 14
Part Number(s): 3461182
Type: Drum
Usage: 1972 Charger, Coronet with power-assisted drum brakes; 1972 Fury, Monaco, Polara with nonpower-assisted drum brakes.

Interchange Number: 15
Part Number(s): 3580146
Type: Disc
Usage: 1973–74 Dart, Duster, and Valiant with *nonpower* disc brakes.

Interchange Number: 16
Part Number(s): 3580112
Type: Disc
Usage: 1973–74 Dart, Duster, and Valiant with *power* disc brakes.

Interchange Number: 17
Part Number(s): 3580184
Type: Disc
Usage: 1973–74 Barracuda, Challenger, Charger, Coronet, and Satellite with *nonpower* disc brakes.

Interchange Number: 18
Part Number(s): 3580209
Type: Drum

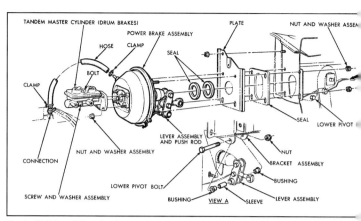

Typical Midland-Ross brake setup.

Usage: 1973–74 Dart, Duster, and Valiant with drum brakes.
Note(s): 10-in drum brakes only. Cars with V-8 engine only.

Chamber, Power Booster

Interchange on booster chambers can become confusing, as two different manufacturers, Bendix and Midland-Ross, were used. The two cannot be interchanged in most cases, and are visually different. Also in some models the same chamber was used with disc and drum brakes, while in other models they are two separate units and are not interchangeable.

Model Identification

Barracuda	Interchange Number
1968 drum brakes	2
1968 disc brakes	2
1969 drum brakes	6
1969 disc brakes	6
1970 drum brakes, except 426 Hemi	18
1970 drum brakes with 426 Hemi	21
1970 disc brakes, except 340-ci triple-two-barrel or 426 Hemi	11
1970 disc brakes with 340-ci triple-two-barrel	12
1970 disc brakes with 426 Hemi	14
1971 drum brakes, except 426 Hemi	
with 10-in drum brakes	19
with 11-in drum brakes	13
with 426 Hemi	21
1971 disc brakes, except 426 Hemi	13
1971 disc brakes with 426 Hemi	15
1972 disc brakes	13
1973 disc brakes	24
1974 disc brakes	13

Belvedere, Charger, Coronet, and Satellite	Interchange Number
1968 drum brakes, except 426 Hemi	3
1968 drum brakes with 426 Hemi	5
1968 disc brakes, except 426 Hemi	1
1968 disc brakes with 426 Hemi	4
1969–70 drum brakes, except 426 Hemi	3
1969–70 drum brakes with 426 Hemi	7
1969–70 disc brakes, except 426 Hemi	1
1969–70 disc brakes with 426 Hemi	8
1971 drum brakes, except 426 Hemi	
with 10-in drum brakes	19
with 11-in drum brakes	13
with 426 Hemi	21
1971 disc brakes, except 426 Hemi	13
1971 disc brakes with 426 Hemi	15
1972 disc brakes	13
1973 disc brakes	24
1974 disc brakes	13

Interchange

Interchange Number: 1
Part Number(s): 2883056
Usage: 1968–70 Belvedere, Charger, and Coronet with power *disc* brakes, except with 426 Hemi.

Interchange Number: 2
Part Number(s): 2881536
Usage: 1967–68 Barracuda, Dart, and Valiant with power brakes.
Note(s): Midland-Ross unit.

Interchange Number: 3
Part Number(s): 3004608
Usage: 1968–70 Belvedere, Charger, and Coronet with power *drum* brakes, except models with 426 Hemi or 1969 station wagon models.

Interchange Number: 4
Part Number(s): 2883074
Usage: 1968 Belvedere, Charger, and Coronet with 426 Hemi and power *disc* brakes.

Interchange Number: 5
Part Number(s): 2883044
Usage: 1968 Belvedere, Charger, and Coronet with 426 Hemi and power *drum* brakes.

Interchange Number: 6
Part Number(s): 2944006
Usage: 1969 Barracuda; 1969–70, Dart, and Valiant; 1970; Duster, with power *drum* or *disc* brakes.
Note(s): Midland-Ross unit

Interchange Number: 7
Part Number(s): 2944160
Usage: 1969–70 Belvedere, Charger, and Coronet with 426 Hemi and power *drum* brakes.

Interchange Number: 8
Part Number(s): 2881801
Usage: 1969–70 Belvedere, Charger, and Coronet with 426 Hemi and power *disc* brakes.

Interchange Number: 9
Part Number(s): 3461104
Usage: 1970 Dart, Duster, and Valiant with power *disc* brakes.

Interchange Number: 10
Part Number(s): 3461110

Usage: 1971 Dart, Duster, and Valiant with power *disc* brakes.

Interchange Number: 11
Part Number(s): 3420987
Usage: 1970 Barracuda, Challenger with power *disc* brakes, except with 426 Hemi or 340-ci triple-two-barrel.

Interchange Number: 12
Part Number(s): 3461118
Usage: 1970 Cuda AAR, Challenger T/A with 340-ci triple-two-barrel with power *disc* brakes.

Interchange Number: 13
Part Number(s): 3579272
Usage: 1971 Challenger T/A with power *disc* brakes; 1971–72 and 1974 Barracuda, Challenger, Charger, Coronet, and Satellite, all models with all engines and models with power *disc* brakes except 1971 models with 426 Hemi; 1971 Barracuda, Challenger, Charger, Coronet, and Satellite with 11-in drum brakes, except models with 426 Hemi.
Note(s): Only one T/A car built.

Interchange Number: 14
Part Number(s): 2944486
Usage: 1970 Barracuda, Challenger with 426 Hemi with power *disc* brakes.

Interchange Number: 15
Part Number(s): 3461301
Usage: 1971 Barracuda, Challenger, Charger, Satellite with 426 Hemi and power *disc* brakes.

Interchange Number: 16
Part Number(s): 3461110
Usage: 1971 Dart, Duster, Demon with 340-ci and power *drum* brakes.

Interchange Number: 17
Part Number(s): 3461109
Usage: 1971 Dart, Duster, Demon, and Valiant and power *drum* brakes, except with 340-ci.

Interchange Number: 18
Part Number(s): 2944489
Usage: 1970 Barracuda, Challenger with power *drum* brakes, except models with 426 Hemi.

Interchange Number: 19
Part Number(s): 3461287
Usage: 1971 Barracuda, Challenger, Charger, Coronet, and Satellite with 10-in power *drum* brakes.

Interchange Number: 20
Part Number(s): 2944309
Usage: 1970 Barracuda, Challenger with 426 Hemi and power *drum* brakes.

Interchange Number: 21
Part Number(s): 3461300
Usage: 1971 Barracuda, Challenger, Charger, and Satellite with 426 Hemi and power *drum* brakes.

Interchange Number: 22
Part Number(s): 3549095
Usage: 1972–73 Dart, Duster, and Valiant with power *disc* or *drum* brakes.

Interchange Number: 23
Part Number(s): 3580083
Usage: 1973 Dart, Duster, and Valiant with power *disc* brakes.

Interchange Number: 24
Part Number(s): 3744466
Usage: 1973 Barracuda, Challenger, Charger, Coronet, and Satellite with power *dsic* brakes.

Interchange Number: 25
Part Number(s): 3580339
Usage: 1974 Dart, Duster, and Valiant with power *drum* or *disc* brakes.

Brake Drums

The important thing to watch for when interchanging brake drums is the diameter of the drum. Several different diameters were used. Some models used more than one diameter in the same year.

For example, the 1968–71 Charger, Coronets, Satellites, and Belvedere models used both 10-inch and 11-inch drums. Those models in muscle car form (R/T, GTX, Road Runner, etc.) used 11-inch drum brakes, only if disc brakes were not ordered; all other models and muscle cars with front disc brakes used the smaller 10-inch-diameter drums. However, 11-inch drum brakes (heavy-duty brakes) were optional on all B-bodies with a V-8 powerplant. The 1968–69 Barracuda, 1968–74 Dart, 1970–74 Duster, and 1968–74 Valiant used 9-inch drums with a six-cylinder powerplant and 10-inch drums with a V-8. Since six-cylinder applications are not covered in this guide due to limited space, only 10-inch drums for these models will be covered.

Note that front and rear drums are not interchangeable, and in some models the drums can not swap sides. In other words, a drum from the passenger's side of the car will not fit the driver's side.

The dimensions given are the size of the drum: The first number is the diameter. The second is the width of the brake lining. Pay particular attention to the model interchange, not the dimensions, as other models may have the same dimensions but may not fit your car. Also, some models after 1972 came standard with front disc brakes, so no front drums are listed for these model years.

Model Identification

Barracuda.....................................Interchange Number
1968–69 drum brakes, front 1
1968–69 drum brakes, rear 15
1968–69 disc brakes, rear 15
1970 drum brakes, except Cuda
  or with trailer package or heavy-duty brakes
    front 2
    rear 16
1970 drum brakes, Cuda or with
  trailer package or heavy-duty brakes
    front 3
    rear 19
1970 disc brakes, all models, rear................................16
1971 drum brakes, except Cuda or
  with trailer package or heavy-duty brakes
    front 10
    rear 22
1971 drum brakes, Cuda or with
  trailer package or heavy-duty brakes
    front 11, 12
    rear 23
1972, except with trailer package or heavy-duty brakes
    front 13
    rear 22
1972 with trailer package or heavy-duty brakes
    front 11, 12
    rear 23
1973 (all models standard with front disc brakes)
    rear drums, standard (10 in) 22
    rear drums, heavy-duty 23
1974 (all models standard with front disc brakes)
    rear drums, standard (10 in) 22
    rear drums, heavy-duty (11 in).......................24

Belvedere, Charger, Coronet, and Satellite......Interchange Number
1968 drum brakes, except Charger R/T,
  Coronet R/T, GTX, Road Runner,
  Super Bee, or models with trailer package
  or heavy-duty brakes
    front 2
    rear 16
1968 drum brakes, Charger R/T,
  Coronet R/T, GTX, Road Runner, or Super Bee
    front 6
    rear 17
1968 drum brakes, with trailer package or heavy-duty brakes
    front 7
    rear 17

1969 drum brakes, except Charger R/T, Coronet R/T,
  GTX, Road Runner, Super Bee, or models with
  trailer package or heavy-duty brakes
    front 2
    rear 16
1969 drum brakes, Charger R/T,
  Coronet R/T, GTX, Road Runner, or Super Bee
    front 3
    rear 17
1970 drum brakes, except Charger R/T,
  Coronet R/T, GTX, Road Runner,
  Super Bee, or models with trailer package
  or heavy-duty brakes
    front 2
    rear 16
1970 drum brakes, Charger R/T,
  Coronet R/T, GTX, Road Runner,
  Super Bee or models with trailer package
  or heavy-duty brakes
    front 3
    rear 19
1970 disc brakes, rear..16
1971 drum brakes, except Charger R/T,
  GTX, Super Bee, Road Runner or
  models with trailer package or heavy-duty brakes
    front 10
    rear 22
1971 drum brakes, Charger R/T,
  GTX, Road Runner, or Super Bee,
  or models with trailer package or heavy-duty brakes
    front 11, 12
    rear 23
1972, except with trailer package or heavy-duty brakes
    front 13
    rear 22
1972 with trailer package or heavy-duty brakes
    front 11, 12
    rear 23
1973 (all models with front disc brakes)
    rear drums, standard (10 in) 22
    rear drums, heavy-duty 23
1974 (all models standard with front disc brakes)
    rear drums, standard (10 in) 22
    rear drums, heavy-duty (11 in).......................24

Challenger..................................Interchange Number
1970 drum brakes, except Challenger R/T
  or models with trailer package or heavy-duty brakes
    front 2
    rear 16
1970 drum brakes, Challenger R/T
  or with trailer package or heavy-duty brakes
    front 3
    rear 19
1970 disc brakes, rear..16
1971 drum brakes, except Challenger R/T
  or models with trailer package or heavy-duty brakes
    front 10
    rear 22
1971 drum brakes, Challenger R/T
  or models with trailer package or heavy-duty brakes
    front 11, 12
    rear 23
1972 drum brakes, except with
  trailer package or heavy-duty brakes
    front 13
    rear 22
1972 drum brakes with trailer package or heavy-duty brakes
    front 11, 12
    rear 23
1973 (all models with front disc brakes)

Interchange

Interchange Number: 1
Part Number(s): 3004730 (right), 3004731 (left)
Position: Front
Dimensions: 10x2 1/4 in
Usage: 1968–69 Barracuda, Dart, and Valiant with V-8 or six-cylinder with heavy-duty brakes.

Interchange Number: 2
Part Number(s): 3004732 (right), 3004733 (left)
Position: Front
Dimensions: 10x2 1/2 in
Usage: 1968–70 Belvedere, Charger, and Coronet, except Super Bee, Coronet R/T, Charger R/T, GTX, or Road Runner with drum brakes or above models with heavy-duty brakes or trailer package; 1970 Barracuda, Challenger, except Challenger T/A, Challenger R/T, Cuda, Cuda AAR models, or Barracuda or Challenger with heavy-duty brakes or trailer package.
Note(s): Motor Wheel housing stamped 35386.

Interchange Number: 3
Part Number(s): 2781564 (right), 2781565 (left)
Position: Front
Dimensions: 11x3 in
Usage: 1969–70 Belvedere, Charger, and Coronet with heavy-duty drum brakes or trailer package; 1969–70 Charger R/T, Coronet R/T, GTX, Super Bee, or Road Runner with drum brakes.

Interchange Number: 4
Part Number(s): 2409858 (right), 2409859 (left)
Position: Front
Dimensions: 10x2 1/2 in
Usage: 1968 Belvedere, Charger, and Coronet with drum brakes, except Charger R/T, Coronet R/T, GTX, Super Bee, Road Runner, or above models with heavy-duty brakes or trailer package.
Note(s): Kelsey-Hayes housing stamped KHE223.

Interchange Number: 5
Part Number(s): 2460610 (right), 2460611 (left)
Position: Front
Dimensions: 10x2 1/2 in
Usage: 1968 Belvedere, Charger, and Coronet with drum brakes, except Charger R/T, Coronet R/T, GTX, Super Bee, Road Runner, or above models with heavy-duty brakes or trailer package.
Note(s): Budd housing stamped CB51.

Interchange Number: 6
Part Number(s): 2266390 (right), 2266391 (left)
Position: Front
Dimensions: 11x3 in
Usage: 1968 Charger R/T, Coronet R/T, GTX, Super Bee, or Road Runner with drum brakes; 1968 Belvedere, Charger, and Coronet with heavy-duty drum brakes but *not* with trailer package.

Interchange Number: 7
Part Number(s): 3004738 (right), 3004739 (left)
Position: Front

Dimensions: 11x3 in
Usage: 1968 Belvedere, Charger, and Coronet with trailer package or taxi or police car packages.

Interchange Number: 8
Part Number(s): 3549836 (right), 3549837 (left)
Position: Front
Dimensions: 10x2 1/4 in
Usage: 1970 Dart, Duster, and Valiant with V-8 or six-cylinder with heavy-duty brakes.

Interchange Number: 9
Part Number(s): 3580534
Position: Front
Dimensions: 10x2 1/4 in
Usage: 1971–72 Dart, Duster, and Valiant with V-8 or six-cylinder with heavy-duty brakes.
Note(s): Fits either side of car.

Interchange Number: 10
Part Number(s): 3580630
Position: Front
Dimensions: 10x2 1/2 in
Usage: 1971 Barracuda, Challenger, Charger, Coronet, and Satellite with drum brakes, except Challenger T/A, Challenger R/T, Charger R/T, GTX, Super Bee, Road Runner, or above models with heavy-duty drum brakes or trailer package.
Note(s): Fits either side of car.

Interchange Number: 11
Part Number(s): 3580546
Position: Front
Dimensions: 11x3 in
Usage: 1971 Charger R/T, Super Bee, GTX, or Road Runner with drum brakes; 1971–72 Charger, Coronet, and Satellite with heavy-duty drum brakes or trailer package.
Note(s): (1) Fits either side of car. (2) Motor Wheel housing stamped MW.

Interchange Number: 12
Part Number(s): 3580692
Position: Front
Dimensions: 11x3 in
Usage: 1971 Charger R/T, Super Bee, GTX, or Road Runner with drum brakes; 1971–72 Charger, Coronet, and Satellite with heavy-duty drum brakes or trailer package.
Note(s): (1) Fits either side of car. (2) Kelsey-Hayes housing stamped KH.

Interchange Number: 13
Part Number(s): 3580704
Position: Front
Dimensions: 10x2 1/2 in
Usage: 1972 Barracuda, Challenger, Charger, Coronet, and Satellite without heavy-duty brakes or trailer package.

Interchange Number: 14
Part Number(s): 3699614
Position: Front
Dimensions: 10x2 1/2 in
Usage: 1973–74 Dart Duster, and Valiant with drum brakes.

Interchange Number: 15
Part Number(s): 2534757
Position: Rear
Dimensions: 10 in
Usage: 1968–69 Barracuda, Dart, and Valiant with V-8 or six-cylinder with heavy-duty brakes.

Interchange Number: 16
Part Number(s): 3004745
Position: Rear
Dimensions: 10x2 1/2 in
Usage: 1968–70 Belvedere, Charger, and Coronet, all models except Charger R/T, Coronet R/T, GTX, Super Bee, or Road Runner with drum brakes, or above models with trailer package. Will fit muscle cars with front disc brakes.
Note(s): Without fins, some 1969 models used drums; with fins see Interchange Number 18.

Interchange Number: 17
Part Number(s): 2405798
Position: Rear
Dimensions: 11 in
Usage: 1968–69 Charger R/T, Coronet R/T, GTX, Super Bee, or Road Runner with drum brakes or Belvedere, Charger, and Coronet with heavy-duty drum brakes or with trailer package. Will *not* fit cars with front disc brakes.

Interchange Number: 18
Part Number(s): 2405798
Position: Rear
Dimensions: 10x2 1/2 in
Usage: 1969 Belvedere, Charger, and Coronet with drum brakes or disc brakes, all models except Charger R/T, Coronet R/T, Charger 500, Daytona, GTX, Super Bee, or Road runner with drum brakes.
Note(s): Drums have fins. Some 1969 models used no fins; see Interchange Number 16.

Interchange Number: 19
Part Number(s): 3004933
Position: Rear
Dimensions: 11x2 1/2 in
Usage: 1969–70 Belvedere, Charger, and Coronet with heavy-duty brakes or trailer package; 1969 Charger R/T, Coronet R/T, Fury, GTX, Monaco, Newport, New Yorker, Chrysler 300, Polara, Road Runner, Super Bee with drum brakes; 1970 Barracuda, Challenger with heavy-duty brakes or trailer package; 1970 Cuda, Challenger R/T with drum brakes. Will *not* fit Charger, Coronet, and Satellite with front disc brakes; this includes muscle cars and those with trailer package. Full-size cars used 11-in drums with or without disc brakes.
Note(s): Drum has cooling fins.

Interchange Number: 20
Part Number(s): 3461685
Position: Rear
Dimensions: 10x1 3/4 in
Usage: 1970 Dart, Duster, and Valiant with V-8 or six-cylinder with heavy-duty brakes.

Interchange Number: 21
Part Number(s): 3580551
Position: Rear
Dimensions: 10x1 3/4 in
Usage: 1971–72 Dart, Duster, and Valiant with V-8 or six-cylinder with heavy-duty brakes.

Interchange Number: 22
Part Number(s): 3580553
Position: Rear
Dimensions: 10x2 1/2 in
Usage: 1971–74 Barracuda, Challenger, Charger, Coronet, and Satellite with drum brakes, except Charger R/T, GTX, Road Runner, or Super Bee models; will fit all above models with front disc brakes; 1973–74 Dart, Duster Valiant with V-8 engine or heavy-duty brakes.

Interchange Number: 23
Part Number(s): 3549842
Position: Rear
Dimensions: 11x2 1/2 in
Usage: 1971–73 Charger, Coronet, and Satellite with heavy-duty brakes or trailer package; 1971 Charger R/T, GTX, Road Runner, or Super Bee with drum brakes; 1971–73 Fury, Monaco, New Port, New Yorker, Chrysler 300, Polara with drum or disc brakes. Will *not* fit mid-sized cars with front disc brakes.

Interchange Number: 24
Part Number(s): 3780526
Position: Rear
Dimensions: 11x2 1/2 in
Usage: 1974 Charger, Coronet, Satellite, Dart, Duster, Valiant, Fury, Monaco with trailer package or with police car package.

Rotor, Disc Brakes
Model Identification

Barracuda..Interchange Number
1968–69..1
1970...4
1971–72...5
1973...6
1974...7

Belvedere, Charger, Coronet,
   and Satellite......................................Interchange Number
1968–69..2
1970...4
1971–72...5
1973...6
1974...7

Challenger...Interchange Number
1970...4
1971–72...5
1973...6
1974...7

Dart, Duster, Demon, and Valiant.............Interchange Number
1968–69..1
1970...1
1971–72...3
1973...6
1974...7

Interchange
Interchange Number: 1
Part Number(s): 2660296 (right), 2660297 (left)
Diameter: 11.04 in
Usage: 1967–69 Barracuda, 1967–70 Dart, Valiant; 1970 Duster with front disc brakes.

Interchange Number: 2
Part Number(s): 282328 (right), 2823285 (left)
Diameter: 11.19 in
Usage: 1967–69 Belvedere, Charger, and Coronet with front disc brakes.

Interchange Number: 3
Part Number(s): 3580502
Diameter: 11.04 in
Usage: 1971–72 Dart, Duster, and Valiant with front disc brakes.
Note(s): Fits either side.

Interchange Number: 4
Part Number(s): 3461818 (right), 3461819 (left)
Diameter: 11.75 in
Usage: 1970 Barracuda, Challenger, Charger, Coronet, and Satellite with front disc brakes.

Interchange Number: 5
Part Number(s): 3580506
Diameter: 11.75 in
Usage: 1971–72 Barracuda, Challenger, Charger, Coronet, and Satellite with front disc brakes.
Note(s): Fits either side.

Interchange Number: 6
Part Number(s): 3580736
Diameter: 10.98 in
Usage: 1973 Barracuda, Challenger, Charger, Coronet, Dart, Duster, Satellite, and Valiant with front disc brakes.

Interchange Number: 7
Part Number(s): 3780527
Diameter: 10.98 in
Usage: 1974 Barracuda, Challenger, Charger, Coronet, Dart, Duster, Satellite, and Valiant with front disc brakes.

Pedals, Brake
Model Identification

Barracuda..Interchange Number
1968–69 manual transmission..1
1968–69 automatic transmission 2

Interchange

Interchange Number: 1
Part Number(s): 2883454
Usage: 1968 Barracuda, Dart, and Valiant with manual transmission and V-8 engine; 1969 Barracuda with four-speed transmission; 1970–72 Dart, Duster with 340-ci and manual transmission; 1973 Dart, Duster with 340-ci and manual transmission *with offset pedal.*
Note(s): (1) A unit from a 1968 model with a six-cylinder will *not* fit. (2) Unit from car with three-speed in 1969 models will not fit. (3) Some 1973 models used a center set pedal, see Interchange Number 12. The two are not interchangeable.

Interchange Number: 2
Part Number(s): 2823618
Usage: 1967–69 Barracuda; 1967–72, Dart, Valiant; 1970–72 Duster with automatic transmission; 1973 Dart, Duster, and Valiant with automatic transmission *with offset pedal.*
Note(s): (1) Fits all models and engines. (2) Some 1973 models used an on-set pedal design; see Interchange Number 13. The two designs are not interchangeable.

Interchange Number: 3
Part Number(s): 2880651
Usage: 1967–69 Belvedere, Charger, and Coronet with automatic transmission; 1970 Charger, Coronet, and Satellite with automatic transmission *without* power brakes.

Interchange Number: 4
Part Number(s): 2880650
Usage: 1967–70 Belvedere, Charger, and Coronet with manual transmission.

Interchange Number: 5
Part Number(s): 2823617
Usage: 1967 Barracuda, Dart, and Valiant with manual transmission; 1968 Barracuda, Dart, and Valiant with six-cylinder and manual transmission; 1969 Barracuda, Dart, and Valiant with three-speed manual transmission; 1970–72 Dart, Duster, and Valiant with manual transmission, except with 340-ci; 1973 Dart, Duster, and Valiant with manual transmission *with offset pedal,* except with 340-ci.
Note(s): Some models used a center set pedal; see Interchange Number 11. The two are not interchangeable.

Interchange Number: 6
Part Number(s): 2996417
Usage: 1970 Charger, Coronet, and Satellite with automatic transmission and *with* power brakes.

Interchange Number: 7
Part Number(s): 2950877
Usage: 1970 Barracuda, Challenger with manual transmission.

Interchange Number: 8
Part Number(s): 3575106
Usage: 1971–72 Barracuda, Challenger, Charger, Coronet, and Satellite with manual transmission.

Interchange Number: 9
Part Number(s): 2950878
Usage: 1970 Barracuda, Challenger with automatic transmission.

Interchange Number: 10
Part Number(s): 3575107
Usage: 1971–72 Barracuda, Challenger, Charger, Coronet, and Satellite with automatic transmission.

Interchange Number: 11
Part Number(s): 3575196
Usage: 1973 Dart, Duster, and Valiant with manual transmission, except with 340-ci.
Note(s): Pedal has center on set. Some models used an offset pedal, see Interchange Number 5. The two are not interchangeable.

Interchange Number: 12
Part Number(s): 3575198
Usage: 1973 Dart, Duster, and Valiant with manual transmission with 340-ci.
Note(s): Pedal has center on set. Some models used an offset pedal, see Interchange Number 1. The two are not interchangeable.

Interchange Number: 13
Part Number(s): 3575200
Usage: 1973 Dart, Duster, and Valiant with automatic transmission.
Note(s): Pedal has center on set. Some models used an offset pedal, see Interchange Number 2. The two are not interchangeable.

Interchange Number: 14
Part Number(s): 3575148
Usage: 1973 Barracuda, Challenger, Charger, and Coronet with manual transmission.

Interchange Number: 15
Part Number(s): 3575178
Usage: 1973 Barracuda, Challenger, Charger, and Coronet with automatic transmission.

Interchange Number: 16
Part Number(s): 3748031

Usage: 1974 Dart, Duster, and Valiant with manual
transmission, except with 360-ci.

Interchange Number: 17
Part Number(s): 3748033
Usage: 1974 Dart, Duster, and Valiant with manual transmission
with 360-ci.

Interchange Number: 18
Part Number(s): 3748032
Usage: 1974 Dart, Duster, and Valiant with automatic
transmission.

Interchange Number: 19
Part Number(s): 3748028
Usage: 1974 Barracuda, Challenger, Charger, Coronet, and
Satellite with manual transmission.

Interchange Number: 20
Part Number(s): 3748055
Usage: 1974 Barracuda, Challenger, Charger, Coronet, and
Satellite with automatic transmission.

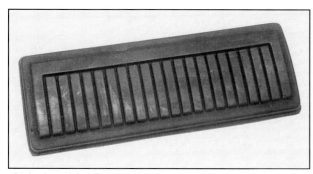

This brake pedal pad was used with 1968–1970 A- and B-bodies with automatic transmission. Year One

1970–1974 B- and E-bodies used this brake pad. Year One

1971–1974 A-bodies used this brake pedal pad.

Pads, Brake Pedal
Model Identification

Barracuda	Interchange Number
1968–69 manual transmission	1
1968–69 automatic transmission	2
1970–72 manual transmission	3
1970–72 automatic transmission	4
1973–74 manual transmission	6
1973–74 automatic transmission	5

Belvedere, Charger, Coronet, and Satellite	Interchange Number
1968–70 manual transmission	1
1968–70 automatic transmission	2
1971–72 manual transmission	3
1971–72 automatic transmission	4
1973–74 manual transmission	6
1973–74 automatic transmission	5

Challenger	Interchange Number
1970–72 manual transmission	3
1970–72 automatic transmission	4
1973–74 manual transmission	6
1973–74 automatic transmission	5

Dart, Duster, Demon, and Valiant	Interchange Number
1968–70 manual transmission	1
1968–70 automatic transmission	2
1971–74 manual transmission	6
1971–74 automatic transmission	5

Interchange

Interchange Number: 1
Part Number(s): 2643712
Usage: 1967–69 Barracuda; 1967–70 Dart, Valiant; 1966–70
Belvedere, Charger, and Coronet, with manual transmission.
Note(s): Clutch pedal pad for these models also fits.

Interchange Number: 2
Part Number(s): 2643707
Usage: 1967–69 Barracuda; 1967–70 Dart, Valiant; 1966–70
Belvedere, Charger, and Coronet with automatic transmission.

Interchange Number: 3
Part Number(s): 2950899
Usage: 1970–72 Barracuda, Challenger; 1971–72 Charger,
Coronet, and Satellite with manual transmission.
Note(s): Clutch pad for these models will also fit.

Interchange Number: 4
Part Number(s): 2950887
Usage: 1970–72 Barracuda, Challenger; 1971–72 Charger,
Coronet, and Satellite with automatic transmission.

Interchange Number: 5
Part Number(s): 3575101
Usage: 1971–74 Dart, Duster, and Valiant with automatic
transmission; 1972–74 Fury, Monaco, Polara, Newport, New
Yorker, Chrysler 300, and Imperial, all models with
automatic transmission; 1973–74 Barracuda, Challenger,
Charger, Coronet, and Satellite.

Interchange Number: 6
Part Number(s): 3467530
Usage: 1971–74 Dart, Duster, and Valiant with manual
transmission; 1970–74 Fury, Monaco, Polara with manual
transmission; 1973–74 Barracuda, Challenger, Charger,
Coronet, and Satellite with manual transmission.

Calipers
Model Identification

Barracuda	Interchange Number
1968, before November 1, 1967	1
1968, November 1, 1967	3
1969	4
1970	6
1971–72	7
1973–74	9

Interchange

Interchange Number: 1
Part Number(s): 2881588 (right), and 2881589 (left)
Usage: 1967–early 1968 Barracuda, Dart, and Valiant with disc brakes.
Note(s): Used until November 1, 1967.

Interchange Number: 2
Part Number(s): 2823216
Usage: 1967–68 Belvedere, Charger, and Coronet with front disc brakes.
Note(s): Fits either side.

Interchange Number: 3
Part Number(s): 2925160 (right), 2925161 (left)
Usage: Late 1968 Barracuda, Dart, and Valiant with disc brakes.
Note(s): Used after November 1, 1967.

Interchange Number: 4
Part Number(s): 2925220 (right), 2925221 (left)
Usage: 1969 Barracuda; 1969–72 Dart, Valiant; 1970–72 Duster with disc brakes.

Interchange Number: 5
Part Number(s): 2925222
Usage: 1969 Belvedere, Charger, and Coronet with disc brakes.
Note(s): Fits either side.

Interchange Number: 6
Part Number(s): 2944712 (right), 2944713 (left)
Usage: 1970 Barracuda, Challenger, Charger, Coronet, and Satellite with disc brakes.

Interchange Number: 7
Part Number(s): 3461964 (right), 3461965 (left)
Usage: 1971–72 Barracuda, Challenger, Charger, Coronet, and Satellite with disc brakes.

Interchange Number: 8
Part Number(s): 3580850 (right), 3580851 (left)
Usage: 1973 Dart, Duster, and Valiant with disc brakes.

Interchange Number: 9
Part Number(s): 3580852 (right), 3580853 (left)
Usage: 1973–74 Barracuda, Challenger with disc brakes.

Interchange Number: 10
Part Number(s): 3580854 (right), 3580855 (left)
Usage: 1973–74 Charger, Coronet, and Satellite with disc brakes.

Interchange Number: 11
Part Number(s): 3699968 (right), 3699969 (left)
Usage: 1974 Dart, Duster, and Valiant with disc brakes.

Parking Brakes
Model Identification

Interchange

Interchange Number: 1
Part Number(s): 2883524
Usage: 1968–69 Barracuda; 1968–71, Dart, Valiant; 1970–71 Duster, all body styles and models.

Interchange Number: 2
Part Number(s): 2534951
Usage: 1967–68 Belvedere, Charger, and Coronet, all body styles and models.

Interchange Number: 3
Part Number(s): 2534952
Usage: 1969–70 Belvedere, Charger, and Coronet, all body styles and models.

Interchange Number: 4
Part Number(s): 2950301
Usage: 1970 Barracuda, Challenger, all body styles and models.

Interchange Number: 5
Part Number(s): 3467922
Usage: 1971–72 Barracuda, Challenger, Charger, Coronet, and Satellite, all body styles and models.

Interchange Number: 6
Part Number(s): 3575622
Usage: 1972–74 Dart, Duster, and Valiant, all body styles and models.

Interchange Number: 7
Part Number(s): 3575631
Usage: 1973–74 Barracuda, Challenger, Charger, Coronet, and Satellite, all body styles and models.

Chapter 8

Wheels and Wheel Covers

Wheels

Determining factors in the interchanging of wheels are diameter, width, and offset. Of these, offset is an important factor to watch for. You may find two wheels that are of the same diameter and width but have different offsets. The offset is the distance that the wheel sits back from the brake drum or rotor. It can be noted by measuring the distance from the centerline of the rim to the inner side of the wheel rim.

Wheels with the wrong offset can interfere with brake operations (especially disc brakes) and can cause tire clearance problems at the wheel well lip. There is generally a 1 "plus" rule in swapping wheels that are a different size than the original units. This means you can usually, but not always, go up one size in the wheel without problems. For example, if your car has 14x6-inch wheels, you can usually install 14x7-inch wheels. Try to avoid large offset changes; for example, if you have a wheel with 1-inch offset, you should not use a wheel with a 3-inch offset. Another factor that can be used in interchanging wheels is if the wheels were available as options on your model, they will usually fit your car.

Also, you may notice some wheels have the same diameter, same width and bolt pattern size, yet they are still not interchangeable, due to the size of the center hub hole. While you can install a wheel with a larger-diameter center hub hole, the reverse is not true. This is why a Chrysler wheel will fit a Ford, but a standard Ford wheel will not fit your Dodge. This information (diameter of the hole) is not given, so be sure to measure, or better yet, test-fit the wheel on your car before you buy.

Up to 1970, Chrysler wheels are stamped with the wheel diameter and width near the valve stem. Also stamped near the valve stem is the manufacture and build date. A typical code will look like this: 14 M39 11 09 69, which will translate to Motor Wheel, built in November 09, 1969. For 1970 and up, the wheel's part number is stamped into the rim near the valve stem. This makes identification easier than the earlier style. All interchanges listed here are according to part number.

Model Identification

Barracuda	Interchange Number
1968–69 13x4	1
1968–69 14x4	2
1968–69 14x5	3
1970–71 14x5	24
1970–71 14x5 1/2	25
1970–71 14x5 1/2 rallye wheel	28
1970–71 14x5 1/2 rallye (spare)	26
1970–71 14x5 1/2 chrome road wheel	29
1970–71 14x6	31
1970–71 15x7	33
1970–71 15x7 slotted rallye wheel	34
1972–74 14x5	10
1972–74 14x5 1/2	11
1972–74 14x5 1/2 slotted rallye wheel	12
1972–74 14x5 1/2 chrome road wheel	18
1972–74 15x7 slotted rallye wheel	21

Belvedere, Charger, Coronet, and Satellite	Interchange Number
1968 14x5	4
1968 14x5 1/2	5
1968 14x5 1/2 chrome road wheel	7
1968 14x5 1/2 deep dish	36, 37
1968 15x6	6
1969 14x5	35, 4
1969 14x5 1/2 deep dish	36, 37
1969 14x5 1/2 chrome road wheel	38
1969 15x6	32
1970–71 14x5	24
1970–71 14x5 1/2	25
1970–71 14x5 1/2 rallye wheel	28
1970–71 14x5 1/2 rallye (spare)	26
1970–71 14x5 1/2 chrome road wheel	29
1970–71 14x6	31
1970–71 15x6	32
1970–71 15x7	33
1970–71 15x7 slotted rallye wheel	34
1972 14x5	10
1972 14x5 1/2	11
1972 14x5 1/2 slotted rallye wheel	12
1972 14x6	13
1972 14x6 chrome road wheel	15
1972 15x6	19
1972 15x7	20
1972 15x7 slotted rallye wheel	34
1973 14x5	10
1973 14x5 1/2	11
1973 14x6	13
1973 14x6 slotted rallye wheel	14
1973 14x6 chrome road wheel	15
1973 15x6	19
1973 15x6 1/2	17
1973 15x7	20
1973 15x7 slotted rallye wheel	21
1974 14x5	10
1974 14x5 1/2	11
1974 14x6	13
1974 14x6 slotted rallye wheel	14
1974 14x6 chrome road wheel	15
1974 15x6 16 slot rallye wheel	16
1974 15x6 1/2	17
1974 15x7	20
1974 15x7 slotted rallye wheel	21

Challenger	Interchange Number
1970–71 14x5	24
1970–71 14x5 1/2	25
1970–71 14x5 1/2 rallye wheel	28
1970–71 14x5 1/2 rallye (spare)	26
1970–71 14x5 1/2 chrome road wheel	29
1970–71 14x6	31
1970–71 15x7	33
1970–71 15x7 slotted rallye wheel	34
1972–74 14x5	10

Interchange

Interchange Number: 1
Part Number(s): 2534167
Diameter/Width: 13x4 1/2
Usage: 1968 Barracuda, Dart, and Valiant, except with air conditioning, disc brakes, or 340-ci or 383-ci.

Interchange Number: 2
Part Number(s): 2660308
Diameter/Width: 14x4 1/2
Usage: 1965–69 Barracuda, Dart, and Valiant with disc brakes or air conditioning but not with air conditioning and disc brakes or with 340-ci or 383-ci; 1970–71 Dart, Duster.

Interchange Number: 3
Part Number(s): 2660312
Diameter/Width: 14x5 1/2
Usage: 1965–69 Barracuda, Dart, and Valiant with 340-ci or 383-ci, or models with air conditioning and disc brakes; 1970–71 Dart, Duster, and Valiant, all models.

Interchange Number: 4
Part Number(s): 2881820
Diameter/Width: 14x5
Usage: 1968–69 Belvedere, Coronet with 318-ci or 383-ci, except Road Runner or Super Bee models.
Note(s): Budd wheel will have the ID code of CB near the valve stem. Will not fit 1968 Charger.

Interchange Number: 5
Part Number(s): 2534702
Diameter/Width: 14x5 1/2
Usage: 1968 Belvedere, Coronet, with F70x14 tires, except station wagon or with 426 Hemi; 1966–68 Charger, all powerplants except 426 Hemi; 1966–68 Fury, Polara, Monaco, and Newport, except station wagon models.
Note(s): (1) Manufactured by Motor Wheel will have the letter M near valve stem. (2) Station wagons have different offset.

Interchange Number: 6
Part Number(s): 2823868
Diameter/Width: 15x6
Usage: 1968 Belvedere, Charger, and Coronet with 426 Hemi; 1967–68 Fury, Polara, Monaco, Newport, New Yorker, and Chrysler 300, all models.

Interchange Number: 7
Part Number(s): 2823840
Diameter/Width: 14x5 1/2
Usage: 1968 Belvedere, Charger, and Coronet, all models except with 426 Hemi.
Note(s): Chrome road wheel.

Interchange Number: 8
Part Number(s): 3621951
Diameter/Width: 14x4 1/2
Usage: 1972–74 Dart, Duster, and Valiant, except with front disc brakes.

Interchange Number: 9
Part Number(s): 3683970
Diameter/Width: 14x5 1/2
Usage: 1973–74 Dart, Duster, and Valiant with front disc brakes.

Interchange Number: 10
Part Number(s): 3621952
Diameter/Width: 14x5
Usage: 1972–74 Barracuda, Challenger, Charger, Coronet, Satellite; 1974 Dart, Duster, and Valiant.

Interchange Number: 11
Part Number(s): 3621953
Diameter/Width: 14x5 1/2
Usage: 1972–74 Barracuda, Challenger, Charger, Coronet, Dart, Duster, Satellite, and Valiant.

Interchange Number: 12
Part Number(s): 3580058
Diameter/Width: 14x5 1/2
Usage: 1972–74 Barracuda, Challenger; 1973–74 Dart, Duster, and Valiant with disc brakes.
Note(s): Slotted rallye wheel.

Wheels are stamped with a date or ID code.

The chrome road wheel.

The slotted Rallye wheel came in two different diameters. The 15-inch-diameter wheel is shown.

Simulated mag wheel for 1968–1969 Plymouths.

Interchange Number: 13
Part Number(s): 3621954
Diameter/Width: 14x6
Usage: 1973–74 Barracuda, Challenger; 1972–74 Charger, Coronet, and Satellite.

Interchange Number: 14
Part Number(s): 3580068
Diameter/Width: 14x6
Usage: 1973–74 Charger, Coronet, Satellite.
Note(s): Slotted rallye wheel.

Interchange Number: 15
Part Number(s): 3580065
Diameter/Width: 14x6
Usage: 1974 Barracuda, Challenger; 1972–74 Charger, Coronet, and Satellite.
Note(s): Chrome road wheel.

Interchange Number: 16
Part Number(s): 3580067
Diameter/Width: 15x6
Usage: 1974 Charger, Coronet, Fury, Monaco, Newport, New Yorker, Satellite, all models and body styles.
Note(s): 16 slot wheel. More common on full-size models.

Interchange Number: 17
Part Number(s): 3621956
Diameter/Width: 15x6 1/2
Usage: 1973–74 Charger, Coronet, Fury, Monaco, Newport, New Yorker, Satellite.

Interchange Number: 18
Part Number(s): 3580059
Diameter/Width: 14x5 1/2
Usage: 1972–73 Barracuda, Challenger.
Note(s): Chrome road wheel.

Interchange Number: 19
Part Number(s): 3580063
Diameter/Width: 15x6
Usage: 1972–73 Charger, Coronet, Fury, Monaco, Newport, and New Yorker.

Interchange Number: 20
Part Number(s): 3580070
Diameter/Width: 15x7
Usage: 1972–73 Charger, Coronet, and Satellite.

Interchange Number: 21
Part Number(s): 3580071
Diameter/Width: 15x7
Usage: 1972–73 Barracuda, Challenger, Charger, Coronet, and Satellite.
Note(s): Slotted rallye wheel.

Interchange Number: 22
Part Number(s): 3420965
Diameter/Width: 14x5 1/2
Usage: 1970–72 Dart, Duster, and Valiant.
Note(s): Wheel manufactured by Norris Thermadore. Look on 1972 models where it is more common.

Interchange Number: 23
Part Number(s): 3580056
Diameter/Width: 14x5 1/2
Usage: 1972 Dart, Duster, and Valiant.
Note(s): Slotted rallye wheel.

Interchange Number: 24
Part Number(s): 3420976
Diameter/Width: 14x5
Usage: 1970–71 Barracuda, Challenger, Charger, Coronet, and Satellite.

Interchange Number: 25
Part Number(s): 3420977
Diameter/Width: 14x5 1/2
Usage: 1970–71 Barracuda, Challenger, Charger, Coronet, and Satellite.

Interchange Number: 26
Part Number(s): 2944395
Diameter/Width: 14x5 1/2
Usage: 1970–71 Barracuda, Challenger, Charger, Coronet, and Satellite.
Note(s): Spare tire originally used with Interchange Number 28.

Interchange Number: 27
Part Number(s): 2944388
Diameter/Width: 14x5 1/2
Usage: 1970–71 Dart, Duster, and Valiant.
Note(s): Slotted rallye wheel.

Interchange Number: 28
Part Number(s): 2944252
Diameter/Width: 14x5 1/2
Usage: 1970–71 Barracuda, Challenger, Charger, Coronet, and Satellite.
Note(s): Slotted rallye wheel.

Interchange Number: 29
Part Number(s): 2944474
Diameter/Width: 14x5 1/2

Usage: 1970–71 Barracuda, Challenger, Charger, Coronet, and Satellite.

Interchange Number: 30
Part Number(s): 3461359
Diameter/Width: 14x6
Usage: 1970–71 Charger, Coronet, and Satellite.
Note(s): Chrome road wheel.

Interchange Number: 31
Part Number(s): 3420978
Diameter/Width: 14x6
Usage: 1970–71 Barracuda, Challenger, Charger, Coronet, and Satellite.

Interchange Number: 32
Part Number(s): 2944169
Diameter/Width: 15x6
Usage: 1969–71 Charger, Coronet, Fury, Monaco, Polara; 1970–71 New Port, New Yorker, Chrysler 300.

Interchange Number: 33
Part Number(s): 2944450
Diameter/Width: 15x7
Usage: 1970–71 Barracuda, Challenger, Charger, Coronet, and Satellite.

Interchange Number: 34
Part Number(s): 2944390
Diameter/Width: 15x7
Usage: 1970–71 Barracuda, Challenger, Charger, Coronet, and Satellite.

Interchange Number: 35
Part Number(s): 3004756
Diameter/Width: 14x5
Usage: 1969 Belvedere, Charger, and Coronet, all models and styles except station wagon.
Note(s): Made by Motor Wheel.

Interchange Number: 36
Part Number(s): 3004892
Diameter/Width: 14x5 1/2
Usage: 1968–69 Belvedere, Charger, and Coronet.
Note(s): (1) Deep dish design. (2) Made by Budd.

Interchange Number: 37
Part Number(s): 3004702
Diameter/Width: 14x5 1/2
Usage: 1968–69 Belvedere, Charger, and Coronet.
Note(s): (1) Deep dish design. (2) Made by Motor Wheel.

Interchange Number: 38
Part Number(s): 2944162
Diameter/Width: 14x5 1/2
Usage: 1969 Belvedere, Charger, and Coronet.
Note(s): Chrome road wheel.

Wheel Covers

Wheel covers should not be confused with hub caps. Hub caps cover only the inner portion of the wheel and the lug nuts, while wheel covers hide the entire face of the wheel. Wheel covers can be identified by their design and size (diameter). In some instances, the part number will be stamped into the underside of the cover, which can also be used for identification.

Model Identification

Nine-slot wheel cover used in 1969.

Six-slot cover used on 1970 Dodges.

Interchange

Interchange Number: 1
Part Number(s): 2881752
Diameter: 13
Description: Raised center dome with the words "Plymouth Division" outlined by eight bars.
Usage: 1968–69 Valiant.

Interchange Number: 2
Part Number(s): 2823016
Diameter: 13
Description: Center dome with Dodge logo, seven slots on outer edge.
Usage: 1967–68 Dart, all models.

Interchange Number: 3
Part Number(s): 2823014
Diameter: 14
Description: Raised center dome. Five slots. Bolt-on design.
Usage: 1967–69 Valiant, Barracuda.

Interchange Number: 4
Part Number(s): 2881787
Diameter: 14
Description: Simulated wire wheel.
Usage: 1968–69 Barracuda, Valiant.

Interchange Number: 5
Part Number(s): 2823010
Diameter: 14
Description: Large flat center dome with Plymouth logo. Five simulated slots. Snap-on type.
Usage: 1967–69 Barracuda, Belvedere, and Valiant.

Interchange Number: 6
Part Number(s): 2881764
Diameter: 14
Description: Depressed center with raised center dome.

Outlined by 11 slots.
Usage: 1968–69 Charger, Coronet, and Dart.

Interchange Number: 7
Part Number(s): 2881769
Diameter: 14
Description: Simulated mag wheel with five spokes and bright, plated lug nuts.
Usage: 1968 Charger, Coronet, Dart, Monaco, and Polara.

Interchange Number: 8
Part Number(s): 2881779
Diameter: 14
Description: Five-spoke design with round raised center dome and Dodge tri-star.
Usage: 1968–69 Charger, Coronet; 1968 Monaco, Polara.

Interchange Number: 9
Part Number(s): 2881773
Diameter: 14
Description: Raised center dome with Plymouth logo. Five slots.
Usage: 1968–69 Belvedere; 1968 Fury.
Note(s): Similar to bolt-on design but snaps into place.

Interchange Number: 10
Part Number(s): 2881753
Diameter: 15
Description: Depressed center dome surrounded by 34 spokes.
Usage: 1968–69 Belvedere, Charger, and Coronet; 1968 Chrysler 300, Fury, Monaco, Newport, New Yorker, and Polara.
Note(s): (1) Look on full-size models. (2) Similar to Interchange Number 11 but does not have the words "Disc Brake" printed on hub.

Interchange Number: 11
Part Number(s): 2881757
Diameter: 15
Description: Depressed center dome surrounded by 34 spokes. Imprint with the words "Disc Brakes" on the center hub.
Usage: 1968–69 Belvedere, Charger, Coronet, Chrysler 300, Fury, Monaco, Newport, New Yorker, and Polara.
Note(s): (1) Look on full-size models.

Interchange Number: 12
Part Number(s): 2881796
Diameter: 13
Description: Larger center dome with Dodge tri-star logo in the center.
Usage: 1969 Dart models with 13-in wheels.

Interchange Number: 13
Part Number(s): 2944165
Diameter: 14
Description: Dominated by a raised center with several bent spines.

Usage: 1969 Barracuda, Belvedere, and Valiant.

Interchange Number: 14
Part Number(s): 2823004
Diameter: 14
Description:. Raised center dome with Dodge tri-star logo bordered by a plain-circle with numerous fins on the outer edge.
Usage: 1969 Coronet, Charger; 1967–68 Polara, Monaco.

Interchange Number: 15
Part Number(s): 2881758
Diameter: 14
Description:. Raised center dome with the words "Plymouth Division" surrounded by nine simulated slots.
Usage: 1969 Belvedere.

Interchange Number: 16
Part Number(s): 2944092
Diameter: 14
Description: Simulated mag wheel with five spokes and knobbed center dome with Dodge tri-star logo.
Usage: 1969 Charger, Coronet, and Dart.

Interchange Number: 17
Part Number(s): 2944433
Diameter: 14
Description: Depressed center with Challenger script surrounded by six slots.
Usage: 1970–71 Challenger.

Interchange Number: 18
Part Number(s): 2944435

Diameter: 14
Description: Depressed center with the words "Dodge Division" surrounded by six slots.
Usage: 1970–71 Charger, Coronet, and Dart.

Interchange Number: 19
Part Number(s): 2944441
Diameter: 14
Description: Simulated mag wheel, five-spoke design separated by several fins. Raised center dome with removable center appliqué with Dodge tri-staR/The words "Dodge Division."
Usage: 1970 Coronet, Charger, and Challenger.

Interchange Number: 20
Part Number(s): 2944400
Diameter: 14
Description: Simulated wire wheel, with-circle in center dome.
Usage: 1970–71 Barracuda, Challenger, Charger, Coronet, Dart, Duster, Satellite, and Valiant.

Interchange Number: 21
Part Number(s): 2944432
Diameter: 14
Description: Looks like a pie tin with 28 holes and raised center dome with the words "Plymouth Division."
Usage: 1970–72 Barracuda, Satellite.

Interchange Number: 22
Part Number(s): 2944426
Diameter: 14
Description: Raised center dome with the Plymouth logo

Fifteen-inch cover used on 1968–1969 Hemis.

Twenty-eight-hole cover used on 1970 Plymouths.

Deluxe cover for 1968–1969 Dodges.

Thirty-three-slot wheel cover used on late 1973–1974 Dodges.

1972–1974 center cap with rallye wheels.

supported by 16 bent legs.
Usage: 1970 Satellite, Duster, and Valiant.

Interchange Number: 23
Part Number(s): 3461401
Diameter: 14
Description: Smooth disk with nine holes in the center.
Usage: 1971 Barracuda, Duster, Satellite, and Valiant.

Interchange Number: 24
Part Number(s): 3580014
Diameter: 14
Description: Eight slots protruding from center dome.
Usage: 1972–74 Duster, Valiant.

Interchange Number: 25
Part Number(s): 3461460
Diameter: 14
Description: 33 slots surrounding center dome with the word "Dodge" imprinted on it.
Usage: 1972 Challenger, Charger, Coronet, and Dart.
Note(s): Area around slots is painted gray. Used until March 1972. After that date, see Interchange Number 26.

Interchange Number: 26
Part Number(s): 3580153
Diameter: 14
Description: 33 slots surrounding center dome with the word "Dodge" imprinted on it.
Usage: Late 1972–74 Challenger, Charger, Coronet, and Dart.
Note(s): Cover is chrome; used until March 1972. After that date, see Interchange Number 26.

Interchange Number: 27
Part Number(s): 3461467
Diameter: 14
Description: Simulated wire wheel.
Usage: 1972–74 Barracuda, Challenger, Charger, Coronet, Dart, Duster, Satellite, and Valiant.

Interchange Number: 28
Part Number(s): 3699017
Diameter: 14
Description: 28 holes. Black center surrounded by five-circles.
Usage: 1973–74 Barracuda, Satellite.

Interchange Number: 29
Part Number(s): 3699003
Diameter: 14
Description: 30 holes, with a multi-blade look.
Usage: 1973–74 Satellite.
Note(s): Very rare cover.

Interchange Number: 30
Part Number(s): Varies (see Notes)
Diameter: 14

Description: Large center dome surrounded by colored spokes.
Usage: 1974 Dart, Duster, and Valiant.
Note(s): Spokes were painted red, black, gold, white, dark green, light green, light parchment or dark parchment. (2) Spokes can be repainted; light parchment the easiest to paint over.

Hub Caps

The caps listed here are for styled wheels. Standard hub caps are not given, as they are not a popular choice with restorers nor that common on muscle cars. There are exceptions: In 1971 a trim ring became available as an option with the standard hub caps, thus an interchange for the standard hub cap for 1971–74 models is given. Also note that no styled wheel option was available for the 1968–69 Barracuda, Dart, or Valiant models, so that information is not listed.

Model Identification

Barracuda ....**Interchange Number**
1968–69 ....option not available
1970 chrome road wheel 1
1970 slotted rallye wheel 2
1970 with trim ring 10
1971 chrome road wheel 1
1971 slotted rallye wheel 5
1971 with trim ring 11
1972–74 chrome road wheel 1
1972–74 slotted rallye wheel 7
1972–74 with trim ring 11

Belvedere and Satellite ....**Interchange Number**
1968–69 chrome road wheel 1
1970 chrome road wheel 1
1970 slotted rallye wheel 2
1970 with trim ring 10
1971 chrome road wheel 1
1971 slotted rallye wheel 5
1971 with trim ring 11
1972–74 chrome road wheel 1
1972–74 slotted rallye wheel 7
1972–74 with trim ring 11

Challenger ....**Interchange Number**
1970 chrome road wheel 1
1970 slotted rallye wheel 2
1970 with trim ring 9
1971 chrome road wheel 1
1971 slotted rallye wheel 5
1971 with trim ring 9
1972 chrome road wheel 1
1972 slotted rallye wheel 7
1972 with trim ring 9
1973–74 chrome road wheel 1
1973–74 slotted rallye wheel 7
1973–74 with trim ring 12

Charger and Coronet ....**Interchange Number**
1968–69 chrome road wheel 1
1970 chrome road wheel 1
1970 slotted rallye wheel 2
1970 with trim ring 9
1971 chrome road wheel 1
1971 slotted rallye wheel 5
1971 with trim ring 9
1972 chrome road wheel 1
1972 slotted rallye wheel 7
1972 with trim ring 9
1973–74 chrome road wheel 1
1973–74 slotted rallye wheel 7
1973–74 with trim ring 12

Dart and Demon ....**Interchange Number**
1968–69 (option not available)
1970 slotted rallye wheel 3
1970 with trim ring 9

Interchange

Interchange Number: 1
Part Number(s): 2823842
Style: Center cap
Usage: 1968–74 Charger, Coronet, and Satellite; 1970–74 Barracuda, Challenger; 1967–68 Fury, Polara, and Monaco, all with chrome road wheel.

Interchange Number: 2
Part Number(s): 3461066
Style: Center cap
Usage: 1970 Barracuda, Challenger, Charger, Coronet, and Satellite with slotted rallye wheel.

Interchange Number: 3
Part Number(s): 3461065
Style: Center cap
Usage: 1970 Dart, Duster, and Valiant with slotted rallye wheel.

Interchange Number: 4
Part Number(s): 3461351
Style: Center cap
Usage: 1971 Dart, Duster, and Valiant with slotted rallye wheels.

Interchange Number: 5
Part Number(s): 3461352
Style: Center cap
Usage: 1971 Barracuda, Challenger, Charger, Coronet, and Satellite with slotted rallye wheels.

Interchange Number: 6
Part Number(s): 3461462
Style: Center cap
Usage: 1972 Dart, Duster, and Valiant with slotted rallye wheels.

Interchange Number: 7
Part Number(s): 3461458
Style: Center cap
Usage: 1972–74 Barracuda, Challenger, Charger, Coronet, and Satellite; 1973–74 Dart, Duster, and Valiant, all with slotted rallye wheels. Used with 14-in and 15-in wheels.

Interchange Number: 8
Part Number(s): 3461041
Style: Center cap
Usage: 1974 Charger, Coronet, and Satellite; 1972–74 Fury, Monaco, Newport, and New Yorker; 1972 Polara, all with 16-slot rallye wheels.
Note(s): Look on full-size models.

Interchange Number: 9
Part Number(s): 2944089
Style: Hub cap
Usage: 1970–72 Challenger, Charger, Coronet, Dart, Polara, and Monaco.
Note(s): Standard cap. Stainless steel aluminum cap also used. (2) Used with trim ring.

Interchange Number: 10
Part Number(s): 2944088
Style: Hub cap
Usage: 1970 Barracuda, Duster, Fury, Satellite, and Valiant.

Note(s): Has the words "Plymouth Division" imprinted into the face. (1) Standard cap. (2) Used with trim ring.

Interchange Number: 11
Part Number(s): 3461450
Style: Hub cap
Usage: 1971–74 Barracuda, Duster, Fury, Satellite, and Valiant.
Note(s): No imprint. (1) Standard cap. (2) Used with trim ring.

Interchange Number: 12
Part Number(s): 2944454
Style: Hub cap
Usage: 1973–74 Challenger, Charger, Coronet, Dart, and Monaco.
Note(s): (1) Standard cap. (2) Used with trim ring.

Trim Rings
Model Identification

Interchange

Interchange Number: 1
Part Number(s): 2944161
Usage: 1968–69 Belvedere, Charger, and Coronet with chrome road wheels.

Interchange Number: 2
Part Number(s): 2944424
Usage: 1970–74 Barracuda, Challenger, Charger, Coronet, Dart, Duster, Satellite Valiant with 14-in slotted rallye wheels or with hub cap; 1970–74 Barracuda, Challenger, Charger, Coronet, and Satellite with chrome road wheel.

Interchange Number: 3
Part Number(s): 3461043
Usage: 1970 Barracuda, Challenger, Charger, Coronet, and Satellite with 15-in slotted rallye wheels.
Note(s): Ring is chrome.

Interchange Number: 4
Part Number(s): 3461222
Usage: 1971–73 Barracuda, Challenger, Charger, Coronet, and Satellite with 15-in slotted rallye wheels.
Note(s): Ring is brushed aluminum.

Interchange Number: 5
Part Number(s): 3461012
Usage: 1974 Charger, Coronet, Satellite; 1972–74 Fury, Monaco, Newport, New Yorker; 1972 Polara, all with 16-slotted rallye wheels.
Note(s): Look on full-size models.

Chapter 9

Electrical

Starter

Most models covered in this manual used a starter with a reduction type of drive. The exception was 1968 cars with a 426 Hemi and four-speed transmission that used a direct drive starter. A direct drive starter was also used in six-cylinder taxis with a manual transmission, but it is different than that used on the 426 and will *not* interchange. And since six-cylinders are not covered in this guide, it is not listed.

Starters can be identified by a part number that is stamped on them. It is this identification number that the interchange is based on.

Model Identification

Barracuda..*Interchange Number*
1968–69, all 1
1970–72, all 3
1973, early 4
1973, late 5
1974, early 5
1974, late 6

Belvedere, Charger, Coronet,
and Satellite..*Interchange Number*
1968–69, except Hemi with four-speed or taxi 1
1968–69 Hemi with four-speed.....................................2
1968–69 taxi..7
1970–72, except taxi 3
1970–72 taxi..7
1973 318 or 340-ci, early...4
1973 318 or 340-ci, late...5
1973 400 or 440-ci...5
1974, early 5
1974 late...6

Challenger..*Interchange Number*
1970–72, all 3
1973, early 4
1973, late 5
1974, early 5
1974, late 6

Dart, Duster, Demon, and Valiant.............*Interchange Number*
1968–69, all 1
1970–72, all 3
1973, early 4
1973, late 5
1974, early 5
1974, late 6

Interchange

Interchange Number: 1
ID Number(s): 2095150
Usage: 1965–69 Barracuda, Belvedere, Charger, Chrysler 300, Coronet, Dart, Fury, Monaco, Newport, New Yorker, Polara, and Valiant, all models and engines, except those with 426 Hemi and four-speed transmission or 170-ci six-cylinder or taxi models with 225-ci six-cylinder and manual transmission.
Note(s): (1) Will fit cars with 426 Hemi and automatic transmission. (2) Be careful when interchanging from 1969

models, as Interchange Number 3 was also used after April 1, 1969.

Interchange Number: 2
ID Number(s): 2642930
Usage: 1967–69 Belvedere, Charger, and Coronet with 426 Hemi and four-speed transmission.
Note(s): Direct drive starter.

Interchange Number: 3
ID Number(s): 2875560
Usage: Late 1969–72 Barracuda, Belvedere, Charger, Chrysler 300, Coronet, Dart Fury, Monaco, Newport, New Yorker, Polara, and Valiant; 1970–72 Challenger; 1970–72 Duster, all models and engines except those with 225-ci six-cylinder and heavy-duty manual transmission.
Note(s): Will fit cars with 426 Hemi.

Interchange Number: 4
ID Number(s): 3656650
Usage: Early 1973 Barracuda, Challenger, Charger, Coronet, Dart, Duster, Fury, Polara, Satellite, and Valiant with 225-ci six-cylinder or 318-ci or 340-ci.
Note(s): Used until January 1973.

Interchange Number: 5
ID Number(s): 3656575
Usage: Late 1973–early 1974 Barracuda, Challenger, Charger, Coronet, Dart, Duster, Fury, Polara, Satellite, and Valiant with 225-ci six-cylinder or 318-ci or 340-ci; 1973–early 1974 Charger, Coronet, Fury, Monaco, Newport, and New Yorker with 360-ci, 400-ci, or 440-ci.
Note(s): Used after January 1973 with six-cylinder and 318-ci and 340-ci powerplants. Used until December 18, 1973, in 1974 models.

Interchange Number: 6
ID Number(s): 3755900
Usage: Late 1974 Barracuda, Challenger, Charger, Coronet, Dart, Duster, Fury, Monaco, Newport, New Yorker, Satellite, and Valiant, all powerplants.
Note(s): Used after December 18, 1973.

Interchange Number: 7
ID Number(s): 1889100
Usage: 1966–72 Coronet, Fury, Polara, and Satellite with 225-ci six-cylinder and heavy-duty manual transmission.
Note(s): Used mostly in taxi and police cars.

Distributor

Engine size and output, transmission type, and in some cases, emission controls will have an effect on the distributor interchange. Distributors can be identified by the part number that is stamped on a tag or the body of the unit itself. There is also a date code on the tag, but it has little importance in the interchange process. Beginning in 1971, electronic ignition became available, which eliminated the points in the distributor. By 1973, all distributors were electronic.

Model Identification

Barracuda..*Interchange Number*
1968 318-ci, manual transmission.................................1

Distributors can be identified by a part number on a tag on the distributor body.

Belvedere, Charger, Coronet, and Satellite.....................Interchange Number

Interchange

Interchange Number: 1
ID Number(s): 2875342
Type: Single points
Usage: 1968 Barracuda, Belvedere, Charger, Coronet, Dart, Fury, Monaco, and Polara with 318-ci, all transmissions.

Interchange Number: 2
ID Number(s): 2875086 or IBS-4015
Type: Dual points
Usage: 1968 Barracuda, Dart with 340-ci and four-speed transmission.
Note(s): IBS-4015 made by Prestolite, other made by Chrysler.

Interchange Number: 3
ID Number(s): 2875105 or IBS-4015A
Type: Dual points
Usage: 1968 Barracuda, Dart with 340-ci and automatic transmission.
Note(s): IBS-4015A made by Prestolite, other made by Chrysler.

Interchange Number: 4
ID Number(s): 2875356
Type: Single
Usage: 1968 Barracuda, Belvedere, Charger, Coronet, Dart, Fury, Polara, and Monaco with 383-ci four-barrel and four-speed transmission.

Interchange Number: 5
ID Number(s): 2875358
Type: Single points
Usage: 1968 Barracuda, Belvedere, Charger, Coronet, Dart, Fury, Monaco, Polara, and Newport with 383-ci four-barrel and automatic transmission.

Interchange Number: 6
ID Number(s): 2875209
Type: Single points
Usage: 1968 Belvedere, Charger, Coronet, Chrysler 300, Fury, Monaco, Newport, and New Yorker with 440-ci high-performance (375 hp) and automatic transmission.

Interchange Number: 7
ID Number(s): 2875102 or IBS-4014
Type: Dual points
Usage: 1968 Belvedere, Charger, Coronet, Fury, Monaco, and Polara with 440-ci four-barrel high-performance (375 hp) with four-speed transmission.
Note(s): ID number IBS-4014 is made by Prestolite.

Interchange Number: 8
ID Number(s): 2875140 or IBS-4014A
Type: Single points
Usage: 1968–69 Belvedere, Charger, and Coronet with 426 Hemi, all transmissions.
Note(s): ID number IBS-4014A is made by Prestolite.

Interchange Number: 9
ID Number(s): 2875982 or IBS-4017A
Type: Dual points
Usage: 1969 Super Bee, Road Runner with 440-ci triple-two-barrel with automatic transmission.

Interchange Number: 10
ID Number(s): 2875981 or IBS-4017
Type: Dual points
Usage: 1969 Super Bee, Road Runner with 440-ci triple-two-barrel and manual transmission.

Interchange Number: 11
ID Number(s): 2875758
Type: Single points
Usage: 1969 Barracuda, Belvedere, Charger, Chrysler 300, Coronet, Dart, Fury, Monaco, Newport, New Yorker, and Polara with 440-ci high-performance (375 hp) four-barrel with automatic transmission.

Interchange Number: 12
ID Number(s): 2875772
Type: Dual points
Usage: 1969 Charger R/T, Charger 500, Coronet R/T, Daytona, GTX with 440-ci four-barrel and four-speed transmission.

Interchange Number: 13
ID Number(s): 2875731
Type: Single points
Usage: 1969 Belvedere, Charger, Coronet, Fury, Monaco, and Newport, with 383-ci four-barrel and automatic transmission.

Interchange Number: 14
ID Number(s): 2875750
Type: Single points
Usage: 1969 Belvedere, Charger, and Coronet with 383-ci four-barrel and four-speed transmission.

Interchange Number: 15
ID Number(s): 2875747
Type: Single points
Usage: 1969 Belvedere, Charger, Coronet, Fury, Monaco, Newport, and Polara with 383-ci two-barrel with automatic transmission.

Interchange Number: 16
ID Number(s): 2875846
Type: Dual points
Usage: 1969 Barracuda, Dart with 383-ci with automatic transmission.

Interchange Number: 17
ID Number(s): 2875715 or IBS-4106A
Type: Dual points
Usage: 1969 Barracuda, Dart with 383-ci and four-speed transmission.

Interchange Number: 18
ID Number(s): 2875779
Type: Single points
Usage: 1969 Barracuda, Dart with 340-ci with automatic transmission

Interchange Number: 19
ID Number(s): 2875782 or IBS-4015B
Type: Dual points
Usage: 1969 Barracuda, Dart with 340-ci with four-speed transmission.

Interchange Number: 20
ID Number(s): 2875796
Type: Single points
Usage: 1969 Barracuda, Belvedere, Charger, Coronet, Dart, Fury, Monaco, and Polara with 318-ci, all transmissions.

Interchange Number: 21
ID Number(s): 3438255
Type: Single points
Usage: 1970–71 Barracuda, Challenger, Charger, Coronet, Dart, Duster, Fury, Monaco, Polara, Satellite, and Valiant with 318-ci with all transmissions, except 1971 California cars with NOX emissions.

Interchange Number: 22
ID Number(s): 3438453
Type: Single points
Usage: 1971 Barracuda, Challenger, Charger, Coronet, Dart, Duster, Fury, Monaco, Polara, Satellite, and Valiant with 318-ci with NOX emissions.

Interchange Number: 23
ID Number(s): 3438317
Type: Dual points
Usage: 1970 Barracuda, Challenger, Dart, Duster with 340-ci and manual transmission.
Note(s): Interchange Number 28 will fit.

Interchange Number: 24
ID Number(s): 3438325
Type: Single points
Usage: 1970 Barracuda, Challenger, Dart, and Duster with 340-ci and automatic transmission.

Interchange Number: 25
ID Number(s): 3438521
Type: Dual points
Usage: 1970 AAR Cuda, Challenger T/A with 340-ci triple-two-barrel with four-speed transmission.

Interchange Number: 26
ID Number(s): 3438523
Type: Dual points
Usage: 1970 AAR Cuda, Challenger T/A with 340-ci triple-two-barrel and automatic transmission.

Interchange Number: 27
ID Number(s): 3438615
Type: Dual points
Usage: 1971 340-ci triple-two-barrel with four-speed transmission.

Interchange Number: 28
ID Number(s): 3438617
Type: Dual points
Usage: 1971 340-ci triple-two-barrel with automatic transmission.

Interchange Number: 29
ID Number(s): 3438522
Type: Dual points
Usage: 1971 Barracuda, Challenger, Charger, Dart, Duster, and Satellite with 340-ci and manual transmission.

Interchange Number: 30
ID Number(s): 3438517
Type: Single points
Usage: 1971 Barracuda, Challenger, Charger, Dart, Duster, and Satellite with 340-ci with automatic transmission.

Interchange Number: 31
ID Number(s): 3656151
Type: Electronic
Usage: 1971 Barracuda, Challenger, Charger, Dart, Duster, and Satellite with 340-ci with electronic ignition and manual transmission.

Interchange Number: 32
ID Number(s): 3438896
Type: Electronic
Usage: 1971 Barracuda, Challenger, Charger, Dart, Duster, and Satellite with 340-ci with electronic ignition and automatic transmission.

Interchange Number: 33
ID Number(s): 3438231
Type: Single points
Usage: 1970 Barracuda, Challenger, Charger, Coronet, Fury, Monaco, Newport, Polara, and Satellite with 383-ci two-barrel, all transmissions.

Interchange Number: 34
ID Number(s): 3438534
Type: Single points
Usage: 1971 Barracuda, Challenger, Charger, Coronet, Fury, Monaco, Newport, Polara, and Satellite with 383-ci two-barrel, all transmissions, except cars with NOX emissions.

Interchange Number: 35
ID Number(s): 3438544
Type: Single points
Usage: 1971 Barracuda, Challenger, Charger, Coronet, Fury, Monaco, Newport, Polara, and Satellite with 383-ci two-barrel, all transmissions with NOX emissions.

Interchange Number: 36
ID Number(s): 3438233 or 3438433
Type: Single points
Usage: 1970 Barracuda, Challenger, Charger, Coronet, Fury, Monaco, Newport, Polara, and Satellite with 383-ci four-barrel, all transmissions.

Interchange Number: 37
ID Number(s): 3438690
Type: Single points
Usage: 1971 Barracuda, Challenger, Charger, Coronet, Fury, Monaco, Newport, Polara, and Satellite with 383-ci four-barrel, all transmissions.

Interchange Number: 38
ID Number(s): 2875987
Type: Dual points

Usage: 1970–71 Barracuda, Challenger, Charger, Coronet, and Satellite with 426 Hemi with four-speed transmission.

Interchange Number: 39
ID Number(s): 2875989
Type: Dual points
Usage: 1970 Barracuda, Challenger, Charger, Coronet, and Satellite with 426 Hemi with automatic transmission.

Interchange Number: 40
ID Number(s): 3438579
Type: Dual points
Usage: 1971 Barracuda, Challenger, Charger, Coronet, and Satellite with 426 Hemi with automatic transmission.

Interchange Number: 41
ID Number(s): 3438891
Type: Electronic
Usage: 1971 Barracuda, Challenger, Charger, Coronet, and Satellite with 426 Hemi with automatic transmission and electronic ignition.

Interchange Number: 42
ID Number(s): 3438893
Type: Electronic
Usage: 1971 Barracuda, Challenger, Charger, Coronet, and Satellite with 426 Hemi with automatic transmission and electronic ignition.

Interchange Number: 43
ID Number(s): 3438222
Type: Single points
Usage: 1970 Barracuda, Challenger, Charger, Coronet, Fury, Monaco, Newport, New Yorker, Polara, and Satellite with 440-ci four-barrel high-performance, all transmissions.

Interchange Number: 44
ID Number(s): 3438694
Type: Single points
Usage: 1971 Charger, Coronet, Fury, Monaco, Newport, New Yorker, Polara, and Satellite with 440-ci four-barrel high-performance, all transmissions.

Interchange Number: 45
ID Number(s): 3438694
Type: Dual points
Usage: Early 1970 Barracuda, Challenger, Charger, Coronet, Fury Satellite with 440-ci triple-two-barrel with four-speed transmission.
Note(s): Used until January 1, 1970.

Interchange Number: 46
ID Number(s): 3438348
Type: Dual points
Usage: Early 1970 Barracuda, Challenger, Charger, Coronet, Fury, and Satellite with 440-ci triple-two-barrel with automatic transmission.
Note(s): Used until January 1, 1970.

Interchange Number: 47
ID Number(s): 2875982
Type: Dual points
Usage: Late 1970 Barracuda, Challenger, Charger, Coronet, Fury, Satellite with 440-ci triple-two-barrel with four-speed transmission.
Note(s): Used after January 1, 1970.

Interchange Number: 48
ID Number(s): 3438349
Type: Dual points
Usage: Late 1970 Barracuda, Challenger, Charger, Coronet, Fury, and Satellite with 440-ci triple-two-barrel with automatic transmission.
Note(s): Used after January 1, 1970.

Interchange Number: 49
ID Number(s): 3438577
Type: Dual points
Usage: 1971 Barracuda, Challenger; 1971–72 Charger, Satellite with 440-ci triple-two-barrel, all transmissions.

Interchange Number: 50
ID Number(s): 3656272
Type: Single points

Usage: 1972 Barracuda, Challenger, Charger, Coronet, Dart, Duster, Satellite, and Valiant with 318-ci with manual transmission, except with California emissions or electronic ignition.

Interchange Number: 51
ID Number(s): 3656390
Type: Single points
Usage: 1972 Barracuda, Challenger, Charger, Coronet, Dart, Duster, Fury, Monaco, Polara, Satellite, and Valiant with 318-ci with automatic transmission, except with California emissions or electronic ignition.

Interchange Number: 52
ID Number(s): 3656275
Type: Single points
Usage: 1972 Barracuda, Challenger, Charger, Coronet, Dart, Duster, Fury, Monaco, Polara, Satellite, and Valiant with 318-ci *with* California emissions, but *without* electronic ignition. Used with all transmission types.

Interchange Number: 53
ID Number(s): 3656429
Type: Electronic
Usage: 1972 Barracuda, Challenger, Charger, Coronet, Dart, Duster, Satellite, and Valiant with 318-ci with manual transmission and electronic ignition.

Interchange Number: 54
ID Number(s): 3656587
Type: Electronic
Usage: 1972 Barracuda, Challenger, Charger, Coronet, Dart, Duster, Fury, Monaco, Polara, Satellite, and Valiant with 318-ci with automatic transmission *without* California emissions.

Interchange Number: 55
ID Number(s): 3656435
Type: Electronic
Usage: 1972 Barracuda, Challenger, Charger, Coronet, Dart, Duster, Fury, Monaco, Polara, Satellite, and Valiant with 318-ci *with* California emissions. Used with both manual and automatic transmissions.

Interchange Number: 56
ID Number(s): 3656278
Type: Electronic
Usage: 1972 Barracuda, Challenger, Charger, Dart, Duster, and Satellite with 340-ci with electronic ignition. Used with both manual and automatic transmissions.

Interchange Number: 57
ID Number(s): 3656283
Type: Dual points
Usage: 1972 Charger, Dart, Duster, and Satellite with 340-ci without electronic ignition. Used with manual transmissions only.

Interchange Number: 58
ID Number(s): 3656335
Type: Electronic
Usage: 1972 Charger, Coronet, and Satellite with 400-ci four-barrel with manual transmission and electronic ignition; 1972 Charger, Coronet, Fury, Monaco, Newport, and Polara with 400-ci four-barrel with automatic transmission, electronic ignition, and California emissions or 400-ci two-barrel with all transmissions and California emissions.

Interchange Number: 59
ID Number(s): 3656329
Type: Single points
Usage: 1972 Charger, Coronet, and Satellite with 400-ci four-barrel with manual transmission; early 1972 Charger, Coronet, Fury, Monaco, Newport, and Polara with 400-ci two-barrel with both manual and automatic transmissions, but without California emissions; 1972 Fury, Monaco, and Polara with 400-ci four-barrel *with* California emissions.
Note(s): Used all year long on 400-ci four-barrel powerplants. Up to November 10, 1971, on cars with 400-ci two-barrel.

Interchange Number: 60
ID Number(s): 3656338
Type: Electronic

Usage: 1972 Charger, Coronet, and Satellite with 400-ci four-barrel with automatic transmission and electronic ignition, except cars with California emissions.

Interchange Number: 61
ID Number(s): 3656593
Type: Electronic
Usage: Late 1972 Charger, Coronet, and Satellite with 400-ci two-barrel with all transmissions and electronic ignition, except cars with California emissions.
Note(s): Used after November 10, 1971.

Interchange Number: 62
ID Number(s): 3656596
Type: Electronic
Usage: 1972 Charger, Coronet, and Satellite with 400-ci four-barrel with electronic ignition except cars with California emissions. Used with both manual and automatic transmissions.

Interchange Number: 63
ID Number(s): 3656353
Type: Electronic
Usage: 1972 Charger, Satellite with 440-ci triple-two-barrel, all transmissions.

Interchange Number: 64
ID Number(s): 3656347
Type: Electronic
Usage: 1972 Charger, Coronet, and Satellite with 440-ci four-barrel with manual transmission and electronic ignition; 1972 Charger, Coronet, and Satellite with 440-ci four-barrel with automatic transmission, electronic ignition, and California emissions.

Interchange Number: 65
ID Number(s): 3656341
Type: Electronic
Usage: 1972 Charger, Coronet, Fury, Monaco, Newport, New Yorker, and Satellite with 440-ci four-barrel with automatic transmission and electronic ignition, except cars with California emissions.
Note(s): Standard unit in full-size models.

Interchange Number: 66
ID Number(s): 3656763
Type: Electronic
Usage: 1972–74 Barracuda, Challenger, Charger, Coronet, Dart, Duster, Fury, Monaco, Satellite, and Valiant with 318-ci, all transmissions, except 1974 Road Runner with manual transmission.

Interchange Number: 67
ID Number(s): 3656771
Type: Electronic
Usage: 1973 Barracuda, Challenger, Charger, Dart, Duster, and Satellite with 340-ci four-barrel with all transmissions.

Interchange Number: 68
ID Number(s): 3656791
Type: Electronic
Usage: 1973 Charger, Coronet, Fury, Monaco, Newport, and Satellite with 400-ci two-barrel with all transmissions.

Interchange Number: 69
ID Number(s): 3755308
Type: Electronic
Usage: 1973 Charger, Coronet, and Satellite with 400-ci four-barrel with manual transmissions.

Interchange Number: 70
ID Number(s): 3652802
Type: Electronic
Usage: 1973 Charger, Coronet, Fury, Monaco, and Satellite with 400-ci four-barrel with automatic transmission.

Interchange Number: 71
ID Number(s): 3755157
Type: Electronic
Usage: 1973 Charger, Coronet, Fury, Monaco, Newport, New Yorker, and Satellite with 440-ci two-barrel with all transmissions.

Interchange Number: 72
ID Number(s): 3755821
Type: Electronic
Usage: 1974 Road Runner with 318-ci and manual transmission.

Interchange Number: 73
ID Number(s): 3755841
Type: Electronic
Usage: 1974 Charger, Coronet, Fury, Monaco, Newport, and Satellite with 360-ci two-barrel with all transmissions.

Interchange Number: 74
ID Number(s): 3755486
Type: Electronic
Usage: 1974 Barracuda, Challenger, Charger, Coronet, Dart, Duster, and Satellite with 360-ci four-barrel high-performance (245 hp) with all transmissions.
Note(s): Do not confuse with Interchange Number 75. They are not the same and performance will suffer.

Interchange Number: 75
ID Number(s): 3755475
Type: Electronic
Usage: 1974 Charger, Coronet, Fury, Monaco, Newport, and Satellite with 360-ci four-barrel (200 hp) with all transmissions, except high-performance.

Interchange Number: 76
ID Number(s): 3755681
Type: Electronic
Usage: 1974 Charger, Coronet, Fury, Monaco, Newport, and Satellite with 400-ci two-barrel or 400-ci four-barrel *without* high-performance. Used with all transmissions.

Interchange Number: 77
ID Number(s): 3755512
Type: Electronic
Usage: 1974 Charger, Satellite with 400-ci four-barrel high-performance (250 hp) with automatic transmission.
Note(s): Do not confuse with Interchange Number 76. Performance will suffer.

Interchange Number: 78
ID Number(s): 3755508
Type: Electronic
Usage: 1974 Charger, Satellite with 400-ci four-barrel high-performance (250 hp) with manual transmission; 1974 Fury, Monaco with 400-ci four-barrel high-performance with California emissions.
Note(s): Do not confuse with Interchange Number 76. Performance will suffer.

Interchange Number: 79
ID Number(s): 3755518
Type: Electronic
Usage: 1972 Charger, Fury, Monaco, Newport, New Yorker, and Satellite with 440-ci four-barrel high-performance with automatic transmission.
Note(s): Watch full-size models with California emissions, the distributor is not the same.

Interchange Number: 80
ID Number(s): 2875352
Type: Single points
Usage: 1968 Belvedere, Charger, Coronet, Fury, Monaco, Newport, and Polara with 383-ci two-barrel and manual transmission.

Interchange Number: 81
ID Number(s): 2875354
Type: Single points
Usage: 1968 Belvedere, Charger, Coronet, Fury, Monaco, Newport, and Polara with 383-ci two-barrel and automatic transmission.

Ignition Coils

Simple interchange here because only one coil was used from 1964–74. Listed as part number 2495531, it as used on all engines from 1964–74 with one exception—the 1964 and 1965 models with a 426 Hemi, which used a different coil. Two identification numbers were used. Those coils manufactured by Prestolite used the identification number of 2444242, while those made by Essex used an identification number of 2444211. There is a slight difference in their resistance, but the two should be interchangeable.

Alternators

Alternators are interchanged by their output rating and their identification number. This number is stamped on the housing. All interchanges are based on the unit without the pulley on 1968 and 1969 models, and the pulley must be swapped to fit your particular application. For 1970 and later models, the interchange includes the pulley. Model or body style have no effect on the interchange, but engine size does. Note higher-rated alternators where available as optional equipment. You can interchange to an alternator that has more output, but you should not use an alternator with a lower rating than your original unit.

Model Identification

Barracuda, Belvedere, Charger, Coronet,
Dart, Duster, Demon, and Satellite ....Interchange Number

1968
  37 amps 1
  46 amps 2
  60 amps 3
1969
  37 amps 1
  46 amps 2
  60 amps 4
1970–71, 37 amps, single-groove pulley
  2 1/2-in pulley 5
  3-in pulley 13
1970–71, 37 amps, dual-groove pulley 8
1970–71, 50 amps
  single-groove pulley
    2 1/2-in pulley 6
    3-in pulley 14
  dual-groove pulley
    2 1/2-in pulley 9
    3-in pulley 10
1970–71, 60 amps
  single-groove pulley 7
  dual-groove pulley
    2 1/2-in pulley 11
    3-in pulley 12
1972, 41 amps, except California cars
  single-groove pulley
    2 1/2-in pulley 15
    2 1/2-in pulley 26
1972, 41 amps, California cars only
  single-groove pulley
    2 1/2-in pulley 29
    2 1/2-in pulley 33
1972, 50 amps, except California cars
  single-groove pulley
    2 1/2-in pulley 16
    2.65-in pulley 27
  dual-groove pulley
    2 3/4-in pulley 24
    2 1/2-in pulley 17
1972, 50 amps, California cars, single-groove pulley
    2 1/2-in pulley 30
    2.65-in pulley 34
1972, 60 amps, except California cars
  single-groove pulley
    2 3/4-in pulley 38
    2.65-in pulley 28
  dual-groove pulley
    2 3/4-in pulley 19, 21, 23, 25
    3-in pulley 20, 22
1972, 60 amps, California Cars, single-groove pulley

Typical coil. Note the ID number on this reproduction from Year One.
Year One

    2 1/2-in pulley 31, 32
    2.65-in pulley 35
1973, 41 amps, single-groove pulley
  2-in pulley
    early 15
    ate 45
  2 3/4-in pulley 26
1973, 50 amps, single-groove pulley
  2-in pulley
    early 16
    late 44
  2 3/4-in pulley
    early 27
    late 42
1973, 50 amps, dual-groove pulley
  2 1/2-in pulley
    early 24
    late 41
1973, 60 amps, single-groove pulley
  2 1/2-in pulley
    early 36, 38
    late 47
  2.65-in pulley
    early 28
    late 43
1973, 60 amps, dual-groove pulley
  2 3/4-in pulley
    early 19, 21, 23, 25
    late 48, 40
1973, 65 amps
  single-groove, 2 1/2-in pulley 37
  dual-groove, 2 3/4-in pulley 48, 39
1974, 41 amps 45
1974, 50 amps
  single-groove pulley 44
  dual-groove pulley 41
1974, 60 amps, dual-groove pulley 40
1974, 65 amps
  single-groove pulley 37
  dual-groove pulley 39
1974, 86 amps 46

Interchange

Interchange Number: 1
Part Number(s): 2642635
Output: 37 amps
Usage: 1968–69 Barracuda, Belvedere, Charger, Coronet, Chrysler 300, Dart, Fury, Monaco, Newport, New Yorker, Polara, and Valiant without air-conditioning, trailer, or heavy-duty alternator packages.

Interchange Number: 2
Part Number(s): 2098535
Output: 46 amps
Usage: 1968–69 Barracuda, Belvedere, Charger, Coronet, Chrysler 300, Dart, Fury, Monaco, Newport, New Yorker, Polara, and Valiant with air conditioning or heavy-duty alternator package.

Interchange Number: 3
Part Number(s): 3000011
Output: 60 amps
Usage: 1968 Barracuda, Belvedere, Charger, Coronet, Chrysler 300, Fury, Monaco, Newport, New Yorker, Polara, and Valiant with air conditioning and heavy-duty alternator; 1968 Fury, Monaco, and Polara with trailer package; 1968 Imperial with air conditioning.

Interchange Number: 4
Part Number(s): 2875439
Output: 60 amps
Usage: 1969 Belvedere, Charger, Coronet, Fury, Monaco, and Polara with heavy-duty alternator.

Interchange Number: 5
Part Number(s): 3438172
Output: 37 amps
Usage: 1970–71 Barracuda, Challenger, Charger, Coronet, Chrysler 300, Fury, Monaco, Newport, New Yorker, Polara, Satellite, and Valiant without air conditioning, with 2 1/2-in single-groove pulley.
Note(s): Interchange Number 6 will fit.

Interchange Number: 6
Part Number(s): 3438173
Output: 50 amps
Usage: 1970–71 Barracuda, Challenger, Charger, Coronet, Chrysler 300, Fury, Newport, New Yorker, Polara, Satellite, and Valiant without air conditioning or power steering.

Interchange Number: 7
Part Number(s): 3438174
Output: 60 amps
Usage: 1970–71 Barracuda, Challenger, Charger, Coronet, Chrysler 300, Fury, Newport, New Yorker, Polara, Satellite, and Valiant with heavy-duty alternator but without air conditioning or power steering.

Interchange Number: 8
Part Number(s): 3438176
Output: 37 amps
Usage: 1970–71 Barracuda, Challenger, Charger, Coronet, Chrysler 300, Fury, Newport, New Yorker, Polara, Satellite, and Valiant with dual-groove pulley.
Note(s): Interchange Number 9 will fit.

Interchange Number: 9
Part Number(s): 3438177
Output: 50 amps
Usage: 1970–71 Barracuda, Challenger, Charger, Coronet, Chrysler 300, Fury, Newport, New Yorker, Polara, Satellite, and Valiant with dual-groove pulley.

Interchange Number: 10
Part Number(s): 3438178
Output: 50 amps
Usage: 1970–71 Barracuda, Challenger, Charger, Coronet, Chrysler 300, Fury, Newport, New Yorker, Polara, Satellite, and Valiant with dual-groove pulley used with air conditioning.

Interchange Number: 11
Part Number(s): 3438179
Output: 60 amps
Usage: 1970–71 Barracuda, Challenger, Charger, Coronet, Chrysler 300, Fury, Newport, New Yorker, Polara, Satellite, and Valiant with 2 1/2-in dual-groove pulley.

Interchange Number: 12
Part Number(s): 3438180
Output: 60 amps
Usage: 1970–71 Barracuda, Challenger, Charger, Coronet, Chrysler 300, Fury, Newport, New Yorker, Polara, Satellite, and Valiant with 3-in dual-groove pulley.

Interchange Number: 13
Part Number(s): 3438780
Output: 37 amps
Usage: 1970–71 Barracuda, Challenger, Charger, Coronet, Chrysler 300, Fury, Newport, New Yorker, Polara, Satellite, and Valiant with 3-in single-groove pulley.

Interchange Number: 14
Part Number(s): 3438782
Output: 60 amps
Usage: 1970–71 Barracuda, Challenger, Charger, Coronet, Chrysler 300, Fury, Newport, New Yorker, Polara, Satellite, and Valiant with 3-in dual-groove pulley.

Interchange Number: 15
Part Number(s): 3438804
Output: 41 amps
Usage: 1972–73 Barracuda, Challenger, Charger, Coronet, Fury, Monaco, Newport, New Yorker, Polara, Satellite, and Valiant with 2 1/2-in single-groove pulley, except California cars.
Note(s): Interchange Number 16 will fit.

Interchange Number: 16
Part Number(s): 3438806
Output: 50 amps
Usage: 1972–73 Barracuda, Challenger, Charger, Coronet, Fury, Monaco, Newport, New Yorker, Polara, Satellite, and Valiant with 2 1/2-in single-groove pulley, except California cars.

Interchange Number: 17
Part Number(s): 3438456
Output: 60 amps
Usage: 1972 Barracuda, Challenger, Charger, Coronet, Fury, Monaco, Newport, New Yorker, Polara, Satellite, and Valiant, with 2 1/2-in single-groove pulley, except California cars.

Interchange Number: 18
Part Number(s): 3438811
Output: 50 amps
Usage: 1972 Barracuda, Challenger, Charger, Coronet, Fury, Monaco, Newport, New Yorker, Polara, Satellite, and Valiant with 3-in dual-groove pulley, except California cars.

Interchange Number: 19
Part Number(s): 3438812
Output: 60 amps
Usage: 1972–73 Barracuda, Challenger, Charger, Coronet, Fury, Monaco, Newport, New Yorker, Polara, Satellite, and Valiant with 2 3/4-in dual-groove pulley, except California cars.

Interchange Number: 20
Part Number(s): 3438813
Output: 60 amps
Usage: 1972 Barracuda, Challenger, Charger, Coronet, Fury, Monaco, Newport, New Yorker, Polara, Satellite, and Valiant with 3-in dual-groove pulley, except California cars.

Interchange Number: 21
Part Number(s): 3656455
Output: 60 amps
Usage: 1972–73 Barracuda, Challenger, Charger, Coronet, Fury, Monaco, Newport, New Yorker, Polara, Satellite, and Valiant with 2 3/4-in dual-groove pulley, except California cars.

Interchange Number: 22
Part Number(s): 3656459
Output: 60 amps
Usage: 1972 Barracuda, Challenger, Charger, Coronet, Fury, Monaco, Newport, New Yorker, Polara, Satellite, and Valiant with 3-in dual-groove pulley, except California cars.

Interchange Number: 23
  Part Number(s): 3656570
  Output: 60 amps
  Usage: 1972–early 1973 Barracuda, Challenger, Charger, Coronet, Fury, Monaco, Newport, New Yorker, Polara, Satellite, and Valiant with 2 3/4-in dual-groove pulley, except California cars.

Interchange Number: 24
  Part Number(s): 3656711
  Output: 50 amps
  Usage: 1972–early 1973 Barracuda, Challenger, Charger, Coronet, Fury, Monaco, Newport, New Yorker, Polara, Satellite, and Valiant with 2 3/4-in dual-groove pulley, except California cars.

Interchange Number: 25
  Part Number(s): 3656713
  Output: 60 amps
  Usage: 1972–early 1973 Barracuda, Challenger, Charger, Coronet, Fury, Monaco, Newport, New Yorker, Polara, Satellite, and Valiant with 2 3/4-in dual-groove pulley, except California cars.

Interchange Number: 26
  Part Number(s): 3656645
  Output: 41 amps
  Usage: 1972–early 1973 Barracuda, Challenger, Charger, Coronet, Fury, Monaco, Newport, New Yorker, Polara, Satellite, and Valiant with 2 3/4-in single-groove pulley, except California cars.

Interchange Number: 27
  Part Number(s): 3656614
  Output: 50 amps
  Usage: 1972–early 1973 Barracuda, Challenger, Charger, Coronet, Fury, Monaco, Newport, New Yorker, Polara, Satellite, and Valiant with 2.65-in single-groove pulley, except California cars.

Interchange Number: 28
  Part Number(s): 3656615
  Output: 60 amps
  Usage: 1972–early 1973 Barracuda, Challenger, Charger, Coronet, Fury, Monaco, Newport, New Yorker, Polara, Satellite, and Valiant with 2.65-in single-groove pulley, except California cars.

Interchange Number: 29
  Part Number(s): 3656217
  Output: 41 amps
  Usage: 1972 Barracuda, Challenger, Charger, Coronet, Dart, Duster, Fury, Monaco, Newport, New Yorker, Polara, Satellite, and Valiant sold in California. Uses a 2 1/2-in single-groove pulley.

Interchange Number: 30
  Part Number(s): 3656218
  Output: 50 amps
  Usage: 1972 Barracuda, Challenger, Charger, Coronet, Dart, Duster, Fury, Monaco, Newport, New Yorker, Polara, Satellite, and Valiant sold in California. Uses a 2 1/2-in single-groove pulley.

Interchange Number: 31
  Part Number(s): 3656219
  Output: 60 amps
  Usage: 1972 Barracuda, Challenger, Charger, Coronet, Dart, Duster, Fury, Monaco, Newport, New Yorker, Polara, Satellite, and Valiant sold in California. Uses a 2 1/2-in single-groove pulley.

Interchange Number: 32
  Part Number(s): 3656471
  Output: 60 amps
  Usage: 1972 Barracuda, Challenger, Charger, Coronet, Dart, Duster, Fury, Monaco, Newport, New Yorker, Polara, Satellite, and Valiant sold in California. Uses a 2 1/2-in single-groove pulley.

Interchange Number: 33
  Part Number(s): 3656617
  Output: 41 amps
  Usage: 1972 Barracuda, Challenger, Charger, Coronet, Dart, Duster, Fury, Monaco, Newport, New Yorker, Polara, Satellite, and Valiant sold in California. Uses a 2 3/4-in single-groove pulley.

Interchange Number: 34
  Part Number(s): 3656618
  Output: 50 amps
  Usage: 1972 Barracuda, Challenger, Charger, Coronet, Dart, Duster, Fury, Monaco, Newport, New Yorker, Polara, Satellite, and Valiant sold in California. Uses a 2.65-in single-groove pulley.

Interchange Number: 35
  Part Number(s): 3656671
  Output: 60 amps
  Usage: 1972 Barracuda, Challenger, Charger, Coronet, Dart, Duster, Fury, Monaco, Newport, New Yorker, Polara, Satellite, and Valiant sold in California. Uses a 2.65-in single-groove pulley.

Interchange Number: 36
  Part Number(s): 3438807
  Output: 60 amps
  Usage: 1973 Barracuda, Challenger, Charger, Coronet, Dart, Duster, Fury, Monaco, Newport, New Yorker, Polara, Satellite, and Valiant. Uses a 2 1/2-in single-groove pulley.

Interchange Number: 37
  Part Number(s): 3755192
  Output: 65 amps
  Usage: 1973–74 Barracuda, Challenger, Charger, Coronet, Dart, Duster, Fury, Monaco, Newport, New Yorker, Polara, Satellite, and Valiant. Uses a 2 1/2-in single-groove pulley.

Interchange Number: 38
  Part Number(s): 3656455
  Output: 60 amps
  Usage: 1972–73 Barracuda, Challenger, Charger, Coronet, Dart, Duster, Fury, Monaco, Newport, New Yorker, Polara, Satellite, and Valiant. Uses a 2 3/4-in single-groove pulley.

Interchange Number: 39
  Part Number(s): 3755191, 3755193
  Output: 65 amps
  Usage: 1973–74 Barracuda, Challenger, Charger, Coronet, Dart, Duster, Fury, Monaco, Newport, New Yorker, Polara, Satellite, and Valiant. Uses a 2 3/4-in single-groove pulley.

Interchange Number: 40
  Part Number(s): 3755413
  Output: 60 amps
  Usage: Late 1973–74 Barracuda, Challenger, Charger, Coronet, Dart, Duster, Fury, Monaco, Newport, New Yorker, Polara, Satellite, and Valiant. Uses a 2 3/4-in dual-groove pulley.

Interchange Number: 41
  Part Number(s): 3755411
  Output: 50 amps
  Usage: Late 1973–74 Barracuda, Challenger, Charger, Coronet, Dart, Duster, Fury, Monaco, Newport, New Yorker, Polara, Satellite, and Valiant. Uses a 2 3/4-in dual-groove pulley.

Interchange Number: 42
  Part Number(s): 3755414
  Output: 50 amps
  Usage: Late 1973 Barracuda, Challenger, Charger, Coronet, Dart, Duster, Fury, Monaco, Newport, New Yorker, Polara, Satellite, and Valiant. Uses a 2.65-in single-groove pulley.

Interchange Number: 43
  Part Number(s): 3755405
  Output: 60 amps
  Usage: Late 1973 Barracuda, Challenger, Charger, Coronet, Dart, Duster, Fury, Monaco, Newport, New Yorker, Polara, Satellite, and Valiant. Uses a 2.65-in single-groove pulley.

Interchange Number: 44
  Part Number(s): 3755406
  Output: 50 amps

Usage: Late 1973–74 Barracuda, Challenger, Charger, Coronet, Dart, Duster, Fury, Monaco, Newport, New Yorker, Polara, Satellite, and Valiant. Uses a 2 1/2-in single-groove pulley.

Interchange Number: 45
Part Number(s): 3755404
Output: 41 amps
Usage: Late 1973–74 Barracuda, Challenger, Charger, Coronet, Dart, Duster, Fury, Monaco, Newport, New Yorker, Polara, Satellite, and Valiant. Uses a 2 1/2-in single-groove pulley.

Interchange Number: 46
Part Number(s): 3755585
Output: 86 amps
Usage: 1974 Barracuda, Challenger, Charger, Coronet, Dart, Duster, Fury, Monaco, Newport, New Yorker, Polara, Satellite, and Valiant. Dual-groove pulley only.

Interchange Number: 47
Part Number(s): 3755407
Output: 60 amps
Usage: Late 1973 Barracuda, Challenger, Charger, Coronet, Dart, Duster, Fury, Monaco, Newport, New Yorker, Polara, Satellite, and Valiant. Uses a 2 1/2-in single-groove pulley.

Interchange Number: 48
Part Number(s): 3755190
Output: 65 amps
Usage: Late 1973 Barracuda, Challenger, Charger, Coronet, Dart, Duster, Fury, Monaco, Newport, New Yorker, Polara, Satellite, and Valiant. Uses a 2 3/4-in dual-groove pulley.

Battery Trays
Model Identification
Barracuda..Interchange Number
1968–69 1
1970–72 4
1973 6
1974 8

Belvedere, Charger, Coronet,
    and Satellite...Interchange Number
1968–69 1
1970–72 4
1973–74 7

Challenger...Interchange Number
1970–72 4
1973 6
1974 8

Dart, Duster, Demon, and Valiant ....Interchange Number
1968–69 1
1970–71 3
1972–74 5

Interchange
Interchange Number: 1
Part Number(s): 2768366
Usage: 1967–69 Barracuda, Dart, and Valiant, all body styles and models.

Interchange Number: 2
Part Number(s): 2530994
Usage: 1966–69 Belvedere, Charger, and Coronet, all body styles and models.

Interchange Number: 3
Part Number(s): 3404432
Usage: 1970–71 Dart, Duster, and Valiant, all body styles and models.

Interchange Number: 4
Part Number(s): 3404436
Usage: 1970–72 Barracuda, Challenger, Charger, Coronet, Satellite, all body styles and models.

Interchange Number: 5
Part Number(s): 3642334
Usage: 1972–74 Dart, Duster, and Valiant, all body styles and models.

Interchange Number: 6
Part Number(s): 2925322
Usage: 1973 Barracuda, Challenger, all models.

Interchange Number: 7
Part Number(s): 3642970
Usage: 1973–74 Charger, Coronet, and Satellite, all body styles and models.

Interchange Number: 8
Part Number(s): 3726551
Usage: 1974 Barracuda, Challenger, all models.

Windshield-Wiper Motors
Things that will affect the interchange are the number of wiper-blade speeds, model, and model year. Chrysler products used a single, a two-speed, and variable-speed wiper motors. Wiper motors can be identified by a number that is stamped into the housing. This number is sometimes hidden under a decal.

Model Identification
Barracuda..Interchange Number
1968
    two-speed 2
    variable-speed 1
1969
    two-speed 4
    variable-speed 3
1970–71
    two-speed 5
    variable-speed 6
1972
    two-speed
        early 9
        late 12
    variable-speed
        early 10
        late 13
1973
    two-speed
        early 12
        late 16
    variable-speed 17
1974
    two-speed 19
    variable-speed 20

Belvedere, Charger, Coronet,
    and Satellite...Interchange Number
1968
    two-speed 2
    three-speed 1
1969
    two-speed 4
    variable-speed 3
1970–71
    two-speed 5
    variable-speed 6
1972
    two-speed
        early 9
        late 12
    variable-speed
        early 10
        late 13
1973
    two-speed
        early 12
        late 16
    variable-speed 17
1974
    two-speed 19
    variable-speed 20

Interchange

Interchange Number: 1
ID/Part Number(s): 300114
Type: Variable-speed
Usage: 1968 Barracuda, Dart, and Valiant, all body styles and models; 1968 Belvedere, Charger, and Coronet with three-speed wipers.

Interchange Number: 2
ID/Part Number(s): 2822252
Type: Two-speed
Usage: 1968 Barracuda, Belvedere, Charger, Coronet, Dart, and Valiant, all body styles and models except with 426 Hemi.

Interchange Number: 3
ID/Part Number(s): 2983116
Type: Variable-speed/three-speed
Usage: 1969 Barracuda; 1969–71 Dart, Valiant; 1970–71 Duster with variable-speed wipers; 1969–70 Belvedere, Charger, and Coronet with three-speed wipers.

Interchange Number: 4
ID/Part Number(s): 2777090
Type: Two-speed
Usage: 1969 Barracuda; 1969–70 Belvedere, Charger, and Coronet, all body styles and models except with 426 Hemi; 1970–71 Dart, Duster, and Valiant; 1970 Challenger, all body styles and models.

Interchange Number: 5
ID/Part Number(s): 2926929
Type: Two-speed
Usage: 1970–71 Barracuda, Challenger; 1971 Charger, Coronet, and Satellite, all models and body styles, except with fresh-air hood.

Wiper motors can be identified by a number stamped into the case.

Interchange Number: 6
ID/Part Number(s): 3431077
Type: Variable-speed
Usage: 1970–71 Barracuda, Challenger; 1971 Charger, Coronet, and Satellite, all models and body styles.

Interchange Number: 7
ID/Part Number(s): 3431531
Type: Two-speed
Usage: Early 1972 Dart, Duster, and Valiant, all models and body styles.
Note(s): Used up to around June 5, 1972.

Interchange Number: 8
ID/Part Number(s): 3431532
Type: Variable-speed
Usage: 1972 Dart, Duster, and Valiant, all models and body styles.

Interchange Number: 9
ID/Part Number(s): 3431533
Type: Two-speed
Usage: Early 1972 Barracuda, Challenger, Charger, Coronet, Fury, Monaco, Newport, New Yorker, Satellite, all models and body styles.
Note(s): Used up to around June 5, 1972.

Interchange Number: 10
ID/Part Number(s): 3431534
Type: Variable-speed
Usage: Early 1972 Barracuda, Challenger, Charger, Coronet, Satellite, all models and body styles.
Note(s): Used until around September 1, 1971.

Interchange Number: 11
ID/Part Number(s): 3431605
Type: Two-speed
Usage: Late 1972–early 1973 Dart, Duster, and Valiant, all models and body styles.
Note(s): Used after June 5, 1972, to approximately February 1, 1973.

Interchange Number: 12
ID/Part Number(s): 3431606
Type: Two-speed
Usage: Late 1972–Early 1973 Barracuda, Challenger, Charger, Coronet, Fury, Monaco, Newport, New Yorker, Polara, and Satellite, all body styles and models.
Note(s): Used from approximately June 2, 1972, to February 1, 1973.

Interchange Number: 13
ID/Part Number(s): 3431624
Type: Variable-speed
Usage: Late 1972 Barracuda, Challenger, Charger, Coronet, Satellite, all body styles and models.
Note(s): Used after around September 1, 1971.

Interchange Number: 14
ID/Part Number(s): 3431730
Type: Two-speed
Usage: Late 1973–74 Dart, Duster, and Valiant, all models and body styles.

Interchange Number: 15
    ID/Part Number(s): 3620877
    Type: Variable-speed
    Usage: 1973 Dart, Duster, and Valiant, all models and body styles.

Interchange Number: 16
    ID/Part Number(s): 3431718
    Type: Two-speed
    Usage: Late 1973 Barracuda, Challenger, Charger, Coronet, Satellite, all models and body styles.
    Note(s): Used after approximately February 1, 1973.

Interchange Number: 17
    ID/Part Number(s): 3431665
    Type: Variable-speed
    Usage: 1973 Barracuda, Challenger, Charger, Coronet, Satellite.

Interchange Number: 18
    ID/Part Number(s): 3431905
    Type: three-speed
    Usage: 1974 Dart, Duster, and Valiant, all models and body styles.

Interchange Number: 19
    ID/Part Number(s): 3431790
    Type: Two-speed
    Usage: 1974 Barracuda, Challenger, Charger, Coronet, Fury, Monaco, Newport, New Yorker, Satellite, all models and body styles.

Interchange Number: 20
    ID/Part Number(s): 3431790
    Type: three-speed
    Usage: 1974 Barracuda, Challenger, Charger, Coronet, Satellite, all models and body styles.

Wiper-Blade Arms

In most lines, the body style will not affect the interchange. The exception is the 1968–70 B-body convertibles, which used a different arm than those used on coupes and hardtops. Another thing to watch for when interchanging is the arm manufacturer. Both Anco and Trico arms were used in the same model year. To identify the arm, look for the company name engraved on the arm. Also, on some models the arm will fit either side, while on others the arm is unique to each side and will not swap positions.

Model Identification

Interchange

Interchange Number: 1
    Part Number(s): 2829951
    Usage: 1968–69 Barracuda, Dart, and Valiant, all models and body styles.
    Note(s): Fits either side.

Interchange Number: 2
    Part Number(s): 2822999
    Usage: 1968–70 Belvedere, Charger, and Coronet, all models and body styles *except* convertible or station wagon.
    Note(s): Fits either side.

Interchange Number: 3
    Part Number(s): 2857903
    Usage: 1967 Belvedere, Charger, and Coronet, all body styles and models; 1968–70 Belvedere, Coronet, convertible or station wagon body styles only.
    Note(s): Fits either side.

Interchange Number: 4
    Part Number(s): 3431041
    Usage: 1970–71 Dart, Duster, and Valiant, all models and body styles.
    Note(s): Fits either side.

Interchange Number: 5
    Part Number(s): 3420816 (passenger)
    Usage: 1970–74 Barracuda, Challenger, all models and body styles.

Interchange Number: 6
    Part Number(s): 3431098 (passenger), 3431097 (driver)
    Usage: 1971 Charger, Coronet, and Satellite, all models and body styles.

Interchange Number: 7
    Part Number(s): 3431622
    Usage: 1972 Dart, Duster, and Valiant, all models and body styles.
    Note(s): (1) Fits either side. (2) Arms made by Anco.

Interchange Number: 8
    Part Number(s): 3431040
    Usage: 1972 Dart, Duster, and Valiant, all models and body styles.
    Note(s): (1) Fits either side. (2) Arms made by Trico.

Interchange Number: 9
    Part Number(s): 3420817 (driver)
    Usage: 1970–early 1972 Barracuda, Challenger, all models and body styles.
    Note(s): Used until approximately November 1, 1971.

Interchange Number: 10
    Part Number(s): 3620828 (driver)
    Usage: Late 1972–74 Barracuda, Challenger, all models and body styles.
    Note(s): Used after approximately November 1, 1971.

Windshield wiper washer reservoirs can be identified by a part number on top of the tank.

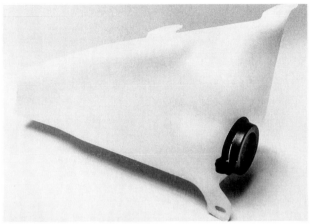

1970–1971 E-bodies and 1971 B-bodies used this washer reservoir. Year One

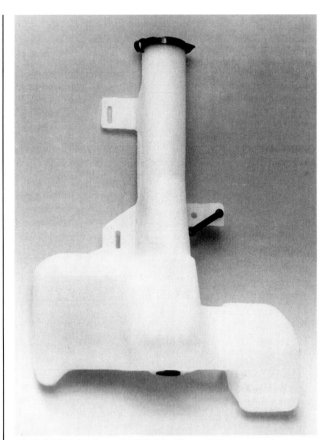

1972–1974 E-bodies and 1972 B-bodies used the same washer reservoir. Year One

Interchange Number: 11
Part Number(s): 3431096 (passenger), 3431095 (driver)
Usage: 1972–73 Charger, Coronet, Satellite, all models and body styles.
Note(s): Arms made by Anco.

Interchange Number: 12
Part Number(s): 3431098 (passenger), 3431097 (driver)
Usage: 1972–73 Charger, Coronet, Satellite, all models and body styles.
Note(s): Arms made by Trico.

Interchange Number: 13
Part Number(s): 3431727
Usage: 1973–early 1974 Dart, Duster, and Valiant, all models and body styles.
Note(s): Fits either side. (2) Used until October 2, 1973.

Interchange Number: 14
Part Number(s): 3431950
Usage: Late 1974 Dart, Duster, and Valiant, all models and body styles.

Interchange Number: 15
Part Number(s): 3431864 (passenger), 3431867 (driver)
Usage: 1974 Charger, Coronet, Satellite, all models and body styles.

Windshield Washer Jars
Model Identification

Interchange
Interchange Number: 1
Part Number(s): 2497502
Usage: 1968–69 Barracuda, Dart, and Valiant with *two-speed* wipers.

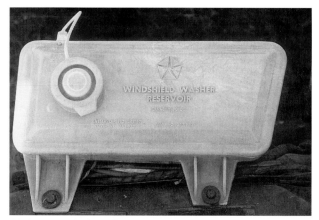

1973–1974 B-body washer reservoir.

Note(s): Will not fit models with variable-speed wipers.

Interchange Number: 2
Part Number(s): 2809011
Usage: 1968–69 Barracuda, 1968–74 Dart, Valiant; 1970–74 Duster with *variable-speed* wipers.
Note(s): Will *not* fit models with two-speed wipers.

Interchange Number: 3
Part Number(s): 2889803
Usage: 1968–70 Belvedere, Charger, and Coronet, all models and options.

Interchange Number: 4
Part Number(s): 2983067
Usage: 1970–74 Dart, Duster, and Valiant with two-speed wipers.

Interchange Number: 5
Part Number(s): 2983092
Usage: 1970–71 Barracuda, Challenger with *two-speed wipers.*
Note(s): Will *not* fit models with variable-speed wipers.

Interchange Number: 6
Part Number(s): 3431074
Usage: 1970–71 Barracuda, Challenger with variable-speed wipers; 1971 Charger, Coronet, and Satellite, all models and options.

Interchange Number: 7
Part Number(s): 3431587
Usage: 1972–74 Barracuda, Challenger with *two-speed* wipers.

Interchange Number: 8
Part Number(s): 3431590
Usage: 1972–74 Barracuda, Challenger with variable-speed wipers; 1972 Charger, Coronet, and Satellite, all models and options.

Interchange Number: 9
Part Number(s): 3431691
Usage: 1973 Charger, Coronet, Satellite, all models and options; 1974 Charger, Coronet, and Satellite *without* speed control.

Interchange Number: 10
Part Number(s): 3431965
Usage: 1974 Charger, Coronet, and Satellite *with* speed control.

Windshield Wiper/Washer Switches

This switch is not as interchangeable as you may first think. Factors that will affect the interchange are the number of wiper-blade speeds and whether or not a separate button was used for the washer system. Also with some B-bodies, those models with a Rallye instrument cluster used a different switch than those models without the option. The switch can be identified by a stamped number, which may not match the part number given.

Model Identification

Interchange

Interchange Number: 1
Part Number(s): 2770378
Type: Wiper control
Usage: 1968–69 Barracuda, Dart, and Valiant with variable-speed wipers.

Interchange Number: 2
Part Number(s): 2864415
Type: Wiper control
Usage: 1968–69 Barracuda, 1968–71 Dart, Valiant; 1970–71 Duster with two-speed wipers.

Interchange Number: 3
Part Number(s): 3004177
Type: Wiper control
Usage: 1968–69 Belvedere, Charger, and Coronet with two-speed wipers, all models and body styles; 1970 Charger, Coronet, and Satellite with Rallye cluster.

Interchange Number: 4
Part Number(s): 2864014
Type: Wiper control
Usage: 1968–69 Belvedere, Charger, and Coronet with variable-speed wipers, all models and body styles; 1970 Charger, Coronet, and Satellite with Rallye cluster and variable-speed wiper.

Interchange Number: 5
Part Number(s): 2983076
Type: Washer control
Usage: 1970–74 Barracuda, Challenger with two-speed wipers.
Note(s): (1) Foot-operated pump. (2) Interchange is with bracket.

Interchange Number: 6
Part Number(s): 2809009
Type: Washer control
Usage: 1968–69 Belvedere, Charger, Coronet, Chrysler 300, Fury, Monaco, Newport, New Yorker, and Polara, all models and body styles; 1968–69 Belvedere, Coronet station wagon with rear window washer; 1968 Fury, Monaco, Newport, and Polara station wagons with rear window washer; 1970 Charger; 1970 Coronet, Satellite with Rallye cluster.

Interchange Number: 7
Part Number(s): 2770380
Type: Wiper/washer control
Usage: 1970–71 Barracuda, Challenger, Dart, Duster, and Valiant with variable-speed wipers.

Interchange Number: 8
Part Number(s): 2947404
Type: Wiper control
Usage: 1970–71 Barracuda, Challenger with two-speed wipers.

Interchange Number: 9
Part Number(s): 3420814
Type: Wiper control
Usage: 1970 Coronet, Satellite with two-speed wipers, except with Rallye cluster.

Interchange Number: 10
Part Number(s): 2947920
Type: Wiper control
Usage: 1970 Coronet, Satellite with variable-speed wipers without Rallye cluster.

Interchange Number: 11
Part Number(s): 3488046
Type: Wiper/washer
Usage: 1971 Charger, Coronet, and Satellite with two-speed wipers, without Rallye cluster.

Interchange Number: 12
Part Number(s): 3488047
Type: Wiper/washer control
Usage: 1971 Charger, Coronet, and Satellite with two-speed wipers with Rallye cluster.

Interchange Number: 13
Part Number(s): 3488073
Type: Wiper/washer control
Usage: 1971 Charger, Coronet, and Satellite with variable-speed wipers without Rallye cluster.

Interchange Number: 14
Part Number(s): 3488043
Type: Wiper/washer control
Usage: 1971 Charger, Coronet, and Satellite with variable-speed wipers and Rallye cluster.

Interchange Number: 15
Part Number(s): 2932807
Type: Washer control
Usage: 1970 Coronet, Satellite without Rallye cluster.

Interchange Number: 16
Part Number(s): 3488781
Type: Wiper control
Usage: 1972 Dart, Duster, and Valiant with two-speed wipers.

Interchange Number: 17
Part Number(s): 3621670
Type: Wiper/washer control
Usage: 1972–74 Barracuda, Challenger, Dart, Duster, and Valiant with variable-speed wipers.

Interchange Number: 18
Part Number(s): 3621666
Type: Wiper control
Usage: 1972–74 Barracuda, Challenger with two-speed wipers.

Interchange Number: 19
Part Number(s): 3621667
Type: Wiper/washer control
Usage: 1972–74 Charger, Coronet, and Satellite with two-speed wipers without Rallye cluster.

Interchange Number: 20
Part Number(s): 3621668
Type: Wiper/washer control
Usage: 1972–74 Charger, Coronet, and Satellite with two-speed wipers and Rallye cluster.

Interchange Number: 21
Part Number(s): 3621671
Type: Wiper/washer control
Usage: 1972–74 Charger, Coronet, and Satellite with variable-speed wipers without Rallye cluster.
Note(s): Stamped number 3488764.

Interchange Number: 22
Part Number(s): 3621672
Type: Wiper/washer control
Usage: 1972–74 Charger, Coronet, and Satellite with variable-speed wipers and Rallye cluster
Note(s): Stamped number is 3488765.

Interchange Number: 23
Part Number(s): 3488839
Type: Wiper control
Usage: 1973–early 1974 Dart, Duster, and Valiant with two-speed wipers.
Note(s): Used until June 3, 1974.

Interchange Number: 24
Part Number(s): 3746851
Type: Wiper control
Usage: Late 1974 Dart, Duster, and Valiant with two-speed wipers.

Interchange Number: 25
Part Number(s): 3431058
Type: Washer control
Usage: Late 1969 Barracuda; late 1969–74 Dart, Valiant; 1970–74 Duster with two-speed wipers.
Note(s): (1) Foot-operated pump. (2) Interchange is with bracket. (3) Used after approximately February 3, 1968.

Interchange Number: 26
Part Number(s): 2889810
Type: Washer control

Usage: 1968 Barracuda, Dart, and Valiant with two-speed wipers.
Note(s): Foot-operated pump.
Interchange Number: 27
Part Number(s): 2926927
Type: Washer control
Usage: Early 1969 Barracuda, Dart, and Valiant with two-speed wipers.
Note(s): (1) Foot-operated pump. (2) Used until approximately February 3, 1969.

Heater Motors

Interchange here is fairly common, but a factor to watch for is whether the car you're interchanging from or to is or was equipped with factory-installed air conditioning. A special motor is used with factory-equipped air-conditioned cars, and it will not fit a car without factory air conditioning or vice versa. Those few models that were equipped with dealer-installed air conditioning used the same motor as models without factory air conditioning.

Model Identification

Barracuda	*Interchange Number*
1968–69	
without air conditioning	1
with air conditioning	11
1970–71	
without air conditioning	3
with air conditioning	10
1972–73	
without air conditioning	5
with air conditioning	7
1974	
without air conditioning	5
with air conditioning	6

Belvedere, Charger, Coronet, and Satellite	*Interchange Number*
1968–70	
without air conditioning	2
with air conditioning	9
1971	
without air conditioning	4
with air conditioning	10
1972–74	
without air conditioning	4
with air conditioning	7

Challenger	*Interchange Number*
1970–71	
without air conditioning	3
with air conditioning	10
1972–73	
without air conditioning	5
with air conditioning	7
1974	
without air conditioning	5
with air conditioning	6

Dart, Duster, Demon, and Valiant	*Interchange Number*
1968–69	
without air conditioning	1
with air conditioning	11
1970	
without air conditioning	2
with air conditioning	9
1971–72	
without air conditioning	2
with air conditioning	8
1973	
without air conditioning	5
with air conditioning	7
1974	
without air conditioning	5
with air conditioning	6

Interchange

Interchange Number: 1
Part Number(s): 2837678
Usage: 1968–69 Barracuda, Dart, and Valiant *without* factory air conditioning.
Interchange Number: 2
Part Number(s): 2837820
Usage: 1968–70 Belvedere, Charger, and Coronet; 1968 Chrysler 300, Fury, Imperial, Monaco, Newport, New Yorker, and Polara *without* factory air conditioning.
Note(s): A motor from a 1969 or 1970 full-size model will *not* fit.
Interchange Number: 3
Part Number(s): 3420859
Usage: 1970–71 Barracuda, Challenger; 1970–72 Dart, Duster, and Valiant *without* factory air conditioning.
Interchange Number: 4
Part Number(s): 3579172
Usage: 1971–74 Charger, Coronet, and Satellite, all models and body styles *without* factory air conditioning.
Interchange Number: 5
Part Number(s): 3621837
Usage: 1972–74 Barracuda, Challenger; 1973–74 Dart, Duster, and Valiant *without* factory air conditioning; 1973 full-size Chrysler with rear compartment heater.
Note(s): On Chrysler model, this is the rear heater motor.
Interchange Number: 6
Part Number(s): 3837343
Usage: 1974 Barracuda, Challenger, Charger, Coronet, Dart, Duster, Satellite, and Valiant *with* factory air conditioning.
Interchange Number: 7
Part Number(s): 3514305
Usage: 1972–73 Barracuda, Challenger, Charger, Coronet, and Satellite; 1973 Dart, Duster, and Valiant *with* factory air conditioning.
Interchange Number: 8
Part Number(s): 3420950
Usage: 1971–72 Dart, Duster, and Valiant, all models and body styles *with* factory air conditioning.
Interchange Number: 9
Part Number(s): 2932709
Usage: 1968–70 Charger, Coronet; 1970 Dart, Duster, Satellite, and Valiant, all models and body styles *with* factory air conditioning.
Interchange Number: 10
Part Number(s): 2936687
Usage: 1970–71 Barracuda, Challenger; 1971 Charger, Coronet, and Satellite *with* factory air conditioning.
Interchange Number: 11
Part Number(s): 2808761
Usage: 1967–69 Barracuda, Dart, and Valiant; 1967 Belvedere, Charger, Coronet, Chrysler 300, Fury, Monaco, Newport, New Yorker, and Polara *with* factory air conditioning.

Rear Window Defrosters
Model Identification

Barracuda, Belvedere, Charger, Coronet, Demon, Duster, Satellite, and Valiant	*Interchange Number*
1968–70	1
1971	2
1972–74	3

Interchange

Interchange Number: 1
Part Number(s): 2096772
Usage: 1968–70 Barracuda, Belvedere, Charger, Coronet, Chrysler 300, Dart, Imperial, Monaco, Newport, New Yorker, and Valiant; 1970 Challenger, Duster, all body styles except station wagon, convertible, or fastback.
Note(s): Interchange is motor and housing only.

Interchange Number: 2
 Part Number(s): 3441526
 Usage: 1971 Barracuda, Belvedere, Charger, Coronet, Chrysler 300, Dart, Imperial, Monaco, Newport, New Yorker, and Valiant; 1970 Challenger, Duster, all body styles except station wagon or convertible.
 Note(s): Interchange is motor and housing only.

Interchange Number: 3
 Part Number(s): 3621814
 Usage: 1972–74 Barracuda, Belvedere, Charger, Coronet, Chrysler 300, Dart, Imperial, Monaco, Newport, New Yorker, and Valiant; 1970 Challenger, Duster, all body styles except station wagon or convertible.
 Note(s): Interchange is motor and housing only.

Heater Core
Model Identification

Barracuda...*Interchange Number*
1968–69
 without air conditioning...1
 with air conditioning..1
1970–73
 without air conditioning...5
 with air conditioning..4
1974
 without air conditioning...5
 with air conditioning...12

Belvedere, Charger, Coronet, and Satellite ......*Interchange Number*
1968–69
 without air conditioning...2
 with air conditioning..8
1970
 without air conditioning...7
 with air conditioning..8
1971–74
 without air conditioning...6
 with air conditioning..4

Challenger...*Interchange Number*
1970–73
 without air conditioning...5
 with air conditioning..4
1974
 without air conditioning...5
 with air conditioning...12

Dart, Demon, Duster, and Valiant
1968–69
 without air conditioning...1
 with air conditioning..1
1970–72
 without air conditioning...3
 with air conditioning..3
1973
 without air conditioning...9
 with air conditioning
  early...10
  late...11
1974
 without air conditioning...9
 with air conditioning...11

Interchange
Interchange Number: 1
 Part Number(s): 2277535
 Usage: 1968–69 Barracuda, Dart, and Valiant *without or with* factory air conditioning.

Interchange Number: 2
 Part Number(s): 2521268
 Usage: 1968–69 Belvedere, Charger, and Coronet; 1968 Fury, Monaco, Newport, New Yorker, and Polara *without* factory air conditioning.

Interchange Number: 3
 Part Number(s): 2933000
 Usage: 1970–72 Dart, Duster, and Valiant *with or without* air conditioning.

Interchange Number: 4
 Part Number(s): 3441180
 Usage: 1970–74 Barracuda, Challenger; 1971–74 Charger, Coronet, and Satellite *with* air conditioning.

Interchange Number: 5
 Part Number(s): 3420815
 Usage: 1970–73 Barracuda, Challenger *without* factory air conditioning.

Interchange Number: 6
 Part Number(s): 3579171
 Usage: 1971–74 Charger, Coronet, and Satellite *without* factory air conditioning.

Interchange Number: 7
 Part Number(s): 2932999
 Usage: 1970 Charger, Coronet, and Satellite *without* factory air conditioning.

Interchange Number: 8
 Part Number(s): 3420577
 Usage: 1968–70 Charger, Coronet, and Satellite *with* factory air conditioning.

Interchange Number: 9
 Part Number(s): 3744266
 Usage: 1973–74 Dart, Duster, and Valiant *without* factory air conditioning.

Interchange Number: 10
 Part Number(s): 3744279
 Usage: Early 1973 Dart, Duster, and Valiant *with* factory air conditioning.
 Note(s): Used until May 15, 1973.

Interchange Number: 11
 Part Number(s): 3780551
 Usage: Late 1973–74 Dart, Duster, and Valiant *with* factory air conditioning.
 Note(s): Used after May 15, 1973.

Interchange Number: 12
 Part Number(s): 3503408
 Usage: 1974 Barracuda, Challenger *without* factory air conditioning.

Air Conditioning Compressors
 Compressors are fairly interchangeable across model lines. However, be careful when interchanging from a full-size model. These models were optional with a slightly different type of compressor. Note that in 1971 the RV2-type compressor was phased into production on the B- and E- bodies. And in 1972 it replaced the V2-type compressor on these models, though A-bodies continued to use the V2-type compressor. The RV2 and the V2 compressors are not interchangeable.

Model Identification
Barracuda, Challenger, Dart,
 Demon, Duster, and Valiant ....*Interchange Number*
1968 1
1969–74...2
Belvedere, Charger, Coronet, and Satellite ......*Interchange Number*
1968 1
1969–71
 V2..2
 RV2..3
1972...3, 4
1973–74...4

Interchange
Interchange Number: 1
 Part Numbers: 2843800, 2843801, 2843802, 2843803, 2843805, 2865391, 2815760
 Usage: 1968 Barracuda, Belvedere, Charger, Coronet, Chrysler

300, Dart, Fury, Monaco, Newport, New Yorker, Polara, and Valiant, except full-sizes models with automatic temperature control or RV2-type compressor.

Note(s): ID number 2815760 is replacement unit.

Interchange Number: 2

Part Number(s): 2951193, 2951194, 2951195, 2951220, 2951268, 2951271, 2953349, 2951268, 2961947, 2953588, 3462019, 2960782, 2941998, 3642350, 3462419, 3462420, 2961920, 3512708, 3462919, 3462420, 3462919, 3462920, 3462998, 3512062, 3512706, 3512707, 3491270, 3491271, 3484552, 3502608, 3502610, 3502716 9982211

Usage: 1969–74 Barracuda; 1969–71 Belvedere, Charger, Coronet, Chrysler 300, Fury, Monaco, Newport, New Yorker, Polara, Satellite; 1969–74 Dart, Valiant; 1970–74 Duster, except with automatic temperature control or RV2-type compressor.

Interchange Number: 3

Part Number(s): 2951269, 2951270, 3462005, 3462020, 3462021, 3512710, 3512711, 3462021, 3462351, 3462352, 9977756

Usage: 1971–72 Charger, Coronet, Fury, Monaco, Newport, New Yorker, Polara, and Satellite with automatic temperature control; 1969 Chrysler 300, Fury, Monaco, Newport, New Yorker, and Polara with RV2-type compressor.

Note(s): Interchange Number 4 was also used, and the two are *not* interchangeable.

Interchange Number: 4

Part Number(s): 3502612, 3502611, 3502609, 3502042, 3502043, 3641238, 3502717, 3502715, 3703601

Usage: 1972–74 Charger, Coronet, Fury, Monaco, Newport, New Yorker, Polara, and Satellite.

Note(s): 1972 models also used Interchange Number 3, and the two are *not* interchangeable.

Air Conditioning Condensers
Model Identification

Interchange
Interchange Number: 1

Part Number(s): 3503546
Usage: 1974 Dart, Duster, and Valiant.

Interchange Number: 2

Part Number(s): 3441934
Usage: 1972–74 Barracuda, Challenger; 1972 Charger, Coronet, and Satellite.

Interchange Number: 3

Part Number(s): 3502548
Usage: 1973–74 Charger, Coronet, and Satellite.

Interchange Number: 4

Part Number(s): 3502569
Usage: 1973 Dart, Duster, and Valiant.

Interchange Number: 5

Part Number(s): 2936778
Usage: 1968–69 Barracuda; 1969–72 Dart, Valiant; 1970–72 Duster.

Interchange Number: 6

Part Number(s): 3441064
Usage: 1970–71 Barracuda, Challenger, Charger, Coronet, and Satellite.
Note(s): Measures 22 in wide with 32 holes in end plates.

Interchange Number: 7

Part Number(s): 3441065
Usage: 1970–71 Barracuda, Challenger, Charger, Coronet, and Satellite.
Note(s): Measures 24 in wide with 32 holes in end plates.

Interchange Number: 8

Part Number(s): 3441065
Usage: 1970–71 Barracuda, Challenger, Charger, Coronet, and Satellite.
Note(s): Measures 24 in wide with 16 holes in end plates.

Interchange Number: 9

Part Number(s): 3441423
Usage: 1970 Charger, Coronet, and Satellite with V-8 engine.

Interchange Number: 10

Part Number(s): 2936780
Usage: 1968–69 Belvedere, Charger, and Coronet with V-8 engine.

Interchange Number: 11

Part Number(s): 2812689
Usage: 1968–69 Barracuda, Dart, and Valiant with dealer-installed air conditioning.

Interchange Number: 12

Part Number(s): 2968361
Usage: 1968–69 Belvedere, Charger, Coronet, Chrysler 300, Fury, Monaco, Newport, New Yorker, and Polara with dealer-installed air conditioning.

Horns
Model Identification

Interchange
Interchange Number: 1

Part Number(s): 2808869 (high note), 2808868 (low note)
Usage: 1966–74 Barracuda, Charger, Coronet, Dart, and Valiant; 1966–69 Belvedere; 1970–74 Duster, Satellite; 1968–74 Fury, Monaco, Newport, New Yorker; 1968–71 Chrysler 300; 1968–72 Polara, except 1968–74 Road Runner or 1974 models sold in New York County in New York.
Note(s): Some models used only the high-note horn.

Interchange Number: 2

Part Number(s): 3746824 (package)
Usage: 1974 Barracuda, Challenger, Charger, Coronet, Dart, Duster, Fury, Monaco, Newport, New Yorker, Satellite, and Valiant, all sold in New York County, New York.

Interchange Number: 3
   Part Number(s): 3488646
   Usage: 1972–74 Road Runner.
Interchange Number: 4
   Part Number(s): 2926233
   Usage: 1968–71 Road Runner

Turn Signal Levers
Model Identification
Barracuda..*Interchange Number*
1968 1
1969 1
1970
   without speed control 4
   with speed control 11
1972–74...4

Belvedere, Charger, Coronet,
   and Satellite..*Interchange Number*
1968
   without speed control 1
   with speed control 2
1970
   without speed control 1
   with speed control 10
1971
   without tilt steering or speed control 4
   with tilt without speed control 9
   without tilt with speed control
      early 5
      late 6
   with tilt with speed control
      early 7
      late 8
1972–73
   without tilt steering...12
   with tilt steering 9
1974
   without speed control 13
   with speed control 14

Challenger..*Interchange Number*
1970
   without speed control 4
   with speed control 11
1972–74...4

Dart, Duster, Demon, Valiant ....*Interchange Number*
1968 1
1969 1
1970
   except with speed control...1
   with speed control 10
1971 3
1972 12
1973–74...13

Interchange
Interchange Number: 1
   Part Number(s): 2889093
   Usage: 1968–69 Barracuda, Belvedere; 1968–70 Charger,
      Coronet, Satellite, Dart, and Valiant; 1969 Chrysler 330,
      Fury, Monaco, Newport, New Yorker, Polara; 1970 Duster,
      except with speed control.
Interchange Number: 2
   Part Number(s): 2857525
   Usage: 1968–69 Belvedere, Charger, and Coronet with speed
      control; 1968 Chrysler 300, Fury, Monaco, Newport, New
      Yorker, and Polara with speed control but with tilt steering.
Interchange Number: 3
   Part Number(s): 2947963
   Usage: 1971 Dart, Duster, and Valiant.
Interchange Number: 4

   Part Number(s): 2947953
   Usage: 1970–74 Barracuda, Challenger; 1971 Charger,
      Coronet, Satellite, except with speed control.
Interchange Number: 5
   Part Number(s): 2947954
   Usage: Early 1971 Charger, Coronet, Fury, Monaco, Polara, and
      Satellite with speed control, without tilt steering.
   Note(s): Used up to approximately February 1971.
Interchange Number: 6
   Part Number(s): 3488538
   Usage: Late 1971 Charger, Coronet, Satellite; late 1971–73
      Fury, Monaco, Polara with speed control, without tilt
      steering.
   Note(s): Used after February 1971.
Interchange Number: 7
   Part Number(s): 2947956
   Usage: Early 1971 Charger, Coronet, Fury, Monaco, Polara, and
      Satellite with speed control and tilt steering.
   Note(s): Used until February 1971.
Interchange Number: 8
   Part Number(s): 3488540
   Usage: Late 1971 Charger, Coronet, Satellite; late 1971–73
      Fury, Monaco, Polara, and Satellite with speed control and
      tilt steering.
   Note(s): Used after February 1971.
Interchange Number: 9
   Part Number(s): 2947952
   Usage: 1971–73 Charger, Coronet, Satellite; 1971–73 Fury,
      Monaco, Polara with tilt steering, without speed control.
Interchange Number: 10
   Part Number(s): 2947500
   Usage: 1970 Charger, Coronet, Chrysler 300, Fury, Monaco,
      Newport, New Yorker, Polara, and Satellite with speed
      control, without tilt steering.
Interchange Number: 11
   Part Number(s): 2984055
   Usage: 1970 Barracuda, Challenger with speed control.
Interchange Number: 12
   Part Number(s): 2947950
   Usage: 1972–73 Charger, Coronet, Dart, Duster, Fury, Monaco,
      Newport, New Yorker, Polara, Satellite, and Valiant, except
      with tilt steering.
Interchange Number: 13
   Part Number(s): 3746683
   Usage: 1974 Charger, Coronet, Dart, Duster, Fury, Monaco,
      Newport, New Yorker, Satellite, and Valiant without tilt
      steering or speed control.
Interchange Number: 14
   Part Number(s): 3746518
   Usage: 1974 Charger, Coronet, Fury, Monaco, Newport, New
      Yorker, and Satellite with auto speed control, without tilt steering.

Headlamp Switches
   Many switches interchange. However, Chargers with hidden
headlamps used a special switch, and those without hidden headlamps will not interchange or vice versa.

Model Identification
Barracuda..*Interchange Number*
1968–69...1
1970–74...6
Belvedere, Charger, Coronet,
   and Satellite..*Interchange Number*
1968–69
   except Charger 2
Charger...3
1970
   without Rallye cluster 4
   with Rallye cluster...2
1971–74...5

Interchange

Interchange Number: 1
   Part Number(s): 2809087
   Usage: 1968–69 Barracuda; 1968–74 Dart, Valiant; 1970–74 Duster.

Interchange Number: 2
   Part Number(s): 3004092
   Usage: 1968–69 Belvedere, Coronet; 1970 Coronet, Satellite with Rallye cluster; 1970 Charger.

Interchange Number: 3
   Part Number(s): 3004113
   Usage: 1968–69 Charger.

Interchange Number: 4
   Part Number(s): 2947763
   Usage: 1970 Coronet, Satellite without Rallye cluster; 1970–71 Fury, Monaco, Newport, New Yorker, and Polara.

Interchange Number: 5
   Part Number(s): 3514427
   Usage: 1971–74 Charger, Coronet, Chrysler 300, Newport, New Yorker, and Satellite; 1972–74 Fury, Monaco, and Polara.

Interchange Number: 6
   Part Number(s): 2947305
         Usage: 1970–74 Barracuda, Challenger.

Convertible Top Motors

   All convertibles from 1967–71 used the same motor. Listed as part number 2573838, it was used in 1967–71 Barracudas, 1970 and 1971 Challengers, 1968–70 Coronets, 1968–70 Belvederes, 1967–70 Furys, 1967–70 Polara 500s, 1967–70 Newports, and 1967–70 Chrysler 300s.

Convertible Top Switches
Model Identification

Interchange

Interchange Number: 1
   Part Number(s): 2820408
   Usage: 1967–69 Barracuda or Dart convertible; 1967 Belvedere, Coronet station wagon with power tailgate window with switch on instrument panel.

Interchange Number: 2
   Part Number(s): 2864007
   Usage: 1968–69 Belvedere, Coronet convertible; 1968–69 Belvedere, Coronet station wagon with power tailgate window with switch on instrument panel; 1969 Coronet R/T without Rallye cluster; 1970 Newport or Chrysler 300 convertible.

Interchange Number: 3
   Part Number(s): 2864489
   Usage: 1969 Coronet R/T with Rallye cluster; 1969 Newport or New Yorker station wagon with power tailgate window with switch on instrument panel; 1970 Coronet, Satellite convertible with or without Rallye cluster; 1970 Chrysler 300, Newport convertible; 1970 Coronet or Satellite station wagon with tailgate window switch on instrument panel.

Interchange Number: 4
   Part Number(s): 2947406
   Usage: 1970–71 Barracuda, Challenger convertible.

Chapter 10

Sheet Metal

Hood

Interchange here is the bare hood, without nameplates, simulated air vents, hinges, or springs, unless otherwise indicated. Note that sport hoods like those used on muscle cars will usually fit other models in the same family group. For example, a Road Runner hood will fit a Satellite coupe, provided it is of the same vintage.

Model Identification

Interchange

Interchange Number: 1
    Part Number(s): 2769190
    Usage: 1967–68 Valiant, all models and body styles.
Interchange Number: 2
    Part Number(s): 2859890
    Usage: 1967–68 Barracuda, all models and body styles.
    Note(s): Interchange is without hood louvers.
Interchange Number: 3
    Part Number(s): 2859181–1968, 2934730–1969
    Usage: 1968–69 Dart, all models and body styles, except GTS or
        Swinger models.

Interchange Number: 4
Part Number(s): 2859379
Usage: 1968–69 Dart GTS; 1969 Dart Swinger.
Note(s): Interchange without hood inserts.

Interchange Number: 5
Part Number(s): 2859052
Usage: 1968 Belvedere, all models and body styles, except Road Runner.
Note(s): Interchange Number 6 will fit. Add a muscle-car look.

Interchange Number: 6
Part Number(s): 2859456
Usage: 1968 GTX, Road Runner, all body styles.
Note(s): Used with or without fresh-air system.

Interchange Number: 7
Part Number(s): 2859114
Usage: 1968 Coronet, all models and body styles, except Coronet R/T or Super Bee models.
Note(s): (1) Interchange Number 11 will fit by removing the extension at the front of the hood. (2) Interchange Number 9 will fiT/Add a muscle-car look.

Interchange Number: 8
Part Number(s): 2859218
Usage: 1968–69 Charger, all models except 1969 Daytona.

Interchange Number: 9
Part Number(s): 2859481
Usage: 1968–69 Coronet R/T, Super Bee, all body styles, without fresh-air option.

Interchange Number: 10
Part Number(s): 3417096
Usage: 1968–69 Coronet R/T, Super Bee with fresh-air option.

Interchange Number: 11
Part Number(s): 2934368
Usage: 1969 Coronet, all models and body style,s except Coronet R/T or Super Bee.
Note(s): (1) Interchange Number 7 will fit by adding the front extension. (2) Interchange Number 9 or 17 will fit. Add a muscle-car look.

Interchange Number: 12
Part Number(s): 2934072
Usage: 1969–70 Valiant; 1970 Duster, all models and body styles.

Interchange Number: 13
Part Number(s): 934086
Usage: 1969 Barracuda, all models and packages.
Note(s): To interchange on or to models with Cuda package, add or remove air scoops.

Interchange Number: 14
Part Number(s): 3417098
Usage: 1969 GTX, Road Runner.
Note(s): Used with or without fresh-air package.

Interchange Number: 15
Part Number(s): 2934495
Usage: 1969 Belvedere, all models and body styles, except GTX or Road Runner.
Note(s): Interchange Number 14 or 15 will fit. Add a muscle-car look.

Interchange Number: 16
Part Number(s): 3412055
Usage: 1969 Road Runner with lift-off fiberglass hood.
Note(s): Will fit all Belvedere models. Hood latch, hinges, catch, and pop-up springs must be removed, and four hood hold-down pins installed to complete the interchange.

Interchange Number: 17
Part Number(s): 3412056
Usage: 1969 Super Bee with lift-off fiberglass hood.
Note(s): Will fit all 1968–69 Coronets. Hood latch, catch, hinges, and pop-up springs must be removed, and four hood hold-down pins installed to complete the interchange.

Interchange Number: 18
Part Number(s): 3417037
Usage: 1969 Charger Daytona; 1970 Charger, all models.

Interchange Number: 19
Part Number(s): 3482862
Usage: 1971 Duster, Valiant, all models and body styles.
Note(s): Salvage-yard dealers say Interchange Number 45 will fit.

Interchange Number: 20
Part Number(s): 3417088
Usage: 1970–71 Dart, 1971 Demon, all models and body styles.
Note(s): Hood scoops are added or deleted to interchange to and from Demon models.

Interchange Number: 21
Part Number(s): 2934856
Usage: 1970 Barracuda, all models except Cuda or AAR Cuda.
Note(s): Interchange Number 22 was optional and will fit.

Interchange Number: 22
Part Number(s): 3417997
Usage: 1970–74 Cuda without fresh-air option.

Interchange Number: 23
Part Number(s): 2988805
Usage: 1970–71 Cuda with fresh-air option package.
Note(s): Has cut in center of hood for air cleaner.

Interchange Number: 24
Part Number(s): 3417996
Usage: 1971–74 Barracuda, all models except Cuda.
Note(s): Interchange Number 22 was optional and will fit.

Interchange Number: 25
Part Number(s): 3443686
Usage: 1970–71 Cuda with fiberglass hood scoop; 1970 Cuda AAR.
Note(s): Standard on AARs but will fit all Barracuda models. Be sure to use low-tension springs.

Interchange Number: 26
Part Number(s): 2934850
Usage: 1970 Challenger, all models, except R/T or T/A.
Note(s): Interchange Number 26 will fiT/Add a muscle-car look.

Interchange Number: 27
Part Number(s): 3417066
Usage: 1970 Challenger R/T without shaker hood.

Interchange Number: 28
Part Number(s): 3443271
Usage: 1970–71 Challenger T/A or 1970–71 Challenger with fiberglass hood.

Interchange Number: 29
Part Number(s): 3482618
Usage: 1971 Challenger R/T; 1971 Challenger with sport hood.

Interchange Number: 30
Part Number(s): 3482614
Usage: 1971 Challenger without shaker hood or sport hood. Will not fit R/T models.
Note(s): Interchange Number 29 was optional and will fit.

Interchange Number: 32
Part Number(s): 3443685
Usage: 1970–71 Challenger with shaker hood.

Interchange Number: 33
Part Number(s): 2934886
Usage: 1970 Satellite, all models except GTX or Road Runner.
Note(s): Interchange Number 35 will fit. Add a muscle-car look.

Interchange Number: 34
Part Number(s): 3417444
Usage: 1970 GTX, Road Runner with fresh-air hood.

Interchange Number: 35
Part Number(s): 3417040
Usage: 1970 GTX, Road Runner without fresh-air hood.

Interchange Number: 36
Part Number(s): 3482024
Usage: 1971–72 Satellite, two-door models only, all except GTX or Road Runner.
Note(s): (1) Warning: Four models will *not* interchange. (2) Interchange Number 37 will fit. Add muscle-car image.

Interchange Number: 37
Part Number(s): 3482468
Usage: 1971 GTX; 1971–72 Road Runner without fresh-air hood.

Interchange Number: 38
Part Number(s): 3482497
Usage: 1971 GTX, Road Runner with fresh-air hood.
Note(s): Will fit 1972 models. Use all 1971 components.

Interchange Number: 39
Part Number(s): 3417037
Usage: 1970 Coronet, all models except Coronet R/T and Super Bee.
Note(s): Interchange Number 40 will fit. Add muscle-car image.

Interchange Number: 40
Part Number(s): 3417051
Usage: 1970 Coronet R/T, Super Bee without fresh-air hood package.

Interchange Number: 41
Part Number(s): 3417779
Usage: 1970 Coronet R/T, Super Bee with fresh-air hood package.

Interchange Number: 42
Part Number(s): 3482018
Usage: 1971–72 Charger, except Charger R/T or Super Bee models.
Note(s): Interchange Number 43 will fit. Add a muscle-car look.

Interchange Number: 43
Part Number(s): 3482535
Usage: 1971 Charger R/T, Charger Super Bee without fresh-air hood package.
Note(s): (1) Interchange without center louvers. (2) Interchange 52 will fit, but looks different.

Interchange Number: 44
Part Number(s): 3482471
Usage: 1971 Charger R/T, Charger Super Bee with fresh-air hood package.
Note(s): Will fit 1972 models. Use all 1971 components.

Interchange Number: 45
Part Number(s): 3611642
Usage: 1972 Duster, Valiant, all models.
Note(s): Drill holes for optional hood scoops. (2) Salvage-yard dealers say Interchange Number 19 will fit.

Interchange Number: 46
Part Number(s): 3611271
Usage: Early 1972 Dart, all models except Sport with scoops.
Note(s): Used until December 1971. (2) Salvage-yard dealers say Interchange Number 20 will fit.

Interchange Number: 47
Part Number(s): 3611266
Usage: Early 1971 Dart Sport with hood scoops.
Note(s): (1) Used until December 1971. (2) Interchange Number 46 can be drilled to fit this application.

Interchange Number: 48
Part Number(s): 3611665
Usage: Late 1972 Dart, except Sport with hood scoops.
Note(s): Used after December 1971.

Interchange Number: 49
Part Number(s): 3611666
Usage: Late 1971 Dart Sport with hood scoops.
Note(s): (1) Used after December 1971. (2) Interchange Number 48 can be modified to fit this application.

Interchange Number: 50
Part Number(s): 3611378
Usage: 1972–74 Challenger, except with Rallye package or high-performance hood.
Note(s): Interchange Number 51 will fit. Add a muscle-car look.

Interchange Number: 51
Part Number(s): 3611368
Usage: 1972–74 Challenger with Rallye package or high-performance hood option.

Interchange Number: 52
Part Number(s): 3611212
Usage: 1972 Charger Rallye with sport hood.

Interchange Number: 53
Part Number(s): 3684274
Usage: 1973–74 Duster, Valiant, all models and body styles.

Interchange Number: 54
Part Number(s): 3684286
Usage: 1973 Dart Sport with hood scoops.
Note(s): Interchange Number 55 can be modified to fit.

Interchange Number: 55
Part Number(s): 3684266
Usage: 1973–74 Dart, all models and body styles, except 1973 Dart Sport with hood scoops.

Interchange Number: 56
Part Number(s): 3684024
Usage: 1973 Satellite two-door models, except Road Runner.
Note(s): (1) Warning: Hood from four-door models will *not* fit. (2) Interchange Number 63 will fit. Add a muscle-car image,

Interchange Number: 57
Part Number(s): 3684033
Usage: 1973 Charger, except with Rallye package.
Note(s): Interchange Number 58 will fit. Add a muscle-car look.

Interchange Number: 58
Part Number(s): 3684031
Usage: 1973 Charger with Rallye package.

Interchange Number: 59
Part Number(s): 3752172
Usage: 1974 Satellite two-door models, except Road Runner.
Note(s): (1) Warning: Hood from four-door models will not fit. (2): Interchange Number 60 will fit. Add a muscle-car look.

Interchange Number: 60
Part Number(s): 3752394
Usage: 1974 Road Runner.

Interchange Number: 61
Part Number(s): 3752743
Usage: 1974 Charger Rallye.

Interchange Number: 62
Part Number(s): 3752174
Usage: 1974 Charger, except with Rallye package.
Note(s): Interchange Number 61 will fit. Add a muscle-car look.

Interchange Number: 63
Part Number(s): 3684027
Usage: 1973 Road Runner

Hood Hinges
Model Identification

Barracuda	Interchange Number
1968–69	1
1970	3
1971	5
1972	8
1973–74	9

Belvedere, Charger, Coronet, and Satellite	Interchange Number
1968–69	2
1970	4
1971–74	6

Challenger	Interchange Number
1970	3
1971	5
1972	8
1973–74	9

Dart, Duster, Demon, and Valiant	Interchange Number
1968–71	1
1972–74	7

Interchange

Interchange Number: 1
Part Numbers: 2802120 (right), 2802121 (left)
Usage: 1967–69 Barracuda; 1967–71 Dart, Valiant; 1970–71 Duster.

Interchange Number: 2
Part Numbers: 2945018 (right), 2945019 (left)
Usage: 1968–69 Belvedere, Charger, and Coronet.

Interchange Number: 3
Part Numbers: 2945842 (right), 2945843 (left)
Usage: 1970 Barracuda, Challenger.

Interchange Number: 4
    Part Numbers: 3454154 (right), 3454155 (left)
    Usage: 1970 Charger, Coronet, and Satellite.
Interchange Number: 5
    Part Numbers: 3548890 (right), 3548891 (left)
    Usage: 1971 Barracuda, Challenger
Interchange Number: 6
    Part Numbers: 3582536 (right), 3582537 (left)
    Usage: 1971–74 Charger, Coronet, Satellite, all models and
        body styles.
Interchange Number: 7
    Part Numbers: 3582972 (right), 3582973 (left)
    Usage: 1972–74 Dart, Duster, and Valiant, all models and body
        styles.
Interchange Number: 8
    Part Numbers: 3548888 (right), 3548889 (left)
    Usage: 1972 Barracuda, Challenger.
Interchange Number: 9
    Part Numbers: 3582926 (right), 3582927 (left)
    Usage: 1973–74 Barracuda, Challenger.

Front Fenders

Due to the natural evolutionary design changes, very few front fenders will interchange. Also in certain models, engine size or tire size will affect the interchange. For example, the 1970 and 1971 Barracuda and Challenger models with the F60x15 tires require a special set of fenders; regular production fenders will not interchange.

Interchange is the bare unit, without nameplate, wheel-well trim, or any side moldings. Note, however, that these factors will have to be weighted in when interchanging used parts, as side trim and nameplates require that holes be drilled. The pre-drilled holes may not match up to your existing fenders. To mount the fender, existing holes may have to be filled or new ones drilled to accommodate your specific application. Remember, it is always easier to drill new holes than it is to fill in existing ones. So look for a fender that matches your particular usage or one without any trim, if possible.

Model Identification

Interchange

Interchange Number: 1
    Part Number(s): 2932152 (right), 2932153 (left)
    Usage: 1968 Valiant, all models and body styles.
Interchange Number: 2
    Part Number(s): 2932154 (right), 2932155 (left)
    Usage: 1968 Barracuda, all models and body styles.
Interchange Number: 3
    Part Number(s): 2932156 (right), 2932157 (left)
    Usage: 1968 Dart, all models and body styles.
Interchange Number: 4
    Part Number(s): 2932158 (right), 2932159 (left)
    Usage: 1968 Belvedere, all models and body styles.
Interchange Number: 5
    Part Number(s): 2932160 (right), 2932161 (left)
    Usage: 1968 Coronet, all models and body styles.
Interchange Number: 6
    Part Number(s): 2932162 (right), 2932163 (left)
    Usage: 1968 Charger, all models.
Interchange Number: 7
    Part Number(s): 2933658 (right), 2933659 (left)
    Usage: 1969 Valiant, all models and body styles.
Interchange Number: 8
    Part Number(s): 2933660 (right), 2933661 (left)
    Usage: 1969 Barracuda, all models and body styles.
Interchange Number: 9
    Part Number(s): 2933662 (right), 2933663 (left)
    Usage: 1969 Dart, all models and body styles.
Interchange Number: 10
    Part Number(s): 2933664 (right), 2933665 (left)
    Usage: 1969 Belvedere, all models and body styles.
Interchange Number: 11
    Part Number(s): 2933666 (right), 2933667 (left)
    Usage: 1969 Coronet, all models and body styles.
Interchange Number: 12
    Part Number(s): 2933668 (right), 2933669 (left)
    Usage: 1969 Charger, all models except Daytona.
Interchange Number: 13
    Part Number(s): 3412762 (right), 3412763 (left)
    Usage: 1969 Charger Daytona.
    Note(s): Regular production Charger fenders will not
        interchange.
Interchange Number: 14
    Part Number(s): 3419872 (right), 3419873 (left)
    Usage: 1970–71 Duster and Valiant, all models and body styles.
Interchange Number: 15
    Part Number(s): 3419874 (right), 3419875 (left)
    Usage: 1970 Barracuda, all models and body styles, except with
        F60x15 tires.

Interchange Number: 16
    Part Number(s): 3579676 (right), 3579677 (left)
    Usage: 1971 Barracuda, all models and body styles, except
        Cuda or models with F60x15 tires.
Interchange Number: 17
    Part Number(s): 3621752 (right), 3621753 (left)
    Usage: 1971 Barracuda with F60x15 tires, all models and body
        styles, except Cuda.
    Note(s): Regular production fenders will not fit.
Interchange Number: 18
    Part Number(s): 3579378 (right), 3579379 (left)
    Usage: 1970 Barracuda with F60x15 tires, all models and body styles.
    Note(s): Larger wheel-well opening. Regular production fenders
        will not fit.
Interchange Number: 19
    Part Number(s): 3579678 (right), 3579679 (left)
    Usage: 1971 Cuda, all models and body styles, except with
        F60x15 tires.
Interchange Number: 20
    Part Number(s): 3579664 (right), 3579665 (left)
    Usage: 1971 Cuda with F60x15 tires, all models and body styles.
    Note(s): Regular production fenders will not fit.
Interchange Number: 21
    Part Number(s): 3419878 (right), 3419879 (left)
    Usage: 1970–71 Challenger, all models and body styles, except
        with F60x15 tires or Challenger T/A models.
Interchange Number: 22
    Part Number(s): 3579380 (right), 3579381 (left)
    Usage: 1970–71 Challenger with F60x15 tires, all models and
        body styles, except Challenger T/A.
    Note(s): Has flare wheel-well openings. Regular production
        fenders will not fit.
Interchange Number: 23
    Part Number(s): 3579624 (right), 3579625 (left)
    Usage: 1970–71 Challenger T/A.
    Note(s): Special wheel-well radius. Production fenders will not fit.
Interchange Number: 24
    Part Number(s): 3419876 (right), 3419879 (left)
    Usage: 1970–71 Dart, all models and body styles, including
        Demon models.
Interchange Number: 25
    Part Number(s): 3419880 (right), 3419881 (left)
    Usage: 1970 Satellite, all models and body styles.
Interchange Number: 26
    Part Number(s): 3579680 (right), 3579681 (left)
    Usage: 1971 Satellite, two-door models only.
    Note(s): Warning: A fender from a four-door or station wagon
        Satellite will not fit.
Interchange Number: 27
    Part Number(s): 3419882 (right), 3419883 (left)
    Usage: 1970 Coronet, all models and body styles.
Interchange Number: 28
    Part Number(s): 3419884 (right), 3419885 (left)
    Usage: 1970 Charger, all models.
Interchange Number: 29
    Part Number(s): 3579684 (right), 3579685 (left)
    Usage: 1971 Charger, all models.
Interchange Number: 30
    Part Number(s): 3621760 (right), 3621761 (left)
    Usage: 1972 Duster, Valiant, all models and body styles.
Interchange Number: 31
    Part Number(s): 3621762 (right), 3621763 (left)
    Usage: 1972 Dart, all models and body styles, includes Demon
        models.
Interchange Number: 32
    Part Number(s): 3621764 (right), 3621765 (left)
    Usage: 1972–74 Barracuda, all models.
Interchange Number: 33
    Part Number(s): 3621768 (right), 3621769 (left)
    Usage: 1972–74 Challenger, all models.

Interchange Number: 34
    Part Number(s): 3621770 (right), 3621772 (left)
    Usage: 1972 Satellite, two-door models only.
    Note(s): Warning: Fender from a four-door or station wagon
        will not fit.
Interchange Number: 35
    Part Number(s): 3621774 (right), 3621775 (left)
    Usage: 1972 Charger, all models.
Interchange Number: 36
    Part Number(s): 3685960 (right), 3685961 (left)
    Usage: 1973 Duster and Valiant, all models and body styles.
Interchange Number: 37
    Part Number(s): 3685962 (right), 3685963 (left)
    Usage: 1973 Dart, all models and body styles.
Interchange Number: 38
    Part Number(s): 3685964 (right), 3658965 (left)
    Usage: 1973–74 Satellite, two-door models only.
    Note(s): *Warning*: Fender from a four-door or station wagon will
        not fit.
Interchange Number: 39
    Part Number(s): 3685968 (right), 3658969 (left)
    Usage: 1973–74 Charger, all models.
Interchange Number: 40
    Part Number(s): 3780370 (right), 3780371 (left)
    Usage: 1974 Duster and Valiant, all models and body styles.
Interchange Number: 41
    Part Number(s): 3780372 (right), 3780373 (left)
    Usage: 1974 Dart, all models and body styles.

Front Doors

Doors were only changed when a major design evolution occurred, so the interchange is larger than it may first appear. Interchange is the complete door minus interior door panel and any exterior trim moldings. When interchanging from a hardtop to a convertible or vice versa, remove the glass. While the door will fit, the glass may not. Because body side molding require holes to be drilled in the sheet metal, trim should be considered when interchanging. A plain door (without trim) is always the best bet, as holes are much easier to drill, and it takes less time than filling previously drilled holes. Note that crash bars were added to the doors in late 1973 models, and they will physically fit the 1972 and earlier 1973 models and have no outward differences.

Model Identification

Interchange

Interchange Number: 1
Part Number(s): 2859504 (right), 2859505 (left)
Usage: 1968 Dart, Valiant two-door coupe models.
Note(s): 1967 Valiant door (from two-door) will fit, but mirror is positioned farther forward. (2) Interchange Number 6 will fit, but locking knobs are positioned farther forward.

Interchange Number: 2
Part Number(s): 2859512 (right), 2859513 (left)
Usage: 1968 Barracuda, all body styles.
Note(s): 1967 Barracuda door will fit, but mirror is positioned farther forward. (2) Interchange Number 7 will fit, but locking knobs are positioned back farther.

Interchange Number: 3
Part Number(s): 2859508 (right), 2859509 (left)
Usage: 1968 Dart, two-door hardtop or convertible.
Note(s): 1967 Dart door (from two-door) will fit, but mirror is positioned farther forward. (2) Interchange Number 8 will fit, but locking knobs are positioned back farther.

Interchange Number: 4
Part Number(s): 2859068 (right), 285909 (left)
Usage: 1968 Belvedere, Coronet two-door coupe, two-door hardtop, or convertible.
Note(s): Interchange Number 9 will fit, but locking knobs are positioned back farther.

Interchange Number: 5
Part Number(s): 2859074 (right), 2859075 (left)
Usage: 1968 Charger.
Note(s): Interchange Number 10 will fit, but locking knobs are positioned back farther.

Interchange Number: 6
Part Number(s): 2934470 (right), 2934471 (left)
Usage: 1969 Dart, Valiant two-door coupe.
Note(s): Interchange Number 1 will fit, but locking knobs are positioned farther back.

Interchange Number: 7
Part Number(s): 2934478 (right), 2934479 (left)
Usage: 1969 Barracuda, all body styles.
Note(s): Interchange Number 2 will fit, but locking knobs are positioned farther back.

Interchange Number: 8
Part Number(s): 2934474 (right), 2934475 (left)
Usage: 1969 Dart convertible; 1969–70 Dart two-door hardtop.
Note(s): Interchange Number 3 will fit, but locking knobs are positioned farther back.

Interchange Number: 9
Part Number(s): 2934462 (right), 2934463 (left)
Usage: 1969–70 Belvedere, Coronet two-door hardtop, coupe, or convertible.
Note(s): Interchange Number 4 will fit, but locking knobs are positioned farther back.

Interchange Number: 10
Part Number(s): 2934468 (right), 2934469 (left)
Usage: 1969 Charger.
Note(s): Interchange Number 5 will fit, but locking knobs are positioned farther back.

Interchange Number: 11
Part Number(s): 3417596 (right), 3417597 (left)
Usage: 1970 Duster.

Interchange Number: 12
Part Number(s): 3482894 (right), 3482895 (left)
Usage: 1971–72 Duster, Demon.

Interchange Number: 13
Part Number(s): 3482890 (right), 3482891 (left)
Usage: 1971–72 Dart, Scamp two-door hardtop.

Interchange Number: 14
Part Number(s): 3482958 (right), 3482959 (left)
Usage: 1971 Barracuda, all models and body styles.

Interchange Number: 15
Part Number(s): 2934748 (right), 2934749 (left)
Usage: 1970 Barracuda, all models and body styles.

Interchange Number: 16
Part Number(s): 2934780 (right), 2934781 (left)
Usage: 1970 Challenger, all models and body styles.

Interchange Number: 17
Part Number(s): 3482674 (right), 3482673 (left)
Usage: 1971 Challenger, all models and body styles.

Interchange Number: 18
Part Number(s): 3482068 (right), 3482069 (left)
Usage: 1971–72 Satellite, all two-door models.

Interchange Number: 19
Part Number(s): 3417740 (right), 3417741 (left)
Usage: 1970 Charger, all models.
Note(s): Charger R/T has scoop on doors

Interchange Number: 20
Part Number(s): 3482050 (right), 3482051 (left)
Usage: 1971–72 Charger, all models except 1971 R/T or 1972 with Rallye package.

Interchange Number: 21
Part Number(s): 3482048 (right), 3482049 (left)
Usage: 1971 Charger R/T, has indentations in doors.
Note(s): Interchange Number 20 will fit, but has no indentation.

Interchange Number: 22
Part Number(s): 3611888 (right), 3611889 (left)
Usage: 1972–early 1973 Barracuda, all models.
Note(s): Used until November 15, 1972. (2) Interchange Number 29 will fit.

Interchange Number: 23
Part Number(s): 3611892 (right), 3611893 (left)
Usage: 1972–early 1973 Challenger, all models.
Note(s): Used until November 15, 1972. (2) Interchange Number 30 will fit.

Interchange Number: 25
Part Number(s): 3611456 (right), 3611457 (left)
Usage: 1972 Charger with Rallye package. Door has indentations.
Note(s): Interchange Number 20 will fit but has no indentations.

Interchange Number: 26
Part Number(s): 3684430 (right), 3684431 (left)
Usage: Early 1973 Duster, Dart, and Valiant two-door.
Note(s): Interchange Number 27 will fit, but has impact bar. No

outer visual difference. (2) When interchange from two-door hardtop to fastback (Duster, Dart, Sport), remove glass.

Interchange Number: 27
Part Number(s): 3684248 (right), 3684249 (left)
Usage: Late 1973 Dart, Duster, and Valiant two-door.
Note(s): Interchange Number 26 will fit but has no impact bar. No outer visual difference. (2) Used after November 15, 1972. (3) When interchange from two-door hardtop to fastback (Duster, Dart, Sport), remove glass.

Interchange Number: 28
Part Number(s): 3752744 (right), 3752745 (left)
Usage: Very late 1973–early 1974 Dart, Duster, and Valiant two-door.
Note(s): Used after May 25, 1973, to February 1, 1974 .(2) When interchange from two-door hardtop to fastback (Duster, Dart, Sport), remove glass.

Interchange Number: 29
Part Number(s): 3684236 (right), 3684237 (left)
Usage: Late 1973–74 Barracuda, all models.
Note(s): Used after November 15, 1972. (2) Has side impact bar. (3) Interchange Number 22 will fit, but has no impact bar.

Interchange Number: 30
Part Number(s): 3684240 (right), 3684241 (left)
Usage: Late 1973–74 Challenger, all models.
Note(s): Used after November 15, 1972. (2) Has side impact bar. (3) Interchange Number 23 will fit, but has no impact bar.

Interchange Number: 31
Part Number(s): 3684520 (right), 3684521 (left)
Usage: Early 1973 Satellite two-door, all models.
Note(s): (1) Used until November 15, 1972. (2) Interchange Number 32 will fit.

Interchange Number: 32
Part Number(s): 3684142 (right), 3684143 (left)
Usage: Late 1973–74 Satellite two-door, all models.
Note(s): (1) Used after November 15, 1972. (2) Interchange Number 31 will fit, but has no side impact bar.

Interchange Number: 33
Part Number(s): 3684516 (right), 3684517 (left)
Usage: Early 1973 Charger, all models.
Note(s): (1) Used until November 15, 1972. (2) Interchange Number 34 will fit.

Interchange Number: 34
Part Number(s): 3684132 (right), 3684133 (left)
Usage: Late 1973–74 Charger, all models.
Note(s): (1) Used after November 15, 1972. (2) Interchange Number 33 will fit, but has no side impact bar.

Interchange Number: 35
Part Number(s): 3752346 (right), 3752347 (left)
Usage: Late 1974 Dart, Duster, and Valiant two-door.
Note(s): Used after February 1, 1974. (2) When interchange from two-door hardtop to fastback (Duster, Dart, Sport), remove glass.

Door Hinges
Model Identification

Interchange

Interchange Number: 1
Part Number(s): 2583796 (passenger), 2583797 (driver)
Location: Upper hinge
Usage: 1967–69 Barracuda; 1967–early 1973, Dart, Valiant; 1970–early 1973 Duster, all body styles. Front door only.
Note(s): Used until July 1, 1973.

Interchange Number: 2
Part Number(s): 2298649 (fits either side)
Location: Upper hinge
Usage: 1966–70 Belvedere, Charger, and Coronet, all body styles. Front door only.

Interchange Number: 3
Part Number(s): 2999368 (passenger), 2999369 (driver)
Location: Upper hinge
Usage: 1970–74 Barracuda, Challenger, all body styles.

Interchange Number: 4
Part Number(s): 3454510
Location: Upper hinge
Usage: 1971–74 Charger, Coronet, Satellite, all models and body styles. Front door only.

Interchange Number: 5
Part Number(s): 3789082 (passenger), 3789083 (driver)
Location: Upper hinge
Usage: Late 1973–74 Dart, Duster, and Valiant, all models and body styles. Front door only.
Note(s): Used after July 1, 1973.

Interchange Number: 6
Part Number(s): 3789084 (passenger), 3789085 (driver)
Location: Lower hinge
Usage: Late 1973–74 Dart, Duster, and Valiant, all models and body styles. Front door only.
Note(s): Used after July 1, 1973.

Interchange Number: 7
Part Number(s): 3788022 (passenger), 3788023 (driver)
Location: Lower hinge
Usage: 1974 Charger, Coronet, and Satellite, all models and body styles. Front door only.

Interchange Number: 8
Part Number(s): 2999370 (passenger), 2999371 (driver)
Location: Lower hinge
Usage: 1970–74 Barracuda, Challenger, all models and body styles.

Interchange Number: 9
Part Number(s): 3454512 (passenger), 3454513 (driver)
Location: Lower hinge
Usage: 1971–73 Charger, Coronet, and Satellite, all models and body styles. Front door only.

Interchange Number: 10
Part Number(s): 2583578 (passenger), 2583579 (driver)
Location: Lower hinge
Usage: 1966–69 Barracuda; 1970–early 1973 Dart, Duster, and Valiant; 1966–70 Belvedere, Charger, Coronet, and Satellite, all models and body styles. Front door only.
Note(s): Used until July 1, 1973.

Outside Door Handle
Exterior door handles are largely interchangeable and will cross car lines and model years. Most models used a handle with a diecast

pushbutton. However, a few early models did use a black plastic push-button. Handles are unique to each side of the car. Thus, a handle from a passenger's door will not fit the driver's side door. Although the handles listed here are for two-door models only, sometimes the same handle can be found on the rear doors of certain models. If this is the case, it is noted, so read the interchange carefully.

Model Identification

Interchange

Interchange Number: 1
  Part Number(s): 2486704
  Location: Passenger's
  Usage: 1968 Barracuda, Belvedere, Charger, Coronet, Chrysler 300, Dart, Fury, Monaco, Newport, New Yorker, Polara, and Valiant, front door only, all body styles; 1968 Belvedere, Coronet station wagon, rear door.
  Note(s): Diecast pushbuttons.

Interchange Number: 2
  Part Number(s): 2486705
  Location: Driver's
  Usage: 1968 Barracuda, Belvedere, Charger, Coronet, Chrysler 300, Dart, Fury, Monaco, Newport, New Yorker, Polara, and Valiant, front door only, all body styles.
  Note(s): Diecast pushbuttons.

Interchange Number: 3
  Part Number(s): 2862972
  Location: Passenger's
  Usage: 1968–69 Barracuda, Belvedere, Charger, Coronet, Dart, and Valiant, front door only, all body styles; 1968–69 Belvedere, Coronet station wagon.
  Note(s): Black pushbuttons.

Interchange Number: 4
  Part Number(s): 2862973
  Location: Driver's
  Usage: 1968–69 Barracuda, Belvedere, Charger, Coronet, Dart, and Valiant, front door only, all body styles.
  Note(s): Black pushbuttons.

Interchange Number: 5
  Part Number(s): 3454390
  Location: Passenger's
  Usage: 1969–70 Belvedere, Charger, and Coronet, front door only, all body styles; 1969 Dart, Valiant four-door sedan, front door only; 1969–70 Coronet, Satellite station wagon, rear door only.
  Note(s): Diecast pushbutton.

Interchange Number: 6
  Part Number(s): 3454391
  Location: Driver's
  Usage: 1969–70 Belvedere, Charger, and Coronet, front door only, all body styles; 1969 Dart, Valiant four-door sedan, front door only.
  Note(s): Diecast pushbutton.

Interchange Number: 7
  Part Number(s): 3454338
  Location: Passenger's
  Usage: 1969 Barracuda; 1969–70 Dart*; 1970 Valiant; 1970 Duster, front door only, all body styles.
  Note(s): *Two-door hardtop or convertible only in 1969 models.

Interchange Number: 8
  Part Number(s): 3454339
  Location: Driver's
  Usage: 1969 Barracuda; 1969–70 Dart*, Valiant; 1970 Duster, front door only, all body styles;

Note(s): *Two-door hardtop or convertible only in 1969 models.

Interchange Number: 9
Part Number(s): 3548036
Location: Passenger's
Usage: 1971–73 Dart, Duster, and Valiant. front door only, all body styles.

Interchange Number: 10
Part Number(s): 3548037
Location: Driver's
Usage: 1971–73 Dart, Duster, and Valiant. front door only, all body styles.

Interchange Number: 11
Part Number(s): 2999816
Location: Passenger's
Usage: 1970–72 Barracuda, all models and body styles.
Note(s): Flush fitting.

Interchange Number: 12
Part Number(s): 2999817
Location: Driver's
Usage: 1970–72 Barracuda, all models and body styles.
Note(s): Flush fitting.

Interchange Number: 13
Part Number(s): 2999882
Location: Passenger's
Usage: 1970–72 Challenger, all models and body styles.
Note(s): Flush fitting.

Interchange Number: 14
Part Number(s): 2999883
Location: Driver's
Usage: 1970–72 Challenger, all models and body styles.
Note(s): Flush fitting.

Interchange Number: 15
Part Number(s): 3621757
Location: Fits either side
Usage: 1971, 1972*–73 Charger, Satellite, two-door models only.
Note(s): *Warning*: Handle from a four-door sedan or station wagon will not fit. (2)*Late 1972 after June 19, 1972. For early 1972 models see Interchange Number 16.

Interchange Number: 16
Part Number(s): 3586024
Location: Fits either side
Usage: Early 1972 Charger, Coronet, and Satellite, front door only, all body styles.
Note(s): Used until June 19, 1972.

Interchange Number: 17
Part Number(s): 3760214
Location: Passenger's
Usage: 1973 Barracuda, Challenger, all models.
Note(s): Flush fitting.

Interchange Number: 18
Part Number(s): 3760215
Location: Driver's
Usage: 1973 Barracuda, Challenger, all models.
Note(s): Flush fitting.

Interchange Number: 19
Part Number(s): 3796130
Location: Passenger's
Usage: 1974 Dart, Duster, and Valiant, front door only, all body styles.

Interchange Number: 20
Part Number(s): 3796131
Location: Driver's
Usage: 1974 Dart, Duster, and Valiant, front door only, all body styles.

Interchange Number: 21
Part Number(s): 3796132
Location: Passenger's
Usage: 1974 Barracuda, Challenger, all models.

Interchange Number: 22
Part Number(s): 3796133
Location: Driver

Usage: 1974 Barracuda, Challenger, all models.

Interchange Number: 23
Part Number(s): 3621755
Location: Fits either side
Usage: 1974 Charger, Coronet, and Satellite, front or rear door, all body styles.

Roof Assembly
Repair Skin

The interchange here is for the complete roof assembly, including the rear pillars. Body style will greatly affect the interchange. If interchanging from a used roof, look for a plain steel roof. Vinyl-covered roofs can hide rust and other signs of damage. Plus those with a vinyl roof will require more prep work to get the roof ready. Note some models like the Challenger S.E. and the Super Bird were made mandatory with a vinyl roof. With these models, take extra time inspecting the roof. A vinyl top was also mandatory with a sunroof, but here no special roofline was used. A standard steel roof can be modified to fit. The roof listed for convertibles is the frame assembly without the canvas top.

Part numbers given here are for the repair skin panel only, which is only the top portion of the roof without sail panels or roof pillars. Here much more interchanging is available. A cross-reference for this repair skin follows this interchange.

Model Identification

Barracuda.....................................Interchange Number
1968–69
    two-door hardtop 1
    fastback...2
    convertible (frame)....................................21
1970–74
    two-door hardtop 10
    convertible (1970–71)................................23

Belvedere, Charger, Coronet,
*   and Satellite.............................Interchange Number*
1968–70, except Charger
    two-door sedan 7
    two-door hardtop 7
    convertible (frame)....................................22
1968–70 Charger, except 1969 500 or Daytona............3
1969 500 and Daytona 8
1971 Charger 13
1971 Satellite 19
1972 Charger
    except S.E. 13
    S.E. 14
    Satellite 19
1973–74 Charger
    except S.E. or Celebrity roof....................17
    S.E. or Celebrity roof 18
    Satellite 20

Challenger................................Interchange Number
1970–71
    except with formal roof............................11
    formal roof...12
    convertible (frame)....................................23
1973–74..11

Dart, Duster, Demon, and Valiant.............Interchange Number
1968–69
  Dart
    two-door hardtop 4
    two-door sedan..6
    convertible (frame)....................................21
  Valiant two-door sedan 6
1970–72
  Dart two-door hardtop...................................4
  Duster 9
  Demon 9
  Valiant two-door hardtop..............................4

Interchange

Interchange Number: 1
Part Number(s): 2842324
Usage: 1968–69 Barracuda two-door hardtop.

Interchange Number: 2
Part Number(s): 2842325
Usage: 1968–69 Barracuda fastback.

Interchange Number: 3
Part Number(s): 2838103
Usage: 1968 Charger, all models; 1969 Charger, all models
except Charger 500 or Daytona; 1970 Charger, all models.

Interchange Number: 4
Part Number(s): 2842323
Usage: 1968–72 Dart two-door hardtop; 1970–72 Valiant two-door hardtop; late 1974 Dart or Valiant two-door hardtop.
Note(s): Used only after September 1973 in 1974 models, was not used in 1973 models.

Interchange Number: 5
Part Number(s): 2842322
Usage: 1968–69 Valiant two-door hardtop.

Interchange Number: 6
Part Number(s): 2842326
Usage: 1968 Dart two-door sedan.

Interchange Number: 7
Part Number(s): 2838573
Usage: 1968–70 Belvedere, Coronet two-door sedan or two-door hardtop.
Note(s): Add or remove center post.

Interchange Number: 8
Part Number(s): 3412567
Usage: 1969 Charger 500; 1969 Charger Daytona.

Interchange Number: 9
Part Number(s): 2965661
Usage: 1970–72 Duster; 1971–72 Demon; late 1974 Dart Sport, Duster.
Note(s): Used after September 1973 in 1974 models. Was not used on 1973 models. For earlier models see Interchange Number 15.

Interchange Number: 10
Part Number(s): 2963296
Usage: 1970–74 Barracuda two-door coupe or hardtop.

Interchange Number: 11
Part Number(s): 2963297
Usage: 1970–74 Challenger, except with formal roofline.

Interchange Number: 12
Part Number(s): 2963297
Usage: 1970 Challenger S.E.; 1971 Challenger with formal roofline.
Note(s): Smaller back window.

Interchange Number: 13
Part Number(s): 3445833
Usage: 1971–72 Charger, all models except 1972 Charger S.E.

Interchange Number: 14
Part Number(s): 3445833
Usage: 1972 Charger S.E.
Note(s): Unique roofline.

Interchange Number: 15
Part Number(s): 3720975
Usage: 1973–early 1974 Dart Sport, Duster.

Note(s): Up to September 1973. For later models see Interchange Number 9.

Interchange Number: 16
Part Number(s): 3720978
Usage: 1973–early 1974 Dart, Valiant two-door hardtop.
Note(s): Used until September 1973.

Interchange Number: 17
Part Number(s): 3445833
Usage: 1973–74 Charger S.E.; 1974 Charger with Celebrity roof.
Note(s): Remove louvers for Celebrity roof.

Interchange Number: 18
Part Number(s): 3445833
Usage: 1973–74 Charger S.E.; 1974 Charger with Celebrity roof.

Interchange Number: 19
Part Number(s): 3445833
Usage: 1971–72 Satellite two-door models.

Interchange Number: 20
Part Number(s): 3445833
Usage: 1973–74 Satellite two-door models.

Interchange Number: 21
Part Number(s): 1981CX9
Usage: 1967–69 Barracuda, Dart convertible frame.

Interchange Number: 22
Part Number(s): 1995DX9
Usage: 1968–70 Belvedere, Coronet convertible.

Interchange Number: 23
Part Number(s): 2964409
Usage: 1970–71 Barracuda, Challenger convertible frame.

Repair Roof Skin Cross-Reference
Model Identification

Quarter Panel

Interchange here is based on a cut-out quarter panel from an original car. A new replacement panel can have an even wider range of interchange, check the Notes section under the individual interchange for more details. Note that body style will greatly influence the interchange, as does minor changes in the model year. If you are salvaging a used panel, try to pick a part that is as close as possible to your original unit in trim and emblem usage. Otherwise there is more prep work needed, with filling pre-drilled holes before you can use it. Better solution is to find a clean part that is free from rust and trim and then drill the holes that are necessary.

Model Identification

Interchange

Interchange Number: 1
Part Numbers: 2842882 (right), 2842883 (left)
Usage: 1968 Barracuda convertible.

Interchange Number: 2
Part Numbers: 2838192 (right), 2838193 (left)
Usage: 1968 Belvedere convertible.

Interchange Number: 3
Part Numbers: 2842884 (right), 2842885 (left)
Usage: 1968 Barracuda two-door hardtop.

Interchange Number: 4
Part Numbers: 2838292 (right), 2838293 (left)
Usage: 1968 Belvedere two-door hardtop.

Interchange Number: 5
Part Numbers: 2604176 (right), 2604177 (left)
Usage: 1968 Valiant two-door sedan.

Interchange Number: 6
Part Numbers: 2838292 (right), 2838293 (left)
Usage: 1968 Belvedere two-door sedan.

Interchange Number: 7
Part Numbers: 2604186 (right), 2604187 (left)
Usage: 1968 Dart two-door sedan.

Interchange Number: 8
Part Numbers: 2838298 (right), 2838299 (left)
Usage: 1968 Coronet two-door sedan or two-door hardtop.
Note(s): When swapping from sedan to hardtop, remove lock pillar.

Interchange Number: 9
Part Numbers: 2604190 (right), 2604191 (left)
Usage: 1968 Dart convertible.

Interchange Number: 10
Part Numbers: 2838194 (right), 2838195 (left)
Usage: 1968 Coronet convertible.

Interchange Number: 11
   Part Numbers: 2604182 (right), 2604183 (left)
   Usage: 1968 Barracuda fastback.
Interchange Number: 12
   Part Numbers: 2783900 (right), 2783901 (left)
   Usage: 1968 Charger.
Interchange Number: 13
   Part Numbers: 2902562 (right), 2902563 (left)
   Usage: 1969 Valiant two-door sedan.
Interchange Number: 14
   Part Numbers: 2902564 (right), 2902565 (left)
   Usage: 1969 Barracuda two-door hardtop.
Interchange Number: 15
   Part Numbers: 2902566 (right), 2902567 (left)
   Usage: 1969 Barracuda fastback.
Interchange Number: 16
   Part Numbers: 2902568 (right), 2902569 (left)
   Usage: 1969 Barracuda convertible.
Interchange Number: 17
   Part Numbers: 2902572 (right), 2902573 (left)
   Usage: 1969 Dart two-door hardtop.
Interchange Number: 18
   Part Numbers: 2902574 (right), 2902575 (left)
   Usage: 1969 Dart convertible.
Interchange Number: 19
   Part Numbers: 2900894 (right), 2900895 (left)
   Usage: 1969 Belvedere convertible.
Interchange Number: 20
   Part Numbers: 2900892 (right), 2900893 (left)
   Usage: 1969 Belvedere two-door sedan or two-door hardtop.
   Note(s): When swapping from sedan to hardtop, remove lock pillar.
Interchange Number: 21
   Part Numbers: 2902628 (right), 2902629 (left)
   Usage: 1969 Coronet two-door sedan or two-door hardtop.
   Note(s): When swapping from sedan to hardtop, remove lock pillar.
Interchange Number: 22
   Part Numbers: 2902634 (right), 2902635 (left)
   Usage: 1969 Charger, except 500 or Daytona.
   Note(s): Repair skin will fit all Charger models.
Interchange Number: 23
   Part Numbers: 2902632 (right), 2902633 (left)
   Usage: 1969 Coronet convertible.
Interchange Number: 24
   Part Numbers: 2965612 (right), 2965613 (left)
   Usage: 1970–71 Duster; 1971 Demon.
Interchange Number: 25
   Part Numbers: 3444666 (right), 3444667 (left)
   Usage: 1970–71 Dart, Valiant two-door hardtop.
Interchange Number: 26
   Part Numbers: 2963144 (right), 2963145 (left)
   Usage: 1970–71 Barracuda two-door hardtop or coupe.
Interchange Number: 27
   Part Numbers: 2963368 (right), 2963369 (left)
   Usage: 1970–71 Barracuda convertible.
Interchange Number: 28
   Part Numbers: 2902646 (right), 2902647 (left)
   Usage: 1970–71 Challenger two-door hardtop, except 1970 Challenger S.E. and 1971 model with formal roof.
   Note(s): Repair skin will fit both Challenger hardtop and S.E. models.
Interchange Number: 29
   Part Numbers: 2902648 (right), 2902649 (left)
   Usage: 1970–71 Challenger convertible.
Interchange Number: 30
   Part Numbers: 2963806 (right), 2963807 (left)
   Usage: 1970 Satellite two-door sedan or two-door hardtop.
   Note(s): When swapping from sedan to hardtop, remove lock pillar.
Interchange Number: 31
   Part Numbers: 2963808 (right), 2963809 (left)
   Usage: 1970 Satellite convertible.

Interchange Number: 32
   Part Numbers: 3444182 (right), 3444183 (left)
   Usage: 1971 Satellite two-door coupe or two-door hardtop.
Interchange Number: 33
   Part Numbers: 3445584 (right), 3445585 (left)
   Usage: 1971 Charger, all models.
Interchange Number: 34
   Part Numbers: 3445304 (right), 3445305 (left)
   Usage: 1970 Charger, all models.
Interchange Number: 35
   Part Numbers: 3615274 (right), 3615275 (left)
   Usage: 1972 Dart, Valiant two-door hardtop.
Interchange Number: 36
   Part Numbers: 3615276 (right), 3615277 (left)
   Usage: 1972 Demon, Duster.
Interchange Number: 37
   Part Numbers: 3615544 (right), 3615545 (left)
   Usage: 1972 Barracuda, two-door hardtop.
Interchange Number: 38
   Part Numbers: 3615548 (right), 3615549 (left)
   Usage: 1972 Challenger two-door hardtop.
Interchange Number: 39
   Part Numbers: 3615206 (right), 3615207 (left)
   Usage: 1972 Satellite two-door coupe or two-door hardtop.
Interchange Number: 40
   Part Numbers: 3615210 (right), 3615211 (left)
   Usage: 1972 Charger two-door coupe or two-door hardtop, except S.E. model.
   Note(s): Repair skin will fit all Charger models, including S.E.
Interchange Number: 41
   Part Numbers: 3756258 (right), 3756259 (left)
   Usage: 1973 Dart, Valiant two-door hardtop.
Interchange Number: 42
   Part Numbers: 3756256 (right), 3756257 (left)
   Usage: 1973 Dart Sport, Duster.
Interchange Number: 43
   Part Numbers: 3616580 (right), 3616581 (left)
   Usage: 1973–74 Barracuda two-door hardtop.
Interchange Number: 44
   Part Numbers: 3616138 (right), 3616139 (left)
   Usage: 1973–74 Challenger two-door hardtop.
Interchange Number: 45
   Part Numbers: 3615410 (right), 3615411 (left)
   Usage: 1973 Satellite two-door coupe or two-door hardtop.
Interchange Number: 46
   Part Numbers: 3615412 (right), 3615413 (left)
   Usage: 1973 Charger, all models except S.E.
   Note(s): Repair skin will fit all Charger models, including the S.E.
Interchange Number: 47
   Part Numbers: 3756016 (right), 3756017 (left)
   Usage: 1974 Dart, Valiant two-door hardtop.
Interchange Number: 48
   Part Numbers: 3756154 (right), 3756155 (left)
   Usage: 1974 Dart Sport, Duster.
Interchange Number: 49
   Part Numbers: 3756756 (right), 3756757 (left)
   Usage: 1974 Satellite two-door coupe or two-door hardtop.
Interchange Number: 50
   Part Numbers: 3756758 (right), 3756759 (left)
   Usage: 1974 Charger two-door coupe, two-door hardtop except S.E. model.
   Note(s): Replacement skin will fit all Charger models, including S.E.
Interchange Number: 51
   Part Numbers: NA
   Usage: 1969 Charger 500, Charger Daytona.
   Note(s): Repair skin will fit all 1969 Chargers.
Interchange Number: 52
   Part Numbers: NA
   Usage: 1970 Challenger S.E.; 1971 Challenger with formal roof package.

Note(s): Repair skin for a two-door hardtop 1970–71
Challenger will fit.
Interchange Number: 53
Part Numbers: NA
Usage: 1972 Charger S.E.
Note(s): Repair skin will fit all Charger models, including S.E. models.
Interchange Number: 54
Part Numbers: NA
Usage: 1973 Charger S.E.
Note(s): Repair skin will fit all Charger models, including S.E. models.
Interchange Number: 55
Part Numbers: NA
Usage: 1974 Charger S.E.
Note(s): Repair skin will fit all Charger models, including S.E. models.
Interchange Number: 56
Part Numbers: 2963730 (right), 2963731 (left)
Usage: 1970 Coronet convertible.
Interchange Number: 57
Part Numbers: 2963728 (right), 2963729 (left)
Usage: 1970 Coronet two-door sedan or two-door hardtop.
Note(s): When swapping from sedan to hardtop, remove lock pillar.
Interchange Number: 58
Part Numbers: 2604188 (right), 2604189 (left)
Usage: 1968 Dart two-door hardtop.
Note(s): When swapping from sedan to hardtop, remove lock pillar.

Deck Lids

Some body styles will greatly influence the interchangeability of deck lids. For example, the Barracuda fastback uses a much narrower lid than does the hardtop or convertible. Also, some lids were made especially for that model and may be difficult to find, such as the 1969 Charger 500/Daytona models, which used a much narrower lid than the production Charger. You should find a deck lid that is clean and free of damage, rust, and, if possible, any additional trim. Interchange below is without any trim or nameplates.

Model Identification

Barracuda......................................**Interchange Number**
1968–69
   two-door hardtop 3
   convertible 3
   fastback 4
1970
  all body styles
    early without rear spoiler................17
    late with or without rear spoiler......18
1971–74...19
Belvedere and Satellite...........**Interchange Number**
1968 all body styles................................6
1969 all body styles................................9
1970 all body styles
   early without spoiler..........................23
   late with or without spoiler 25
1971 –72 two-door...................................24
1973–74 two-door...................................30
Challenger.................................**Interchange Number**
1970
   early without spoiler..........................20
   late with or without spoiler 21
1971–74...22
Charger......................................**Interchange Number**
1968 5
1969
   except 500 or Daytona 5
   Daytona and 500 11
1970
   early without spoiler............................5
   late with or without spoiler 32
1971–72...28

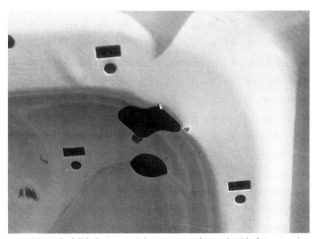
Late-1970 deck lids have special cutouts on the underside for mounting the rear-wing spoiler.

1973–74...31
Coronet..**Interchange Number**
1968 7
1969 10
1970
   early without spoiler..................................26
   late with or without spoiler 27
Dart and Demon ....**Interchange Number**
1968 2
1969 8
1970
   early without rear spoiler..........................15
   late with or without rear spoiler 16
1971–72
   except Demon 16
  Demon
    early 13
    late 14
1973–74
   except Dart Sport......................................29
   Dart Sport..14
Duster and Valiant.......................**Interchange Number**
1968 1
1969 1
1970
  Duster
    early without spoiler..........................12
    late with or without spoiler 13
  Scamp..16
1971–72
   except Duster..16
  Duster
    early 13
    late 14
1973–74
   except Duster..29
   Duster 14

Interchange

Interchange Number: 1
Part Number(s): 2934074
Usage: 1968–69 Valiant, all models and body styles.
Interchange Number: 2
Part Number(s): 2859546
Usage: 1968 Dart, all models and body styles.
Interchange Number: 3
Part Number(s): 2859428

Usage: 1968–69 Barracuda, two-door hardtop and convertible.
Interchange Number: 4
Part Number(s): 2859432
Usage: 1968–69 Barracuda fastback.
Interchange Number: 5
Part Number(s): 2859146
Usage: 1968 Charger, all models; 1969 Charger, all models except 500 and Daytona; early 1970 Charger without rear spoiler.
Note(s): Use Interchange Number 32 if installing rear spoiler on these models.
Interchange Number: 6
Part Number(s): 2859150
Usage: 1968 Belvedere, all models and body styles except station wagon.
Interchange Number: 7
Part Number(s): 2859174
Usage: 1968 Coronet, all models and body styles except station wagon.
Interchange Number: 8
Part Number(s): 2934727
Usage: 1969 Dart, all models and body styles.
Interchange Number: 9
Part Number(s): 2934036
Usage: 1969 Belvedere, all models and body styles except station wagon.
Interchange Number: 10
Part Number(s): 2934040
Usage: 1969 Coronet, all models and body styles except station wagon.
Interchange Number: 11
Part Number(s): 3412154
Usage: 1969 Charger 500; 1969 Charger Daytona.
Interchange Number: 12
Part Number(s): 3417167
Usage: Early 1970 Duster without rear spoiler.
Note(s): Use Interchange Number 13 if installing spoiler.
Interchange Number: 13
Part Number(s): 3482625
Usage: Late 1970–early 1971 Duster; early 1971 Demon with or without rear spoiler.
Note(s): Used until June 15, 1971.
Interchange Number: 14
Part Number(s): 3611553
Usage: Late 1971–74 Duster; 1971–72 Demon; 1973–74 Dart Sport.
Note(s): Used after June 15, 1971..
Interchange Number: 15
Part Number(s): 3417160
Usage: Early 1970 Dart two-door hardtop, four-door sedan.
Note(s): Used without rear spoiler. Switch to Interchange Number 16 for use with spoiler.
Interchange Number: 16
Part Number(s): 3482861
Usage: Late 1970–72 Dart two-door hardtop, four-door sedan; 1970–72 Valiant Scamp two-door hardtop.
Note(s): Used with or without rear deck spoiler.
Interchange Number: 17
Part Number(s): 2934744
Usage: Early 1970 Barracuda, all body styles.
Note(s): Used only without a spoiler. Use Interchange Number 18 with spoiler.
Interchange Number: 18
Part Number(s): 3482628
Usage: Late 1970 Barracuda, all models and body styles.
Note(s): Used with or without rear spoiler.
Interchange Number: 19
Part Number(s): 3482802
Usage: 1971–74 Barracuda, all models and body styles.
Interchange Number: 20
Part Number(s): 2934950

Usage: Early 1970 Challenger, all models and body styles.
Note(s): Used without rear spoiler. Use Interchange Number 21 with spoiler.
Interchange Number: 21
Part Number(s): 3482623
Usage: Late 1970 Challenger, all models and body styles.
Note(s): Used with or without rear spoiler.
Interchange Number: 22
Part Number(s): 3482687
Usage: 1971–74 Challenger, all models and body styles.
Interchange Number: 23
Part Number(s): 2934970
Usage: Early 1970 Satellite, all models and body styles except station wagon.
Note(s): Used without rear spoiler. Use Interchange Number 25 with spoiler.
Interchange Number: 24
Part Number(s): 3482010
Usage: 1971–72 Satellite two-door models only.
Note(s): *Warning*: Deck lid from a four-door model will not fit.
Interchange Number: 25
Part Number(s): 3482629
Usage: Late 1970 Satellite, all models and body styles except station wagon.
Note(s): Used with or without rear spoiler.
Interchange Number: 26
Part Number(s): 2934958
Usage: Early 1970 Coronet, all models and body styles except station wagon.
Note(s): Used without spoiler. Use Interchange Number 27 with spoiler.
Interchange Number: 27
Part Number(s): 2959146
Usage: Late 1970 Coronet, all models and body styles except station wagon.
Interchange Number: 28
Part Number(s): 3482013
Usage: 1971–72 Charger, all models.
Interchange Number: 29
Part Number(s): 3684497
Usage: 1973–74 Dart two-door hardtop, four-door sedan; 1973–74 Valiant two-door hardtop; 1974 Valiant four-door sedan.
Interchange Number: 30
Part Number(s): 3684491
Usage: 1973–74 Satellite two-door models only.
Note(s): *Warning*: Deck lid from four-door models will *not* fit.
Interchange Number: 31
Part Number(s): 3684494
Usage: 1973–74 Charger, all models.
Interchange Number: 32
Part Number(s): 3482627
Usage: Late 1970 Charger, use with or without rear wing spoiler.

Deck-Lid Hinges

All hinges here are the bare hinges with mounting brackets, but without the torque rods. Some body styles will affect the interchange. Some hinges are universal fit, meaning they will fit either side of the car, while others have specific usage and cannot swap sides.

Model Identification

Interchange

Interchange Number: 1
Part Number(s): 2769289
Usage: 1968–70 Belvedere, all body styles except station wagon; 1968–73 Valiant, except Scamp; 1968 Coronet, all body styles except station wagon.
Note(s): (1) Fits either side. (2) Hinges from 1969–70 Coronet will *not* fit.

Interchange Number: 2
Part Number(s): 2783552
Usage: 1968–69 Barracuda, all body styles except fastback.
Note(s): Fits either side.

Interchange Number: 3
Part Number(s): 2765758 (right), 2765759 (left)
Usage: 1968 Barracuda fastback only.

Interchange Number: 4
Part Number(s): 2769274
Usage: 1968 Dart, all body styles except convertible.
Note(s): Fits either side.

Interchange Number: 5
Part Number(s): 2782734 (right), 2782735 (left)
Usage: 1968 Dart convertible.
Note(s): Some models used a hinge with a cam. The two are not interchangeable.

Interchange Number: 6
Part Number(s): 2841320 (right), 2841321 (left)
Usage: 1968 Charger. (See Notes and Interchange Number 7).
Note(s): Hinges have no holes. Some models used Interchange Number 7.

Interchange Number: 7
Part Number(s): 2842708
Usage: 1968 (See Notes and Interchange Number 6); 1969 Charger, all except 500 and Daytona; 1970 Charger, all models.
Note(s): Have 2-in holes. Some 1968 models used Interchange Number 6.

Interchange Number: 8
Part Number(s): 2945034 (right), 2945035 (left)
Usage: 1969 Barracuda fastback only.

Interchange Number: 9
Part Number(s): 3417080 (right), 3417081 (left)
Usage: 1969 Dart convertible only.

Interchange Number: 10
Part Number(s): 3417078 (right), 3417079 (left)
Usage: 1969–74 Dart, all body styles except convertible or fastback; 1970–74 Valiant Scamp; 1974 Valiant, all body styles and models except Duster.

Interchange Number: 11
Part Number(s): 2901990 (right), 2901991 (left)
Usage: 1969 Coronet, all body styles except station wagon.

Interchange Number: 12
Part Number(s): 3412156
Usage: 1969 Charger 500; 1969 Charger Daytona.
Note(s): Fits either side.

Interchange Number: 13
Part Number(s): 3417768 (right), 3417769 (left)
Usage: 1970–74 Duster; 1971–72 Demon; 1973–74 Dart Sport.

Interchange Number: 14
Part Number(s): 2963364
Usage: 1970 Barracuda, Challenger, all models and body styles.

Interchange Number: 15
Part Number(s): 3615014 (right), 3615015 (left)
Usage: 1971–74 Barracuda, Challenger, all models and body styles.

Interchange Number: 16
Part Number(s): 3446520 (right), 3446521 (left)
Usage: 1970 Coronet, all models and body styles except station wagon.

Interchange Number: 17
Part Number(s): 3482536 (right), 3482537 (left)
Usage: 1971–73 Charger, Coronet, and Satellite, all models and body styles except station wagon.

Interchange Number: 18
Part Number(s): 3752748 (right), 3752749 (left)
Usage: 1974 Charger, Coronet, Fury, Monaco, Newport, New Yorker, Satellite, all models and body styles except station wagon.

Front Bumpers
Interchange is without back braces. In some models a rear bumper from one model will fit another model as the front bumper, so read the interchange carefully.

Model Identification

Interchange

Interchange Number: 1
  Part Number(s): 2768575
  Usage: 1968–early 1971 Valiant, all models and body styles; 1970–early 1971 Duster.
  Note(s): Used until June 1971.

Interchange Number: 2
  Part Number(s): 2768602
  Usage: 1968–69 Barracuda, all body styles. Rear bumper from this model will also fit.

Interchange Number: 3
  Part Number(s): 2768625
  Usage: 1968–69 Dart, all models and body styles.

Interchange Number: 4
  Part Number(s): 2856550
  Usage: 1968–69 Belvedere, all models and body styles *without* bumper guards.

Interchange Number: 5
  Part Number(s): 2856551
  Usage: 1968 Belvedere, all models and body styles *with* bumper guards.

Interchange Number: 6
  Part Number(s): 2856600
  Usage: 1968–69 Coronet, all models and body styles.

Interchange Number: 7
  Part Number(s): 2856650
  Usage: 1968–69 Charger, all except 1969 Daytona.

Interchange Number: 8
  Part Number(s): 2931125
  Usage: 1969 Belvedere, all models and body style *with* bumper guards.

Interchange Number: 9
  Part Number(s): 3595025
  Usage: Late 1971–72 Duster, Valiant, all models and body styles.

Interchange Number: 10
  Part Number(s): 2962400
  Usage: 1970–early 1971 Dart, all models and body styles; early 1971 Demon.
  Note(s): Used until June 1971.

Interchange Number: 11
  Part Number(s): 3595032
  Usage: Late 1971–72 Dart, Demon, all models and body styles.

Interchange Number: 12
  Part Number(s): 2962275
  Usage: 1970 Barracuda, all models and body styles, without colored bumper.
  Note(s): Interchange Numbers 13 to 20 will fit, but may have to be repainted to match car.

Interchange Number: 13
  Part Number(s): 2962375
  Usage: 1970 Barracuda, all models and body styles with colored bumper.
  Note(s): Bright, blue metallic in color.

Interchange Number: 14
  Part Number(s): 2962376
  Usage: 1970 Barracuda, all models and body styles with colored bumper.
  Note(s): Light bright, red in color.

Interchange Number: 15
  Part Number(s): 2962377
  Usage: 1970 Barracuda, all models and body styles with colored bumper.
  Note(s): Medium dark green metallic in color.

Interchange Number: 16
  Part Number(s): 2962378
  Usage: 1970 Barracuda, all models and body styles with colored bumper.
  Note(s): Medium burnt orange metallic in color.

Interchange Number: 17
  Part Number(s): 2962380
  Usage: 1970 Barracuda, all models and body styles with colored bumper.
  Note(s): White in color.

Interchange Number: 18
  Part Number(s): 2962381
  Usage: 1970 Barracuda, all models and body styles with colored bumper.
  Note(s): Black in color.

Interchange Number: 19
  Part Number(s): 2962294
  Usage: 1970 Barracuda, all models and body styles with

colored bumper.

Note(s): Cadmium yellow in color.

Interchange Number: 20
Part Number(s): 2962295

Usage: 1970 Barracuda, all models and body styles with colored bumper.

Note(s): Purple metallic in color.

Interchange Number: 21
Part Number(s): 364052

Usage: Early 1971 Barracuda, all models and body styles *without* colored bumper.

Note(s): (1) Used until June 1971. (2) Interchange Numbers 23–28 will fit, but may have to be repainted to match the car.

Interchange Number: 22
Part Number(s): 3595035

Usage: Late 1971–72 Barracuda, all models and body styles *without* colored bumper.

Note(s): (1) Used after June 1971. (2) Interchange Numbers 23–28 will fit, but will have to be repainted to match the car.

Interchange Number: 23
Part Number(s): 3464250

Usage: 1971 Barracuda, all models and body styles *with* colored bumper.

Note(s): Bright, blue metallic in color.

Interchange Number: 24
Part Number(s): 3464875

Usage: 1971 Barracuda, all models and body styles *with* colored bumper.

Note(s): Avocado in color.

Interchange Number: 25
Part Number(s): 3464876

Usage: 1971 Barracuda, all models and body styles *with* colored bumper.

Note(s): Citron yella in color.

Interchange Number: 26
Part Number(s): 3464877

Usage: 1971 Barracuda, all models and body styles *with* colored bumper.

Note(s): Plum in color.

Interchange Number: 27
Part Number(s): 3464878

Usage: 1971 Barracuda, all models and body styles *with* colored bumper.

Note(s): Tor red (Hemi orange) in color.

Interchange Number: 28
Part Number(s): 3464879

Usage: 1971 Barracuda, all models and body styles *with* colored bumper.

Note(s): Red in color.

Interchange Number: 29
Part Number(s): 2962348

Usage: 1970–early 1971 Challengers *without* colored bumpers.

Note(s): (1) Used until February 1971. (2) Interchange Numbers 32 to 35 will fit, but may have to be repainted to match car.

Interchange Number: 30
Part Number(s): 3595062

Usage: Late 1971 Challengers, all models and body styles *without* colored bumpers.

Note(s): Used from February 1971 to June 1971. (2) Interchange Numbers 32 to 35 will fit, but will have to be repainted to match car.

Interchange Number: 31
Part Number(s): 3595032

Usage: Very late 1971 Challenger, all models and body styles *without* colored bumpers.

Note(s): Used after June 1971. (2) Interchange Numbers 32 to 35 will fit, but may have to be repainted to match car.

Interchange Number: 32
Part Number(s): 3464077

Usage: 1971 Challenger, all models and body styles *with* colored bumpers.

Note(s): Bright, blue metallic in color.

Interchange Number: 33
Part Number(s): 3464889

Usage: 1971 Challenger, all models and body styles *with* colored bumpers.

Note(s): Citron yella in color.

Interchange Number: 34
Part Number(s): 3464890

Usage: 1971 Challenger, all models and body styles *with* colored bumpers.

Note(s): Plum crazy in color.

Interchange Number: 35
Part Number(s): 3464891

Usage: 1971 Challenger, all models and body styles *with* colored bumpers.

Note(s): Ceramic red in color.

Interchange Number: 36
Part Number(s): 2962450

Usage: 1970 Satellite, all models and body styles.

Interchange Number: 37
Part Number(s): 3464100

Usage: Early 1971 Satellite, two-door models only *without* colored bumper.

Note(s): (1) Used until June 1971. (2) Bumper from four-door or station wagon will *not* fit. Interchange Numbers 38 to 43 will fit, but may have to be repainted to match car.

Interchange Number: 38
Part Number(s): 3464143

Usage: 1971 Satellite two-door *with* colored bumpers.

Note(s): Ceramic red in color.

Interchange Number: 39
Part Number(s): 3464144

Usage: 1971 Satellite two-door *with* colored bumpers.

Note(s): Avocado in color.

Interchange Number: 40
Part Number(s): 3464145

Usage: 1971 Satellite two-door *with* colored bumpers.

Note(s): Yellow green metallic in color.

Interchange Number: 41
Part Number(s): 3464146

Usage: 1971 Satellite two-door *with* colored bumpers.

Note(s): Bright, blue metallic in color.

Interchange Number: 42
Part Number(s): 3464147

Usage: 1971 Satellite two-door *with* colored bumpers.

Note(s): Dark gold metallic in color.

Interchange Number: 43
Part Number(s): 3464148

Usage: 1971 Satellite two-door *with* colored bumpers.

Note(s): Citron yella in color.

Interchange Number: 44
Part Number(s): 2962506 (right), 2962504 (center), 2962507 (left)

Usage: 1970 Coronet, all models and body styles.

Note(s): Three-part design.

Interchange Number: 45
Part Number(s): 3664325

Usage: Early 1971 Charger *without* colored bumpers.

Note(s): (1) Used until June 1971. (2) Interchange Number 47 to 52 will fit, but will have to be repainted to match car.

Interchange Number: 46
Part Number(s): 3595107

Usage: Late 1971–early 1972 Charger, all models *without* colored bumpers.

Note(s): (1) Used after June 1971 to August 1971. (2) Interchange Number 47 to 52 will fit, but will have to be repainted to match car.

Interchange Number: 47
Part Number(s): 3464379

Usage: 1971 Charger *with* colored bumpers.

Note(s): Ceramic red in color.

Interchange Number: 48
　Part Number(s): 3464380
　Usage: 1971 Charger *with* colored bumpers.
　Note(s): Avocado in color.
Interchange Number: 49
　Part Number(s): 3464381
　Usage: 1971 Charger *with* colored bumpers.
　Note(s): Citron yella in color.
Interchange Number: 50
　Part Number(s): 3464382
　Usage: 1971 Charger *with* colored bumpers.
　Note(s): Bright, blue metallic in color.
Interchange Number: 51
　Part Number(s): 3464383
　Usage: 1971 Charger *with* colored bumpers.
　Note(s): Plum crazy in color.
Interchange Number: 52
　Part Number(s): 3464384
　Usage: 1971 Charger *with* colored bumpers.
　Note(s): Medium yellow green metallic in color.
Interchange Number: 53
　Part Number(s): 3595039
　Usage: 1972 Challenger, all models.
Interchange Number: 54
　Part Number(s): 3595100
　Usage: Late 1971–72 Satellite two-door models only.
　Note(s): Warning: Bumper from four-door or station wagon model will *not* fit.
Interchange Number: 55
　Part Number(s): 3595130
　Usage: Late1972 Charger, all models.
Interchange Number: 56
　Part Number(s): 3686002
　Usage: 1973 Duster, Valiant, all models and body styles; late 1974 Duster, Valiant two-door hardtop.
　Note(s): (1) Used after November 14, 1973, in 1974 models. (2) Not found on four-door 1974 models. (3) Has absorber.
Interchange Number: 57
　Part Number(s): 3686026
　Usage: 1973 Dart, all models and body styles; late 1974 Dart two-door hardtop and Sport models.
　Note(s): (1) Used after November 14, 1973. (2) Was not used on 1974 four-door sedans. (3) Has no absorber.
Interchange Number: 58
　Part Number(s): 3686050
　Usage: 1973–74 Barracuda, all models.
Interchange Number: 59
　Part Number(s): 3686075
　Usage: 1973–74 Challenger, all models and body styles.
Interchange Number: 60
　Part Number(s): 3686100
　Usage: 1973–74 Satellite two-door models only.
　Note(s): Warning: Bumper from a four-door or two-door model will *not* fit.
Interchange Number: 61
　Part Number(s): 3686150
　Usage: 1973–74 Charger, all models.
Interchange Number: 62
　Part Number(s): 3753100
　Usage: Early 1974 Duster, Valiant two-door hardtop; 1974 Valiant four-door sedan.
　Note(s): (1) Used until November 14, 1973, on two-door models, all year long on four-door sedan. (2) With absorber.
Interchange Number: 63
　Part Number(s): 3753150
　Usage: Early 1974 Dart, two-door hardtop; early Dart Sport; 1974 Dart four-door sedan.
　Note(s): (1) Used until November 14, 1973, on two-door models, all year long on four-door models. (2) Has absorber.

Interchange Number: 64
　Part Number(s): 2962576
　Usage: 1970 Charger, all models.

Rear Bumper
Model Identification

Interchange

Interchange Number: 1
Part Number(s): 2768600
Usage: 1968–69 Valiant, all models and body styles; 1970–early 1971 Duster; early 1971 Demon.
Note(s): Used until June 1971 in 1971 models.

Interchange Number: 2
Part Number(s): 2768602
Usage: 1968–69 Barracuda, all models and body styles. Front and rear bumper will interchange.

Interchange Number: 3
Part Number(s): 2856525
Usage: 1968–69 dart *without* bumper guards, all models and body styles.

Interchange Number: 4
Part Number(s): 2856526
Usage: 1968–69 Dart *with* guards, all models and body styles.

Interchange Number: 5
Part Number(s): 2856575
Usage: 1968 Belvedere *without* bumper guards, all models and body styles except station wagon.

Interchange Number: 6
Part Number(s): 2856576
Usage: 1968 Belvedere *with* bumper guards, all models and body styles except station wagon.

Interchange Number: 7
Part Number(s): 2856625
Usage: 1968–69 Coronet, all models and body styles except station wagon.

Interchange Number: 8
Part Number(s): 2856675
Usage: 1968–70 Charger, all models.

Interchange Number: 9
Part Number(s): 2931140
Usage: 1969 Belvedere *without* bumper guards, all models and body styles except station wagon.

Interchange Number: 10
Part Number(s): 2931141
Usage: 1969 Belvedere *with* bumper guards, all models and body styles except station wagon.

Interchange Number: 11
Part Number(s): 3595028
Usage: Late 1971–72 Duster, Demon.
Note(s): (1) Used after June 1971. (2) Other body styles will *not* fit.

Interchange Number: 12
Part Number(s): 2962325
Usage: 1970–early 1971 Valiant two-door hardtop.
Note(s): (1) Used until June 1971. (2) Bumper from Duster will *not* fit.

Interchange Number: 13
Part Number(s): 3595027
Usage: Late 1971–72 Valiant two-door hardtop.
Note(s): (1) Used after June 1971. (2) Bumper from Duster will *not* fit.

Interchange Number: 14
Part Number(s): 2962425
Usage: 1970 Dart, all models and body styles.

Interchange Number: 15
Part Number(s): 3464050
Usage: Early 1971 Dart, all models and body styles except Demon.
Note(s): Used until June 1971.

Interchange Number: 16
Part Number(s): 3595034
Usage: Late 1971–72 Dart, all models and body styles except Demon.
Note(s): Used after June 1971.

Interchange Number: 17
Part Number(s): 2962300
Usage: 1970–71 Barracuda, all models and body styles *without* colored bumper.
Note(s): Interchange Numbers 18–26 and 29–30 will fit, but may have to be repainted to match car.

Interchange Number: 18
Part Number(s): 2962391
Usage: 1970–71 Barracuda, all models and body styles *with* colored bumper.
Note(s): Light bright, red in color.

Interchange Number: 19
Part Number(s): 2962421
Usage: 1970 Barracuda, all models and body styles *with* colored bumper.
Note(s): Lemon twist in color.

Interchange Number: 20
Part Number(s): 2962422
Usage: 1970 Barracuda, all models and body styles *with* colored bumper.
Note(s): Lime light in color.

Interchange Number: 21
Part Number(s): 2962423
Usage: 1970 Barracuda, all models and body styles *with* colored bumper.
Note(s): Violet metallic in color.

Interchange Number: 22
Part Number(s): 2962390
Usage: 1970 Barracuda, all models and body styles *with* colored bumper.
Note(s): Blue fire metallic in color.

Interchange Number: 23
Part Number(s): 2962392
Usage: 1970 Barracuda, all models and body styles *with* colored bumper.
Note(s): Ivy green metallic in color.

Interchange Number: 24
Part Number(s): 2962393
Usage: 1970 Barracuda, all models and body styles *with*

colored bumper.

Note(s): Deep burnt orange metallic in color.

Interchange Number: 25
Part Number(s): 2962395
Usage: 1970 Barracuda, all models and body styles *with* colored bumper.
Note(s): Alpine white in color.

Interchange Number: 26
Part Number(s): 2962396
Usage: 1970 Barracuda, all models and body styles *with* colored bumper.
Note(s): Black in color.

Interchange Number: 27
Part Number(s): 3595037
Usage: Late 1971–72 Barracuda, all models and body styles *without* colored bumpers.

Interchange Number: 28
Part Number(s): 3464883
Usage: 1971 Barracuda, all models and body styles *with* colored bumper.
Note(s): (1) Citron yella in color. (2) Will fit 1970 Barracudas but not originally offered on this model.

Interchange Number: 29
Part Number(s): 3464884
Usage: 1971 Barracuda, all models and body styles *with* colored bumper.
Note(s): (1) Plum metallic in color. (2) Will fit 1970 Barracudas but not originally offered on this model.

Interchange Number: 30
Part Number(s): 3464885
Usage: 1971 Barracuda, all models and body styles *with* colored bumper.
Note(s): (1) Tor red (Hemi orange) in color. (2) Will fit 1970 Barracudas but not originally offered on this model.

Interchange Number: 31
Part Number(s): 2962350
Usage: 1970 Challenger, all models and body styles.

Interchange Number: 32
Part Number(s): 3464073
Usage: Early 1971 Challenger, all models and body styles *without* colored bumpers.
Note(s): (1) Used until June 1971. (2) Interchange Numbers 34–37 will fit but may have to be repainted to match car.

Interchange Number: 33
Part Number(s): 3595038
Usage: Late 1971–72 Challenger, all models and body styles *without* colored bumpers.
Note(s): Used after June 1971.

Interchange Number: 34
Part Number(s): 3464092
Usage: 1971 Challenger, all models and body styles *with* colored bumpers.
Note(s): Bright, blue metallic in color.

Interchange Number: 35
Part Number(s): 3464895
Usage: 1971 Challenger, all models and body styles *with* colored bumpers.
Note(s): Citron yella in color.

Interchange Number: 36
Part Number(s): 3464896
Usage: 1971 Challenger, all models and body styles *with* colored bumpers.
Note(s): Plum crazy in color.

Interchange Number: 37
Part Number(s): 3464897
Usage: 1971 Challenger, all models and body styles *with* colored bumpers.
Note(s): Ceramic red in color.

Interchange Number: 38
Part Number(s): 2962475

Usage: 1970 Satellite, all models and body styles except station wagon.

Interchange Number: 39
Part Number(s): 3464200
Usage: 1971 Satellite, two-door models *without* bumper guards or colored bumper group.
Note(s): Bumper from four-door model will *not* fit.

Interchange Number: 40
Part Number(s): 3464201
Usage: 1971 Satellite, two-door models *with* bumper guards *without* colored bumper group.
Note(s): (1) Bumper from four-door or station wagon model will *not* fit. (2) Interchange Numbers 41–46 will fit but may have to be repainted to match the car.

Interchange Number: 41
Part Number(s): 3464168
Usage: 1971 Satellite, two-door models *with* colored bumper group.
Note(s): Ceramic red in color.

Interchange Number: 42
Part Number(s): 3464169
Usage: 1971 Satellite, two-door models *with* colored bumper group.
Note(s): Avocado in color.

Interchange Number: 43
Part Number(s): 3464170
Usage: 1971 Satellite, two-door models *with* colored bumper group.
Note(s): Medium yellow green in color.

Interchange Number: 44
Part Number(s): 3464171
Usage: 1971 Satellite, two-door models *with* colored bumper group.
Note(s): Bright, blue metallic in color.

Interchange Number: 45
Part Number(s): 3464172
Usage: 1971 Satellite, two-door models *with* colored bumper group.
Note(s): Dark gold in color.

Interchange Number: 46
Part Number(s): 3464173
Usage: 1971 Satellite, two-door models *with* colored bumper group.
Note(s): Citron yella in color.

Interchange Number: 47
Part Number(s): 2962550
Usage: 1970 Coronet, all models and body styles except station wagon.

Interchange Number: 48
Part Number(s): 3464425
Usage: Early 1971 Charger *without* colored bumper group.
Note(s): Used until June 1971. (2) Interchange Numbers 49–55 will fit but may have to be repainted to match car.

Interchange Number: 49
Part Number(s): 3595189
Usage: Late 1971 Charger *without* colored bumper group.
Note(s): Used after June 1971.

Interchange Number: 50
Part Number(s): 3464466
Usage: Charger *with* colored bumper group.
Note(s): Ceramic red in color.

Interchange Number: 51
Part Number(s): 3464467
Usage: 1971 Charger *with* colored bumper group.
Note(s): Avocado in color.

Interchange Number: 52
Part Number(s): 3464468
Usage: 1971 Charger *with* colored bumper group.
Note(s): Citron yella in color.

Interchange Number: 53
Part Number(s): 3464469
Usage: 1971 Charger *with* colored bumper group.
Note(s): Bright, blue metallic in color.

Interchange Number: 54
Part Number(s): 3464470
Usage: 1971 Charger *with* colored bumper group.
Note(s): Plum crazy in color.

Interchange Number: 55
   Part Number(s): 3464471
   Usage: 1971 Charger *with* colored bumper group.
   Note(s): Medium yellow green in color.
Interchange Number: 56
   Part Number(s): 3595150
   Usage: 1972 Satellite two-door models only, *without* bumper guards.
   Note(s): Warning: Bumper from four-door or station wagon will *not* fit.
Interchange Number: 57
   Part Number(s): 3595151
   Usage: 1972 Satellite two-door models only, with bumper guards.
   Note(s): Warning: Bumper from four-door or station wagon will *not* fit.
Interchange Number: 58
   Part Number(s): 3595105
   Usage: 1972 Charger, all models.
Interchange Number: 59
   Part Number(s): 3686500
   Usage: 1973 Duster, Dart Sport.
Interchange Number: 60
   Part Number(s): 3686525
   Usage: 1973 Valiant two-door hardtop, except Duster.
Interchange Number: 61
   Part Number(s): 3686526
   Usage: 1973 Dart, all body styles except fastback.
Interchange Number: 62
   Part Number(s): 3686550
   Usage: 1973 Barracuda, all models.
Interchange Number: 63
   Part Number(s): 3686575
   Usage: 1973 Challenger, all models.
Interchange Number: 64
   Part Number(s): 3686600
   Usage: Early 1973 Satellite two-door models only.
   Note(s): (1) Used until April 16, 1973. (2) Bumper from four-door or station wagon will *not* fit.
Interchange Number: 65
   Part Number(s): 3686602
   Usage: Late 1973 Satellite two-door models only.
   Note(s): (1) Used after April 16, 1973. (2) Bumper from four-door or station wagon will *not* fit.
Interchange Number: 66
   Part Number(s): 3686650
   Usage: 1973–74 Charger, all models.
Interchange Number: 67
   Part Number(s): 3754104
   Usage: 1974 Dart, Valiant, all models and body styles except Duster and Sport.
Interchange Number: 68
   Part Number(s): 3754052
   Usage: 1974 Duster, Dart Sport.
Interchange Number: 69
   Part Number(s): 3754152
   Usage: 1974 Barracuda, all models.
Interchange Number: 70
   Part Number(s): 3754202
   Usage: 1974 Challenger, all models.
Interchange Number: 71
   Part Number(s): 37541252
   Usage: 1974 Satellite two-door models only.
   Note(s): Bumper from four-door or station wagon will *not* fit.

Grilles

   Grilles were usually changed each yea, and will differ between different models and some submodels, like R/T models. However, some grilles can be modified (painted) to adapt them to other models. If this is the case, it is noted under the heading Modification Notes.

Model Identification

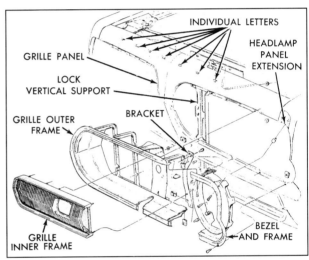

1968 Barracuda grille.

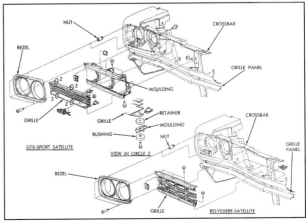

1968 Belvedere grille.

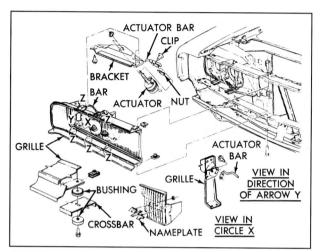

1968 Charger grille.

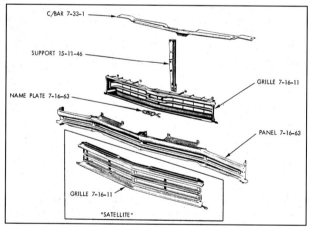

1969 Belvedere, Satellite, and GTX grille.

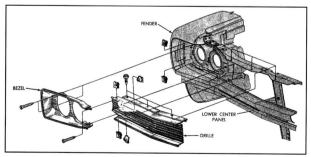

1969 Coronet grille.

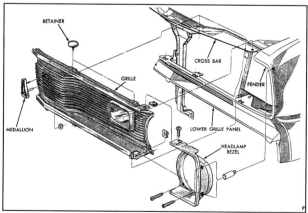

1970–1972 Duster/Valiant grille attachment.

Interchange

Interchange Number: 1
  Part Number(s): 2786548 (right), 2786549 (left)
  Usage: 1968 Barracuda, all models and body styles.

Interchange Number: 2
  Part Number(s): 2786047
  Usage: 1968 Dart, all body styles and models except GT or GTS.

Interchange Number: 3
  Part Number(s): 2786475
  Usage: 1968 Dart GTS models.
  Modification Note(s): Interchange Number 2 can be adapted by painting inserts and adding center ornament.

Interchange Number: 4
  Part Number(s): 2786567
  Usage: 1968 Dart GT.
  Modification Note(s): Interchange Number 2 will fit by painting inserts.

Interchange Number: 5
  Part Number(s): 2786445
  Usage: 1968 Belvedere, all models except Sport Satellite, GTX, or Road Runner.

Interchange Number: 6
  Part Number(s): 2785880
  Usage: 1968 Road Runner
  Modification Note(s): Interchange Number 5 will fit if inserts are painted dark gray.

Interchange Number: 7
  Part Number(s): 2786513
  Usage: 1968 GTX, Sport Satellite, all body styles including station wagon.

Interchange Number: 8
  Part Number(s): 2786801
  Usage: 1968 Coronet, all models and body styles except Coronet 500 or R/T.

Interchange Number: 9
  Part Number(s): 2786857
  Usage: 1968 Coronet 500, Coronet R/T; 1969 Charger 500.
  Modification Note(s): Interchange Number 8 will fit if inserts are painted flat black.

Interchange Number: 10
  Part Number(s): 2785590

Usage: 1968 Charger, all models.

Interchange Number: 11
  Part Number(s): 2786022 (right), 2768023 (left)
  Usage: 1968 Valiant, all models except Signet.

Interchange Number: 12
  Part Number(s): 278810 (right), 276811 (left)
  Usage: 1968 Valiant Signet.
  Modification Note(s): Interchange Number 11 will fit if inserts are painted flat black.

Interchange Number: 13
  Part Number(s): 2898110
  Usage: 1969 Valiant, all models and body styles.

Interchange Number: 14
  Part Number(s): 2898808 (right), 2898809 (left)
  Usage: 1969 Barracuda, all models and body styles except with Formula S package.

Interchange Number: 15
  Part Number(s): 2998196 (right), 2998197 (left)
  Usage: 1969 Barracuda with Formula S package.

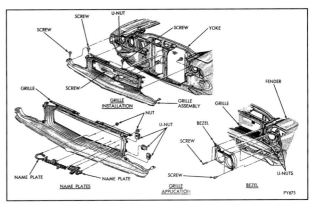

1970 Challenger grille.

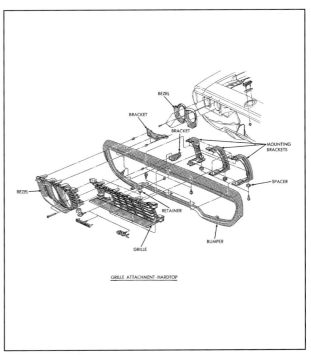

1971 Satellite grille.

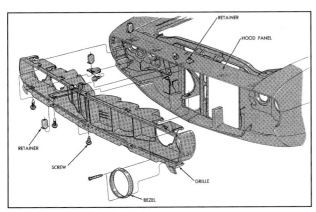

1971 Barracuda grille.

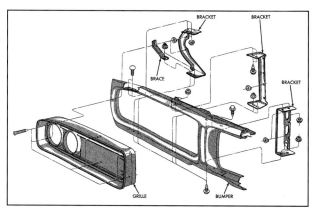

1971 Charger grille attachment. Typical of 1972–1974.

Modification Note(s): Interchange Number 14 will fit if inserts are painted flat black.

Interchange Number: 16
Part Number(s): 2898242
Usage: 1969 Dart GT and GTS.
Modification Note(s): Interchange Number 17 will fit if inserts are painted flat black.

Interchange Number: 17
Part Number(s): 2898114
Usage: 1969 Dart, all models and body styles except GT or GTS.

Interchange Number: 18
Part Number(s): 2947007
Usage: 1969 Road Runner.
Modification Note(s): Interchange Number 19 will fit if inserts are painted flat black.

Interchange Number: 19
Part Number(s): 2898116
Usage: 1969 Belvedere, all models and body styles except Sport Satellite, GTX, or Road Runner.

Interchange Number: 20
Part Number(s): 289116
Usage: 1969 GTX, Sport Satellite, all body styles.

Interchange Number: 21
Part Number(s): 28998120
Usage: 1968 Coronet, all models except R/T, Super Bee, or 500 models.

Interchange Number: 22
Part Number(s): 2898872
Usage: 1969 Coronet R/T, Coronet 500, Super Bee.

Interchange Number: 23
Part Number(s): 2786362 (right), 289638 center, 2786363 (left)
Usage: 1969 Charger, except 500 or Daytona.

Interchange Number: 24
Part Number(s): 2949526
Usage: 1970 Valiant, all models and body styles except Duster.

Interchange Number: 25
Part Number(s): 2998364
Usage: 1970 Duster
Modification Note(s): Interchange Number 24 will fit if inserts are painted dark gray.

Interchange Number: 26
Part Number(s): 3573721
Usage: 1971–72 Valiant, all models except Duster 340 or Twister.

Interchange Number: 27
Part Number(s): 3442739
Usage: 1971–72 Duster 340 and Duster Twister.

Interchange Number: 28
Part Number(s): 2949558
Usage: 1970 Barracuda, all models except AAR.

Interchange Number: 29
Part Number(s): 3443808

Usage: 1970 Cuda AAR.
Modification Note(s): Interchange Number 28 will fit if inserts and frame are painted flat black.

Interchange Number: 30
Part Number(s): 3442647
Usage: 1971 Barracuda, all models except with colored grille.

Interchange Number: 31
Part Number(s): Varies
Usage: 1971 Cuda, with colored grille.
Modification Note(s): Interchange Number 30 will fit if frame is painted to match car. Grille inserts are still painted argent silver.

Interchange Number: 32
Part Number(s): 2949577
Usage: 1970 Challenger, all models except Challenger R/T.

Interchange Number: 33
Part Number(s): 2998216
Usage: 1970 Challenger R/T or Challenger T/A.
Modification Note(s): Interchange Number 32 will fit if painted flat black.

Interchange Number: 34
Part Number(s): 3443276
Usage: 1971 Challenger with decor group; 1971 Challenger R/T or T/A.
Note(s): Interchange Number 35 will fit if painted flat black.

Interchange Number: 35
Part Number(s): 3443278
Usage: 1971 Challenger without decor group.

Interchange Number: 36
Part Number(s): 2949548
Usage: 1970 Dart, all models.

Interchange Number: 37
Part Number(s): 3573667
Usage: 1971 Dart, Demon, all models.

Interchange Number: 38
Part Number(s): 2949860
Usage: 1970 Satellite, except Satellite Sport, GTX, or Road Runner.

Interchange Number: 39
Part Number(s): 2949997
Usage: 1970 Road Runner.
Modification Note(s): Interchange Number 38 will fit if inserts are painted dark gray.

Interchange Number: 40
Part Number(s): 2998002
Usage: 1970 Sport Satellite, GTX.

Interchange Number: 41
Part Number(s): 3442207
Usage: 1971 Satellite two-door, all models except Sebring.
Modification Note(s): *Warning:* Grille from four-door will *not* fit.

Interchange Number: 42
Part Number(s): 3443014
Usage: 1971 Satellite Sebring.

Interchange Number: 43
Part Number(s): 2949808 (right), 2949809 (left)
Usage: 1970 Coronet, all models except Coronet R/T, Coronet 500, Super Bee.

Interchange Number: 44
Part Number(s): 2998200 (right), 2998201 (left)
Usage: 1970b Coronet R/T, Coronet 500, Super Bee.
Modification Note(s): Interchange Number 43 will fit if painted dark gray.

Interchange Number: 45
Part Number(s): 3442378 (right), 3442379 (left)
Usage: 1971 Charger R/T, Super Bee without concealed headlamps.
Modification Note(s): Interchange Number 46 will fit if painted dark gray.

Interchange Number: 46
Part Number(s): 3442984 (right), 3442985 (left)
Usage: 1971 Charger, without concealed headlamps except R/T or Super Bee.

Interchange Number: 47
Part Number(s): 3442864 (frame part number)
Usage: 1971 Charger with concealed headlamps.
Note(s): When swapping to a car originally built without this option, it is easier to swap with front bumper or entire front end.

Interchange Number: 48
Part Number(s): 2998440
Usage: 1970 Charger, all models.

Interchange Number: 49
Part Number(s): 3573214
Usage: 1972 Barracuda, all models.

Interchange Number: 50
Part Number(s): 3573216
Usage: 1972–74 Challenger, all models except Rallye.

Interchange Number: 51
Part Number(s): 3573589
Usage: 1972–74 Challenger Rallye.
Modification Note(s): Interchange Number 50 will fit if painted dark gray.

Interchange Number: 52
Part Number(s): 3573143
Usage: 1972 Dart, all models and body styles.

Interchange Number: 53
Part Number(s): 3573409
Usage: 1972 Road Runner.

Interchange Number: 54
Part Number(s): 3574139
Usage: 1972 Satellite two-door models, except Road Runner.

Interchange Number: 55
Part Number(s): 3573356 (right), 3573357 (left)
Usage: 1972 Charger, all models without concealed headlamps.

Interchange Number: 56
Part Number(s): 3442864 (right), 3442865 (left) (frame part number)
Usage: 1972 Charger with concealed headlamps. Standard on S.E. models.

Interchange Number: 57
Part Number(s): 3672929
Usage: 1973–74 Duster, Scamp, and Valiant, all models and body styles, except 1974 Valiant Brougham.

Interchange Number: 58
Part Number(s): 3672673
Usage: 1973–74 Barracuda, all models.

Interchange Number: 59
Part Number(s): 3672931
Usage: 1973 Dart, all models and body styles.

Interchange Number: 60
Part Number(s): 3672209
Usage: 1973–74 Satellite two-door, all models.
Note(s): *Warning*: Bumper form four-door or station wagon will *not* fit.

Interchange Number: 61
Part Number(s): 3672318 (right), 3672319 (left)
Usage: 1973–74 Charger, all models except S.E.

Interchange Number: 62
Part Number(s): 3672322 (right), 3672323 (left)
Usage: 1973–74 Charger S.E. models.

Interchange Number: 63
Part Number(s): 3691476
Usage: 1974 Dart, all models and body styles except Special Edition.

Interchange Number: 64
Part Number(s): 3691649
Usage: 1974 Dart Special Edition.

Outside Rearview Mirror
Model Identification

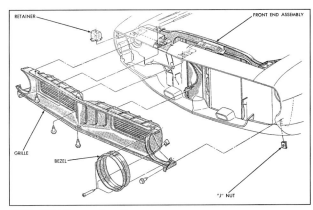

1972–1974 Barracuda grille.

This standard mirror was used on nearly all models.

Body-colored mirrors for the Duster/Dart line.

Body-colored mirrors used on the E-body.

Interchange

Interchange Number: 1
Part Number(s): 2802710
Style/Shape: Round-head
Type: Non-remote
Usage: 1968–69 Barracuda; 1968–70 Belvedere, Charger, Coronet, Satellite; 1968–73 Dart and Valiant, all models; 1970–73 Duster; 1971–72 Demon; 1968 Chrysler 300, Fury, Monaco, Newport, and New Yorker, all models and body styles without remote-control mirror.
Note(s): (1) Fits either driver's or passenger's side. (2) 1968 full-size only; mirror from 1969 full-size model will *not* interchange.

Interchange Number: 2
Part Number(s): 2935217
Style/Shape: Round-head
Type: Remote control
Usage: 1968–69 Barracuda; 1968–70 Belvedere, Charger, Coronet, Satellite; 1968–70 Dart, Valiant; 1970 Duster; 1968 Chrysler 300, Fury, Newport, New Yorker, and Polara; all models and body styles with remote-control mirror.

Note(s): (1) Standard on Imperial models. (2) 1968 full-size models only; 1969 or 1970 models will *not* fit.

Interchange Number: 3
Part Number(s): 2802869
Style/Shape: Round-head
Type: Non-remote
Usage: 1967–69 Barracuda; 1967–70 Belvedere, Charger, Coronet, Satellite; 1967–74 Dart, Valiant; 1970–74 Duster; 1971–72 Demon; 1967–68 Chrysler 300, Fury, Monaco, Newport, New Yorker, and Polara, all models and body styles. Passenger-side mirror. Used with remote-control left-hand round-headed mirror.
Note(s): 1967–68 full-size models only; mirror from 1969 full-size models will *not* interchange. Used on driver's side in 1967 models.

Interchange Number: 4
Part Number(s): 3586175
Style/Shape: Chrome racing
Type: Remote control
Usage: 1970 Charger, Coronet, Dart, Duster, Satellite, and Valiant.

Interchange Number: 5
Part Number(s): 3586655
Style/Shape: Colored racing
Type: Remote control
Usage: 1970 Charger, Coronet, Satellite; 1970–72 Dart, Duster, and Valiant; 1971 Demon.
Note(s): Paint to match car.

Interchange Number: 6
Part Number(s): 2945955
Style/Shape: Round-head
Type: Remote control
Usage: 1970 Charger, Coronet, and Satellite; 1970–72 Dart Valiant, all body styles except Duster or Demon; 1973 Dart, Valiant four-door models only.
Note(s): Standard mirror.

Interchange Number: 7
Part Number(s): 2999875
Style/Shape: Chrome round-head
Type: Remote control
Usage: 1970 Duster.

Interchange Number: 8
Part Number(s): 3548053
Style/Shape: Colored racing
Type: Remote control
Usage: 1970 Barracuda, Challenger.

Interchange Number: 9
Part Number(s): 2999549
Style/Shape: Chrome racing
Type: Remote control
Usage: 1970 Barracuda, Challenger.

Interchange Number: 10
Part Number(s): 3586174
Style/Shape: Chrome racing
Type: Non-remote
Usage: 1970 Charger, Coronet, and Satellite; 1970–74 Dart, Duster, and Valiant, all models; 1971–72 Demon. Passenger-side mirror.

Interchange Number: 11
Part Number(s): 3586176
Style/Shape: Colored racing
Type: Non-remote
Usage: 1970 Charger, Coronet, and Satellite; 1970–74 Dart, Duster, and Valiant, all models; 1971–72 Demon. Passenger-side mirror.
Note(s): 1973 Dart taxi cab used a different mirror and will not interchange to these models.

Interchange Number: 12
Part Number(s): 3508990
Style/Shape: Colored racing
Type: Non-remote
Usage: 1970 Barracuda, Challenger.

Chrome racing mirror for the 1972 B-body.

Chrome racing mirror for the 1970 E-body.

Interchange Number: 13
Part Number(s): 3508989
Style/Shape: Chrome racing
Type: Non-remote
Usage: 1970 Barracuda, Challenger.

Interchange Number: 14
Part Number(s): 2999553
Style/Shape: Chrome round-head
Type: Non-remote
Usage: 1970 Barracuda, Challenger. Driver's side only.

Interchange Number: 15
Part Number(s): 3586087
Style/Shape: Chrome round-head
Type: Remote control
Usage: 1971–72 Duster, Demon.

Interchange Number: 16
Part Number(s): 3586654
Style/Shape: Chrome racing
Type: Remote control
Usage: 1971–72 Dart, Duster, Demon, and Valiant.

Interchange Number: 17
Part Number(s): 3586642
Style/Shape: Chrome racing
Type: Remote control
Usage: 1971–74 Barracuda, Challenger.

Interchange Number: 18
Part Number(s): 3586649
Style/Shape: Colored racing
Type: Remote control
Usage: 1971–74 Barracuda, Challenger.

Interchange Number: 19
Part Number(s): 3586976
Style/Shape: Colored racing
Type: Remote control
Usage: 1971–72 Charger, Satellite.

Interchange Number: 20
Part Number(s): 3586977
Style/Shape: Chrome racing
Type: Remote control
Usage: 1971–72 Charger, Satellite.

Interchange Number: 21
    Part Number(s): 3586645
    Style/Shape: Chrome round-head
    Type: Non-remote
    Usage: 1971–74 Barracuda, Challenger; 1971–72 Charger, Satellite.
    Note(s): Swap from two-door models only. Mirror from four-door models will *not* fit.

Interchange Number: 22
    Part Number(s): 3586644
    Style/Shape: Chrome racing
    Type: Non-remote control
    Usage: 1971–74 Barracuda, Challenger; 1971–72 Charger, Satellite. Passenger-side mirror.

Interchange Number: 23
    Part Number(s): 3586650
    Style/Shape: Colored racing
    Type: Non-remote
    Usage: 1971–74 Barracuda, Challenger; 1971–72 Charger, Satellite.

Interchange Number: 24
    Part Number(s): 3695507
    Style/Shape: Chrome racing
    Type: Remote control
    Usage: 1973–74 Dart Sport, Duster.
    Note(s): Mirror from other models or body styles will *not* fit.

Interchange Number: 25
    Part Number(s): 3695506
    Style/Shape: Colored racing
    Type: Remote control
    Usage: 1973–74 Dart Sport, Duster.
    Note(s): Mirror from other models or body styles will *not* fit.

Interchange Number: 26
    Part Number(s): 3695508
    Style/Shape: Chrome round-head
    Type: Remote control
    Usage: 1973 Dart, Valiant, all models except Duster or Dart Sport; 1974 Dart, Duster, and Valiant, all models and body styles.

Interchange Number: 27
    Part Number(s): 3695514
    Style/Shape: Chrome racing
    Type: Remote control
    Usage: 1973–74 Charger, Satellite (two-door models only).
    Note(s): Mirror from four-door models will *not* fit.

Interchange Number: 28
    Part Number(s): 3695513
    Style/Shape: Colored racing
    Type: Remote control
    Usage: 1973–74 Charger, Satellite (two-door models only).
    Note(s): Mirror from four-door models will *not* fit.

Interchange Number: 29
    Part Number(s): 2802869
    Style/Shape: Chrome round-head
    Type: Non-remote control
    Usage: 1970 Charger, Coronet, and Satellite; 1970–73 Dart, Duster, and Valiant, all models and body styles.

Interchange Number: 30
    Part Number(s): 3695511
    Style/Shape: Chrome racing
    Type: Non-remote control
    Usage: 1973–74 Charger, Satellite (two-door models only). Passenger-side mirror.
    Note(s): Mirror from four-door model will *not* fit.

Interchange Number: 31
    Part Number(s): 3695512
    Style/Shape: Colored racing
    Type: Non-remote control
    Usage: 1973–74 Charger, Satellite (two-door models only). Passenger-side mirror.

Interchange Number: 32
    Part Number(s): 3695517
    Style/Shape: Chrome round-head
    Type: Non-remote control
    Usage: 1973–74 Charger, Coronet, and Satellite (two and four-door models only).
    Note(s): Station wagon used a different mirror and will *not* fit.

Interchange Number: 33
    Part Number(s): 2802834
    Style/Shape: Chrome round -head
    Type: Non-remote
    Usage: 1973–74 Dart, Duster, and Valiant, all models and body styles.

Glass

Interchange here is "physical fit." There are two types of glass used, tinted and non-tinted. Tinted glass came in three forms: all-tinted glass; tinted windshield with the other glass untinted; and tinted side glass with windshield and back glass untinted. Tinted glass was standard on cars with air conditioning, unless the customer specifically requested it to be replaced with non-tinted glass. The interchanges do not consider tint, but you should match the glass to the rest of the car. For example, if your 1972 Charger has all-tinted glass, you should not replace the driver's door glass with non-tinted glass. Tinted glass can be determined on 1969 to 1974 models by the option code on the fender tag. If your car has the following codes—G11 (all glass tinted), G1 (tinted side glass), G15 (tinted windshield)—you may also find these codes—G18 (clear windshield) or G21 (all glass clear). These later codes were used in cars with air conditioning, when the customer requested untinted glass only. All part numbers given are for tinted glass only; they should be used for reference only.

Windshield
Model Identification

Interchange
Interchange Number: 1
    Part Number(s): 2663142
    Usage: 1967–68 Dart, Valiant two-door sedan; 1967–74 Dart or Valiant four-door sedan.

Interchange Number: 2
    Part Number(s): 2663150
    Usage: 1967–69 Barracuda; 1967–74 Dart, except fastback or sedan; 1970–74 Valiant two-door hardtop, except Duster.

Interchange Number: 3
    Part Number(s): 2811266
    Usage: 1968–70 Belvedere, Charger, Coronet, Satellite, all models and body styles except station wagon, four-door sedan, or convertible.

Interchange Number: 4
    Part Number(s): 2570606
    Usage: 1968–70 Belvedere, Coronet, and Satellite convertible.

Interchange Number: 5

Part Number(s): 2895593
Usage: 1970–74 Barracuda, Challenger, all body styles.
Interchange Number: 6
Part Number(s): 2895863
Usage: 1970–76 Duster; 1971 Demon; 1973–76 Dart Sport.
Interchange Number: 7
Part Number(s): 3439473
Usage: 1971–74 Charger, Satellite. Two-door models only.
Note(s): Glass from four-door Satellite and Coronets will *not* fit.

Door Glass
Model Identification

Barracuda..*Interchange Number*
1968
two-door hardtop 5
convertible 8
fastback..7
1969
two-door hardtop 1
convertible 3
fastback..21
1970–74
except convertible..16
convertible (1970–71)....................................17

Belvedere, Charger, Coronet,
and Satellite...*Interchange Number*
1968
two-door sedan..9
two-door hardtop 10
Charger..10
convertible 11
1969–70
two-door sedan..12
two-door hardtop 13
Charger..13
convertible 14
1971–74..18

Challenger..*Interchange Number*
1970–74
except convertible..16
convertible (1970–71)....................................17

Dart, Duster, Demon, and Valiant
1968
two-door sedan..4
two-door hardtop 6
convertible 8
1969–72
except Duster and Demon
two-door hardtop 2
convertible (1969 only)..................................3
Duster and Demon..15
1973–74
two-door hardtop 19
Duster and Sport..20

Interchange
Interchange Number: 1
Part Number(s): 2861908 (passenger), 2861909 (driver)
Usage: 1969 Barracuda two-door hardtop only.
Note(s): Interchange with rear frame.
Interchange Number: 2
Part Number(s): 2861900 (passenger), 2861901 (driver)
Usage: 1969–72 Dart two-door hardtop.
Note(s): Interchange with rear frame.
Interchange Number: 3
Part Number(s): 2861902 (passenger), 2861903 (driver)
Usage: 1969 Barracuda, Dart convertible.
Interchange Number: 4
Part Number(s): 2663496 (passenger), 2663497 (driver)
Usage: 1967–68 Dart Valiant two-door; 1968 Dart two-door sedan.

Interchange Number: 5
Part Number(s): 2811974 (passenger), 2811975 (driver)
Usage: 1967–68 Barracuda two-door hardtop only.
Note(s): Interchange with rear frame.
Interchange Number: 6
Part Number(s): 2663484 (passenger), 2663485 (driver)
Usage: 1967–68 Dart two-door hardtop.
Note(s): Interchange with rear frame.
Interchange Number: 7
Part Number(s): 2664798 (passenger), 2664799 (driver)
Usage: 1967–68 Barracuda fastback.
Note(s): Interchange with rear frame.
Interchange Number: 8
Part Number(s): 2663510 (passenger), 2663511 (driver)
Usage: 1967–68 Barracuda, Dart convertible.
Note(s): Interchange with rear frame.
Interchange Number: 9
Part Number(s): 2860390 (passenger), 2863091 (driver)
Usage: 1968 Belvedere, Coronet two-door sedan.
Interchange Number: 10
Part Number(s): 2811640 (passenger), 2811641 (driver)
Usage: 1968 Belvedere, Coronet two-door hardtop; 1968 Charger.
Note(s): Interchange with rear frame.
Interchange Number: 11
Part Number(s): 2860070 (passenger), 2860071 (driver)
Usage: 1968 Belvedere, Coronet convertible.
Note(s): Interchange with rear frame.
Interchange Number: 12
Part Number(s): 2895288 (passenger), 2895289 (driver)
Usage: 1969–70 Belvedere, Coronet two-door sedan.
Interchange Number: 13
Part Number(s): 2895296 (passenger), 2895297 (driver)
Usage: 1969–70 Belvedere, Coronet two-door hardtop; 1968–70 Charger.
Note(s): Interchange with rear frame.
Interchange Number: 14
Part Number(s): 2895300 (passenger), 2895301 (driver)
Usage: 1969–70 Belvedere, Coronet convertible.
Note(s): Interchange with rear frame.
Interchange Number: 15
Part Number(s): 2895890 (passenger), 2895891 (driver)
Usage: 1970–72 Duster; 1971–72 Demon.
Interchange Number: 16
Part Number(s): 2895688 (passenger), 2895689 (driver)
Usage: 1970–74 Barracuda, Challenger, all models except convertible.
Interchange Number: 17
Part Number(s): 3440322 (passenger), 3440323 (driver)
Usage: 1970–71 Barracuda, Challenger convertible.
Interchange Number: 18
Part Number(s): 3439902 (passenger), 3439903 (driver)
Usage: 1971–74 Charger, Satellite two-door models only.
Interchange Number: 19
Part Number(s): 3582748 (passenger), 3582749 (driver)
Usage: 1973–74 Dart, Valiant two-door hardtop, except Duster or Sport.
Interchange Number: 20
Part Number(s): 3582752 (passenger), 3582753 (driver)
Usage: 1973–74 Dart Sport, Duster.
Interchange Number: 21
Part Number(s):
Usage: 1969 Barracuda fastback.

Quarter-Window Glass
Model Identification
Barracuda..*Interchange Number*
1968–69
two-door hardtop 1
convertible 3

Interchange

Interchange Number: 1
    Part Number(s): 2840810 (passenger), 2840811 (driver)
    Usage: 1968–69 Barracuda two-door hardtop.
    Note(s): Interchange with front frame.

Interchange Number: 2
    Part Number(s): 2840804 (passenger), 2840805 (driver)
    Usage: 1968–72 Dart two-door hardtop, except Demon.
    Note(s): Interchange with front frame.

Interchange Number: 3
    Part Number(s): 2604362 (passenger), 2604363 (driver)
    Usage: 1967–69 Barracuda, Dart convertible.
    Note(s): Interchange with lower frame.

Interchange Number: 4
    Part Number(s): 2604352 (passenger), 2604353 (driver)
    Usage: 1967–69 Barracuda fastback.

Interchange Number: 5
    Part Number(s): 2838436 (passenger), 2838437 (driver)
    Usage: 1968–70 Belvedere two-door sedan.

Interchange Number: 6
    Part Number(s): 2840710 (passenger), 2840711 (driver)
    Usage: 1968–70 Coronet two-door sedan.

Interchange Number: 7
    Part Number(s): 2838440 (passenger), 2838441 (driver)
    Usage: 1968–70 Belvedere, Coronet two-door hardtop; 1968 Charger.

Interchange Number: 8
    Part Number(s): 2603702 (passenger), 2603703 (driver)
    Usage: 1968–70 Belvedere, Coronet convertible.

Interchange Number: 9
    Part Number(s): 2965592 (passenger), 2965593 (driver)
    Usage: 1970–72 Duster; 1971–72 Demon.

Interchange Number: 10
    Part Number(s): 3505732 (passenger), 3505733 (driver)
    Usage: 1970 Barracuda two-door hardtop.

Interchange Number: 11
    Part Number(s): 3505740 (passenger), 3505741 (driver)
    Usage: 1970 Challenger two-door hardtop, includes S.E. models.

Interchange Number: 12
    Part Number(s): 3505736 (passenger), 3505737 (driver)
    Usage: 1970 Barracuda, Challenger convertible.

Interchange Number: 13
    Part Number(s): 3500274 (passenger), 3500275 (driver)
    Usage: 1971–74 Barracuda two-door hardtop.

Interchange Number: 14
    Part Number(s): 3500282 (passenger), 3500283 (driver)
    Usage: 1971–74 Challenger two-door hardtop.

Interchange Number: 15
    Part Number(s): 3500278 (passenger), 3500279 (driver)
    Usage: 1971 Barracuda, Challenger convertible.

Interchange Number: 16
    Part Number(s): 3445570 (passenger), 3445571 (driver)
    Usage: 1971–72 Satellite two-door hardtop.
    Note(s): Windows roll down.

Interchange Number: 17
    Part Number(s): 3581762 (passenger), 3581763 (driver)
    Usage: 1971–72 Satellite two-door coupe.
    Note(s): Windows won't roll down.

Interchange Number: 18
    Part Number(s): 3445572 (passenger), 3445573 (driver)
    Usage: 1971–72 Charger two-door hardtop, except 1972 S.E.
    Note(s): Windows roll down.

Interchange Number: 19
    Part Number(s): 3581766 (passenger), 3581767 (driver)
    Usage: 1971–72 Charger two-door coupe.
    Note(s): Windows won't roll down.

Interchange Number: 20
    Part Number(s): 3696562 (passenger), 3696563 (driver)
    Usage: 1973–74 Dart, Valiant two-door hardtop.
    Note(s): Interchange with front frame and weather strip.

Interchange Number: 21
    Part Number(s): 3696624 (passenger), 3696625 (driver)
    Usage: 1973–74 Dart Sport, Duster.

Interchange Number: 22
    Part Number(s): 3582988 (passenger), 3582989 (driver)
    Usage: 1973–74 Charger, Satellite two-door coupe.
    Note(s): (1) Windows won't roll down. (2) Interchange with front frame and weather strip.

Interchange Number: 23
    Part Number(s): 3582980 (passenger), 3582981 (driver)
    Usage: 1973–74 Satellite two-door coupe with electric windows; 1973–74 Charger, Satellite two-door hardtop; 1973 Charger with halo roof.
    Note(s): Interchange with front frame and weather strip.

Interchange Number: 24
    Part Number(s): 3674880 (passenger), 3674881 (driver)

Usage: 1973–74 Charger S.E., except with halo top.
Note(s): Windows won't roll down.
Interchange Number: 25
Part Number(s): 2604340 (passenger), 2604341 (driver)
Usage: 1967–68 Dart two-door sedan; 1967–69 Valiant two-door sedan.

Back Glass
Model Identification

Interchange
Interchange Number: 1
Part Number(s): 2604011
Usage: 1968–69 Valiant two-door or four-door sedan.
Interchange Number: 2
Part Number(s): 2603691
Usage: 1968 Dart two-door sedan; 1968–69 Dart four-door sedan.
Interchange Number: 3
Part Number(s): 2842512
Usage: 1968–69 Barracuda two-door hardtop.
Interchange Number: 4
Part Number(s): 2604009
Usage: 1968–69 Barracuda, fastback.
Note(s): This glass is not available without tint.
Interchange Number: 5
Part Number(s): 2842345
Usage: 1968–70 Belvedere, Coronet two-door sedan or two-door hardtop.
Interchange Number: 6
Part Number(s): 2838131
Usage: 1968–70 Charger, except 1969 500 or Daytona.

Interchange Number: 7
Part Number(s): 3412161
Usage: 1969 Charger 500, Daytona.
Interchange Number: 8
Part Number(s): 2963971
Usage: 1969 Valiant two-door sedan; 1969–73 Valiant four-door sedan.
Interchange Number: 9
Part Number(s): 2965658
Usage: 1970–74 Duster; 1971–72 Demon; 1973–74 Dart Sport.
Interchange Number: 10
Part Number(s): 2604007
Usage: 1968–74 Dart two-door hardtop; 1970–74 Valiant two-door hardtop.
Interchange Number: 11
Part Number(s): 2963273
Usage: 1970–74 Barracuda two-door hardtop.
Interchange Number: 12
Part Number(s): 3444078
Usage: 1970 Challenger S.E.; 1971 Challenger with formal roof package.
Interchange Number: 13
Part Number(s): 2963275
Usage: 1970–74 Challenger, except S.E. or with formal roof package.
Interchange Number: 14
Part Number(s): 3445828
Usage: 1971–74 Charger, Satellite two-door models only.

Vent Glass
Model Identification

Interchange
Interchange Number: 1
Part Number(s): 2861636 (passenger), 2861637 (driver)
Usage: 1967–69 Barracuda, all body styles; 1967–74 Dart or Valiant four-door sedan; 1967–72, Dart two-door hardtop; 1968 Dart two-door coupe; 1968–69 Valiant two-door coupe; 1970–72 Valiant two-door hardtop; 1967–74 Valiant four-door sedan.
Interchange Number: 2
Part Number(s): 2811360 (passenger), 2811361 (driver)
Usage: 1968–70 Belvedere, Charger, Coronet, Satellite, all models and body styles except convertible, four-door sedan, or station wagon.
Interchange Number: 3
Part Number(s): 2861622 (passenger), 2861623 (driver)
Usage: 1968–70 Belvedere, Coronet convertible, four-door sedan, or station wagon.

Moldings
There were many different types of moldings used on Dodge and Plymouth cars. Thus, to more easily help you find the molding you are looking for, different moldings have been grouped together.

When interchanging a molding, it is always a good idea to interchange it with all the holding clips. Also look for moldings that are free of deep scratches, pits, or abuse. Remove moldings carefully, as they are easily damaged.

Interchange range will vary. Items like body side moldings are usually limited to that particular model, body style, and model year, while parts such as window moldings will cross different lines, years, and body styles.

Windshield Moldings
Model Identification

Interchange

Interchange Number: 1
Part Number(s): 2932450 (passenger), 2932451 (driver)
Location: Upper
Usage: 1967–69 Barracuda, all body styles except convertible; 1967–74 Dart two-door hardtop; 1970–74 Valiant two-door hardtop.

Interchange Number: 2
Part Number(s): 2807776 (passenger), 2807777 (driver)
Location: Upper
Usage: 1967–69 Barracuda, Dart convertible.

Interchange Number: 3
Part Number(s): 2932446 (passenger), 2932447 (driver)
Location: Sides
Usage: 1967–69 Barracuda, all body styles except convertible; 1968–74 Dart two-door hardtop; 1970–74 Valiant two-door hardtop.

Interchange Number: 4
Part Number(s): 2782018 (passenger), 2782019 (driver)
Location: Sides
Usage: 1967–69 Barracuda, Dart convertible.

Interchange Number: 5
Part Number(s): 2932445
Location: Lower
Usage: 1967–69 Barracuda, all body styles except convertible; 1967–74 Valiant, all models and body styles; 1967–74 Dart, all models and body styles except convertible.

Interchange Number: 6
Part Number(s): 2839148
Location: Lower
Usage: 1967–69 Barracuda, Dart convertible.
Note(s): Includes weather strip.

Interchange Number: 7
Part Number(s): 2932452 (passenger), 2932453 (driver)
Location: Upper
Usage: 1968–69 Valiant, all models and body styles; 1968 Dart coupe and four-door sedan, except 270 series; 1970–74 Dart, Valiant four-door sedan.

Interchange Number: 8
Part Number(s): 2932448 (passenger), 2932449 (driver)
Location: Sides
Usage: 1968–69 Valiant, all models and body styles; 1968 Dart coupe; 1968–74 Dart four-door sedan, except 270 series; 1970–74 Valiant four-door sedan.

Interchange Number: 9
Part Number(s): 2811259
Location: Upper
Usage: 1968–70 Belvedere, Coronet, and Satellite two-door coupe or hardtop only; 1968–70 Charger.

Interchange Number: 10
Part Number(s): 2586272 (passenger), 2586273 (driver)
Location: Upper
Usage: 1968–70 Belvedere, Coronet, and Satellite convertible.

Interchange Number: 11
    Part Number(s): 2811260 (passenger), 2811261 (driver)
    Location: Sides
    Usage: 1968–70 Belvedere, Coronet, and Satellite two-door coupe or hardtop only; 1968–70 Charger, except 1969 Charger 500 or Daytona.
Interchange Number: 12
    Part Number(s): 2586274 (passenger), 2586275 (driver)
    Location: Sides
    Usage: 1968–70 Belvedere, Coronet, and Satellite convertible.
.**Interchange Number: 13**
    Part Number(s): 2585852 (passenger), 2585853 (driver)
    Location: Lower
    Usage: 1968–70 Belvedere, Coronet, and Satellite convertible, four-door sedan or station wagon.
Interchange Number: 14
    Part Number(s): 2811888 (passenger), 2811889 (driver)
    Location: Lower
    Usage: 1968–70 Belvedere, Coronet, and Satellite two-door coupe or hardtop; 1968–70 Charger.
Interchange Number: 15
    Part Number(s): 3412150 (passenger), 3412151 (driver)
    Location: Sides
    Usage: 1969 Charger 500, Charger Daytona.
Interchange Number: 16
    Part Number(s): 3481772 (passenger), 3481773 (driver)
    Location: Upper and sides.
    Usage: 1970–74 Duster; 1971–72 Demon; 1973–74 Dart Sport.
Interchange Number: 17
    Part Number(s): 3481771
    Location: Lower
    Usage: 1970–74 Duster; 1971–72 Demon; 1973–74 Dart Sport.
Interchange Number: 18
    Part Number(s): 3444796 (passenger), 3444797 (driver)
    Location: Lower corners
    Usage: 1970–74 Duster; 1971–72 Demon; 1973–74 Dart Sport.
Interchange Number: 19
    Part Number(s): 3419807
    Location: Lower
    Usage: 1970–73 Barracuda, Challenger, all models and body styles.
Interchange Number: 20
    Part Number(s): 3419816 (passenger), 3419817 (driver)
    Location: Upper
    Usage: 1970–early 1971 Barracuda, Challenger convertible.
    Note(s): Used until October 1970.
Interchange Number: 21
    Part Number(s): 3419814 (passenger), 3419815 (driver)
    Location: Sides
    Usage: 1970–71 Barracuda, Challenger convertible.
Interchange Number: 22
    Part Number(s): 3419818 (passenger), 3419819 (driver)
    Location: Upper and sides
    Usage: 1970–74 Barracuda, Challenger, all models except convertible.
Interchange Number: 23
    Part Number(s): 3419820 (passenger), 3419821 (driver)
    Location: Lower corner
    Usage: 1970–73 Barracuda, Challenger, all models and body styles.
Interchange Number: 24
    Part Number(s): 3570966 (passenger), 3570967 (driver)
    Location: Upper
    Usage: Late 1971 Barracuda, Challenger convertible.
    Note(s): Used after October 1970.
Interchange Number: 25
    Part Number(s): 3579580 (passenger), 3579581 (driver)
    Location: Upper and sides
    Usage: 1971–74 Charger, Satellite two-door models only.
Interchange Number: 26
    Part Number(s): 3579533
    Location: Lower

Interchange Number: 27
    Part Number(s): 3579578 (passenger), 3579579 (driver)
    Location: Lower corner
    Usage: 1971–73 Charger, Satellite two-door models only.
Interchange Number: 28
    Part Number(s): 2895565
    Location: Lower
    Usage: 1974 Barracuda, Challenger, all models.
Interchange Number: 29
    Part Number(s): 3444786 (passenger), 3444787 (driver)
    Location: Lower corner
    Usage: 1974 Barracuda, Challenger, all models.
Interchange Number: 30
    Part Number(s): 3439432
    Location: Lower
    Usage: 1974 Charger, Coronet, and Satellite, all models and body styles.
Interchange Number: 31
    Part Number(s): 3505024 (passenger), 3505025 (driver)
    Location: Lower corner
    Usage: 1974 Charger, Coronet, and Satellite, all models and body styles.

Drip Rail Moldings
Model Identification

Interchange

Interchange Number: 1
Part Number(s): 2783026 (passenger), 2783027 (driver)
Usage: 1968 Dart two-door sedan; 1968–73 Dart four-door sedan; 1968–69 Valiant two-door sedan; 1970–69–73 Valiant four-door sedan without vinyl roof, all models.

Interchange Number: 2
Part Number(s): 2840980 (passenger), 2840981 (driver)
Usage: 1968–69 Valiant two-door sedan with vinyl roof; 1967–73 Valiant four-door sedan with vinyl roof, all models.

Interchange Number: 3
Part Number(s): 2839190 (passenger), 2839191 (driver)
Usage: 1968–69 Barracuda two-door hardtop without vinyl roof.

Interchange Number: 4
Part Number(s): 2840976 (passenger), 2840977 (driver)
Usage: 1968–69 Barracuda two-door hardtop with vinyl roof.

Interchange Number: 5
Part Number(s): 2784828 (passenger), 2784829 (driver)
Usage: 1968–69 Barracuda fastback.
Note(s): Used with or without vinyl roof.

Interchange Number: 6
Part Number(s): 2840282 (passenger), 2840283 (driver)
Usage: 1968–70 Belvedere, Coronet, and Satellite two-door sedan or hardtop without vinyl roof; 1968 Charger without vinyl roof, all models.

Interchange Number: 7
Part Number(s): 2841504 (passenger), 2841505 (driver)
Usage: 1968–70 Belvedere, Coronet, and Satellite two-door sedan, or hardtop with vinyl roof; 1968 Charger with vinyl roof, all models.

Interchange Number: 8
Part Number(s): 2783020 (passenger), 2783021 (driver)
Usage: 1968–74 Dart two-door hardtop without vinyl roof; 1970–74 Valiant two-door hardtop without vinyl roof.

Interchange Number: 9
Part Number(s): 2840982 (passenger), 2840983 (driver)
Usage: 1968–74 Dart two-door hardtop with vinyl roof; 1970–74 Valiant with vinyl roof.

Interchange Number: 10
Part Number(s): 3444932 (passenger), 3444933 (driver)
Usage: 1970–74 Duster; 1971–72 Demon; 1973–74 Dart Sport, without vinyl roof.

Interchange Number: 11
Part Number(s): 3445934 (passenger), 3445935 (driver)
Usage: 1970–74 Duster; 1971–72 Demon; 1973–74 Dart Sport with vinyl roof.

Interchange Number: 12
Part Number(s): Front molding: 3549190 (passenger), 3549191 (driver)
Rear molding: 3549192 (passenger), 3549193 (driver)
Usage: 1970–73 Barracuda with or without vinyl roof.

Interchange Number: 13
Part Number(s): 3612914 (passenger), 3612915 (driver)
Usage: 1971–72 Charger without vinyl top.

Interchange Number: 14
Part Number(s): 3612912 (passenger), 3612913 (driver)
Usage: 1971–72 Charger with vinyl roof.
Note(s): Used with full vinyl or canopy top.

Interchange Number: 15
Part Number(s): 3549194 (passenger), 3549195 (driver)
Usage: 1970–73 Challenger with or without vinyl roof.

Interchange Number: 16
Part Number(s): 3504832 (passenger), 3504833 (driver)
Usage: 1971–72 Satellite two-door without vinyl roof.

Interchange Number: 17
Part Number(s): 3504834 (passenger), 3504835 (driver)
Usage: 1971–72 Satellite two-door with vinyl roof.
Note(s): Used with both full vinyl and canopy vinyl roof.

Interchange Number: 18
Part Number(s): 3749062 (passenger), 3749063 (driver)
Usage: 1973–74 Satellite two-door without vinyl roof.

Interchange Number: 19
Part Number(s): 3749060 (passenger), 3749061 (driver)
Usage: 1973–74 Satellite two-door with vinyl roof.

Interchange Number: 20
Part Number(s): 3749068 (passenger), 3749069 (driver)
Usage: 1973–74 Charger without vinyl roof, with or without opera window roofline.

Interchange Number: 21
Part Number(s): 3749070 (passenger), 3749071 (driver)
Usage: 1973–74 Charger with vinyl roof, except S.E. models with standard roof or models with opera window. Will fit S.E. models with halo roof; 1973–74 Charger with canopy vinyl roof and opera window roofline.

Interchange Number: 22
Part Number(s): 1944JX9* (passenger), 1945JX9* (driver)
Usage: 1973 Charger S.E. with standard roof.
Note(s): * Part number for black moldings. Green or white moldings were also used.

Interchange Number: 23
Part Number(s): E524JX9 (passenger), E525JX9 (driver)
Usage: 1974 Charger S.E.; 1974 Charger with Celebrity roofline.[1]
Note(s): Moldings are in color. Part number for black-colored moldings are given. Other colors were white, parchment, green, or gold. [1] Charger with Celebrity roof used only the parchment-colored molding, but all molding in this Interchange will fit and can be repainted.

Interchange Number: 24
Part Number(s): Front: 3444584 (passenger), 3444585 (driver)
Rear: 2964632 (passenger), 2964633 (driver)
Usage: 1974 Barracuda with or without vinyl roof.

Interchange Number: 25
Part Number(s): 2965412 (passenger), 2965413 (driver)
Usage: 1974 Challenger with or without vinyl top.

Back-Window Moldings
Model Identification

Interchange

Interchange Number: 1
  Part Number(s): 2932464 (passenger), 2932465 (driver)
  Location: Upper and sides
  Usage: 1967–69 Valiant, all models and body styles; 1970–73 Valiant four-door sedan.

Interchange Number: 2
  Part Number(s): 2932466 (passenger), 2932467 (driver)
  Location: Lower
  Usage: 1967–69 Valiant, all models and body styles; 1970–73 Valiant four-door sedan.

Interchange Number: 3
  Part Number(s): 2932460 (passenger), 2932461 (driver)
  Location: Upper and sides
  Usage: 1967–69 Barracuda two-door hardtop.

Interchange Number: 4
  Part Number(s): 2932462 (passenger), 2932463 (driver)
  Location: Lower
  Usage: 1967–69 Barracuda two-door hardtop.

Interchange Number: 5
  Part Number(s): 2932458 (passenger), 2932459 (driver)
  Location: Lower and sides
  Usage: 1967–69 Barracuda fastback.

Interchange Number: 6
  Part Number(s): 2932456 (passenger), 2932457 (driver)
  Location: Upper
  Usage: 1967–69 Barracuda fastback.

Interchange Number: 7
  Part Number(s): 3004390 (passenger), 3004391 (driver)
  Location: Upper and sides
  Usage: 1968–70 Belvedere, Coronet, and Satellite two-door coupe or two-door hardtop only.
  Note(s): Moldings from a four-door sedan mount differently and will not correctly interchange.

Interchange Number: 8
  Part Number(s): 3004392 (passenger), 3004393 (driver)
  Location: Lower
  Usage: 1968–70 Belvedere, Coronet, and Satellite two-door coupe or hardtop only.
  Note(s): Moldings from four-door sedan mount differently and will not correctly interchange.

Interchange Number: 9
  Part Number(s): 2807610 (passenger), 2807611 (driver)
  Location: Upper and sides
  Usage: 1968 Dart two-door sedan; 1968–74 Dart four-door sedan; 1973–early 1974 Valiant Scamp four-door.
  Note(s): Stainless steel trim. Used until March 1, 1974. Later models up to 1976 will fit, but trim is aluminum.

Interchange Number: 10
  Part Number(s): 2807612 (passenger), 2807613 (driver)
  Location: Lower
  Usage: 1968 Dart two-door sedan; 1968–early 1974 Dart four-door sedan; 1973–74 Valiant Scamp four-door.

Note(s): Stainless steel trim. Used until March 1, 1974. Later trim up to 1976 models will fit but is aluminum.

Interchange Number: 11
Part Number(s): 2807616 (passenger), 2807617 (driver)
Location: Upper and sides
Usage: 1968–early 1974 Dart two-door hardtop; 1970–early 1974 Valiant two-door hardtop.
Note(s): Stainless steel trim. Used until March 1, 1974. Interchange Number 31 will fit but is aluminum.

Interchange Number: 12
Part Number(s): 2932218 (passenger), 2932219 (driver)
Location: Lower corner
Usage: 1968–70 Charger, except 1969 500 and Daytona.

Interchange Number: 13
Part Number(s): 2932220 (passenger), 2932221 (driver)
Location: Upper
Usage: 1968–70 Charger, except 1969 Charger 500 and Daytona.

Interchange Number: 14
Part Number(s): 2932217
Location: Lower
Usage: 1968–70 Charger, except 1969 500 and Daytona.

Interchange Number: 15
Part Number(s): 2807614 (passenger), 2807615 (driver)
Location: Lower
Usage: 1968–early 1974 Dart two-door hardtop; 1970–early 1974 Valiant two-door hardtop.
Note(s): Stainless stee trim. Used until March 1, 1974. Interchange Number 30 will fit but is aluminum.

Interchange Number: 16
Part Number(s): 3412152 (passenger), 3412153 (driver)
Location: Upper and sides
Usage: 1969 Charger 500; 1969 Charger Daytona.

Interchange Number: 17
Part Number(s): 3412582 (passenger), 3412582 (driver)
Location: Lower
Usage: 1969 Charger 500; 1969 Charger Daytona.

Interchange Number: 18
Part Number(s): 3419990 (passenger), 3419991 (driver)
Location: Lower
Usage: 1970–early 1974 Duster; 1971–72 Demon; 1973–early 1974 Dart Sport.
Note(s): Stainless steel trim. Used until March 1, 1974. Interchange Number 32 will fit but is aluminum.

Interchange Number: 19
Part Number(s): 3419988 (passenger), 3419989 (driver)
Location: Upper and sides
Usage: 1970–74 Duster; 1971–72 Demon; 1973–74 Dart Sport.

Interchange Number: 20
Part Number(s): 3419806
Location: Upper
Usage: 1970–74 Barracuda two-door hardtop.
Note(s): (1) Chrome part. Black molding was used with rear window louvers. (2) 1971 Gran coupe models used moldings that matched the vinyl roof.

Interchange Number: 21
Part Number(s): 3419802 (passenger), 3419803 (driver)
Location: Upper corner
Usage: 1970–74 Barracuda two-door hardtop.
Note(s): Chrome part number. Black molding used with rear window louvers. Chrome part can be used if painted flat black. (2) 1971 Gran coupe models used moldings that matched the vinyl roof.

Interchange Number: 22
Part Number(s): 3419804 (passenger), 3419805 (driver)
Location: Lower and sides
Usage: 1970–74 Barracuda two-door hardtop.
Note(s): (1) Chrome part number. Black molding used with rear window louvers. Chrome can be painted flat black. (2) 1971 Gran coupe models used moldings that matched the vinyl roof.

Interchange Number: 23
Part Number(s): 3419808 (passenger), 3419809 (driver)
Location: Lower
Usage: 1970–74 Challenger two-door hardtop, except S.E. or 1971 models with formal roof.

Interchange Number: 24
Part Number(s): 3419810 (passenger), 3419811 (driver)
Location: Upper and sides
Usage: 1970–74 Challenger two-door hardtop, except S.E. or 1971 models with formal roof.

Interchange Number: 25
Part Number(s): 3549626 (passenger), 3549627 (driver)
Location: Upper and sides
Usage: 1970 Challenger S.E.; 1971 Challenger with formal roof.

Interchange Number: 26
Part Number(s): 3549601
Location: Lower
Usage: 1970 Challenger S.E.; 1971 Challenger with formal roof.

Interchange Number: 27
Part Number(s): 3446710 (passenger), 34446711 (driver)
Location: Lower corner
Usage: 1970 Challenger S.E.; 1971 Challenger with formal roof.

Interchange Number: 28
Part Number(s): 3579576 (passenger), 3579577 (driver)
Location: Upper and sides
Usage: 1971–74 Charger, all models; 1971–74 Satellite, two-door models only.

Interchange Number: 29
Part Number(s): 3579588 (passenger), 3579589 (driver)
Location: Lower
Usage: 1971–74 Charger, all models; 1971–74 Satellite two-door models only.
Note(s): Moldings from a four-door Satellite will *not* fit.

Interchange Number: 30
Part Number(s): 3749980 (passenger), 3749981 (driver)
Location: Lower
Usage: Late 1974–76 Dart, Valiant two-door hardtop.
Note(s): (1) Aluminum. Used after March 1, 1974. (2) Interchange Number 15 will fit but is stainless steel.

Interchange Number: 31
Part Number(s): 3749976 (passenger), 3749977 (driver)
Location: Upper and sides
Usage: Late 1974 Dart, Valiant two-door hardtop.
Note(s): (1) Aluminum. Used after March 1, 1974. (2) Interchange Number 11 will fit but is stainless steel.

Interchange Number: 32
Part Number(s): 3749986 (passenger), 3749987 (driver)
Location: Lower
Usage: Late 1974 Duster, Dart Sport.
Note(s): (1) Aluminum. Used after March 1, 1974. (2) Interchange Number 18 will fit but is stainless steel.

Wheel-Well Moldings

Wheel lip moldings, both front and back, are not interchangeable between makes or models. Thus, wheel trim from a Coronet will not fit a Belvedere. Nor will Barracuda moldings fit a Valiant. However, there is interchanging between the various submodels: For example, those from a Coronet 500 will fit your Super Bee. Note that on low-priced models, like Road Runner and Super Bee, wheel-well trim was optional.

Model Identification

Barracuda...*Interchange Number*
1968–69
   front 2
   rear...13
1970–74
   front 24
   rear...31

Interchange

Interchange Number: 1
    Part Number(s): 3004208 (right), 3004209 (left)
    Location: Front
    Usage: 1968 Valiant, all models and body styles.

Interchange Number: 2
    Part Number(s): 2807876 (right), 2807877 (left)
    Location: Front
    Usage: 1968–69 Barracuda, all models and body styles.

Interchange Number: 3
    Part Number(s): 2932354 (right), 2932355 (left)
    Location: Front
    Usage: 1968 Belvedere, all models and body styles except Sport
        station wagon.

Interchange Number: 4
    Part Number(s): 3004238 (right), 3004239 (left)
    Location: Front
    Usage: 1968 Dart GT. Will not fit GTS models.

Interchange Number: 5
    Part Number(s): 2807766 (right), 2807767 (left)
    Location: Front
    Usage: 1968–74 Dart, all models and body styles except 1968
        GT (will fit 1968 GTS models); 1971–72 Demon; 1973–74
        Dart Sport.

Interchange Number: 6
    Part Number(s): 2932284 (right), 2932285 (left)
    Location: Front
    Usage: 1968 Coronet, all models and body styles except station
        wagon.

Interchange Number: 7
    Part Number(s): 3004370 (right), 3004371 (left)
    Location: Front
    Usage: 1968–70 Charger, all models.

Interchange Number: 8
    Part Number(s): 2932110 (right), 2932111 (left)
    Location: Rear
    Usage: 1968–69 Charger, all models.

Interchange Number: 9
    Part Number(s): 2932112 (right), 2932113 (left)
    Location: Rear
    Usage: 1968–70 Coronet, all models and body styles except
        station wagon or Coronet 500 four-door sedan.

Interchange Number: 10
    Part Number(s): 2807630* (right), 2807631* (left), 2932594 #
        (right), 2932595 # (left)
    Location: Rear
    Usage: 1968–74 Dart, all models and body styles except 1968
        GT; 1970–74 Valiant two-door hardtop.
    Note(s): *Stainless steel moldings; #Aluminum moldings. Both
        styles were used.

Interchange Number: 11
    Part Number(s): 3004270 (right), 3004271 (left)
    Location: Rear
    Usage: 1968 Dart GT only. Will not fit GTS models.

Interchange Number: 12
    Part Number(s): 2932354 (right), 2932355 (left)
    Location: Rear
    Usage: 1968 Belvedere, all models except sport station wagon.

Interchange Number: 13
    Part Number(s): 2809692 (right), 2809693 (left)
    Location: Rear
    Usage: 1968–69 Barracuda, all models and body styles.

Interchange Number: 14
    Part Number(s): 3004218 (right), 3004219 (left).
    Location: Rear
    Usage: 1968 Valiant, all models and body styles.

Interchange Number: 15
    Part Number(s): 2933550 (right), 2933551 (left)
    Location: Front
    Usage: 1969 Valiant, all models and body styles.

Interchange Number: 16
    Part Number(s): 2933548 (right), 2933549 (left)
    Location: Rear
    Usage: 1969 Valiant, all models and body styles.

Interchange Number: 17
    Part Number(s): 2933558 (right), 2933559 (left)
    Location: Front
    Usage: 1969 Satellite, all models and body styles. Will not fit Road
        Runner, GTX, Sport Satellite, or base Belvedere models.

Interchange Number: 18
    Part Number(s): 2933560 (right), 2933561 (left)
    Location: Front
    Usage: 1969 Sport Satellite, all body styles except
        station wagon.

Interchange Number: 19
Part Number(s): 3419064 (right), 3419065 (left)
Location: Front
Usage: 1969 GTX, all body styles.

Interchange Number: 20
Part Number(s): 2932260 (right), 2932261 (left)
Location: Rear
Usage: 1969 GTX, all body styles.

Interchange Number: 21
Part Number(s): 3419038 (right), 3419039 (left)
Location: Rear
Usage: 1969 Sport Satellite, all body styles except station wagon.

Interchange Number: 22
Part Number(s): 3419036 (right), 3419037 (left)
Location: Rear
Usage: 1969 Satellite, all body styles except station wagon. Will not fit Road Runner, GTX, or Sport Satellite.

Interchange Number: 23
Part Number(s): 2807896 (right), 2807897 (left)
Location: Front
Usage: 1970–74 Duster, Valiant, all models and body styles.

Interchange Number: 24
Part Number(s): 3419702 (right), 3419703 (left)
Location: Front
Usage: 1970–74 Barracuda, all models and body styles.

Interchange Number: 25
Part Number(s): 3443108 (right), 3443109 (left)
Location: Front
Usage: 1970 Road Runner, Satellite, Sport Satellite, except station wagon, GTX.

Interchange Number: 26
Part Number(s): 3419868 (right), 3419869 (left)
Location: Front
Usage: 1970 Coronet, all models and body styles except Cornet 440 four-door sedan or Coronet 500 station wagon.

Interchange Number: 27
Part Number(s): 3419710 (right), 3419711 (left)
Location: Front
Usage: 1970–73 Challenger, all model and body styles except for T/A.

Interchange Number: 28
Part Number(s): 3419790 (right), 3419791 (left)
Location: Rear
Usage: 1970–73 Challenger, all models and body styles.

Interchange Number: 29
Part Number(s): 3419918 (right), 3419919 (left)
Location: Rear
Usage: 1970 Sport Satellite, all body styles except station wagon.

Interchange Number: 30
Part Number(s): 2932262 (right), 2932263 (left)
Location: Rear
Usage: 1970 GTX, Road Runner, Satellite, all models and body styles.

Interchange Number: 31
Part Number(s): 3419784 (right), 3419785 (left)
Location: Rear
Usage: 1970–74 Barracuda, all models and body styles.

Interchange Number: 32
Part Number(s): 3419768 (right), 3419769 (left)
Location: Rear
Usage: 1970–74 Duster; 1971–72 Demon; 1973–74 Dart Sport.

Interchange Number: 33
Part Number(s): 3579304 (right), 3579305 (left)
Location: Front
Usage: 1971–72 Satellite, all two-door models.

Interchange Number: 34
Part Number(s): 3579344 (right), 3579345 (left)
Location: Rear
Usage: 1971–72 Satellite, all two-door models.

Interchange Number: 35
Part Number(s): 3579384 (right), 3579385 (left)
Location: Front
Usage: 1970–71 Dart Swinger.

Interchange Number: 36
Part Number(s): 3579362 (right), 3579363 (left)
Location: Front
Usage: 1971–72 Charger, all models.

Interchange Number: 37
Part Number(s): 3579440 (right), 3579441 (left)
Location: Rear
Usage: 1971–72 Charger, all models.

Interchange Number: 38
Part Number(s): 3685866 (right), 3865867 (left)
Location: Front
Usage: 1973–74 Satellite, all two-door models.

Interchange Number: 39
Part Number(s): 3685892 (right), 3685893 (left)
Location: Rear
Usage: 1973 Satellite, all two-door models.

Interchange Number: 40
Part Number(s): 3685900 (right), 3685901 (left)
Location: Front
Usage: 1973–74 Charger, all models.

Interchange Number: 41
Part Number(s): 3685904 (right), 3685905 (left)
Location: Rear
Usage: 1973–74 Charger, all models.

Rocker Panel Moldings
Model Identification

Interchange

Interchange Number: 1
    Part Number(s): 3004216 (right), 3004217 (left)
    Usage: 1968 Valiant Signet two-door or four-door sedans.
Interchange Number: 2
    Part Number(s): 3004228 (right), 3004229 (left)
    Usage: 1968 Barracuda, all models and body styles.
Interchange Number: 3
    Part Number(s): 2932268 (right), 2932269 (left)
    Usage: 1968–70 Belvedere, all models except for Road Runner, Satellite, Sport Satellite, or GTX.
    Note(s): Interchange Number 4 will fit but looks slightly different.
Interchange Number: 4
    Part Number(s): 2932272 (right), 2932273 (left)
    Usage: 1968 GTX, Satellite, Sport Satellite, all body styles; 1968–70 Road Runner
    Note(s): Wide molding. Interchange Number 3 will fit but is narrower.
Interchange Number: 5
    Part Number(s): 2807906 (fits either side)
    Usage: 1968 Dart two-door sedan; 1968–71 Dart two-door hardtop or four-door sedan, except Demon.
Interchange Number: 6
    Part Number(s): 2932184 (right), 2932185 (left)
    Usage: 1968 Coronet two-door sedan or hardtop without wide moldings.
Interchange Number: 7
    Part Number(s): 2932180 (right), 2932181 (left)
    Usage: 1968–70 Coronet two-door sedan or two-door hardtop with wide moldings, except 1969 Coronet 500 models; 1968 Charger, all models.
    Note(s): Wide moldings were standard on 1968 Coronet 500 and 1968–70 R/T models.
Interchange Number: 8
    Part Number(s): 2933914 (right), 2933915 (left)
    Usage: 1969–70 Charger, all models except 500 and Daytona.

Interchange Number: 10
    Part Number(s): 2933858 (right), 2933859 (left)
    Usage: 1969 Sport Satellite two-door hardtop.
Interchange Number: 11
    Part Number(s): 2933236 (right), 2933237 (left)
    Usage: 1969 Barracuda, all models and body styles except with Cuda package.
Interchange Number: 12
    Part Number(s): 2933501 (fits either side)
    Usage: 1969 Valiant, all body styles.
Interchange Number: 13
    Part Number(s): 3514074 (fits either side)
    Usage: 1970–72 Duster, Valiant, all models and body styles except Scamp.
Interchange Number: 14
    Part Number(s): 3549646 (right), 3549647 (left)
    Usage: 1970 Cuda, all body styles.
Interchange Number: 15
    Part Number(s): 3419786 (right), 3419787 (left)
    Usage: 1970 Barracuda Gran coupe, all body styles.
Interchange Number: 16
    Part Number(s): 3419922 (right), 3419923 (left)
    Usage: 1970 Sport Satellite, all body styles except station wagon.
Interchange Number: 17
    Part Number(s): 3419792 (right), 3419793 (left)
    Usage: 1970–71 Challenger, all models and body styles, except T/A.
Interchange Number: 18
    Part Number(s): 3620512 (right), 3620513 (left)
    Usage: 1970–72 Valiant Scamp.
Interchange Number: 19
    Part Number(s): 3579148 (fits either side)
    Usage: 1971–72 Barracuda, all body styles; 1972 Challenger, all models.
Interchange Number: 20
    Part Number(s): 3579146 (right), 3579147 (left)
    Usage: 1971 Barracuda Gran coupe.
Interchange Number: 21
    Part Number(s): 3579123 (fits either side)
    Usage: 1971–72 Satellite two-door models, except for 1971 Sebring Plus or 1971 GTX.
Interchange Number: 22
    Part Number(s): 3579342 (right), 3579343 (left)
    Usage: 1971 Satellite Sebring Plus.
Interchange Number: 23
    Part Number(s): 3620096 (right), 3620097 (left)
    Usage: 1971 GTX.
Interchange Number: 24
    Part Number(s): 3506036 (fits either side)
    Usage: 1971 Demon.
Interchange Number: 25
    Part Number(s): 3579554 (fits either side)
    Usage: 1971–73 Charger, all models except 1972–73 S.E.
Interchange Number: 26
    Part Number(s): 3683466 (right), 3683467 (left)
    Usage: 1972 Dart, all models and body styles except Demon.
Interchange Number: 27
    Part Number(s): 3549196 (right), 3549197 (left)
    Usage: 1972 Demon.
Interchange Number: 28
    Part Number(s): 3744365 (fits either side)
    Usage: 1973–74 Duster, Valiant, all models and body styles; 1973 Dart, all models and body styles except Dart Sport or Special Edition.
    Note(s): Used until April 29, 1974, on Valiant four-door or Brougham sedan model. Used all year long on other models.
Interchange Number: 29
    Part Number(s): 3744364
    Usage: 1973–74 Dart Sport; 1973–74 Barracuda; 1973–74 Challenger, all models.

Interchange Number: 30
  Part Number(s): 3685894 (right), 3685895 (left)
  Usage: 1973–74 Satellite two-door models.
Interchange Number: 31
  Part Number(s): 3685902 (right), 365903 (left)
  Usage: 1973 Charger S.E. models; 1974 Charger, all models.
Interchange Number: 32
  Part Number(s): 3810220 (right), 3810221 (left)
  Usage: 1974 Dart Special Edition, all body styles.

Exterior Decoration

This section covers decor nameplates and emblems. Due to the vast number of emblems on each car, the interchange has been broken down by location (grille, fender, etc.) Part numbers given will appear on the back of most of the nameplates, which can also be used as a method of identification. Photos and descriptions will further help you identify the nameplates. Note some nameplates may have been used on a different model in a different location. For example, an emblem used on the grille of a Charger may have been used on the hood of a Dart. So read the interchange carefully.

Emblems, Grille
Model Identification

1970 Challenger grille script.

Interchange
Interchange Number: 1
  Part Number(s): 2786044
  Design or Style: Plymouth
  Usage: 1968 Valiant, all models.
Interchange Number: 2
  Part Number(s): 2786730
  Design or Style: GTX
  Usage: 1968 GTX.
Interchange Number: 3
  Part Number(s): D-2786574, O-2786575, D (center) 2786927, G-2786576, E-2786577
  Design or Style: DODGE
  Usage: 1968 Coronet, except for Coronet 500 and R/T models.
  Note(s): Individual letters.
Interchange Number: 4
  Part Number(s): 2786635 (2786636 lower portion)
  Design or Style: 500
  Usage: 1968 Coronet 500 models.
  Note(s): Two-part design.
Interchange Number: 5
  Part Number(s): 2786711
  Design or Style: R/T
  Usage: 1968 Coronet R/T.
Interchange Number: 6
  Part Number(s): 2786773
  Design or Style: Charger (script)
  Usage: 1968 Charger, base models only.
Interchange Number: 7
  Part Number(s): 2786772
  Design or Style: Charger (script)
  Usage: 1968 Charger R/T.
  Note(s): Used with Interchange Number 8 only. Interchange Number 6 will fit, but is slightly different in length.
Interchange Number: 8
  Part Number(s): 2785830
  Design or Style: R/T
  Usage: 1968 Charger R/T.
Interchange Number: 9

Part Number(s): 2898303
Design or Style: GTX
Usage: 1969 GTX.

Interchange Number: 10
Part Number(s): 2898335
Design or Style: DODGE
Usage: 1969 Coronet, except for Super Bee, R/T, and Coronet 500 models.

Interchange Number: 11
Part Number(s): 2949303
Design or Style: Bumble Bee
Usage: 1969 Super Bee.

Interchange Number: 12
Part Number(s): 2898334
Design or Style: 500
Usage: 1969 Coronet 500 models.

Interchange Number: 13
Part Number(s): 2786711
Design or Style: R/T
Usage: 1969 Coronet R/T.

Interchange Number: 14
Part Number(s): 2898929
Design or Style: Charger (script)
Usage: 1969 Charger, all models except Charger 500 and Daytona.

Interchange Number: 15
Part Number(s): 2898930
Design or Style: Sideways arrow
Usage: 1968–69 Charger, except for Charger R/T, 1969 Charger 500 or Daytona.

Interchange Number: 16
Part Number(s): 2898931
Design or Style: R/T
Usage: 1969 Charger R/T.

Interchange Number: 17
Part Number(s): 2998278
Design or Style: Charger (script)
Usage: 1970 Charger, all models.

Interchange Number: 18
Part Number(s): 3443554
Design or Style: DODGE
Usage: 1971 Challenger, Charger, all models and body styles; 1973 Coronet on hood.

Interchange Number: 19
Part Number(s): 2998547
Design or Style: R/T
Usage: 1970–71 Challenger R/T.

Interchange Number: 20
Part Number(s): 2998546
Design or Style: Challenger
Usage: 1970 Challenger, all models and body styles.

Interchange Number: 21
Part Number(s): 2998282
Design or Style: Plymouth
Usage: 1970 Barracuda, all models and body styles.

Interchange Number: 22
Part Number(s): 2949992
Design or Style: GTX
Usage: 1970 GTX.

Interchange Number: 23
Part Number(s): 3443541
Design or Style: GTX
Usage: 1971 GTX.

Interchange Number: 24
Part Number(s): 2949862
Design or Style: Plymouth
Usage: 1970 Satellite, except GTX and Sport Satellite models.

Interchange Number: 25
Part Number(s): 2949993
Design or Style: Multiple-colored badge
Usage: 1970 Sport Satellite models.

Interchange Number: 26
Part Number(s): 3445250
Design or Style: Plymouth
Usage: 1971 Satellite, all two-door models. Also on rear deck lids of both two-door and four-door models.

Interchange Number: 27
Part Number(s): 3443513
Design or Style: Bird's head
Usage: 1971 Road Runner.

Interchange Number: 28
Part Number(s): 3443362
Design or Style: Multiple-colored bar
Usage: 1971 Satellite Sebring Plus; 1972 Satellite two-door, all models except Road Runner.

Interchange Number: 29
Part Number(s): 3573505
Design or Style: Challenger
Usage: 1972–74 Challenger.

Interchange Number: 30
Part Number(s): 3573534
Design or Style: Road Runner
Usage: 1972 Road Runner.

Interchange Number: 31
Part Number(s): 3573458
Design or Style: DODGE
Usage: 1972 Charger, except S.E. or with hideaway headlamps.

Interchange Number: 32
Part Number(s): 3613151
Design or Style: DODGE
Usage: 1973–74 Dart, all models; 1972 Dart, all models and body styles on hood and deck lid.

Interchange Number: 33
Part Number(s): 3444927
Design or Style: Multiple-colored bar
Usage: 1973 Satellite Sebring, Satellite Sebring Plus; 1974 Satellite two-door, all models except Road Runner.

Interchange Number: 34
Part Number(s): 2998279
Design or Style: Sideways arrow
Usage: 1970 Charger, except Charger 500 or Charger R/T.

Interchange Number: 35
Part Number(s): 2998510
Design or Style: R/T
Usage: 1970 Charger R/T.

Interchange Number: 36
Part Number(s): 3443093
Design or Style: 500
Usage: 1970 Charger 500.

Interchange Number: 37
Part Number(s): 2898302
Design or Style: Multiple-colored badge
Usage: 1969 Sport Satellite, all models and body styles.

Emblems, Hood or Front Panel
Model Identification

1970–1971 Cuda hood engine call out.

Charger script for 1968–1970 sail panels

Interchange

Interchange Number: 1
Part Number(s): 2785791
Design or Style: "Plymouth"
Usage: 1968–69 Barracuda, all models and body styles, positioned on the header panel; 1968–69 Belvedere, Fury, all models and body styles; 1969–72 Valiant, all models and body styles; 1970–72 Duster, positioned on front edge of hood; 1971–72 Plymouth Satellite four-door models only, positioned on hood; 1970–71 Plymouth Fury station wagon, positioned on tailgate; 1968–69 Valiant, positioned on rear deck; 1968–69 Belvedere, positioned on rear deck lid on all models except Satellite, Sport Satellite, or GTX.

Interchange Number: 2
Part Number(s): 2786642 right, 2786643 left
Design or Style: Plain simulated air vents.
Usage: 1968 Barracuda with six-cylinder or 318-ci V-8. On hood.

Interchange Number: 3
Part Number(s): 2786640 right, 2786641 left
Design or Style: Simulated air vents with "340-S" wording
Usage: 1968 Barracuda with 340-ci. On hood.

Interchange Number: 4
Part Number(s): 2785746 right, 2785747 left
Design or Style: simulated air vents with "383-S" wording.
Usage: 1968 Barracuda with 383-ci. On hood.

Interchange Number: 5
Part Number(s): 2785874 right, 2785875 left
Design or Style: 383 call outs

Usage: 1968 Road Runner. On hood.

Interchange Number: 6
Part Number(s): 2785828 right, 2785829 left
Design or Style: 440 call outs
Usage: 1968 GTX. On sides of hood.

Interchange Number: 7
Part Number(s): 2785826 right, 2785827 left
Design or Style: Hemi
Usage: 1968 GTX, Road Runner with 426 Hemi.

Interchange Number: 8
Part Number(s): 2785861
Design or Style: 318
Usage: 1968–69 Belvedere, Fury III, all models with 318-ci.
    Positioned on front center of hood.

Interchange Number: 9
Part Number(s): 2785862
Design or Style: 383 two-barrel
Usage: 1968–69 Belvedere, Fury III, VIP with 383-ci two-barrel.
    Positioned on front center of hood.

Interchange Number: 10
Part Number(s): 2785862
Design or Style: 383 four-barrel
Usage: 1968–69 Belvedere, Fury III, VIP with 383-ci four-barrel,
    except Road Runner. Positioned front on center of hood.

Interchange Number: 11
Part Number(s): 2786482
Design or Style: Dodge (script)
Usage: 1968 Dart, all models and body styles except GT and
    GTS, positioned on center front edge of hood; 1970 Dart,
    except Swinger.

Interchange Number: 12
Part Number(s): D-2785202, O-2785203, G-2785204, E-
    2785205
Design or Style: DODGE individual letters
Usage: 1968 Dart GT models only.

Interchange Number: 13
Part Number(s): Red letters G-2786527, T-2786528, S-
    2786529; Black letters G-2840889, T-2840890, S-2842786
Design or Style: GTS
Usage: 1968 GTS models only. Used on hood and rear deck lid.
Note(s): Both red and black inset letters were used.

Interchange Number: 14
Part Number(s): 2949240
Design or Style: 383
Usage: 1969 Road Runner with or without ram air; 1969–70
    Super Bee with ram air.

Interchange Number: 15
Part Number(s): 2898876
Design or Style: Hemi
Usage: 1969 Road Runner, GTX, Coronet R/T, Super Bee with
    426 Hemi.

Interchange Number: 16
Part Number(s): 2898878
Design or Style: 440
Usage: 1969 GTX with or without ram-air hood; 1969–70
    Coronet with ram-air hood.

Interchange Number: 17
Part Number(s): 2898866
Design or Style: DODGE
Usage: 1969 Dart, all models except GT or GTS.

Interchange Number: 18
Part Number(s): 2898868
Design or Style: GT
Usage: 1969 Dart GT models.

Interchange Number: 19
Part Number(s): 2898867
Design or Style: GTS
Usage: 1969 GTS models.

Interchange Number: 20
Part Number(s): 2949150 right, 2949151 left

1971–1972 hood call out for Chargers.

Design or Style: 340
Usage: 1969 Dart GTS with 340-ci.

Interchange Number: 21
Part Number(s): 2949148 right, 2949149 left
Design or Style: 383
Usage: 1969 Dart GTS with 383-ci.

Interchange Number: 22
Part Number(s): 2998798 (fits either side)
Design or Style: Cuda 440-6
Usage: 1970 Cuda with 440 triple-two-barrel with or without
    fresh-air hood.

Interchange Number: 23
Part Number(s): 3462269 (fits either side)
Design or Style: Hemi Cuda
Usage: 1970 Cuda with 426 Hemi with fresh-air hood only.
Note(s): Fresh-air hood standard.

Interchange Number: 24
Part Number(s): 3577361 (fits either side)
Design or Style: 340 four-barrel
Usage: 1970 Barracuda with 340-ci, except Cuda models.

Interchange Number: 25
Part Number(s): 3443159 (fits either side)
Design or Style: Cuda 340
Usage: 1970–71 Cuda models with 340-ci with fresh-air hood,
    except AAR; 1972–73 Barracuda.

Interchange Number: 26
Part Number(s): 2988796 (fits either side)
Design or Style: Cuda 383
Usage: Cuda models with 383-ci.

Interchange Number: 27
Part Number(s): 2998797
Design or Style: Cuda 440
Usage: 1970 Cuda with 440-ci four-barrel with or without fresh-
    air hood.

Interchange Number: 28
Part Number(s): 3443159
Design or Style: Cuda 340
Usage: 1970–71 Cuda with 340-ci without fresh-air hood.

Interchange Number: 29
Part Number(s): 2898629
Design or Style: 383 four-barrel
Usage: 1970 Belvedere, Satellite with 383-ci four-barrel, except
    Road Runner.

Interchange Number: 30
Part Number(s): 2898630
Design or Style: 383 two-barrel
Usage: 1970 Belvedere, Satellite with 383-ci two-barrel.

Interchange Number: 31
Part Number(s): 2449932
Design or Style: Dodge tri-star medallion
Usage: 1970–71 Challenger, except T/A or with shaker hood, or
    performance hood; 1968 Dodge passenger car with vinyl
    top, placed on roof sail panels; 1968 Dart, positioned on
    rear deck lid.

Interchange Number: 32
Part Number(s): 3443247 (fits either side)
Design or Style: 340 four-barrel
Usage: 1970 Challenger with 340-ci with or without fresh-air hood.

Interchange Number: 33
Part Number(s): 2998801

Design or Style: 383 Magnum
Usage: 1970 Challenger R/T with 383-ci four-barrel.

Interchange Number: 34
Part Number(s): 2998800 (fits either side)
Design or Style: 426 Hemi
Usage: 1970–71 Challenger with 426 Hemi without fresh-air hood.

Interchange Number: 35
Part Number(s): 3462491 right, 3462492 left
Design or Style: 440
Usage: 1970 Challenger R/T with 440-ci four-barrel with or without fresh-air hood.

Interchange Number: 36
Part Number(s): 3462489 left 3462490 right
Design or Style: 426 Hemi
Usage: 1970–71 Challenger with 426 Hemi with fresh-air hood.

Interchange Number: 37
Part Number(s): D-2579655, O-2998231, G-2579657, E-2579658
Design or Style: DODGE individual letters
Usage: 1970–71 Challenger with fresh-air or performance hood; 1972 Challenger, all models.

Interchange Number: 38
Part Number(s): 2998302
Design or Style: Dart
Usage: 1970 Dart Swinger.

Interchange Number: 39
Part Number(s): 2998065
Design or Style: Bumble Bee
Usage: 1970 Super Bee.

Interchange Number: 40
Part Number(s): 2998749
Design or Style: Super Bee
Usage: 1970 Super Bee without ram-air hood.

Interchange Number: 41
Part Number(s): 2998062
Design or Style: 500
Usage: 1970 Coronet 500 models.

Interchange Number: 42
Part Number(s): 2998066
Design or Style: R/T
Usage: 1970 Coronet R/T.

Interchange Number: 43
Part Number(s): 2998042
Design or Style: Plymouth
Usage: 1971–74 Barracuda, all models and body styles.

Interchange Number: 44
Part Number(s): 3442005
Design or Style: Dodge
Usage: 1971 Dart, all models and body styles.

Interchange Number: 45
Part Number(s): 2998804
Design or Style: 440 Six Pack
Usage: 1970–71 Challenger; 1971 Charger.

Interchange Number: 46
Part Number(s): 3443516
Design or Style: 440 Magnum
Usage: 1971–74 Charger R/T, Rallye models only.

Interchange Number: 47
Part Number(s): 3443627
Design or Style: 383 Magnum
Usage: 1971 Charger.

Interchange Number: 48
Part Number(s): 3573632
Design or Style: 340 Magnum
Usage: 1971–73 Charger R/T, Super Bee, or Rallye models only.

Interchange Number: 49
Part Number(s): 3574059
Design or Style: 400 Magnum
Usage: 1972–74 Charger with Rallye package.

Interchange Number: 50

Part Number(s): 2965502
Design or Style: Dodge
Usage: 1973–74 Charger.

Interchange Number: 51
Part Number(s): D-3749006, O-3749007, G-3749008, E-3749009
Design or Style: DODGE (individual letters)
Usage: 1973–74 Challenger.

Interchange Number: 52
Part Number(s): 3680160
Design or Style: GTX
Usage: 1973–74 Road Runner with 440-ci.

Interchange Number: 53
Part Number(s): 3691470
Design or Style: Cuda 360
Usage: 1974 Cuda with 360-ci.

Interchange Number: 54
Part Number(s): 3691468
Design or Style: 360 four-barrel
Usage: 1974 Barracuda with 360-ci four-barrel.

Interchange Number: 55
Part Number(s): 3691667
Design or Style: Magnum
Usage: 1974 Charger with Rallye package and 360-ci.

Interchange Number: 56
Part Number(s): 2898876
Design or Style: Hemi
Usage: 1971 Charger.

Emblems, Front-Fender
Model Identification

1969 Coronet 500 fender nameplates.

Interchange

Interchange Number: 1
   Part Number(s): 2786924
   Style/Design: Valiant 100
   Usage: 1968 Valiant 100 models.
Interchange Number: 2
   Part Number(s): 2786925
   Style/Design: Valiant 200
   Usage: 1968–69 Valiant 200 models.
Interchange Number: 3
   Part Number(s): 2786926
   Style/Design: Valiant Signet
   Usage: 1968–69 Valiant Signet.
Interchange Number: 4
   Part Number(s): 2786559
   Style/Design: Barracuda
   Usage: 1968 Barracuda.
Interchange Number: 5
   Part Number(s): 2579443
   Style/Design: Formula S badge
   Usage: 1967–68 Barracuda with Formula S package.
Interchange Number: 6
   Part Number(s): 2786590 (right), 2786591 (left)
   Style/Design: Fish with V-8
   Usage: 1968 Barracuda with V-8 but without Formula S package.
Interchange Number: 7
   Part Number(s): 2785320 (right), 2785321 (left)

1970 Challenger script used on the front fenders.

1968 Barracuda fender nameplate. Year One

Style/Design: Fish
Usage: 1967 Barracuda, all models and body styles; 1968 Barracuda, with six-cylinder.

Interchange Number: 8
Part Number(s): 2786954
Style/Design: Belvedere
Usage: 1968 Belvedere sedan or station wagon models only; 1970 Belvedere two-door or four-door sedans only.

Interchange Number: 9
Part Number(s): 2785870
Style/Design: Satellite script
Usage: 1968 Satellite, all models and body styles except Sport Satellite models.

Interchange Number: 10
Part Number(s): 2785602
Style/Design: Satellite script
Usage: 1968 Sport Satellite, except station wagon.

Interchange Number: 11
Part Number(s): 2785867
Style/Design: SPORT
Usage: 1968 Sport Satellite, except station wagon.

Interchange Number: 12
Part Number(s): 2579748
Style/Design: V-8
Usage: 1968–69 Dart with V-8; 1970 Challenger with V-8.

Interchange Number: 13
Part Number(s): G-2786894, T-2786895
Style/Design: GT
Usage: 1968 Dart GT.

Interchange Number: 14
Part Number(s): Red Letters: G-2786531, T-2786532, S-2786533; Black Letters: G-2786894, T-2786895, S-2786896
Style/Design: GTS
Usage: 1968 GTS.

Interchange Number: 15
Part Number(s): 2579804
Style/Design: 383 four-barrel
Usage: 1968 Dart GTS with 383-ci; 1969 Coronet with 383-ci four-barrel; 1970 Barracuda with 383-ci four-barrel, except Cuda models.

Interchange Number: 16
Part Number(s): 2785540

Style/Design: Pentastar
Usage: 1967–71 Barracuda, Challenger, Charger, Coronet, Dart, Duster, Chrysler 300, Fury, Monaco, Newport, New Yorker, Polara, Satellite, and Valiant, all models and body styles.

Interchange Number: 17
Part Number(s): 2785579
Style/Design: R/T
Usage: 1968 Coronet R/T.

Interchange Number: 18
Part Number(s): 2579612
Style/Design: V-Eight
Usage: 1969–71 Valiant with V-8.

Interchange Number: 19
Part Number(s): 2901852
Style/Design: Barracuda script
Usage: 1969 Barracuda.

Interchange Number: 20
Part Number(s): 2901859
Style/Design: 340-S
Usage: 1969 Barracuda with 340-ci.

Interchange Number: 21
Part Number(s): 2901858
Style/Design: 383-S
Usage: 1969 Barracuda with 383-ci.

Interchange Number: 22
Part Number(s): 2963656 (right), 2963657 (left)
Style/Design: Fish
Usage: 1969 Barracuda without Formula S package.

Interchange Number: 23
Part Number(s): 2963433
Style/Design: Belvedere
Usage: 1969 Belvedere.

Interchange Number: 24
Part Number(s): 2902789
Style/Design: Satellite script
Usage: 1969–70 Satellite, all models and body styles.

Interchange Number: 25
Part Number(s): 2902788
Style/Design: Sport
Usage: 1969–70 Sport Satellite, all body styles.
Note(s): Used in front of Interchange Number 24.

Interchange Number: 26
Part Number(s): 2901894
Style/Design: Dart
Usage: 1969–70 Dart.

Interchange Number: 27
Part Number(s): 2901895
Style/Design: GTS
Usage: 1969 Dart GTS.

Interchange Number: 28
Part Number(s): 2901751
Style/Design: Coronet
Usage: 1969–70 Coronet, all models and body styles except Super Bee.

Interchange Number: 29
Part Number(s): 3444957
Style/Design: 383 Magnum
Usage: 1969–70 Super Bee.

Interchange Number: 30
Part Number(s): 2901810
Style/Design: 440
Usage: 1969 Coronet 440, all body styles.

Interchange Number: 31
Part Number(s): 3504077
Style/Design: Valiant script
Usage: 1970 Valiant, all models except Duster.

Interchange Number: 32
Part Number(s): 3505787
Style/Design: Valiant
Usage: 1970 Duster, except Duster 340; 1971 Valiant, all models.

Interchange Number: 33
Part Number(s): 2786559
Style/Design: Barracuda script
Usage: 1970 Barracuda, except Cuda or AAR models.

Interchange Number: 34
Part Number(s): 2949240
Style/Design: 383
Usage: 1970–71 Barracuda with 383-ci two-barrel.

Interchange Number: 35
Part Number(s): 3504075
Style/Design: Gran coupe badge
Usage: 1970 Gran coupe Barracuda.

Interchange Number: 36
Part Number(s): 3444938
Style/Design: Challenger script
Usage: 1970–73 Challenger, all models.
Note(s): On rear quarters on 1972 models. Also on deck lid on 1970 models.

Interchange Number: 37
Part Number(s): 3504233
Style/Design: 383-ci four-barrel
Usage: 1970 Challenger with 383-ci four-barrel except R/T models.

Interchange Number: 38
Part Number(s): 3445223
Style/Design: R/T
Usage: 1970 Challenger R/T.

Interchange Number: 39
Part Number(s): 2785558
Style/Design: Hemi
Usage: 1969–70 Super Bee, Coronet R/T, Charger R/T with 426 Hemi.

Interchange Number: 40
Part Number(s): 2901811
Style/Design: 500
Usage: 1969–70 Coronet 500, all models.

Interchange Number: 41
Part Number(s): 3505419
Style/Design: Dart
Usage: 1971–74 Dart, all models except Demon, will fit Dart Sport, also on deck lid.

Interchange Number: 42
Part Number(s): 3613359
Style/Design: Demon
Usage: 1971 Demon, used on front fender and rear panel, except Demon 340.

Interchange Number: 43
Part Number(s): 3549645
Style/Design: Swinger
Usage: 1971–74 Dart Swinger.

Interchange Number: 44
Part Number(s): 3570983
Style/Design: Special
Usage: 1971–74 Dart Swinger Special.

Interchange Number: 45
Part Number(s): 3504804
Style/Design: Super Bee
Usage: 1971 Super Bee.

Interchange Number: 46
Part Number(s): 3504807
Style/Design: Charger script
Usage: 1971 Charger, except Super Bee.

Interchange Number: 47
Part Number(s): 3506410
Style/Design: Charger medallion
Usage: 1971 Charger, except R/T, Super Bee, 500 ,or S.E.

Interchange Number: 48
Part Number(s): 3504810
Style/Design: 500
Usage: 1971 Charger 500.

Interchange Number: 49
Part Number(s): 3506410
Style/Design: S.E. medallion
Usage: 1971 Charger S.E.

Interchange Number: 50
Part Number(s): 3504809
Style/Design: R/T
Usage: 1971 Charger R/T, also used on deck lid of this model.

Interchange Number: 51
Part Number(s): 3505444
Style/Design: 383-ci four-barrel
Usage: 1971 Challenger with 383 four-barrel.

Interchange Number: 52
Part Number(s): 3680462
Style/Design: Valiant
Usage: 1972–74 Valiant, except Duster or Scamp models; early 1974 Valiant Brougham.
Note(s): Used until January 23, 1974, on Brougham models.

Interchange Number: 53
Part Number(s): 3680304
Style/Design: Duster
Usage: 1972–73 Duster, except Gold Duster.

Interchange Number: 54
Part Number(s): 3680038
Style/Design: Valiant
Usage: 1972 Valiant Scamp; late 1974 Valiant Brougham models.
Note(s): Used after January 23, 1974, on Brougham models.

Interchange Number: 55
Part Number(s): 3680160
Style/Design: GTX
Usage: 1972 Road Runner with 440-ci; 1973–74 Road Runner with 440-ci on header panel.

Interchange Number: 56
Part Number(s): 3680322
Style/Design: Demon
Usage: 1972 Demon.

Interchange Number: 57
Part Number(s): 3680297
Style/Design: 400 Magnum
Usage: 1972 Charger with 400-ci four-barrel, except models with Rallye package.

Interchange Number: 58
Part Number(s): 3680997
Style/Design: Scamp
Usage: Early 1973 Valiant Scamp.
Note(s): Used until March 1, 1973.

Interchange Number: 59
Part Number(s): 3810058
Style/Design: Scamp
Usage: Late 1973–74 Valiant Scamp.
Note(s): Used after March 1, 1973.

Interchange Number: 60
Part Number(s): 3749083
Style/Design: Sport
Usage: 1973–74 Dart Sport.

Interchange Number: 61
Part Number(s): 3505056
Style/Design: Custom
Usage: 1973 Dart Custom.

Interchange Number: 62
Part Number(s): 3810255
Style/Design: 360
Usage: 1974 Dart Sport with 360-ci.

Interchange Number: 63
Part Number(s): 3505020
Style/Design: Satellite script
Usage: 1971–74 Satellite four-door models on front fenders; 1971–74 Satellite two-door models on rear quarters or roof sail panels. Also used on deck lids of two-door models.

Emblems, Rear-Quarter and Roof
Model Identification

Interchange

Interchange Number: 1
  Part Number(s): D-2784578, A-2784579, R-2784580, T-2784581
  Style/Design: D-A-R-T
  Usage: 1967 Dart, all models except GT; 1968 Dart, all models except Dart 270 series or GTS.

Interchange Number: 2
  Part Number(s): C-2840622, O-2840574, R-2840623, N-2840624, E-2840625, T-28040626
  Style/Design: C-O-R-O-N-E-T
  Usage: 1968 Coronet, all models and body styles except Super Bee.

Interchange Number: 3
  Part Number(s): 2840621
  Style/Design: Tri-star
  Usage: 1968 Coronet, all models except Coronet 440, Coronet 500, Coronet R/T, or Super Bee. Interchange from hardtop or sedans only. Station wagons used a different medallion.

Interchange Number: 4
  Part Number(s): 2840620
  Style/Design: 440
  Usage: 1968 Coronet 440, all body styles except station wagon.

Interchange Number: 5
  Part Number(s): 5-2840618, 0-2840619
  Style/Design: 500
  Usage: 1968 Coronet 500, all body styles except station wagon.

Interchange Number: 6
  Part Number(s): 2841866 right, 2841867 left
  Style/Design: Charger script
  Usage: 1968–70 Charger, all models. On roof sail panels.

Interchange Number: 7
  Part Number(s): 2841849
  Style/Design: Charger medallion
  Usage: 1968 Charger, except Charger R/T models. On roof sail panels.

Interchange Number: 8
  Part Number(s): 2449932
  Style/Design: Tri-star
  Usage: 1967–69 Coronet, Dart, Polara, Monaco with vinyl top, place on roof sail panels; 1970–71 Challenger hood, except with performance or shaker hood; 1968 Dart, on rear deck lid.

1971–1972 Charger Special Edition wreath.

1971 Charger Special Edition script.

Interchange Number: 9
Part Number(s): 2901812
Style/Design: R/T
Usage: 1969 Coronet R/T; 1969 Charger R/T. Used only when rear stripes were deleted.

Interchange Number: 10
Part Number(s): 3504289
Style/Design: GTX
Usage: 1970–71 GTX.

Interchange Number: 11
Part Number(s): 3446801
Style/Design: S.E. medallion
Usage: 1970 Challenger S.E.; 1971 Charger S.E. On roof sail panels.

Interchange Number: 12
Part Number(s): 3612859
Style/Design: Sebring
Usage: 1971–74 Satellite Sebring, all except Sebring Plus models. Also on deck lid of this model and Sebring Plus.

Interchange Number: 13
Part Number(s): 3445985
Style/Design: Dart
Usage: 1970 Dart, all two-door models.

Interchange Number: 14
Part Number(s): 3446861
Style/Design: Swinger (script)
Usage: 1970 Dart Swinger two-door.

Interchange Number: 15
Part Number(s): 3446052 right, 3446053 left
Style/Design: R/T
Usage: 1970 Coronet R/T, on rear quarters; 1970 Charger R/T on doors.

Interchange Number: 16
Part Number(s): 2782966
Style/Design: Special Edition badge
Usage: 1969–70 Charger with S.E. package.

Interchange Number: 17
Part Number(s): Road-3505944, Runner-3505945
Style/Design: Road Runner
Usage: 1971–74 Road Runner.

Interchange Number: 18
Part Number(s): 3505020
Style/Design: Satellite (script)
Usage: 1971–72 Satellite two-door models on rear quarters; 1971–74 Satellite four-door models on front fenders; 1973 Satellite two-door models on roof sail panels.

Interchange Number: 19
Part Number(s): 3612863
Style/Design: Sebring Plus
Usage: 1971–72 Satellite Sebring plus.

Interchange Number: 20
Part Number(s): 2964624
Style/Design: GTX
Usage: 1969 GTX.

Interchange Number: 21
Part Number(s): 2842330
Style/Design: GTX
Usage: 1968 GTX.

Interchange Number: 22
Part Number(s): 3613794 right, 3613795 left
Style/Design: Charger (script)
Usage: 1972 Charger without vinyl roof.

Interchange Number: 23
Part Number(s): 3680354 right, 3680355 left
Style/Design: Charger (script)
Usage: 1972 Charger with vinyl roof.

Interchange Number: 24
Part Number(s): 3680357
Style/Design: Charger medallion
Usage: 1972 Charger without vinyl roof.

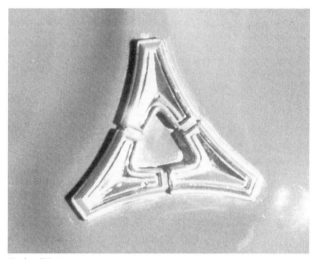

Dodge Tri-star.

1974 Dart Special Edition script.

Interchange Number: 25
Part Number(s): 3613696
Style/Design: Charger medallion
Usage: 1972 Charger with vinyl roof.

Interchange Number: 26
Part Number(s): 3613273
Style/Design: Special Edition
Usage: 1972 Charger S.E. with vinyl roof.

Interchange Number: 27
Part Number(s): 3680358
Style/Design: Special Edition
Usage: 1972 Charger S.E. without vinyl roof.

Interchange Number: 28
Part Number(s): 3444938
Style/Design: Challenger (script)
Usage: 1970–74 Challenger, on front fenders on 1970–71 models.

Interchange Number: 29
Part Number(s): 3680872
Style/Design: Sebring Plus
Usage: 1973–74 Satellite Sebring Plus.

Interchange Number: 30
Part Number(s): 3680828
Style/Design: S.E. medallion
Usage: 1973–74 Charger S.E.

Interchange Number: 31
Part Number(s): 3810287
Style/Design: Brougham
Usage: 1974 Valiant Brougham, all body styles. On roof sail panels.

Interchange Number: 32
Part Number(s): 3613273
Style/Design: Special Edition
Usage: 1974 Dart with Special Edition.

Interchange Number: 33
  Part Number(s): 3505419
  Style/Design: Dart
  Usage: 1973–74 Dart two-door models; 1971–74 Dart four-door on front fenders.
Interchange Number: 34
  Part Number(s): 2901896
  Style/Design: Dart GT
  Usage: 1969 Dart GT.

Emblems, Door
Model Identification

Interchange

Interchange Number: 1
  Part Number(s): 3504807
  Style/Design: Charger (script)
  Usage: 1973–74 Charger, all models.
Interchange Number: 2
  Part Number(s): 3506410
  Style/Design: Charger medallion
  Usage: 1974 Charger, all models.
Interchange Number: 3
  Part Number(s): 3505456
  Style/Design: Barracuda
  Usage: 1971–74 Barracuda. Used on door and rear deck lid.
Interchange Number: 4
  Part Number(s): 3505457
  Style/Design: Gran coupe medallion
  Usage: 1971 Gran coupe Barracuda.
Interchange Number: 5
  Part Number(s): 2785558
  Style/Design: Hemi
  Usage: 1968–69 Charger with 426 Hemi.
Interchange Number: 6
  Part Number(s): 3445919
  Style/Design: R/T
  Usage: 1970 Charger R/T on doors; 1970 Coronet R/T on rear quarters.

Emblems, Rear Deck
Model Identification

1970 Challenger script and R/T badge used the rear deck lid.

1970 Cuda nameplate.

1971 Cuda rear-end nameplate.

1969 Barracuda with 340-ci V-8. Year One

Interchange

Interchange Number: 1
   Part Number(s): 2785791
   Style/Design: Plymouth
   Usage: 1968–69 Valiant rear deck lid, except Signet; 1968–69 Belvedere rear deck lid, all models and body styles, except 1968 Satellite, 1968 Sport Satellite, or 1968 GTX; 1969 Fury deck lid, all models and body styles; 1968–69 Barracuda, all models and body styles, positioned on the header panel; 1968–69 Belvedere, Fury, all models and body styles; 1969–72 Valiant, all models and body styles; 1970–72 Duster, positioned on front edge of hood; 1971–72 Plymouth Satellite four-door models only. Positioned on hood; 1970–71 Plymouth Fury station wagon, on tailgate.

Interchange Number: 2
   Part Number(s): 2840876
   Style/Design: Barracuda
   Usage: 1968 Barracuda, all models and body styles.

Interchange Number: 3
   Part Number(s): 2840877
   Style/Design: Fish in-circle
   Usage: 1968 Barracuda, all models and body styles.

Interchange Number: 4
   Part Number(s): 2840867
   Style/Design: Hemi
   Usage: 1968–69 Belvedere, with 426 Hemi.

Interchange Number: 5
   Part Number(s): 2449932
   Style/Design: Tri-Star
   Usage: 1968 Dart, rear deck lid except GT or GTS models;

1968 Formula S badge. Year One

1970–1971 Gran Coupe badge. Year One

1970–71 Challenger hood, except with shaker hood or performance hood; 1968–69 Dodge passenger car with vinyl top, placed on roof sail panels.

Interchange Number: 6
Part Number(s): 2786482
Style/Design: DODGE (script)
Usage: 1968 Dart, on rear deck lid except GTS; 1969 Dart on hood, except GTS or GT models.

Interchange Number: 7
Part Number(s): G-2840889; T-2840890
Style/Design: GT
Usage: 1968 Dart GT.

Interchange Number: 8
Part Number(s): Red letters—G-2786527, T-2786528, S-2786529; Black letters—G-2840889, T-2840890, S-2842786
Design or Style: GTS
Usage: 1968 GTS models only. Used on deck lid and hood.
Note(s): Both red and black inset letters were used.

Interchange Number: 9
Part Number(s): D-2840573, O-2840574, D-2840575, G-2840576, E-2840577
Style/Design: DODGE
Usage: 1968 Coronet, all models except Coronet 440 or 500 station wagon.

Interchange Number: 10
Part Number(s): 2840066
Style/Design: Charger (script)
Usage: 1968 Charger, all models.

Interchange Number: 11
Part Number(s): 2842016
Style/Design: Charger medallion
Usage: 1968 Charger, except R/T.

Interchange Number: 12
Part Number(s): 2842346
Style/Design: R/T
Usage: 1968 Charger R/T.

Interchange Number: 13
Part Number(s): 2901746
Style/Design: Sport Satellite
Usage: 1969 Sport Satellite.

Interchange Number: 14
Part Number(s): 2901813
Style/Design: DODGE

Usage: 1969 Dart, all models except Custom, GT, or GTS models; 1969 Coronet, except Coronet 440, Super Bee, Coronet 500, and Coronet R/T.

Interchange Number: 15
Part Number(s): 2964635
Style/Design: Bumble bee
Usage: 1969 Super Bee, all models.

Interchange Number: 16
Part Number(s): D-2784488, O-2784489, G-2784490, E-2784491
Style/Design: D O D G E
Usage: 1969 Coronet 500, all body styles; 1969 Coronet R/T.

Interchange Number: 17
Part Number(s): 2902306
Style/Design: Charger (script)
Usage: 1969–70 Charger, all except 1969 Charger R/T.

Interchange Number: 18
Part Number(s):
Style/Design: R/T
Usage: 1969 Charger R/T.

Interchange Number: 19
Part Number(s): 3445250
Style/Design: Plymouth
Usage: 1970–72 Valiant, except Duster; 1971–74 Satellite.

Interchange Number: 20
Part Number(s): 3444927
Style/Design: Plymouth
Usage: 1970–74 Duster; 1971–74 Valiant Scamp.

Interchange Number: 21
Part Number(s): 2786559
Style/Design: Barracuda
Usage: 1970 Barracuda, except Cuda or AAR models.

Interchange Number: 22
Part Number(s): 3446960
Style/Design: Cuda
Usage: 1970 Cuda, AAR Cuda.

Interchange Number: 23
Part Number(s): 3454767
Style/Design: Gran coupe medallion
Usage: 1970–71 Barracuda Gran coupe.

Interchange Number: 24
Part Number(s): P-2528974, L-2528975, Y-2528976, M-2528977, U-2528979, T-2528978, H-2528981

S T A T U S

STATUS OF UNSHIPPED MERCHANDISE

TOS — Temporarily Out of Stock-expect
to ship within 30 days

NPO — New Publication on Order-will
ship when initial stock is received

OP — Out of Print-no longer being printed

NA — No longer Available from us

OSI — Out of Stock Indefinitely-may be
available in 6-12 months-Please reorder

CREDIT CARD CUSTOMERS — You have been charged only for items shipped plus postage & handling
and sales tax where applicable.

R E T U R N S

If for any reason you are not completely satisfied with your purchase, return it **within 14 days**
of receipt for replacement, exchange or refund.

1. Complete information below and return with package.
2. Address your package with return label provided below.
3. For your protection we suggest you return items via UPS or Insured Parcel Post.

Qty	Item #	Description	Desired Action	Reason Code	Unit Price	Total Credit

DESIRED ACTION

1. Please replace
2. Reorder different and/or additional merchandise
3. Please refund by original method of payment

REASON CODE — Please Explain Below

1. Received damaged/defective
2. Received incorrect merchandise
3. Merchandise on back-order too long
4. Unsatisfactory service
5. Other

R E O R D E R

If Desired Action is option 1 or 2 above please complete below:

Qty	Item #	Description	Price	Total

Ship to: If Different

Name

Address

City

State   Zip Code

☐ Check or Money order enclosed
☐ Visa   ☐ American Express
☐ Mastercard   ☐ Discover
Card # _____
Expiration date _____
Signature _____

Please indicate form of payment for any amount due.

*Residents of CA, CT, D.C., HI, IL, KS, MA, MN, NE, NM, NV & WI please add your state sales tax.

Return explanation and customer
concerns suggestions or comments.

_____
_____
_____
_____
_____
_____

Use this label to return merchandise. Fasten with cellophane tape.

FROM

_____
_____
_____
_____

TO

Classic Motorbooks T.M.

729 PROSPECT AVENUE
OSCEOLA, WI 54020, U.S.A.

Classic Motorbooks ™

729 PROSPECT AVENUE
OSCEOLA, WI 54020, U.S.A. • 1-800-826-6600

ORDER NUMBER
216723-001
CUSTOMER NUMBER
036558
DATE
11/24/97

SOLD
TO

JOHN G CLANTON JR

1024 S 16TH
MOUNT VERNON   WA   98274-0000

LOCATION	ITEM NUMBER	QUANTITY	DESCRIPTION	PRICE	STATUS
10-J2	125497	1	CHRY MUSC PT INTRCH MNL US		

MERCHANDISE	SHIPPING/HANDLING	STATE TAX	TOTAL AMOUNT	AMOUNT PAID	BALANCE DUE	CREDIT

SHIP VIA:

FX2   (PH @ 3604241720   12:57 PM

226716001

THANK YOU FOR YOUR ORDER.   WE LOOK FORWARD TO
SERVING YOU AGAIN IN THE FUTURE.   IF WE CAN BE OF
SERVICE TO YOU, PLEASE CALL US ON OUR TOLL FREE
HOT LINE – 1-800-826-6600.

MASTER CHARGE

SEE REVERSE SIDE FOR RETURN AND REORDER INFORMATION AND **STATUS** OF UNSHIPPED MERCHANDISE

UT 2

Classic Motorbooks ™

729 PROSPECT AVENUE • OSCEOLA, WI 54020, U.S.A.

FORWARDING AND RETURN POSTAGE GUARANTEED

DATE
11/24/97
ORDER #
216723-001
SHIP VIA
FX2

PKGID   226716003

TO ▶ JOHN G CLANTON   JR
C/O BROWN LINE
1763 HWY 99 S
MOUNT VERNON   WA 98273-0000

226716003

Classic Motorbooks ™

729 PROSPECT AVENUE • OSCEOLA, WI 54020, U.S.A.

FORWARDING AND RETURN POSTAGE GUARANTEED

DATE
11/24/97
ORDER #
216723-001
SHIP VIA
FX2

PKGID   226716004

TO ▶ JOHN G CLANTON   JR
C/O BROWN LINE
1763 HWY 99 S
MOUNT VERNON   WA 98273-0000

1971 GTX rear-quarter panel nameplates.

1972–1976 Dusters used this nameplate

Style/Design: P L Y M O U T H
Usage: 1970 Plymouth Belvedere, all models and body styles
   except station wagon.
Interchange Number: 25
   Part Number(s): 2965261
   Style/Design: Sport Satellite
   Usage: 1970 Sport Satellite, all models except station wagon.
Interchange Number: 26
   Part Number(s): 2840214
   Style/Design: GTX
   Usage: Early 1970 GTX.
Interchange Number: 27
   Part Number(s): 3506363
   Style/Design: GTX
   Usage: Late 1970 GTX.
Interchange Number: 28
   Part Number(s): 3444938
   Style/Design: Challenger (script)
   Usage: 1970 Challenger, also used on front fenders in 1970–71
      Challengers.
Interchange Number: 29
   Part Number(s): 3445223
   Style/Design: R/T
   Usage: 1970 Challenger R/T, also used on front fenders.
Interchange Number: 30
   Part Number(s): 3504199
   Style/Design: DODGE (Script)
   Usage: 1970 Dart, all models except Dart Swinger.
   Interchange Number: 31
   Part Number(s): 3445985
   Style/Design: Dart
   Usage: 1970 Dart Swinger, also found on rear quarters of this
      model.
Interchange Number: 32
   Part Number(s): 3505330
   Style/Design: Swinger
   Usage: 1970 Dart Swinger. Deck lid only.
Interchange Number: 33
   Part Number(s): D-2840324, O-2840325, D-3446454, G-
      2840326, E-2840327
   Style/Design: D O D G E
   Usage: 1970 Coronet, all models except Coronet 440, Coronet
      500, or Coronet R/T, all body styles except station wagon.
Interchange Number: 34
   Part Number(s): 3444609
   Style/Design: R/T
   Usage: 1970 Coronet R/T; 1970 Charger R/T.
Interchange Number: 35
   Part Number(s): 3505338
   Style/Design: 500
   Usage: 1970 Charger 500; 1970 Coronet 500.
Interchange Number: 36
   Part Number(s): 3505456
   Style/Design: Barracuda
   Usage: 1971–74 Barracuda, used on deck lid and front doors, all
      models except Cuda.

1971–1972 Demon nameplate.

Interchange Number: 37
   Part Number(s): 3570075
   Style/Design: By Plymouth
   Usage: 1971 Barracuda, all models.
Interchange Number: 38
   Part Number(s): 3570071
   Style/Design: Cuda
   Usage: 1971–74 Cuda.
Interchange Number: 39
   Part Number(s): 3505020
   Style/Design: Satellite
   Usage: 1971–74 Satellite, rear deck lid, all models, also on front
      fenders and rear quarter panels.
Interchange Number: 40
   Part Number(s): 3505433
   Style/Design: DODGE
   Usage: 1971 Dart, all except Demon; 1973 Coronet station
      wagon.
Interchange Number: 41
   Part Number(s): 2965502
   Style/Design: DODGE
   Usage: 1971 Demon; 1971 Challenger; 1973 Coronet four-door
      sedans on deck lid; 1974 Coronet station wagon, except
      Crestwood.
Interchange Number: 42
   Part Number(s): 3570035
   Style/Design: Charger Dodge Division
   Usage: 1971 Charger, all models.
Interchange Number: 43
   Part Number(s): 3506413
   Style/Design: 500
   Usage: 1971 Charger 500.
Interchange Number: 44
   Part Number(s): 3504811
   Style/Design: S.E. medallion
   Usage: 1971 Charger S.E.
Interchange Number: 45
   Part Number(s): 3504809
   Style/Design: R/T

1972–1973 Dart Sports used this nameplate.

1969 Road Runner tail-end nameplate.

Usage: 1971 Charger R/T, also used on front fender of this model.

Interchange Number: 46
Part Number(s): 3569542
Style/Design: By Plymouth
Usage: 1972–74 Barracuda.

Interchange Number: 47
Part Number(s): 3680160
Style/Design: GTX
Usage: 1972 Road Runner with GTX package and 440-ci.

Interchange Number: 48
Part Number(s): 3612859
Style/Design: Sebring
Usage: 1971–74 Satellite Sebring; 1971–72 Sebring Plus.

Interchange Number: 49
Part Number(s): 3613151
Style/Design: DODGE
Usage: 1972–74 Dart, all models except 1972 models with boxed-in style nameplate or 1974 Swinger or Special Edition. Also used on hood of this model.

Interchange Number: 50
Part Number(s): 3506412
Style/Design: Charger
Usage: 1972 Charger.

Interchange Number: 51
Part Number(s): 3613272
Style/Design: Dodge
Usage: 1972–74 Charger.

Interchange Number: 52
Part Number(s): 3680687
Style/Design: Charger
Usage: 1973–74 Charger.

Interchange Number: 53
Part Number(s): 3680997
Style/Design: Scamp
Usage: Early 1973 Scamp.
Note(s): Used until March 1, 1973.

Interchange Number: 54
Part Number(s): 3810058
Style/Design: Scamp
Usage: Late 1973–74 Scamp.
Note(s): Used after March 1, 1973.

Interchange Number: 55
Part Number(s): 3613272
Style/Design: DODGE (boxed in)
Usage: 1972 Dart Demon.

Interchange Number: 56
Part Number(s): 3505419
Style/Design: Dart
Usage: 1972 Demon, also on front fenders of Dart models.

Interchange Number: 57
Part Number(s): 3680804
Style/Design: Sebring Plus
Usage: 1973–74 Satellite Sebring Plus.

Interchange Number: 58
Part Number(s): 3505944 Road, 3505945 Runner
Style/Design: Road Runner
Usage: 1971–73 Road Runner, also used on rear quarters or roof sail panels.

Interchange Number: 59
Part Number(s): Road-305490, Runner-3505491
Style/Design: Road Runner
Usage: 1974 Road Runner.

Interchange Number: 60
Part Number(s): D-3612986, O-3612987, G-3612988, E-3612989
Style/Design: DODGE
Usage: 1972–74 Challenger.

Interchange Number: 61
Part Number(s): D-3443365, O-3443367, D 3443369, G-3443371, E-3443373
Style/Design: D O D G E
Usage: 1974 Dart Swinger, Special Edition; 1974 Dart four-door sedan.

Interchange Number: 62
Part Number(s): 3749326
Style/Design: PLYMOUTH
Usage: 1974 Valiant, except Scamp or Duster.

Interchange Number: 63
Part Number(s): 2901811
Style/Design: 500
Usage: 1969 Charger 500; 1969 Coronet 500. Also on front fenders of 1969 Coronet 500.

Interchange Number: 64
Part Number(s): 3613880
Style/Design: Plymouth
Usage: 1973 Valiant, except Duster or Scamp; 1974 Plymouth Fury Suburban station wagon.

Interchange Number: 65
Part Number(s): 2902767
Style/Design: Barracuda
Usage: 1969 Barracuda *without* Formula S package, all body styles.
Note(s): Part of trim panel. Silver in color.

Interchange Number: 66
Part Number(s): 2902772
Style/Design: Barracuda
Usage: 1969 Barracuda *with* Formula S package, all body styles.
Note(s): Part of trim panel. Black in color.

Interchange Number: 67
Part Number(s): 2963391
Style/Design: Dart GT
Usage: 1969 Dart GT models.
Note(s): Part of trim panel. Black in color.

Interchange Number: 68
Part Number(s): 2901890
Style/Design: DODGE
Usage: 1969 Dart Custom.
Note(s): Part of trim panel.

Interchange Number: 69
Part Number(s): 2963392

Style/Design: GTS
Usage: 1969 Dart GTS.
Note(s): Part of trim panel. Black in color.

Interchange Number: 70
Part Number(s): 2902881
Style/Design: Dodge
Usage: 1969 Coronet 440, all body styles except station wagon.
Note(s): Part of trim panel. Silver in color.

Interchange Number: 71
Part Number(s): 2964857
Style/Design: Dodge
Usage: 1969 Coronet Super Bee.
Note(s): (1) Part of trim panel. Black in color. (2) Interchange Number 70 can be painted flat black and will fit.

Interchange Number: 72
Part Number(s): 2901844
Style/Design: Plymouth
Usage: 1969 Valiant Signet, all body styles.
Note(s): Part of trim panel.

Interchange Number: 73
Part Number(s): 2902911
Style/Design: GTX
Usage: 1969 GTX, all body styles.
Note(s): Part of trim panel. Black in color.

Interchange Number: 74
Part Number(s): 2783011
Style/Design: Medallion
Usage: 1970 Valiant, except Duster models.

Interchange Number: 75
Part Number(s): 2965254
Style/Design: Dodge
Usage: 1970 Coronet Super Bee.
Note(s): Part of trim panel.

Interchange Number: 76
Part Number(s): 2965256
Style/Design: Dodge
Usage: 1970 Coronet 440, all body styles except station wagon.

Interchange Number: 77
Part Number(s): 2965259
Style/Design: Dodge
Usage: 1970 Coronet R/T, all body styles.
Note(s): Part of trim panel. Black in color.

Interchange Number: 78
Part Number(s): 2965258
Style/Design: Dodge
Usage: 1970 Coronet 500, all body styles except station wagon.
Note(s): Part of trim panel. Black in color.

Add-On Accessories

This section deals with bolt-on accessories that were options or part of option packages. These include air scoops, front and rear spoilers. and luggage racks.

Hood Scoops and Bezels
Model Identification

Interchange

Interchange Number: 1
Part Number(s): 3672605
Description: Bolt-on hood scoop
Usage: 1973–74 Dart, all models.
Note(s): Not originally offered but will fit 1970–74 Duster models.

Interchange Number: 2
Part Number(s): 2998034 (right), 2998035 (left)
Description: Bezel for sport-hood air scoops
Usage: 1972–74 Barracuda with sport hood.

Interchange Number: 3
Part Number(s): 2998182 (right), 2998183 (left)
Description: Bezels for hood scoops
Usage: 1972–74 Challenger with sport hood.

Interchange Number: 4
Part Number(s): 3672258 (right), 3672259 (left)
Description: Air scoops
Usage: 1973–74 Road Runner.

Interchange Number: 5
Part Number(s): 2949146 (right), 2949147 (left)
Description: Bezels for scoops
Usage: 1972 Valiant with sport hood.

Interchange Number: 6
Part Number(s): 3443442 (right), 3443443 (left)
Description: Simulated air vents
Usage: 1972 Road Runner.

Interchange Number: 7
Part Number(s): 2949336 (right), 2949337 (left)
Description: Bezels for air scoops
Usage: 1973–74 Valiant with sport hood.

Interchange Number: 8
Part Number(s): 3443426 (right), 3443427 (left)
Description: Air scoops
Usage: 1972 Valiant.

Interchange Number: 9
Part Number(s): 3573698
Description: Bolt-on hood scoop
Usage: 1972 Dart.

Interchange Number: 10
Part Number(s): 2949194 (right), 2949195 (left)
Description: Hood scoops
Usage: 1969–70 Coronet R/T, Super Bee with ram air.

Interchange Number: 11
Part Number(s): 2949336 (right), 2949337 (left)
Description: Hood scoops
Usage: 1969 Barracuda with Cuda package.
Note(s): Will fit all Barracuda models.

Interchange Number: 12
Part Number(s): 3443130 (right), 3443131 (left)
Description: Hood scoops
Usage: 1970–71 Valiant or Dart models.
Note(s): Not originally offered but will fit 1968–69 models.

Rear Spoilers

There were only three rear spoilers used on Mopar models. Part number 3570208 was a wing type and was used on the following models: 1970–71 Barracuda, Challenger, Charger, Coronet, Dart, Duster, Demon, and Valiant two-door models. This spoiler was canceled after 1971, but it will fit these models: 1971–74 Barracuda, Challenger, Charger, and Satellite two-door models; Dart Sport/Demon, Duster, with only minor modifications to the deck lid. Due to deck design, problems may occur if interchanging this wing to 1968 and 1969 models. Interchange this spoiler without the mounting brackets, as brackets differ between models.

Part number 3570369 was a lip type of spoiler and was used only on the 1970 AAR Cuda. This spoiler will fit all 1970–74 Barracuda models without any problems. Interchange with the mounting plates. The third spoiler is also a lip type. It was used on the 1970 Challenger T/A models. This spoiler will fit all 1970–74 Challengers if it is interchanged with its mounting brackets. The 1969 Daytona and the 1970 Super Bird models used special rear-wing spoilers. Although they look similar, they are not interchangeable with each other.

Front Spoilers

Front spoilers were designed to fit only four models. Part numbers 3443352 right, 3443353 left were available on the 1970 and 1971 Barracuda models. Due to their design, interference may occur when swapping them to a later model. They will not fit earlier Barracudas.

Challengers used part 3443354 (right), 3443355 (left). They, too, were available for 1970 and 1971 models. They will fit 1972–74 models with a little modification. A one-piece style of spoiler was used on 1971 Chargers. Listed as part number 3443180, it will fit 1972–74 Chargers without any modification.

A two-part front spoiler was used on 1971 two-door Satellite models. Listed as part numbers 3442954 right, 344295 left, it will fit 1972 models, but due to a redesign in front sheet metal, it won't fit 1973 or 1974 models.

Luggage Racks
Model Identification

Interchange

Interchange Number: 1
Part Number(s): 3419382
Usage: 1968–69 Barracuda, except fastback; 1968–70 Charger.

Interchange Number: 2
Part Number(s): 3419498
Usage: 1970–74 Barracuda, Challenger, all body styles; 1973–74 Charger, Coronet, and Satellite, all body styles except station wagon.

Interchange Number: 3
Part Number(s): 3620518
Usage: 1971–72 Charger, Satellite two-door models only, except Charger S.E. models.

Interchange Number: 4
Part Number(s): 3419382
Usage: 1972 Charger S.E. models only.

Chapter 11

Interior

Instrument Panel
Model Identification

Interchange
Interchange Number: 1
  Part Number(s): 2857605
  Usage: 1968 Valiant, all models and body styles, with or
    without air conditioning.
Interchange Number: 2

Part Number(s): 2857134
Usage: 1968 Barracuda, all body styles, with or without air
  conditioning.
Interchange Number: 3
  Part Number(s): 2857132
  Usage: 1968 Dart, all models and body styles, with or without
    air conditioning.
Interchange Number: 4
  Part Number(s): 2927303
  Usage: 1968 Belvedere, Coronet, all models and body styles,
    with or without air conditioning, without Rallye instrument
    cluster.
Interchange Number: 5
  Part Number(s): 2927306
  Usage: 1968 Charger, all models, with or without air

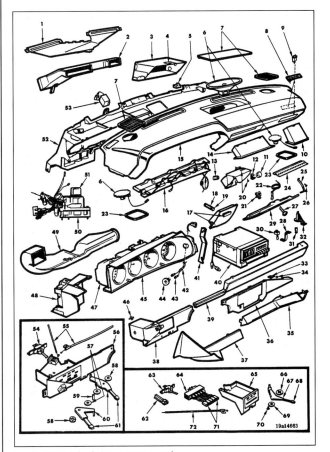

1970–1974 E-body instrument panel.

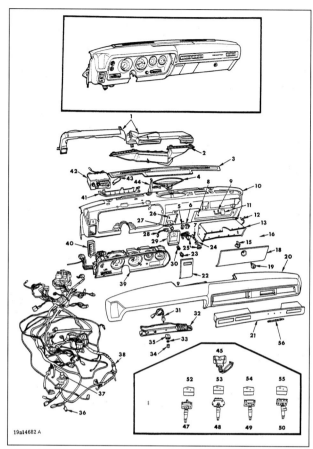

1971–1974 B-body instrument panel.

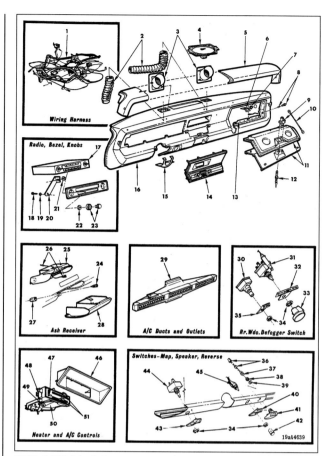

1971–1974 B-body instrument panel.

conditioning; 1968 Belvedere, Coronet with Rallye instrumentation, with or without air conditioning.

Interchange Number: 6
Part Number(s): 2984641
Usage: 1969 Valiant, all models and body styles, with or without air conditioning.

Interchange Number: 7
Part Number(s): 2984642
Usage: 1969 Barracuda, all models and body styles, with or without air conditioning.

Interchange Number: 8
Part Number(s): 2984643
Usage: 1969 Dart, all models and body styles, with or without air conditioning.

Interchange Number: 9
Part Number(s): 2927580
Usage: 1969 Belvedere, all models and body styles, with or without air conditioning; 1969 Coronet, all models except Super Bee, Coronet R/T, and Coronet 500 with Rallye instrumentation.

Interchange Number: 10
Part Number(s): 2927582
Usage: 1969 Charger, all models, with or without air conditioning; 1969 Coronet with Rallye instrumentation, with or without air conditioning.

Interchange Number: 11
Part Number(s): 2984574
Usage: 1970–72 Duster, Valiant, all models and body styles, except Duster 340, with or without air conditioning.

Interchange Number: 12
Part Number(s): 2984576

Usage: 1970 Dart, all models and body styles, except Swinger 340, with or without air conditioning.

Interchange Number: 13
Part Number(s): 2985452
Usage: 1970 Dart Swinger 340; 1970 Duster 340, with or without air conditioning.

Interchange Number: 14
Part Number(s): 2984290
Usage: 1970 Charger without air conditioning; 1970 Coronet, and Satellite with Rallye instrumentation, without air conditioning.

Interchange Number: 15
Part Number(s): 2984292
Usage: 1970 Charger with air conditioning; 1970 Coronet, and Satellite with Rallye instruments and air conditioning.

Interchange Number: 16
Part Number(s): 2984288
Usage: 1970 Coronet, Satellite, all models and body styles, without air conditioning, without Rallye instrumentation.

Interchange Number: 17
Part Number(s): 2984019
Usage: 1970–73 Barracuda, Challenger, all models with or without air conditioning, with or without Rallye instruments.

Interchange Number: 18
Part Number(s): 2985018
Usage: 1971–72 Charger, Coronet, Satellite, all models and body styles, with air conditioning.

Interchange Number: 19
Part Number(s): 2985016
Usage: 1971–72 Charger, Coronet, Satellite, all models and body styles, without air conditioning, with or without Rallye instrumentation.

Interchange Number: 20
 Part Number(s): 3590242
 Usage: 1973 Dart, Duster, and Valiant, all models and body styles, with or without air conditioning.
Interchange Number: 21
 Part Number(s): 3590286
 Usage: 1973 Charger, Coronet, Satellite, all models and body styles, with or without Rallye instrumentation, with air conditioning.
Interchange Number: 22
 Part Number(s): 3590284
 Usage: 1973 Charger, Coronet, and Satellite with or without Rallye instrumentation, without air conditioning.
Interchange Number: 23
 Part Number(s): 3590349
 Usage: Early 1974 Dart, Duster, and Valiant, all models and body styles, with or without air conditioning.
 Note(s): Used until June 1, 1974.
Interchange Number: 24
 Part Number(s): 3590651
 Usage: Late 1974 Dart, Duster, and Valiant, all models and body styles.
 Note(s): Used after June 1, 1974.
Interchange Number: 25
 Part Number(s): 3590460
 Usage: 1974 Barracuda, Challenger, with or without Rallye instrumentation.
Interchange Number: 26
 Part Number(s): 3590310
 Usage: 1974 Charger, Coronet, Satellite, with or without Rallye instrumentation, with air conditioning, all models and body styles.
Interchange Number: 27
 Part Number(s): 3590310
 Usage: 1974 Charger, Coronet, Satellite, with or without Rallye instrumentation, without air conditioning, all models and body styles.

Glovebox Compartment
Model Identification

Interchange
Interchange Number: 1
 Part Number(s): 2829773
 Usage: 1968 Barracuda, Dart, and Valiant, all models and body styles, with or without air conditioning.
Interchange Number: 2
 Part Number(s): 2822821
 Usage: 1968 Belvedere, Charger, and Coronet, all models and body styles, with or without air conditioning.
Interchange Number: 3
 Part Number(s): 2889773

Usage: 1969 Barracuda; 1969–72 Dart, Valiant; 1970–72 Duster, all models and body styles, with or without air conditioning.
Interchange Number: 4
 Part Number(s): 2927940
 Usage: 1969 Belvedere, Charger, and Coronet, all models and body styles, with or without air conditioning.
Interchange Number: 5
 Part Number(s): Upper–2984457, Lower–2984819
 Usage: 1970–71 Barracuda, Challenger, all models and body styles, with or without air conditioning.
Interchange Number: 6
 Part Number(s): 2984716
 Usage: 1970 Charger, Coronet, and Satellite, all models and body styles, with or without air conditioning.
Interchange Number: 7
 Part Number(s): 2985747
 Usage: 1971–74 Charger, Coronet, and Satellite, all models and body styles, with or without air conditioning.
 Note(s): Solid plastic.
Interchange Number: 8
 Part Number(s): 2984819
 Usage: 1972–74 Barracuda, Challenger, all models, with or without air conditioning.
Interchange Number: 9
 Part Number(s): 3590298
 Usage: 1973–early 1974 Dart, Duster, and Valiant, all models and body styles, with or without air conditioning.
 Note(s): Up to December 5, 1973.
Interchange Number: 10
 Part Number(s): 3590655
 Usage: Late 1974 Dart, Duster, and Valiant, all models and body styles, with or without air conditioning.
 Note(s): Used after December 5, 1973.

Glovebox Doors
Model Identification

Interchange
Interchange Number: 1
 Part Number(s): 3590656
 Usage: 1974 Dart, Duster, and Valiant, all models and body styles.
Interchange Number: 2
 Part Number(s): 3590222
 Usage: 1972–74 Barracuda, Challenger, all models.
Interchange Number: 3
 Part Number(s): 3590280

Usage: 1973–74 Charger, Coronet, and Satellite, all models and body styles.

Interchange Number: 4
Part Number(s): 3590207
Usage: 1972–73 Dart, Duster, and Valiant, all models and body styles.

Interchange Number: 5
Part Number(s): 2985747
Usage: 1972 Charger, Coronet, and Satellite, all models and body styles.
Note(s): Interchange Number 3 will fit but uses a strap instead of an arm for support.

Interchange Number: 6
Part Number(s): 2984468
Usage: 1970–71 Dart, Duster, and Valiant, all models and body styles.

Interchange Number: 7
Part Number(s): 2984029
Usage: 1970–71 Barracuda, Challenger, all models and body styles.

Interchange Number: 8
Part Number(s): 2889638
Usage: 1968–69 Barracuda, Dart, and Valiant, all models and body styles except Signet.

Interchange Number: 9
Part Number(s): 2857130
Usage: 1968–69 Valiant Signet models only.
Note(s): Interchange with spacer.

Interchange Number: 10
Part Number(s): 4250DX9 (inner), 4251DX9 (outer)
Usage: 1968–69 Belvedere, Coronet, all models and body styles, without Rallye instrumentation.
Note(s): Originally molded in colored vinyl, repaint to match trim.

Interchange Number: 11
Part Number(s): 4284DX9 (inner), 4285DX9 (outer)
Usage: 1968–69 Charger, Coronet with Rallye instrumentation.
Note(s): Originally molded in colored vinyl. Repaint to match trim.

Interchange Number: 12
Part Number(s): 2984720
Usage: 1970 Coronet, Satellite without Rallye instrumentation.

Interchange Number: 13
Part Number(s): 2984721
Usage: 1970 Charger, Coronet, and Satellite with Rallye instrumentation.

Interchange Number: 14
Part Number(s): 2985037
Usage: Early 1971 Charger, Coronet, and Satellite, all models and body styles, with or without Rallye Instrumentation.
Note(s): Used before January 1, 1971.

Interchange Number: 15
Part Number(s): 2985973
Usage: Late 1971 Charger, Coronet, Satellite, all models and body styles, with or without Rallye Instrumentation.
Note(s): Used after January 1, 1971.

Seat Adjustment Rails

Seat type, model, and seat position will have the greatest effects on the interchange here. Rails are in matched pairs, so a set from the driver's side will not fit the passenger's side in most cases. Nor will those from a bench seat fit bucket seats.

Model Identification

Barracuda...*Interchange Number*
1968
  bench seats 1
  bucket seats
    driver's side 5
    passenger's side 3
1969
  bench seats 7
  bucket seats
    driver's side 11
    passenger's side 9
1970
  bench seats 13
  bucket seats
    driver's side 21
    passenger's side 20
1971
  bench seats 14
  bucket seats
    driver's side 21
    passenger's side 20
1972–74
    driver's side 34
    passenger's side 33

***Belvedere, Charger, Coronet,
and Satellite***...*Interchange Number*
1968
  bench seats 2
  bucket seats
    driver's side 6
    passenger's side 4
1969
  bench seats 8
  bucket seats
    driver's side 12
    passenger's side 10
1970
  bench seats 8
  bucket seats
    driver's side 25
    passenger's side 23
  six-way seats..28
1971
  bench seat...22
  bucket seats
    driver's side 26
    passenger's side 24
  six-way seats..29
1972–74
  bench seat...35
  bucket seat
    driver's side 37
    passenger's side 36

Dart, Duster, Demon, and Valiant............*Interchange Number*
1968
  bench seats 1
  bucket seats
    driver's side 5
    passenger's side 3
1969
  bench seats 7
bucket seats
driver's side 11
    passenger's side 9
1970
  bench seats 7
  bucket seats
    driver's side 17
    passenger's side 16
1971
  bench seats 15
  bucket seats
    driver's side 19
    passenger's side 18
1972–74
  bench seats 30
  bucket seats
    driver's side 32
    passenger's side 31

Interchange

Interchange Number: 1
Part Numbers: 2935054 (right), 2935055 (left)
Seat Type: Bench seat
Usage: 1968 Barracuda, Dart, and Valiant, all models and body styles.

Interchange Number: 2
Part Numbers: 2862232 (right), 2862233 (left)
Seat Type: Bench seat
Usage: 1968 Belvedere, Charger, and Coronet two-door models only.

Interchange Number: 3
Part Numbers: 2935946 (inner), 2935947 (outer)
Seat Type: Passenger's bucket seat
Usage: 1968 Barracuda, Dart, and Valiant, all models and body styles.

Interchange Number: 4
Part Numbers: 2862058 (inner), 2862059 (outer)
Seat Type: Passenger's bucket seat
Usage: 1968 Belvedere, Charger, and Coronet, all models and body styles.

Interchange Number: 5
Part Numbers: 2935947 (inner), 2935948 (outer)
Seat Type: Driver's bucket seat
Usage: 1968 Barracuda, Dart, and Valiant, all models and body styles.

Interchange Number: 6
Part Numbers: 2862059 (inner), 2862061 (outer)
Seat Type: Driver's bucket seat
Usage: 1968 Belvedere, Charger, and Coronet, all models and body styles.

Interchange Number: 7
Part Numbers: 2935758 (right), 2935759 (left)
Seat Type: Bench seat
Usage: 1969 Barracuda; 1969–70, Dart, Valiant; 1970 Duster, all models and body styles.

Interchange Number: 8
Part Numbers: 2935744 (right), 2935745 (left)
Seat Type: Bench seat
Usage: 1969–70 Belvedere, Charger, Coronet, Satellite two-door models only.

Interchange Number: 9
Part Numbers: 2935769 (inner), 2935771 (outer)
Seat Type: Driver's bucket seat
Usage: 1969 Barracuda, Dart, and Valiant, all models and body styles.

Interchange Number: 10
Part Numbers: 2935781 (inner), 2935783 (outer)
Seat Type: Driver's bucket seat
Usage: 1969 Belvedere, Charger, Coronet, and Satellite, all models and body styles.

Interchange Number: 11
Part Numbers: 2935768 (inner), 2935770 (outer)
Seat Type: Passenger's bucket seat
Usage: 1969 Barracuda, Dart, and Valiant, all models and body styles.

Interchange Number: 12
Part Numbers: 2935780 (inner), 2935782 (outer)
Seat Type: Passenger's bucket seat
Usage: 1969 Belvedere, Charger, Coronet, Satellite, all models and body styles.

Interchange Number: 13
Part Numbers: 2999518 (right), 2999521 (left)
Seat Type: Bench seat
Usage: 1970 Barracuda, Challenger, all models except convertible.

Interchange Number: 14
Part Numbers: 3586134 (right), 3586135 (left)
Seat Type: Bench seat
Usage: 1971 Barracuda, Challenger, all models except convertible.

Interchange Number: 15
Part Numbers: 3586388 (right), 3586389 (left)
Seat Type: Bench seat
Usage: 1971 Dart, Duster, and Valiant, all models and body styles.

Interchange Number: 16
Part Numbers: 3454068 (inner), 3454072 (outer)
Seat Type: Passenger's bucket seat
Usage: 1970 Dart, Duster, and Valiant, all models and body styles.

Interchange Number: 17
Part Numbers: 3454069 (inner), 3454073 (outer)
Seat Type: Driver's bucket seat
Usage: 1970 Dart, Duster, and Valiant, all models and body styles.

Interchange Number: 18
Part Numbers: 3586148 (inner), 3454072 (outer)
Seat Type: Passenger's bucket seat
Usage: 1971 Dart, Duster, and Valiant, all models and body styles.
Note(s): Outer rail is also used in Interchange Number 16.

Interchange Number: 19
Part Numbers: 3586149 (inner), 3454073 (outer)
Seat Type: Driver's bucket seat
Usage: 1971 Dart, Duster, and Valiant, all models and body styles.
Note(s): Outer rail is also used in Interchange Number 17.

Interchange Number: 20
Part Numbers: 2999522 (inner), 2999520 (outer)
Seat Type: Passenger's bucket seat
Usage: 1970–71 Barracuda, Challenger, all models and body styles.

Interchange Number: 21
Part Numbers: 2999523 (inner), 2999521 (outer)
Seat Type: Driver's bucket seat
Usage: 1970–71 Barracuda, Challenger, all models and body styles.

Interchange Number: 22
Part Numbers: 3586132 (right), 3586133 (left)
Seat Type: Bench seat
Usage: 1971 Charger, Satellite, two-door models only.

Interchange Number: 23
Part Numbers: 3454070 (inner), 3454072 (outer)
Seat Type: Passenger's bucket seat
Usage: 1970 Charger, Coronet, Satellite, all models and body styles.

Interchange Number: 24
Part Numbers: 3586144 (inner), 3586136 (outer)
Seat Type: Passenger's bucket seat
Usage: 1971 Charger, Satellite two-door models only.

Interchange Number: 25
Part Numbers: 3454071 (inner), 3454075 (outer)
Seat Type: Driver's bucket seat
Usage: 1970 Charger, Coronet, and Satellite, all models and body styles.

Interchange Number: 26
Part Numbers: 3586145 (inner), 3586137 (outer)
Seat Type: Driver's bucket seat
Usage: 1971 Charger, Satellite, two-door models only.

Interchange Number: 27
Part Numbers: 3454443, left only
Seat Type: Six-way power seat driver's side
Usage: 1970–71 Barracuda, Challenger with power seats.
Note(s): Inner rail is the same as standard.

Interchange Number: 28
Part Numbers: 3454445, left only
Seat Type: Six-way power seat driver's side
Usage: 1970 Charger, Coronet, and Satellite with power seats, all models.
Note(s): Inner rail is the same as standard.

Interchange Number: 29
Part Numbers: 3508217 (left)
Seat Type: Six-way power seat driver's side

Usage: 1971 Charger, Coronet, and Satellite, all models and body styles with power seat.
Note(s): Inner rail same as standard.

Interchange Number: 30
Part Numbers: 3670234 (right), 3670235 (left)
Seat Type: Bench seat
Usage: 1972–74 Dart, Duster, and Valiant, all models and body styles.

Interchange Number: 31
Part Numbers: 3670230 (inner), 3670232 (outer)
Seat Type: Passenger's bucket seat
Usage: 1972–74 Dart, Duster, and Valiant, all models and body styles.

Interchange Number: 32
Part Numbers: 3670231 (inner), 3670233 (outer)
Seat Type: Driver's bucket seat
Usage: 1972–74 Dart, Duster, and Valiant, all models and body styles.

Interchange Number: 33
Part Numbers: 3670228 (inner), 3670226 (outer)
Seat Type: Passenger's bucket seat
Usage: 1972–74 Barracuda, Challenger.
Note(s): Inner rail is also used in Interchange Number 34.

Interchange Number: 34
Part Numbers: 3670228 (inner), 3670227 (outer)
Seat Type: Driver's bucket seat
Usage: 1972–74 Barracuda, Challenger.
Note(s): Inner rail is also used in Interchange Number 33.

Interchange Number: 35
Part Numbers: 3670242 (right), 3670243 (left)
Seat Type: Bench seat
Usage: 1972–74 Charger, Coronet, and Satellite, all models and body styles.

Interchange Number: 36
Part Numbers: 3670238 (inner), 3670240 (outer)
Seat Type: Passenger's bucket seat
Usage: 1972–74 Charger, Coronet, and Satellite, all models and body styles.

Interchange Number: 37
Part Numbers: 3670239 (inner), 3670241 (outer)
Seat Type: Driver's bucket seat
Usage: 1972–74 Charger, Coronet, and Satellite, all models and body styles.

Front-Seat Frame

Even though there are certain similarities between certain seats, other factors must be weighted in when swapping seats. The fender tag on your car will tell you the color seat type and color the original units were. Carefully inspect the frame, look for signs of repair or damage. Next, make sure the springs are tight and not broken or sagging. Then carefully inspect the headrest slide, seat latch, hinges, and the seatbelt guides. It is these factors that can affect the interchange. When swapping out bench seats, a center armrest can also affect your interchange. Note that many seats are sold with the seat adjustment rails, so you may want to cross-reference that section in this chapter. All interchanges here are the bare seat frame, stripped of all upholstery padding and cotton stuff.

Model Identification

bucket seats
    driver's side 21
    passenger's side. 22

Challenger...***Interchange Number***

1970
  bench seats
    without center armrest...31
    with center armrest 32
  bucket seats
    driver's side 17
    passenger's side. 18

1971–72
  bench seats
    without center armrest...33
    with center armrest 34
  bucket seats
    driver's side 17
    passenger's side. 18

1973–74
  bucket seats
    driver's side 19
    passenger's side. 20

Dart, Duster, Demon, and Valiant ....***Interchange Number***

1968
  bench seats without center armrest
    without headrests...11
    with headrests 9
  bench seats with center armrest
    without headrests...12
    with headrests 10
  bucket seats, driver's side
    without headrest 7
    with headrest 5
  bucket seats, passenger's side
    without headrest 8
    with headrest 6

1969
  bench seats
    without center armrest...9
    with center armrest 10
  bucket seats
    driver's side 5
    passenger's side. 6

1970–72
  bench seats
    without center armrest...35
    with center armrest 36
  bucket seats
    driver's side 17
    passenger's side. 18

1973–74
  bench seats
    without center armrest...37
    with center armrest 38
  bucket seats
    driver's side 19
    passenger's side. 20

Interchange

Interchange Number: 1
Seat Type/Position: Bucket driver
Usage: 1968–69 Belvedere, Charger, and Coronet two-door models only.
Note(s): With headrests. Models up to January 1, 1968, were optional with headrest. Seat without headrest will not fit, see Interchange Number 3.

Interchange Number: 2
Seat Type/Position: Bucket passenger
Usage: 1968–69 Belvedere, Charger, and Coronet two-door models only.

Note(s): With headrests. Models up to January 1, 1968, were optional with headrest. Seat without headrest will not fit; see Interchange Number 4.

Interchange Number: 3
Seat Type/Position: Bucket driver
Usage: Early 1968 Belvedere, Charger, and Coronet two-door models only, without headrest.
Note(s): For models up to January 1, 1968, *without* headrest. After this date, headrests are mandatory.

Interchange Number: 4
Seat Type/Position: Bucket passenger
Usage: Early 1968 Belvedere, Charger, and Coronet two-door models only.
Note(s): For models up to January 1, 1968, *without* headrest. After this date, headrests are mandatory.

Interchange Number: 5
Seat Type/Position: Bucket driver
Usage: 1968–69 Barracuda, Dart with headrests.
Note(s): Some early (up to January 1, 1968) models came without headrests and will *not* fit. See Interchange Number 7.

Interchange Number: 6
Seat Type/Position: Bucket passenger
Usage: 1968–69 Barracuda, Dart with headrest.
Note(s): Some early (up to January 1, 1968) models came without headrests and will *not* fit. See Interchange Number 8.

Interchange Number: 7
Seat Type/Position: Bucket driver
Usage: Early 1968 Barracuda, Dart without headrest.
Note(s): Only up to January 1, 1968; after this date, headrests are mandatory.

Interchange Number: 8
Seat Type/Position: Bucket passenger
Usage: Early 1968 Barracuda, Dart without headrest.
Note(s): Only up to January 1, 1968; after this date, headrests are mandatory.

Interchange Number: 9
Seat Type/Position: Bench seats
Usage: 1968–69 Barracuda, Dart, and Valiant two-door models without center armrest.
Note(s): Some early (up to January 1, 1968) models came without headrests and will *not* fit. See Interchange Number 11.

Interchange Number: 10
Seat Type/Position: Bench seats
Usage: 1968–69 Barracuda, Dart, and Valiant two-door models with center armrest.
Note(s): Some early (up to January 1, 1968) models came without headrests and will *not* fit. See Interchange Number 12.

Interchange Number: 11
Seat Type/Position: Bench seats
Usage: Early 1968 Barracuda, Dart, and Valiant two-door models without center armrest.
Note(s): Until January 1, 1968; after this date headrests are mandatory.

Interchange Number: 12
Seat Type/Position: Bench seats
Usage: Early 1968 Barracuda, Dart, and Valiant two-door models with center armrest.
Note(s): Up to January 1, 1968; after this date, headrests are mandatory.

Interchange Number: 13
Seat Type/Position: Bench seats
Usage: 1968–69 Belvedere, Coronet two-door models only; 1968–69 Charger, all models, without center armrest.
Note(s): Some early (up to January 1, 1968) models came without headrests and will *not* fit. See Interchange Number 15.

Interchange Number: 14
Seat Type/Position: Bench seats
Usage: 1968–69 Belvedere, Coronet two-door models only; 1968–69 Charger, all models with center armrest.
Note(s): Some early (up to January 1, 1968) models came without headrests and will *not* fit. See Interchange Number 16.

Interchange Number: 15
Seat Type/Position: Bench seats
Usage: Early 1968 Belvedere, Coronet two-door models only; 1968–69 Charger, all models without center armrest.
Note(s): Up to January 1, 1968; after this date, headrests are mandatory.

Interchange Number: 16
Seat Type/Position: Bench seats
Usage: Early 1968 Belvedere, Coronet two-door models only; 1968–69 Charger, all models with center armrest.
Note(s): Up to January 1, 1968; after this date, headrests are mandatory.

Interchange Number: 17
Seat Type/Position: Bucket driver
Usage: 1970–72 Barracuda, Challenger, Charger, Dart, Duster, Satellite, and Valiant; 1970 Coronet two-door models.
Note(s): High-back bucket seats.

Interchange Number: 18
Seat Type/Position: Bucket passenger
Usage: 1970–72 Barracuda, Challenger, Charger, Dart, Duster, Satellite, and Valiant; 1970 Coronet two-door models.
Note(s): High-back bucket seats.

Interchange Number: 19
Seat Type/Position: Bucket driver
Usage: 1973–74 Barracuda, Challenger, Dart, Duster, and Valiant.
Note(s): High-back bucket seats.

Interchange Number: 20
Seat Type/Position: Bucket passenger
Usage: 1973–74 Barracuda, Challenger, Dart, Duster, and Valiant.
Note(s): High-back bucket seats.

Interchange Number: 21
Seat Type/Position: Bucket driver
Usage: 1973–74 Charger, Satellite, two-door models only.
Note(s): High-back bucket seats.

Interchange Number: 22
Seat Type/Position: Bucket passenger
Usage: 1973–74 Charger, Satellite, two-door models only.
Note(s): High-back bucket seats.

Interchange Number: 23
Seat Type/Position: Bench seats
Usage: 1970 Charger, Coronet, and Satellite without center armrest.

Interchange Number: 24
Seat Type/Position: Bench seats
Usage: 1970 Charger, Coronet, and Satellite with center armrest.

Interchange Number: 25
Seat Type/Position: Bench seats
Usage: 1971–72 Charger, Coronet, and Satellite without center armrest, except high-back seats.

Interchange Number: 26
Seat Type/Position: Bench seats
Usage: 1971–72 Charger, Coronet, and Satellite with center armrest. High-back seats.
Note(s): More common in Charger S.E. and Satellite Brougham models.

Interchange Number: 27
Seat Type/Position: Bench seats
Usage: 1971–72 Charger, Coronet, and Satellite with center armrest, except high-back seats.

Interchange Number: 28
Seat Type/Position: Bench seats
Usage: 1973–74 Charger, Coronet, and Satellite without center armrest.

Interchange Number: 29
Seat Type/Position: Bench seats
Usage: 1973–74 Charger, Coronet, and Satellite with center armrest, except high-back seats.

Interchange Number: 30
Seat Type/Position: Bench seats
Usage: 1973–74 Charger, Coronet, and Satellite with center armrest. High-back seats.

Interchange Number: 31
Seat Type/Position: Bench seats
Usage: 1970 Barracuda, Challenger without center armrest.

Interchange Number: 32
Seat Type/Position: Bench seats
Usage: 1970 Barracuda, Challenger with center armrest.

Interchange Number: 33
Seat Type/Position: Bench seats
Usage: 1971–72 Barracuda, Challenger without center armrest.

Interchange Number: 34
Seat Type/Position: Bench seats
Usage: 1971–72 Barracuda, Challenger with center armrest.

Interchange Number: 35
Seat Type/Position: Bench seats
Usage: 1970–72 Dart, Duster, and Valiant without center armrest.

Interchange Number: 36
Seat Type/Position: Bench seats
Usage: 1970–72 Dart, Duster, and Valiant with center armrest.

Interchange Number: 37
Seat Type/Position: Bench seats
Usage: 1973–74 Dart, Duster, and Valiant without center armrest.

Interchange Number: 38
Seat Type/Position: Bench seats
Usage: 1973–74 Dart, Duster, and Valiant with center armrest. High-back seats.

Sun Visors

Sun visors are covered in vinyl trim. Color varies with color of interior and usually matches the headliner. No interchange is given regarding color; rather the concern here is the usage of a particular visor. The interchange is based on white or black only. Visors can be repainted or recovered to match your car's trim. Body style has little effect on usage with two exemptions—convertibles and station wagons. Convertibles require a special set of visors, and those with a steel roof will not fit. In most cases the visor is reversible, meaning it will fit either the driver's or passenger's side.

Model Identification

Interchange
Interchange Number: 1
Part Number(s): 1112DX9
Usage: 1968–69 Barracuda; 1968–70 Belvedere, Charger, and Coronet; 1968–71 Dart and Valiant, all models and styles except convertible or Duster.
Interchange Number: 2
Part Number(s): 1109DX9
Usage: 1968–70 Belvedere, Coronet convertible.
Interchange Number: 3
Part Number(s): 1107EW1
Usage: 1968–69 Barracuda, Dart convertible.
Interchange Number: 4
Part Number(s): 1103FX9
Usage: 1970–71 Duster; 1971 Demon.
Note(s): Fastback only; other body styles will not fit.
Interchange Number: 5
Part Number(s): 1102FX9
Usage: 1970–73 Barracuda, Challenger, except convertible.
Interchange Number: 6
Part Number(s): 1120FX9
Usage: 1970–71 Barracuda, Challenger convertible.
Interchange Number: 7
Part Number(s): 1123GX9
Usage: 1971 Charger, Coronet, and Satellite, all body styles.
Interchange Number: 8
Part Number(s): 1138GX9
Usage: 1972–73 Dart, Valiant, all body styles except fastback (Duster/Demon/Dart Sport).
Interchange Number: 9
Part Number(s): 1137GX9
Usage: early 1972 Duster, Demon.
Note(s): Used until December 1, 1971.
Interchange Number: 10
Part Number(s): 1139HX9
Usage: Late 1972–73 Duster, Demon.
Note(s): Used after December 1, 1971.
Interchange Number: 11
Part Number(s): 1141GX9
Usage: 1972–73 Charger, Coronet, and Satellite, all models and body styles.
Interchange Number: 12
Part Number(s): H502KX9
Usage: 1974–75 Dart, Valiant, all models except Dart Sport or Duster.
Interchange Number: 13
Part Number(s): H503KX9
Usage: 1974–75 Dart Sport, Duster.
Interchange Number: 14
Part Number(s): H501KX9
Usage: 1974 Barracuda, Challenger.
Interchange Number: 15
Part Number(s): H504KX9
Usage: 1974 Charger, Coronet, and Satellite, all models and body styles.

Inside Door Handles
Model Identification

Interchange
Interchange Number: 1
Part Number(s): 2935214 (right), 2935215 (left)
Usage: 1968–69 Barracuda; 1968–70 Belvedere, Charger; 1968–74 Coronet; 1968–74 Dart, Valiant; 1970–74 Duster; 1971–72 Demon; 1968 Chrysler 300, Fury, Monaco, Newport, New Yorker, Polara; 1971–74 Satellite four-door or station wagon; All models and body styles. Both front and rear doors.
Interchange Number: 2
Part Number(s): 3454842 (right), 3454843 (left)
Usage: 1970–74 Barracuda.
Interchange Number: 3
Part Number(s): 3454170 (right), 3454171 (left)
Usage: 1970–74 Challenger.
Interchange Number: 4
Part Number(s): 3508916 (right), 3508917 (left)
Usage: 1971–74 Charger, Satellite, two-door models only.

Headrests
Model Identification

Interchange
Interchange Number: 1
Part Number(s): 8496DX9
Usage: 1968–69 Barracuda, Belvedere, Charger, Coronet, Chrysler 300, Fury, Monaco, Newport, New Yorker, Polara, and Valiant with bucket seats. Fits either side.
Interchange Number: 2
Part Number(s): 8498DX9
Usage: 1968–69 Barracuda, Belvedere, Charger, Coronet,

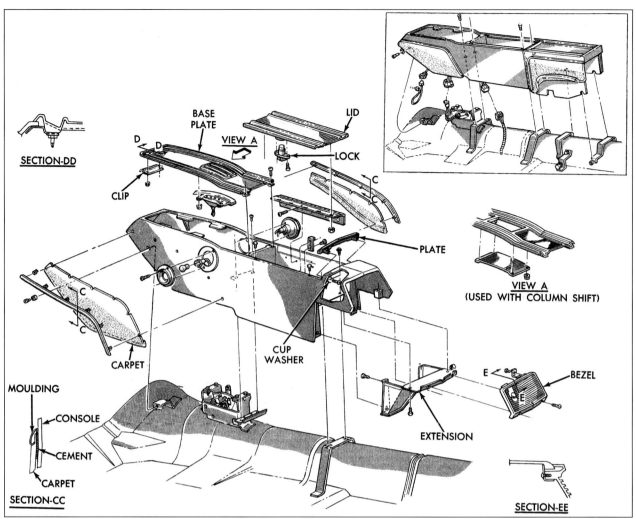

1968–1970 B-body and 1968–1974 A-body console.

Chrysler 300, Fury, Monaco, Newport, New Yorker, Polara, and Valiant with bench seats. Fits either side.

Interchange Number: 3
Part Number(s): 2789GX9
Usage: 1970–72 Charger, Coronet, and Satellite with bench seats. Fits either side.

Interchange Number: 4
Part Number(s): 2788GX9
Usage: 1970–72 Dart, Duster, and Valiant; 1970–71 Chrysler 300, Fury, Monaco, Newport, New Yorker, and Polara with bench seats. Fits either side.

Interchange Number: 5
Part Number(s): 2791GX9
Usage: 1970 Charger, Coronet, Satellite; 1970–71 Chrysler 300, Fury, Monaco, and Polara with bucket seats. Fits either side.

Interchange Number: 6
Part Number(s): 2790JF6
Usage: 1973 Dart, Duster, and Valiant with bench seats. Fits either side.

Interchange Number: 7
Part Number(s): 2789JX9
Usage: 1973 Charger, Coronet, and Satellite with bench seats. Fits either side.

Interchange Number: 8
Part Number(s): S505JX9

Usage: 1974 Charger, Coronet, and Satellite with bench seats. Fits either side.

Interchange Number: 9
Part Number(s): S506JX9
Usage: 1974 Dart, Duster, Fury, Monaco, Newport, New Yorker, and Valiant with bench seats. Fits either side.

Inside-Window Regulator Handle
Model Identification
All Models .... ***Interchange Number***
All 1

Interchange Number: 1
Part Number(s): 2862167
Usage: 1968–74 Barracuda, Belvedere, Charger, Coronet, Dart, Satellite, and Valiant; 1968 Chrysler 300, Fury, Monaco, and Polara, all body styles, both front and rear windows.

Consoles
There are many different components involved in a console swap, including the base and upper trim parts, console door, and trim. Of these only the upper and lower parts are given in this interchange. However, most other parts will usually interchange with them. The big consideration in interchanging most consoles is the

transmission type. Most models used a different console with a manual transmission than they did with an automatic. Some bases were molded in color, but no consideration to color is included in this interchange: All part numbers are based on a black color console. Consoles can be repainted to match your car's interior trim.

Model Identification

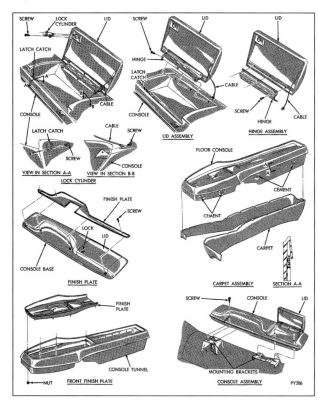

1971–1974 B-body and E-body console.

Interchange

Interchange Number: 1
> Part Numbers: 2788859 (base)
> Transmission Type: Manual
> Usage: 1968–69 Barracuda, Dart.

Interchange Number: 2
> Part Numbers: 2589594 (base)
> Transmission Type: Automatic
> Usage: 1968–69 Barracuda, Dart.

Interchange Number: 3
> Part Numbers: 2788366 (base)
> Transmission Type: Automatic
> Usage: 1968–69 Belvedere, Charger, Coronet, Chrysler 300, Fury, Monaco, Newport, and New Yorker.
> Note(s): Interchange base only in full-size models.

Interchange Number: 4
> Part Numbers: 2877234 Top
> Transmission Type: Manual
> Usage: 1969 Barracuda, 1969–74 Dart; 1970–74 Duster, Valiant.
> Note(s): Has vinyl insert. Some 1969 and 1970 models used Interchange Number 8.

Interchange Number: 5
> Part Numbers: 2877233 Top
> Transmission Type: Automatic
> Usage: 1969 Barracuda; 1969–74 Dart; 1970–74 Duster, Valiant.
> Note(s): With vinyl insert. Some 1969 and 1970 models used Interchange Number 9.

Interchange Number: 6
> Part Numbers: Top plate—2675572 (front), 2657573 (rear)
> Transmission Type: Manual
> Usage: 1969 Belvedere, Charger, Coronet.

Interchange Number: 7
> Part Numbers: Top plate—2657580 (front), 2657571 (rear)
> Transmission Type: Automatic
> Usage: 1969–70 Belvedere, Charger, and Coronet.

Interchange Number: 8
> Part Numbers: 2589600 (top plate)
> Transmission Type: Manual
> Usage: 1968–70 Barracuda, Dart; 1970 Duster, Valiant.
> Note(s): Plain. No insert. Some 1968–70 models used Interchange Number 4.

Interchange Number: 9
> Part Numbers: 2589599 (top plate)
> Transmission Type: Automatic
> Usage: 1968 Barracuda, Dart; 1970 Duster, Valiant.
> Note(s): Plain. No insert. Some 1968–70 models used Interchange Number 5.

Interchange Number: 10
> Part Numbers: 2657585 (top plate)
> Transmission Type: Manual
> Usage: 1968 Belvedere, Charger, and Coronet.

Interchange Number: 11
> Part Numbers: 2657584 (top plate)
> Transmission Type: Automatic
> Usage: 1968 Belvedere, Charger, and Coronet.

Interchange Number: 12
> Part Numbers: 3415844 (base)
> Transmission Type: All
> Usage: 1970–74 Dart, Duster, and Valiant.

Interchange Number: 13
> Part Numbers: 2788367 (base)
> Transmission Type: Manual
> Usage: 1968–70 Charger, Coronet, and Satellite.

Interchange Number: 14
> Part Numbers: 2788366 (base)
> Transmission Type: Automatic
> Usage: 1970 Charger, Coronet, Chrysler 300, Monaco, Newport, New Yorker, and Satellite; 1970–72 Fury Sport.

Interchange Number: 15
> Part Numbers: 3526FX9 (base)
> Transmission Type: Manual
> Usage: 1970–71 Barracuda, Challenger; 1971 Charger, Satellite.

Interchange Number: 16
> Part Numbers: 3505FX9 (base)
> Transmission Type: Automatic
> Usage: 1970–71 Barracuda, Challenger; 1971 Charger, Satellite.

Interchange Number: 17
> Part Numbers: 3504FX9 (top plate)
> Transmission Type: All
> Usage: 1970 Barracuda, Challenger; 1971 Charger, Satellite.
> Note(s): Simulated woodgrain trim plate differs between automatic and manual transmissions and will *not* interchange. Top plate here is the plastic shell.

Interchange Number: 18
> Part Numbers: 3540GX9
> Transmission Type: All
> Usage: 1971 Barracuda, Challenger.
> Note(s): Simulated woodgrain trim plate differs between automatic and manual transmissions and will *not* interchange. Top plate here is the plastic shell.

Interchange Number: 19
> Part Numbers: 2879813 (top plate)
> Transmission Type: Manual
> Usage: 1970 Charger, Coronet, and Satellite.

Interchange Number: 20
> Part Numbers: 3500HX9 (top plate)
> Transmission Type: All
> Usage: 1972–74 Barracuda, Challenger, Charger, Satellite.
> Note(s): Simulated woodgrain trim plate differs between automatic and manual transmissions and will *not* interchange. Top plate here is the plastic shell.

Interchange Number: 21
> Part Numbers: 3542GX9 (base)
> Transmission Type: Manual
> Usage: 1972–74 Barracuda, Challenger, Charger, and Satellite.

   Part Numbers: 3541GX9 (base)
   Transmission Type: Automatic
   Usage: 1972–74 Barracuda, Challenger, Charger, and Satellite.

Inside Rearview Mirrors
Model Identification

Barracuda...Interchange Number
1968–69..1
1970–71..2
1972 ....2, 3
1973–74..3

Belvedere, Charger, Coronet,
   and Satellite..Interchange Number
1968–69..1
1970–71..2
1972
   without Prismatic mirror......................................4, 5
   with Prismatic mirror...2, 3
1973–74
   without Prismatic mirror...5
   with Prismatic mirror...3

Challenger......................................Interchange Number
1970–71..2
1972 ....2, 3
1973–74..3

Dart, Duster, Demon, and Valiant ....Interchange Number
1968–69..1
1970–71..2
1972
   without Prismatic mirror......................................4, 5
   with Prismatic mirror...2, 3
1973–74
   without Prismatic mirror...5
   with Prismatic mirror...3

Interchange
Interchange Number: 1
   Part Number(s): 2935490
   Usage: 1968–69 Barracuda, Belvedere, Charger, Coronet,
      Chrysler 300, Dart, Fury, Monaco, Newport, New Yorker,
      Polara, and Valiant, all models and body styles.
   Note(s): Interchange without bracket.
Interchange Number: 2
   Part Number(s): 3454875
   Usage: 1970–early 1972 Barracuda, Challenger, Charger,
      Coronet, Dart, Duster, Satellite, and Valiant, all models and
      body styles; 1970 Chrysler 300, Fury, Monaco, Newport,
      New Yorker, and Polara, all models and body styles.
   Note(s): Interchange without bracket. Used until December 1, 1971.

Interchange Number: 3
   Part Number(s): 3695130
   Usage: Late 1972–74 Barracuda, Challenger, Charger, Coronet,
      Dart, Duster, Demon, Satellite, and Valiant, all models and
      body styles. Mirror has Prismatic view.
   Note(s): Interchange without bracket.
Interchange Number: 4
   Part Number(s): 3548447
   Usage: Early 1972 Charger, Satellite coupe (fixed rear windows);
      early 1972 Dart, Duster, Demon, and Valiant, without
      Prismatic view mirror.
   Note(s): Used until December 15, 1971.
Interchange Number: 5
   Part Number(s): 3695132
   Usage: Late 1972–74 Charger, Satellite coupe (fixed rear
      windows); late 1972–73 Dart, Duster, Demon, and Valiant,
      without Prismatic view mirror.
   Note(s): Used after December 15, 1971.

Interior Locking Knobs
Model Identification

Barracuda...Interchange Number
1968 1
1969 2
1970–74..3

Belvedere, Charger, Coronet,
   and Satellite..Interchange Number
1968 1
1969–74..2

Challenger......................................Interchange Number
1970–74..3

Dart, Duster, Demon, and Valiant ....Interchange Number
1968 1
1969–74..2

Interchange
Interchange Number: 1
   Part Number(s): 4346BX9
   Usage: 1967–68 Barracuda, Belvedere, Charger, Coronet, Dart,
      Chrysler 300, Fury, Monaco, Newport, New Yorker, Polara,
      and Valiant, all models and body styles.
   Note(s): Knob was molded in color to match trim. Part number
      is for black knob. Knobs can be refinished.
Interchange Number: 2
   Part Number(s): 3419209
   Usage: 1969 Barracuda; 1969–76 Belvedere, Charger, Coronet,
      Dart, Chrysler 300, Fury, Monaco, Newport, New Yorker,
      Polara, and Valiant, all models and body styles.
   Note(s): Knob was chrome.
Interchange Number: 3
   Part Number(s): 2999950
   Usage: 1970–74 Barracuda, Challenger.

Index